Jane —

Enjoy —

Bonnie Moore

MIZ FANCY

By

Bonnie Moore

authorHOUSE™

1663 LIBERTY DRIVE, SUITE 200
BLOOMINGTON, INDIANA 47403
(800) 839-8640
WWW.AUTHORHOUSE.COM

First published by AuthorHouse 01/28/05

ISBN: 1-4184-5322-6 (e)
ISBN: 1-4184-5321-8 (sc)

Library of Congress Control Number: 2004097223

Printed in the United States of America
Bloomington, Indiana

This book is printed on acid-free paper.

MIZ FANCY

By

Bonnie Moore

authorHOUSE™

1663 LIBERTY DRIVE, SUITE 200
BLOOMINGTON, INDIANA 47403
(800) 839-8640
WWW.AUTHORHOUSE.COM

© 2004 Bonnie Moore.
All Rights Reserved.

No part of this book may be reproduced, stored in a retrieval system, or transmitted by any means without the written permission of the author.

First published by AuthorHouse 01/28/05

ISBN: 1-4184-5322-6 (e)
ISBN: 1-4184-5321-8 (sc)

Library of Congress Control Number: 2004097223

Printed in the United States of America
Bloomington, Indiana

This book is printed on acid-free paper.

ACKNOWLEDGMENTS

With great appreciation, I thank …
My friend Ron, who first suggested
that I should write a novel;
My writing class at Bethesda's Writers' Center,
who took my idea and crafted it into a real story;
My writing coach, Peter, who kept me going;
My companion and soul mate, my husband Dennis,
who helped build each of the characters;
The many who read, critiqued, and edited,
including, but not limited to: Jane, Frank,
Doug, Mary, Pat, Mare, Dori, and Madeleine.

. . . .

And I thank the real person who inspired
Bucky, may he find his peace.

The front cover was designed by Mike Lehman.

The photograph on the back cover was taken by
Patricia Clark, Photography.

DEDICATION

This book is dedicated to my granddaughter, Jessica, who has shown an enormous will to live from the moment she was born.

TABLE OF CONTENTS

PART ONE

1. THE FATEFUL ENCOUNTER

Perhaps there are angels who watch over us, angels who know that we must complete an earthly mission before our souls can take their places in eternity. Perhaps these angels, with their heavenly duty, bring us together with our past for this purpose.

They must have been watching over me when I met an old black woman named Emmaline in a nursing home. As I learned about her, and as she became important to me, I recognized the blindness and the pain caused by the way we treat people who are different from us. This fateful encounter changed my life and created an opportunity for the angel's healing balm to ease painful moments in both her life and mine. I have also rediscovered my essence and have learned to be proud of who I am.

In writing this saga, I will divulge secrets and portray others in ways that are not kind. I am driven by a need to gather up the intricately woven tapestries of my life and offer them to others who might benefit from these experiences.

I am getting ahead of myself, though. Let me take you back to the day of our first meeting and let you share my story.

. . . .

1

Bonnie Moore

It is Christmas 1993. My husband, Bucky, and I have belonged to a Southern Baptist congregation in the upscale Georgetown district of Washington, D.C., since we moved here from Richmond, Virginia, many years ago. Our women's group at the church has adopted a large nursing home on Wisconsin Avenue, the Northwest Convalescent Center. Northwest, a ten-story, hospital-like facility partially funded by the District, is for the benefit of lower-income elderly and disabled people. We collect small gifts and visit on several holidays; this year we're meeting there at ten-thirty on Christmas morning.

With my daughter away at college and alienated from us, my involvement in the church group and various charities has become more important, and the Christmas holidays have become a time to focus on others instead of my own family. Bucky, along with some of the other spouses, attends the visitation more because he is easy-going and, as a local political leader, he relishes mingling with his voting friends.

There are fifteen in the group, ten women and five men. The conversation is lively with holiday greetings as each person or couple arrives. We take off our coats, hats, gloves, and scarves in the softly lit visitor's lounge on the first floor and put on nametags. We're well-dressed, white, and mostly middle-aged. Several are shop owners and restaurateurs on Georgetown's trendy M Street. One couple is important in national affairs, while the older single women are primarily widows of politicians and matriarchs of local families.

Our group leader, Pauline Boothe-Sheppard, one of the political widows, has brought single, red roses for us to give to the residents and is trying, unsuccessfully, to distribute them to the group in the midst of the holiday greetings.

2

"Here, let me help you pass those out." Bucky takes a bundle, flashes a smile, and seamlessly ingratiates himself into the group. He stands several inches taller than me, and is striking in his black turtleneck, slacks, and brushed-camel sports jacket. Even at forty-eight, he is dashing with his salt-and-pepper hair and Rhett Butler mustache. With amusement, I watch him turn on his charm, using an unusually strong accent as he mingles, "Why, Miz Stevens, it's so nice to see you today ... and Flora, Merry Christmas to you too ...."

He greets an elderly couple standing next to me. Pressing flowers into their hands, he gently touches my elbow, "Mr. Secretary, y'all know my lovely wife, don't you?" Bending over, he whispers in my ear, "Smile, sugar plum, it'll be good for us."

"Winfred ...." I pretend to be annoyed with him as I turn to the secretary's wife with a greeting.

He moves on to the next couple to hand out flowers, while whispering to me, "You only call me that when you're mad. You're not goin' to be mad today, are you, sugar?"

I playfully mock him, "Bucky, it's Christmas. It's not a day for politics."

"Darlin'," he coos back, his eyes laughing, "this is Washington. Every day is a day for politics." He nuzzles close to my head, speaking through my short curly hair, "I was just doin' harmless flirtin'. You're still the prettiest woman here." Taking a rose from the bundle, he presses it against my shoulder and spills some of the loose greenery on me. "Wouldn't that look nice right there? Is there a way you can pin it on?"

Taking the rose and carefully putting it back, I sigh, "Bucky, it's red and my sweater is peach; it doesn't match. Besides, a pin would snag my sweater, and I can't have that. You paid too much for it!" I brush the leaves from my slacks and wipe water from my loafers.

"You know I'd buy you another one in a minute. 'Course, you'd be as cute as a button even if you had nothin' on."

"Hush up now, we're with church folks." I always love the way we shamelessly flirt with each other, even after years of marriage. I guide him toward the elevators, "Come on, silly, let's go be kind and generous to folks who aren't voters. Think you can do that?"

"Darlin', it's my pleasure to oblige." He grins and exaggerates his accent as he adjusts his jacket, "I shall be in my element with all these fine, older ladies who have sons and daughters who do vote." He kisses me quickly on the cheek. Laughing together, we enter the elevator with the group.

The visitation begins in the seventh-floor day room, a large, bright area, where twenty to thirty people sit around on functional, metal furniture that is arranged in conversation groups against the pale green walls. Some are in small groups; others are alone in their wheelchairs. Almost all are black and most are women. A young couple with a child is visiting one woman, and two other residents have visitors. In one corner sits a TV, quietly playing *Miracle on 34ᵗʰ Street,* but no one watches. A sparsely decorated Christmas tree is near the window, tinsel garlands frame the doors, and cardboard cutouts of the manger scene are taped to the wall. A mild antiseptic scent floats in the air.

Four women sit at a table, playing cards. They are wearing housedresses and cotton robes, and one of them has a portable IV next to her, with a tube taped to her left arm. Reading the nametag of the woman with the IV, I say, "Ruth, I've brought you a flower. It's Christmas today, and we've come to visit."

4

"What day is it?" Ruth is momentarily puzzled, "Oh … I don't care much for Christmas anymore." She puts her cards down and raises her chin. She is a tall woman, with a rectangular face and a commanding presence. Taking the rose, she absently puts it down, then gazes into the distance and reminisces about her life as a schoolteacher for forty-two years, and how her students were always nice to her and loved her. With pride, she adds, "They still do, you know, they still love me." I hear loneliness and a sense of being abandoned in her voice.

Like the other church members, I listen, respond when I can, and gradually move on. The next resident is by herself and in a wheelchair. Approaching her, I read her nametag aloud, "Emmaline?" I gently put a rose in her hand, "Emmaline, may I give you a rose for Christmas?"

Emmaline has a strap around her waist holding her in the wheelchair. Her head tilts to one side. She takes a handkerchief and wipes the corner of her mouth as she raises her head, "What?" She sniffs the rose, "Oh, thank you, deary, thank you. It's so nice of you." She looks at me vacantly. As her focus becomes clearer, her eyes change and grow larger. She stares. Her mouth opens but she says nothing. Finally, she whispers, "Fancy," and continues to stare at me, speaking in a barely audible voice and in a slow, soft manner, "Fancy. You shur is pretty now, Miz Fancy."

"Oh goodness, that's mighty kind of you. My name is Mary Frances, not Fancy. See," I point, "here on my nametag?" I'm embarrassed.

Emmaline is quiet, but more resolute when she says, "You're Fancy." Her face is ashen, her eyes suggest words that she does not speak, and I don't comprehend. She seems to collect herself a little. A sense of dignity emanates from her face, from the softness of her dark eyes, and from her carriage. Her shoulders remain erect even when her head moves with uncertainty. Her skin is the color of café au lait and is tautly stretched over large bones. Her small eyes are sunken, with circles of aging skin around them, and she holds her chin high with a sense of elegance. Hairpins secure her frizzy, white hair in a small bun.

I sit down next to the wheelchair and take Emmaline's hand. Her fingers are long, with dry, rough skin, and her nails need attention. I feel strength in her hand. My glance moves from her hands to her face. The tension of proudly holding her head up causes the veins in her neck to protrude. Her nose is long but not wide, and her lips are thin. A small mole high on her left cheek has a few hairs growing out of it. Rows and rows of fine lines spread horizontally across her forehead. Her face touches me emotionally, and I am overwhelmed with compassion. I do not understand why, but I feel a connection to her.

She continues to stare. Finally speaking again, a little more audibly, she says, "I been waitin' fo' you, just like we said. I knowed …" she stops, "I knowed … I knowed my li'l darlin' would come for me…." Her voice trails off.

I cannot find words for her. She appears to be remembering something painful. I begin to absorb her heartache. Without warning, my own painful memories surface. I lost my mother when I was young and never found an adequate replacement. I didn't develop a closeness with my own child, who now seems to hate me. I feel uncomfortable. Shifting, I withdraw my hand and begin to stand up.

Emmaline leans over, takes my hand again, and whispers quietly, "Don't leave me again, li'l Miz Fancy. There's no need, this time." She stares into space. Her face shows concern and her eyes

6

narrow. She squints and shakes her head, then turns and speaks to me again, more resolutely, "You is my li'l baby chile an' you's come for your manny."

I sit down again and continue holding her hand. We're silent. Emmaline's grip becomes stronger. My stomach hurts and my shoulders feel heavy. I begin to feel the bond that must exist between all women who suffer and think that this woman must have lost a child. In a way, I have also lost my child. I want to reach out and hug her, but she's a stranger and I can't. I feel afraid, but I don't know why. Something about this woman is hauntingly familiar to me. I collect myself by turning to listen to the group leader, Pauline, who is nearby, chatting with a resident, comparing grandchildren. Emmaline notices and nods toward the others. "I's talks about my grandbaby, too. I's always been talkin' about her."

"How old is your granddaughter?"

"You knows, she be's about … mebbee about … oh, these years pass so fast. Last time I saw her, she was graduatin' high school, I saw her then." Her head twists a little as she looks at me intently, her eyes twinkling with the pleasure of remembering. "It weren't too long before I came here." Her face clouds over and she looks away, apologetically. "I ain't been able to see her since I been here."

I stay with Emmaline while the other members of the group mill around from resident to resident, listening to their stories. Bucky is chatting and flirting with several of the elderly women and has them laughing. He catches my eye and winks.

A short time later, an orderly who has been watching from the doorway comes over. "Time for our Miz Emmaline to get her lunch." He speaks gently, "Now say goodbye to the nice lady," and waits for her to collect herself. Shyly, she lifts her face and says goodbye. I gently lay Emmaline's large hand on the armrest of the wheelchair. He guides her toward the door. She turns, looking back at me. Tears fill her eyes and begin to fall from the corners. She brushes them aside as the wheelchair passes from my view.

With the other visitors, I step aside as the nursing staff and orderlies begin to assist the residents in moving toward the dining room a few doors away. Those who can, walk slowly, shuffling alone and in small groups. Some use walkers, canes, or hold on to each other.

The members of the church group congregate at the elevator. When the orderly who assisted Emmaline finishes with his residents and returns to the nearby nursing station, I approach him. "I'm so sorry, sir. I don't want to be a nuisance, but could you tell me anything about Emmaline?"

"You ain't gonna be a nuisance. We enjoys havin' ya'll visit." His eyes sparkle and his smile is infectious. He is a middle-aged, black man whose badge identifies him as Benjamin Mitchell. Tall and thin with rounded shoulders, he is dressed in a green hospital uniform and speaks in a melodic baritone with a slow drawl. As we talk, he casually straightens a few papers, "We don't rightly know too much about these here ladies." He gives me a knowing look over the rim of his wire-framed glasses. "I do think she might have been a domestic. Most of them was, y'know."

"I'm concerned that I might have upset her, maybe brought up some sad memories. Has she confused me with someone else by chance, someone who comes to visit?"

"No, Miz Emmaline don't have no visitors. She don't talk much neither," he says. "She's still mighty sharp, though, and she ain't lost her mind, that's for sure. But she's beginnin' to have trouble with her memory now and again and she's quite embarrassed about it. We's havin' to watch her a bit closer now."

"Is this something she does because of her age, maybe? Confuses people, that is?" I pause and turn to him, feeling confused myself, silently wonder why I know her face, and speaking as if I am talking to myself. "It's strange. It seems like she might know me. Is it possible that she does?"

"I ain't never seen her like this before. You certainly had some kind of effect on her." He sighs and shakes his head slightly, "We sure ain't never seen her cry before."

I'm aware of how easy and comfortable it is talking to him. "What's even stranger, I have a feeling I might know her, that maybe I've met her before." I try to shrug it off. "I don't know. Maybe it's just my imagination."

"Could she have been a domestic in your household?"

"I don't think so. My aunt's had the same maid since I was a child, still does." And an afterthought, "I was raised by my aunt in Richmond."

"Why don't you give it some thinkin' time, an' if you want, come on back and visit her sometime. We put y'all together, and you jus' might remember." He gives me a wide grin, with a twinkle in his eyes. "It'd be real nice of you."

"Thank you so much. That's a good idea. I might do that." I pat him lightly on the arm in the Southern fashion, "I hope to see you again, and Merry Christmas to you," and catch up with the group as we head for another floor.

Afterwards, as we drive home, I tell Bucky about my encounter with Emmaline and how she seemed to recognize me. He replies, "You don't really plan to go back and visit that ol' colored woman, do you?"

"Now, why do you say that?"

"Well, it just isn't too seemly, I don't think."

"Is it unseemly for us to visit on Christmas Day?"

"That's somethin' nice for people to do because it's Christmas. Goin' back and spendin' time would make it a little too personal, don't you think?"

"Sorta like feeding the homeless when it isn't Thanksgiving? Is that about right?"

"Darlin', you know what I mean. Regularly visitin' a stranger in a nursing home doesn't make too much sense, now does it, especially with everythin' else more important that you have to do. You really don't have time for fiddlin' around."

"Well, I am a bit curious about her. I'm puzzled about the possibility that she might know me. I keep thinking about where that could have come from." Reaching over, I turn up the music. The oldies station is playing Dylan's "Blowing in the Wind," one of my favorites, and I begin to quietly sing along.

He doesn't pay attention. "That old lady didn't recognize you, darlin', she was just hallucinatin'. Anybody could see that; probably had too many pills this mornin'. You're just another white lady to her, and she probably worked for dozens of 'em." He pushes the button to change the radio to a news station, "You should just get that visitin' outta' your mind."

"I wonder if it goes back to school? I've been trying to remember if there were domestics at school, or if only the nuns took care of us. I certainly don't remember being close to someone like her, except for Martha, and she's still with Aunt Beatrice."

"Well, you weren't close enough to any of them to bother with a crazy ol' colored woman, so don't you fuss about it now." He turns his head toward me with a gentle but authoritative tone, "Mary Frances, I'd prefer that you drop this."

"Bucky, that's not nice of you." Looking out the car window, I feel annoyed, dissatisfied. I feel a hunger for something that food cannot fulfill, and I momentarily dwell on the fact that I will never be able to care for my own mother in her old age.

A strange voice, somewhere deep inside of me, seems to quietly whisper to Bucky, but it's so soft that only I hear it. *I'll thank you to let me make my own decisions about how I spend my time, if you don't mind.*

2.   MEMORIES AND ATTITUDES

Bucky and I have invited a small, congenial group of local, Washington politicians, political consultants, and Georgetown businesspeople to our home for a late-night buffet on New Year's Eve. We live on a quiet, tree-lined street a few blocks from the intersection of M Street and Wisconsin Avenue in the heart of old Georgetown. Our house is called the Beall Mansion, but it really isn't a mansion, just a large, comfortable, old house on N Street between Thirtieth and Thirty-First. It is said to be the oldest brick home in the area, with the original section dating back to the year 1751. Well-kept and brightly painted Federalist-era townhouses add to the neighborhood ambiance. Distinctive, old, wrought-iron fences, magnificent, ivy-covered magnolia trees, and sparsely paved, cobblestone streets give the neighborhood a rustic feeling and an expectation of dignified elderly men in morning coats and genteel grandmothers in hoop skirts floating along the sidewalk.

Bucky and I moved into this house soon after he graduated from Georgetown Law School and joined a local law firm. We raised our daughter here in an atmosphere of social and political prominence, with its attendant cultural artifacts. Sometimes I worry that we gave her too many benefits, too much privilege, and a life with no struggle. She is now attending Columbia University in New York City, and this is our second Christmas without her at home. She and I talk occasionally, but the umbilical cord has been cut, and our communication is often terse. In a temperamental fit, she chose to spend the holidays this year with her friends in New York.

I feel a sense of loss as I adjust to life without my child nearby, and I no longer have the opportunity to express instinctive maternal love. Motherhood defined my life for so many years, and I quietly, confidently, and comfortably merged it into the partnership of my marriage. Unlike many women around me, once I married I did not hear a Greek chorus in the background urging me to strive for a separate personal recognition. My role, which I took seriously, was to inspire my family to better themselves.

For the first time in years, we are having the traditional New Year's gathering at our home, and I am pleased to play the role of a political hostess. I know that Bucky has ambitions in the Washington political scene and I feel important in those plans, if only in a social sense. Living in Washington, D.C., has given me a panoramic view of world cultures and foreign affairs, and my life has been uniquely enriched through involvements with the community. Yet occasionally, I find myself wondering about this cacophony of life. In those moments, I question whether I have actually succeeded in doing something important, or whether I exist only through my husband and his ambitions. In quieter times, I wonder if I could be denying who I am, or if I am downplaying the valuable contributions that I have made to his life.

As I prepare for the party, I take pleasure in working with the decorations of maroon and ivory, creating homage to elegant, Victorian-era styles and arranging background music of traditional Christmas carols. Old, wicker doll furniture sets off a collection of brown teddy bears and lacy china dolls in the foyer. The spacious parlor, through the archway to the left, is aglow with candlelight and evergreen garlands. Old-fashioned, candle-shaped lights flicker on a large Christmas tree that takes up one corner and bulges with ornaments, ribbons, popcorn, and cranberry strings. And, of course, I match the mood by dressing in a high-necked, Victorian, lace blouse and a long, dark green, velvet skirt.

"You look jus' like my sweet li'l wife is supposed to look," Bucky ogles before adjusting his holiday tie in the bedroom mirror. As always, he has dressed his six-foot-one-inch frame impeccably. Today, he has chosen a custom-made, dark blue, double-breasted jacket with a striped shirt and gray slacks. Pulling out a pocket watch and opening it, he laughs jovially, "My grandfather's fine gold watch tells me it's about time for our guests to arrive." He leans over and kisses me lightly. "I certainly expect you'll be the perfect hostess tonight."

"Sweetheart, have I ever failed you?" I grin at his joke about the antique watch that I had just given him for Christmas, brush his shoulders for imaginary lint, and pause to admire how good we look together in the mirror, the successful man with his faithful wife hugging him. The reflection that I see of myself is a shadow, someone whose life and ambitions center on Bucky and the quiet reverie of our life together. Although sometimes I fear being on the proverbial pedestal reserved for Southern women, I feel lucky to be with him and to give back the love that I feel coming from him.

"Absolutely not," he says as he turns and kisses my cheek. "I predict that when I become mayor of this fine city, and beyond that, when I have reached my highest pinnacle, y'all will be the next major social hostess. We might even make you into an Alice Roosevelt Longworth."

"Now, don't you go expecting too much of me! I like being in the background. I couldn't play at her level." Socially, he has always pushed me a little beyond my own expectations. His pull has always been upward, toward success, clarity, and progress. I've always known that Bucky would be a good mayor, or whatever else he chooses, and I'm proud of his successes. For his sake, I try hard to keep up and to be a more social person than is my nature. He talks a great deal about fulfilling his destiny of governing with honor and showing compassion for all of his constituents. During my college years in the late sixties, I gained an appreciation for social issues, and I have always been pleased that my husband has the same inclination.

"Why not? We do great things together. You've always been an important part of my success. Tell me now, would you prefer to be the wife of the mayor of the District of Columbia, or maybe," his arms spread with a flourish, and he bows graciously, "the secretary's wife, or even the ambassador's wife? Nothing is beyond our reach!" He laughs and reaches for me. Nuzzling and hugging, he talks to me in the mirror, "I promised you once that we would soar with the eagles, and I'm looking forward to it happenin' soon. An', sugar, you're better than you think … I imagine you'll even keep ol' Katherine herself in line tonight!"

I laugh at the thought of my feminist, Jewish friend from New York and her reputation for causing scenes. "Now, darlin', I'm sure she'll be fine." Bucky and Katherine have never liked each other, and he barely tolerates our friendship, which has lasted since college. She annoys him because she is an outspoken journalist who enjoys egging on politicians and downsizing the more flamboyant ones.

"I swear, that woman has me in the sights of her shotgun, and you're the only reason she's not pulling the trigger."

"Don't be silly. She's my friend and she respects you more than you think. She's just that way, and besides, you have nothing to worry about anyway."

"Yes, dear, that's what I keep telling myself." He kisses my cheek, exaggerates a sigh, and goes downstairs with a bounce in his step to answer the first doorbell. Our guests begins to arrive in earnest around ten o'clock, and Bucky and I take turns greeting them.

Bucky's nemesis, Katherine, a correspondent for the Associated Press, is one of the first to arrive when I take over at the door. Her husband, Peter, a political consultant from North Carolina, greets me with a hug. In appearance, he reminds me of a mature Kenny Rogers, with a full head of snowy white hair and a beard. I notice how handsome he is in evening wear and playfully compliment him with a whistle.

Katherine, who normally wears subdued colors and somewhat masculine styles, is stunning in a glittering, long-sleeved, red-sequined top and straight, floor-length, red skirt. Her long, dark blonde hair has been pulled into a braided chignon at the nape of her neck. I have always admired Katherine's combination of tall lankiness inherited from her Midwestern, Nordic ancestors; her cultural warmth gained from her Jewish heritage; and, in spite of myself, her straightforward brusqueness born of a New York City upbringing. Her mother was from Chicago, moved to Washington to work during World War II, and migrated to New York when she married a Jewish publisher and assimilated into his culture.

"Katherine, dear, you are stunning!" I greet her with a warm hug as I take her heavy woolen shawl. "Perhaps you missed your calling as a fashion model!"

"I prefer being a model of other things. This is camouflage." She feigns fear, "Do you think Bucky will recognize me?"

"I don't understand you two," I laugh, "he's harmless."

"Mary Frances, you are *sooo* innocent. I love you dearly," she kisses my cheek, "but someday I will crack Bucky's phony exterior."

"Just liked she cracked mine years ago," Peter says warmly, handing me his white scarf, coat, and umbrella, and straightening his tie in the hall mirror. "I have to keep her away from my clients, though!"

She turns to him, "My dear, the threat of a scathing Katherine Schuller-Jones investigation has kept your clients well behaved and successful. You have me to thank for it."

"They hire me just to keep in your good graces, I'm sure of that." He bows to her briefly, his eyes beaming with affection. Taking her arm and strolling into the living room, he teases, sounding a little like W. C. Fields, "My little sweet pea, how should we behave tonight?"

She shrugs playfully, speaking with a twist of her wrist and a husky flare in her voice, reminiscent of Hepburn, "Well, let's see. Tonight, I'm in the mood for rakish … maybe frisky … oh, you know, might as well go all the way … let's be the life of the party with our *mishegoss*."

"All right." He stands still, touches his nose with the point of his index finger as he thinks, then turns the finger toward her and says quietly with pretentiously hooded eyes and tone, "You can be Patricia Ireland, and I'll be Colonel Sanders."

She whispers back, "Good show, ol' man! N.O.W. vs. The South. What a poignant idea! I'm on, if you are."

I know these two well, and always enjoy their playful bantering, but cringe slightly at the thought of what they might stir up tonight.

A short time later, another close friend, Patricia, a gentle-natured hypnotherapist, arrives with her husband, Phillip, who is a professional campaign manager and political strategist. He recently began working with Bucky to map out a political future. Phillip, who is a smidgen shorter than Patricia, definitely rounder, and rapidly losing his hair, helps her off with her coat.

"You did it ... I thought you were joking," I quip, admiring her dress. She has surprised me with the boldness of a deep purple crepe dress with a long, red, silk scarf gently wrapped around her neck, the ends elegantly trailing down her back. A small, red, pillbox hat sits on her stylishly coifed, prematurely white hair. It is exactly like a poem she recently found in a women's magazine, entitled "When I Am 50, I Shall Wear Purple."

"Never underestimate me," she grins. "Do I look like it or not?"

"Absolutely!" She poses, and in that fleeting moment, I see someone very different from the person I have known since we were neighbors as children ... there is a hint of sophistication and worldliness in her attitude. "Now that I am fifty, I can dress as I please. It's allowed; the poem says so." There seems to be more truth than witty sarcasm in her voice.

"Where's our boy?" her husband asks, ignoring us.

"Oh Phillip, always on the job are you? He's probably back in the library with the rest of the boys." I wave him off as I see Katherine coming over to greet Patricia.

The festivities are alive with laughter and political chatter as tuxedoed waiters silently move through the crowd serving drinks. It is the end of 1993, and the District political landscape is awash with scandals concerning mismanagement of public funds. These issues have touched many of our guests, including several members of the District and Georgetown City Councils. Politicians, however difficult their public lives, have a way of smoothing these things over in personal gatherings, and there are no signs of rancor as the evening progresses.

It is a few minutes before eleven and snowing lightly when a limousine arrives with our final guests, the city's former mayor and current member of the city council, Marion Barry, who has suffered through substantial personal and professional legal difficulties with the undying support of his loyal constituents. The mayor is accompanied by his wife, Effi, who is another one of my close friends. We are the final stop in the Barrys' tour of New Year's Eve parties, and a crowd gathers in the foyer to greet them with splendid aplomb. In spite of everything, Mayor Barry has not lost his public appeal and seems to be making a comeback. Bucky has worked with the mayor on numerous projects over the years, and they have an affable relationship, even though Bucky now serves on an advisory committee for the Control Board, which was appointed to usurp the mayor's power.

Marion enters first with the outstretched hand of a professional politician, discarding his overcoat and umbrella between handshakes. He's a fairly large man from my perspective, but shorter than Bucky. Several in the group exclaim over his bright-yellow-and-orange African dashiki with gold thread trimming. "I understand this is the latest in formal attire in this city," he jokes as he mingles. Bucky seizes the moment and boisterously escorts the mayor back to where many of the men have gathered.

Effi, a well-educated and beautiful woman, who is part black, part Cherokee, and part Italian, comes through the door close behind Marion. She is always poised in spite of her recent public humiliations as Marion's wife, and greets the gathered women with grace. Stepping forward with a hug, I comment, "Effi, dear, you are lovely as usual." Helping her with her coat and escorting her into the party, I notice how impressive she is, wearing a black Chinese cheongsam dress with brilliant embroidery and red piping along the side where the buttons are.

Effi, Katherine, Patricia, and I soon congregate around the tree to discuss the success of our Christmas activities. I enjoy telling them about our church visit to the nursing home, ending with a comment that one of the patients, an elderly black woman, seemed to recognize me, and I am both intrigued and confused by this.

"What do you think it's about?" Katherine asks.

"I really don't know. When I grew up, we didn't have much contact with the black culture. I can't even imagine how she would know me. Bucky thinks she was hallucinating and it's nonsense." I stop for a minute to share a recollection. "However, since meeting her, I have been haunted by a peculiar dream where she and I are counting stars in the night together, and then I fall asleep in her arms."

"Could she have been your nurse?" Effi interjects. "You could be remembering something you did with her. The old mammies did most of the childrearing, and strong bonds often developed between their charges and them."

"Martha was my mammy."

Patricia contemplates, "What about when you lived with your parents before they died?"

"I was a small child then. She couldn't possibly recognize me from so long ago." We continue to discuss the possibilities, but can't come up with an answer. I also tell them that the hospital orderly suggested I come back for a visit, but Bucky opposes the idea.

"Screw Bucky." This is Katherine's style of talking. "Do you want to go back?"

I look to Patricia and Effi for their comments. Patricia offers, "If this is important enough for you to keep thinking about it, you should probably try for a resolution." After a long pause, Effi speaks what she seems to have been pondering. "It sounds like this might also be important to that old woman. And who knows what will happen … you'll never know unless you go."

I know that each speaks the truth, in her own way, but feel uneasy about what Bucky's reaction might be and retreat to my hostess role, backing away slightly. "Y'all are such good friends. As always, thank you for your comments. I'll have to sleep on it, I'm afraid." Another guest turns to me and I fade into the crowd. Slowly, I ease my way toward the library to observe the men and quietly lean against the doorway.

In our home, the library is the traditional bastion for men, their brandy snifters, and their cigars. True to form, our male guests have gravitated here to discuss their views of Clinton's first year in office and to assess local business and political strategies. Marion's and Bucky's voices are heard most frequently.

Katherine finds her way over. After a few minutes of observation while sipping her drink, she muses, "Reminds you of know-it-all, high school sophomores, doesn't it?"

I laugh, "Oh, give them a little more credit—college sophomores at least."

"They aren't going to like it when I walk in and disturb their one-upmanship, are they?"

"Katherine, you wouldn't, would you?"

"Watch me. I bet I find an opening soon." She eases in while exchanging a knowing look with her husband and settles on an ottoman near where he is seated.

I watch more closely, anticipating that I may have to dampen Katherine's spirits. Although she has learned to talk our talk, she is not a native Washingtonian, and her Northern personality sometimes stirs up more than she might want to cope with.

Our guests who are members of the District and Georgetown City Councils have much to say about recent political maneuverings, and Bucky, in particular, is quizzed about his role with the Control Board, while Marion is vehement about the necessity for true local control and the lack of a congressional vote for District citizens, a very sore spot for District residents.

I've watched these political events very closely from the sidelines, cognizant of how the changes affect Bucky's career and ambitions. Standing in the doorway, I reminisce about how the District was on the verge of a financial meltdown and was politically immobile when the new president arrived in early 1993. The blacks had gained substantial political control of the District during the eighties, but much of this control collapsed amid rumors and allegations of malfeasance that reached a crescendo when Mayor Barry was convicted of a misdemeanor drug charge and sent to jail for six months. Crime was rampantly increasing. Affluent residents were moving to safer homes in Virginia and Maryland and leaving the city cash poor. Almost immediately after taking office, and to the relief of many local businesses, Clinton created the Financial Control Board and vested it with absolute authority. The board bypasses all local control and is beginning to show signs of flexing its muscles. There is much to talk about, and the opportunity to second-guess the board is seldom missed. Those of our guests who benefited under the old system are, of course, horrified at this display of federal force, while those who pay the local taxes quietly sigh with relief. I've watched Bucky use his ability to charm many times, even in the most difficult of these situations. It has made him adroit at remaining friendly with the old guard, while facilitating a difficult transition and making inroads for his own future.

Marion's enthusiasm for his point of view finally seems to get the best of him, and the political discussion becomes poignant and terse. I smile with admiration as Bucky breaks the tension by cheerfully turning toward our piano and capturing a small entourage. "Gentlemen, gentlemen, we have a local election coming up this year, and I promise you I won't run," he takes a breath and lowers his tone, "at least for the moment." A couple of heads turn away from Marion.

Bucky puts his drink on the piano with a mild thump to attract more attention and raises his voice with good humor, "And because of my rousing non-campaign promise, I suggest a round of 'For He's a Jolly Good Fellow.'" He seats himself, gesturing to Marion to join him, "It'll be for both of us," and raises his hands over the keys. "And I will lead the chorus." He strikes the first chord with only a small audience just as Marion begins another political assertion.

Marion gets the message, ceases in mid-sentence, smiles broadly, and walks to the piano, leaning against the edge. He knowingly raises his glass to Bucky, "Let's drink to our collective health, wealth, long life, happiness, and prosperity." Bucky begins playing, and the entire group stands, gathers around, and breaks out in song. Marion's rich voice becomes louder than the rest.

Bucky and Marion laugh good-naturedly as the group transitions to a Rodgers and Hammerstein song, "Getting to Know You."

After the singing breaks up, Bucky and Marion amble toward the parlor. Some women join the remaining group and they gather around three hangings on the library wall that are mementos of my family connection with the tobacco industry. There are two displays of antique silkies and a larger framed piece that had originally been a table decoration.

Well-bred, antebellum women were not allowed to smoke, but they often collected the small, woven silk inserts that came in cigar boxes, similar to present day baseball cards. The silkies, as they were called, were of sports figures, hunting scenes, local schools, lodges, and the like. They were collected and sewn together to become runners, tablecloths, or throws. The individual, small, rectangular silk pieces were stitched together and shaped with cotton backing. Each finished piece is about the size of a man's handkerchief. One of my hangings depicts early horseless carriages, and the other one shows hunting dogs.

The seamstress who made the third hanging collected almost five hundred yellow, silk, ribbons that had originally been wrapped around cigars. Each yellow ribbon had the name of the manufacturer printed in black down its center. They were artfully sewn together along the edges, using a prominent herringbone stitch in black thread and arranged so that the brand names made a pleasing pattern in the finished piece. These names represent many old Southern manufacturers, including a cigar factory owned by my mother's ancestors.

Commenting on the hangings, several men, cigars in hand, joke about the current civil war being waged on the tobacco industry by the government and the anti-smoking forces and how the Northerners are still intent on destroying the Southern economy like they did in the War Between the States. They are thankful that the battle is only in the court system this time and predict a great legal success for the tobacco industry.

"Well now, that may not always be good. You gotta remember that the first efforts to resolve the slavery issue were in the courts back then, too," muses a black councilman named Jerome. Several people look at him quizzically. "You remember, ol' Dred Scott," he responds. "Well, there was mor'n one like him who tried to get his freedom by petitionin' the courts in the free states. But most of the judges, they weren't gonna have anythin' to do with it. If the judges back then had listened to their conscience, 'stead of being tied to the politicians, we wouldn't have had a war at all. Same thing might happen because of tobacco."

"The tobacco money will keep anything from happening, count on it; an' besides, it benefits the blacks and the whites now—they all gain a livelihood from tobacco," volunteers another man. "Tobacco is still the mainstay of the South's economy, and no one is gonna destroy the South again—there's too much power in that lobby." He intentionally taps his ashes into a tray. "Besides, our good citizens who smoke will keep them going."

"Back then, the decisions were really made by the white men who were afraid of losing their power, weren't they?" This comes from Katherine, who had risen from the ottoman when the conversation started. She moves in toward the middle of the group. "Actually, it was peer pressure to see who could be the most patronizing." The eyebrows of two nearby women arch in a moment of jovial agreement, while the faces of the men cloud over, especially her husband's. Their eyes lock with electricity as if she is expecting a response from him.

"Katherine," he slowly rises, moves closer to the group, and says, "I don't believe y'all have a good understandin' of the proper culture of those times."

"Culture, smulture," she retorts with confidence. "Darling, it's all about the white men and their need for power as the basis of everything else. Always has been. 'Course, we women are starting to do something about it, which makes us feel just fine."

"You go right on feelin' fine all you want," he nods his head in a mock bow, "while we continue runnin' the country and takin' care of y'all. It's us men who know how to manage and earn the money while all that feelin' is goin' on. Doin' the serious thinkin' is not somethin' that womenfolk are good at." I know these two well and quietly chuckle as they create havoc and concern on the faces of their audience.

"Balderdash, darling. Look how much money we're raising for Emily's List and how powerful the women's political groups are becoming."

"Darlin', that's a li'l bit of bunk, if you don't mind my sayin' so. Emily's List is far from being powerful. An', let me remind you, Anita Hill did herself no good at all tryin' to be powerful. That ol' boy, Clarence Thomas, is still our man."

"Well, now," she crosses her arms in front of her, "look at how Hillary is taking such a prominent role in fixing the health care system."

"Why, that Miz Clinton is an upstart who don't know which side her jacket is buttoned on. She ain't a part of Congress an' neva will be, an' she ain't neva gonna get her ideas through the ol' boy's club. We'll see to that." The men standing around her husband guffaw loudly, and two older men concurrently begin to speak. One nods to the other in a moment of intuitive decision-making as to who will go first.

I sense the beginning of a personal attack that may get beyond Katherine's sense of fun and will certainly overreach the party atmosphere, and decide to step into the conversation, saying, "Now before y'all get all riled up over here, let's go in and fix our plates." I link one arm with Katherine's and the other with her husband's, leading them toward the dining room while the other guests follow. Bucky, who has been leaning against the mantel in deep conversation with Patricia's husband, spots us. With a slight nod and a beckoning look, I make him aware of the two people on my arms and motion toward the dining room.

The quick movement of his eyes from me to Katherine indicates that he immediately sizes up the situation. With the ease of a chameleon, he transitions, linking with her other arm and pecking her cheek with exaggerated charm. "Kate, darlin'! I'm so pleased to see you made it over here this fine evening … we are always glad to have you as our guest."

Katherine leans over and whispers loudly into his ear with pretended seriousness and twinkling eyes, "Bucky, darling, you are such a schmuck. You know better than to ever call me 'Kate.'" I know how much she loves to banter with him. She is the only woman I know who does not pander to his "Southern gentleman" style.

"Katherine, dear, such language. I meant it as an endearment. You cut me to the quick with your swift disapproval of me!" He feigns offense in his tone and laughs with her as he skillfully and gently begins to guide our guests into the softly lit dining room. An elegant Christmas flower arrangement made with red roses commands the center of the table and holds court over tempting displays of salmon, shrimp, turkey, and six different salads and pasta. On the sideboard are platters of elaborate appetizers surrounding a huge bowl filled with red champagne punch, with exotic puffs of dry ice rising from the bowl.

Bucky begins ladling out punch and places each glass cup on a small matching glass tray, handing it to a guest, and inviting each to begin the buffet. His political skill is apparent as he schmoozes each person with a personal familiarity. He is typical of his breeding: Trained as a lawyer, but also a scholar of local history, a lover of fine wines, an epicure, and a gentleman who takes his social responsibilities seriously and does them very well.

As the midnight hour nears, I gather our guests together in the library for the traditional toast and make sure everyone has a freshly filled champagne flute. Turning on a television so that we can count down along with the rest of Times Square, I hand out party whistles. Seeing Effi alone, I am puzzled and approach her. "Should I try to find your husband?"

"Oh, girl, you may find his body, but you won't find his head. He lost that a long time ago." Her face is set in a grim expression and her arms are folded across her body with determination.

I hand her a full glass of champagne. "Don't you fret; let me see what I can do."

I go to the front door to see if Marion has stepped outside for fresh air. As I am about to close it, I see him walking along the sidewalk back to the house. He has an umbrella, but he has not put on his coat and is using the fences and trees to steady himself. I step out and call, "Marion ... Marion ...," and wait for him to reach our gate and slowly find his way back to the porch. "Are you all right?"

"Yes, yes. I'm fine, just had to go to the car for a minute." I look at him closely and wonder, but quickly take his umbrella and bring him in.

Effi walks up behind me. "Mary Frances, you're being very kind, but would you leave us alone for a minute?" Her voice is stern, almost angry.

I quietly back away, but before I am out of earshot, she says angrily, "You promised you wouldn't do this! You promised…."

"Woman, you keep out of this!" he snaps at her.

I worry about my friend, but move away so that I can't hear any more. I am just in time for Bucky to count the final minutes on his pocket watch. In between each minute, he jokes about how his grandfather used the watch every year for counting down the final seconds of the year, and how he is pleased to continue the family tradition. He grabs me quickly for a midnight kiss, and I decide not to tell him about the friction between Marion and Effi as they join the party, each adopting a presence that nothing is wrong.

Our guests begin to say their goodbyes around one-thirty in the morning. Bucky, in spite of an ample interest in champagne over the course of the evening, is still the congenial host as he warmly shakes hands with the men and kisses the women's cheeks. I make sure all coats are retrieved along with hats, gloves, and umbrellas. A northern weather front, known locally as an Alberta Clipper, is coming through and is dropping a dusting of snow for New Year's Eve, and a few flakes are blowing in the door each time it opens. Several of the guests have drivers who have waited or who are picking them up, and our narrow street is filled with long, black automobiles. In the distance we hear gaiety on M Street, probably coming from Nathan's Bar and Grill, and the wailing of sirens.

"Now, Miz Barry, don't you go getting wet, y'hear?" Bucky says as he helps her with her coat and opens the door for the mayor and his wife. "Let me help you." He takes their big, black umbrella, steps out onto our front veranda ahead of them, opens it, and hovers over her as she steps into the night air. As Effi moves in front of her husband, Bucky offers his arm to steady her. He walks ahead of them on the old sidewalk and opens the iron gate, escorting Effi down the slippery, semicircular, brick steps to the sidewalk. "There you go, ma'am." And to the driver he shouts and waves, "They're all yours, and drive carefully now."

This scene is repeated several times until he closes the door for the last time with an exaggerated sigh of relief. Grabbing my hand and pulling me along, he collapses on the lower steps of the staircase. "Now little woman, it's you and me, and we're gonna start the new year off right!" As I fall into his lap, he plants a big kiss on my lips and wraps me in his arms. "Miz Andrews, you're a mighty fine woman, and I sure do love you, even mor'n I did last year about this time." He starts to get up, "Now, let's go get some of that lovin' that you're so good at."

"Bucky, darling, that's just fine with me, but the caterers are gone, and you have to let me put a couple of things away before I go to bed. Why don't you go on up, and I'll be right with you." I pull away and start for the kitchen.

He gets up and starts up the stairs. About halfway, he turns and says, "Don't you be long now, and sugar," he pauses and chuckles, "don't forget to count the silverware."

I whirl around, stunned, "What did you say?"

"Count the silverware. We had those colored folks in the house, y'know."

I can't believe my ears. "I am astonished at you! That was the mayor and his wife! She's one of my friends! And the councilmen! What in the world prompted you to say that?"

He staggers a little bit, chuckling, "My mama always tol' me that the nigras would steal the silverware if you don't watch them." He puts both hands on the railing to steady himself, chuckling. "And darlin', remember, you can take a nigra off of welfare, but you ain't neva gonna stop 'em from stealing from white folks. Even His Honor, the former mayor of this fine city, stole every dime he could get jus' by running a crooked government, and you know that!"

"Bucky, you're being drunk and disorderly right now, and I'm certainly glad that Effi and her husband can't hear you say that. You politicians all steal from the ordinary folks. You know that as well as I do, and it doesn't matter what color skin the folks have, or the politicians."

He raises his hands and shoulders in a playful shrug, "I'm just tellin' you the Lord's honest truth as my mama taught me a long time ago." He awkwardly starts to unfasten his tie as he resumes his attempt to climb. "I'll see you in a few minutes, sugar plum, and don't you be long now 'cause I'm wantin' you real bad."

I stare after him in disbelief. I've known Bucky for twenty-three years and I know that he had a typical segregationist upbringing before the civil rights movement, just like me, but I have never known him to be so blatantly racist. He and I were both born into a segregated society, and our impressionable early training was in the old rules of the South, but times changed and the Southern way of thinking changed. Slowly, and painfully at times, new attitudes developed, and most Southerners don't talk this way anymore. I know many fine black people and appreciate the opportunity for their acquaintance. Bucky does not normally drink to excess, and I can only imagine that the alcohol has dimmed his wits and loosened his tongue. His words feel like an insult to me and to many of our friendships. It takes some time in the kitchen for me to calm down.

A few minutes later, I quietly open the bedroom door, undress in the dark, and gently lie down on my side of the king-size bed, pulling the thick quilt over my shoulders. Bucky seems to be passed out from the champagne or asleep, but he hears me, or perhaps feels the bed move, and groggily rolls over toward me, putting his arm around my waist.

"Bucky, darling," I whisper, "perhaps we should wait until morning. I'm awfully tired, too." What I didn't say is that I'm still upset with him.

"No, no," he grumbles as he tries to wake up, "gotta have my girl on New Year's Eve." He fumbles with my nightgown and awkwardly attempts foreplay. "We've got a great year ahead of us, darlin', and we want to start it out right." His touch is clumsy but I accept it as I always have.

I know that I can't talk to him now. I barely have time to set aside my anger, try to relax, and begin to enjoy the stimulation when he rolls over on top of me. "That's it, baby doll, give your man what he needs." With little concern for me, he concentrates on himself and his desires, talking in a groggy, drunken manner. "Move with me, baby, that's my girl, talk to me, give me those sexy sounds that you make." His body is very tense in spite of the alcohol, and I can tell he is close. "Yes, sugar, yes, oh that feels so good." He finishes, his body relaxes, and he falls to my side and hugs me. I have just begun to feel aroused, and his closeness is still stimulating to me. I savor the touch of his body and the warmth and tingle that I feel, and console myself with memories of other times when he has been more sensitive to my needs. We fall asleep the same way we have slept together for twenty-one years—his arms engulfing me, protecting me—and I feel the rhythm of his breathing as if we are one.

. . . .

In the morning on New Years Day, Bucky and I leave around nine-thirty to visit my Aunt Beatrice in Richmond, Virginia. It's an easy, two-hour trip from our home to hers. As we drive, I notice that the Alberta Clipper from the night before has left a layer of beautiful confectioner's sugar on the foliage along the highway and its high clouds are still in the sky.

Beatrice's annual custom is to have an open house for all the important people in town, where she serves a traditional New Year's Day brunch buffet. Among the splendor, she has faithfully kept the Southern superstition that black-eyed peas mixed with rice must be served in abundance on New Year's Day in order to bring good luck in the new year. Although I have grown to dislike some aspects of our culture, steeped in its traditions, I feel duty bound to attend every year, especially since Bucky enjoys the camaraderie of his fellow Virginians and politicians. We lived in Richmond when we were first married, and his political career started there, so the annual brunch feels like a homecoming for him.

Driving to Beatrice's brings back childhood memories as we drive, not all of them pleasant. I lived with my mother's only sister and her late husband, George, after my parents were killed in a hurricane in the late summer of 1954, when I was five years old. I was their only child. My father had been a prominent Richmond attorney and my mother had been involved in the social culture of Richmond, much like Beatrice. I don't remember anything of my life with my parents, nor do I remember the hurricane.

Beatrice and George didn't have children of their own and welcomed me with an effervescence that was overwhelming to a small child who had just lost both parents. Her words from those early years still ring in my ears: "Now, darlin' child, I know it's hard on you, but I want you to consider this your home, and we're gonna be your parents, an' we're all gonna be right happy now, aren't we?" It was usually followed by a request for me to call her "mommy" or "mama" any time that I felt like it. I never did. The words stuck in my throat every time I attempted.

Beatrice's house never felt like home, either. She still lives in the upscale, older section of Richmond and has made the preservation of Southern history and traditions, and especially her fine, old home, the focus of her attention. It has become a personal and private museum of culture and artifacts open only to friends and invitees.

As we drive, I remember the Thanksgiving dinner when I was six. I knocked over and broke an antique crystal water goblet, cutting my finger, and Beatrice was furious. I was banished to my room, with screams about being an ungrateful, inconsiderate, selfish child. She never noticed the blood on my hand. As soon as she could, Martha, Beatrice's live-in maid, came upstairs and bandaged it, then brought dessert for me. Beatrice always used those words when she was angry, "ungrateful, inconsiderate and selfish." I never had the sense that I pleased her about anything.

"Sugar plum, you're bein' awful quiet," Bucky breaks the silence. He reaches down and picks up a penny from the car floor and hands it to me, "A penny for your thoughts?" I felt much like an orphan in Beatrice's home, but I know Bucky doesn't like to hear this. When I don't answer, he coaxes, "What's on your mind that's keepin' you a thousand miles away from me?"

I'm pensive. "I wish I had had a real mother growing up. I sometimes think that my problems with Betty Susanne come from that. I didn't want to be like Aunt Beatrice, but I never learned how to be a mother and how to instill in her the goodness of our life. So now Betty Susanne has turned her back on her culture and her opportunities, and I'm afraid it's my fault."

"Oh, don't you fret about Boopsie, she's in a phase. She's been through lots of them. Our little girl'll be all right by the time she gets out of school. An' don't you ever think that you did poorly by her, y'hear now?"

"You think so?" Inwardly, I fear that my daughter will always dislike me the way I dislike Beatrice.

"Of course, don't you fret your pretty li'l head. She's just an emotional young girl. You were there once, remember, and you turned out jus' fine … she'll come around. I'm her father, trust me."

"I know," I sigh, feeling that my concerns don't really count and wondering if my emptiness is the natural way a woman feels when her child is gone. My feelings of despair about Betty Susanne are something that Bucky has never understood. Bucky has been right so often that I have to believe him. After a moment's hesitation, I raise another issue.

"Bucky, darling, something you said last night really bothers me."

"What's that, sugar?"

"That comment you made just before going to bed, about the silverware. I'm glad no one else heard you, but I'm very disturbed that you would say that in this day and age."

He's very nonchalant. "I'd never say anything like that in front of anyone, you know that."

"You said it in front of me, and I was insulted on behalf of my friends."

"You're different, though, you're my wife. You understand these things."

I pause in order to decide whether or not I have just become a non-person. My Southern persona emerges along with my old accent, "No, I don't understan' 'these things.' Your mama may have made comments like that a long time ago when times were different, but if she were alive now, she wouldn't be saying what you said, and I don't think she would even be thinkin' it."

"I'm not so sure. My mama was a true plantation lady."

"Your mama was a fine, true lady of the South whose morals were above reproach and whose thoughts were pure. She did not go around insulting folks behind their backs. And she was able to change with the times when it became the right thing to do, far better than Aunt Beatrice, I might say."

"Mary Frances, your understandin' of Beatrice is marred by your feelings about her, an' I don't think you're giving her a fair shake." His tone changes and he turns to me with contrite eyes and an exaggerated humble expression. "Darlin', if I tweaked your pretty li'l nose, I am so sorry. I suppose I was out of line, and a true gentleman always apologizes to a lady."

"You were very much out of line. I don't expect to hear that kind of language ever again. And, apology accepted. I hope you hold your tongue a little better in the future."

Even though I know there is some playacting in this little repartee, I appreciate the idea, but I feel a nagging sense of concern. It has been years since I felt compelled to contemplate the issue of racism. I thought that Bucky had advanced beyond the old-style bigotry, and I have been pleased to see his warm acceptance of our

36

multicultural lifestyle. I'm very disappointed to learn that this is not true; that he has only masked it. I stare out the window, wondering if there is any way to change him, and wondering how important I should make this.

After fussing at Bucky about his attitude, I began to feel a pang of guilt as I remember an old conversation with Martha about my new elementary school one morning as she was dressing me in the navy blue uniform. I didn't understand why I had to change schools and why I couldn't wear my own clothes.

"Dumplin'," Martha had said, "there ain't no use fightin' it. White folks just don't like the new law an' they's gonna find a way around it." She finished buttoning the blouse in the back.

"Whatcha mean, Martha?" I lifted my arms for the jumper to be pulled on over my head.

"There's a new law out there that says li'l colored children gets to go to the same school as you do." She tugged, pulling it into place.

"Martha, Aunt Beatrice says that's not right … that colored children have got schools just as good and shouldn't be hornin' in on ours … that they are just trying to take over everythin' and push us out, and make us pay for private schools while they get the free schools."

"Dumplin', you's a lucky one, and you's got everythin' you will want for, and don't ever forget that, but don't think for one minute that li'l colored children gets the same. On the other side of those tracks yonder, there ain't nothing so good as the fine school you is agoin' to." Martha finished buttoning the three small buttons on the back of the uniform, patted my behind, and told me to sit down and get my braids done up. "Dumplin', they's a whole lot you just ain't gonna understand for a long time, but you be good, do as your aunt says, an' everythin' will go fine for you."

I had fine, dark, curly hair, even as a child. Aunt Beatrice had insisted that it be kept very short, almost boyish, but I wanted braids like the other girls, and pleaded with Martha not to cut it. We finally worked out a secret between us ... Martha wouldn't cut it when she was told to; instead, she would curl it tight for a while, then when it was long enough, she would make two ponytails. I wore a cap a lot. Finally, I started appearing in braids, and Aunt Beatrice didn't seem to notice.

My favorite pastime while having my hair done up was to catch the early morning light rays from the window in a hand mirror and redirect them to Martha's face. She always fussed and pretended to brush them away like someone brushes away the summer flies, and I would laugh. "You stop that, chile, you hear? And use that mirror the way it's suppos' ta' be used."

I would peer at myself carefully in the mirror while I was making "flies" on Martha's face. Aunt Beatrice had told me several times that I looked like my roguish, Irish father, with his flashy eyes and dark, wavy hair. I knew I didn't look like Aunt Beatrice, and often wondered which physical attributes I had inherited from my mother's side of the family. Martha often told me that she could see my real mama's face in the mirror, and if I peered carefully, I could see it, too. All I saw was someone who couldn't look at her parents straight on and see for herself.

Even in the mirror, Martha was a commanding presence because she was tall and dark. Even though she was thinner then, I always had a sense of her being round, and sometimes teased her about being a colored Mrs. Santa Claus because she was so warm and kind. I remember asking her if the Santa for little colored children was also colored, and if she was his wife, because she always went away at Christmas. As she braided, I said, "Well, I still think it ain't right for them to make us pay all that money so's we don't have to go to school with the riffraff."

"Hush up," Martha pulled as the bundles of hair in her nimble fingers began to form into braids. "That's not a charitable thing to say, and you also gotta think about bein' charitable." She wove a white ribbon into the plaits and tied it into a bow. "Don't you never let me hear you say them kinda trashy words again." Martha's words echoed. They always did. She was the voice of my conscience.

As we drive toward Richmond, I stare out the car window as my memories toss and tumble like the never-ending waves of an ocean. I have often wished that I could remember the time before I lived with Aunt Beatrice and Uncle George. When I concentrate on these memories, the nightmare that I used to have as a child returns and I tremble with fear. I hear loud, crashing winds and feel a gigantic, dark bear smothering and suffocating me. The nightmare always ends the same way, with a red hawk swooping down and taking me away from the bear and suffocating me again. Thinking about it brings back chills.

Martha had stayed in a room close to mine so that she could come when I woke up screaming. It took years before the comfort of Martha's warm body and her gentle rocking eased the pain enough that I could sleep through the night. Even now, the summer thunderstorms and lightning awaken the same fear, and I curl up in fright, feeling an overpowering despondency and suffocation that I cannot identify.

Thoughts of my very early school years begin to surface. I was a very frightened child when I started kindergarten a month after the hurricane had killed my parents. Beatrice was proud to walk me to the neighborhood school and show off because she finally had a child to care for. She made a big fuss as she installed me in the classroom and kissed my forehead. Other new students were clinging to their mothers and crying, but I didn't cling or cry, and she was embarrassed. But she pretended and fawned over me, saying the same things that the other mothers were saying. I stood in the shadows stoically, absorbing the moment, confused about Aunt Beatrice's behavior and reeling from the changes that were occurring in my life. 'Course that was only the first day. Martha walked me to school thereafter.

My first school was a public school, and I started making friends there, but it was hard with my delicate emotional situation. It was a typical Southern school setting … we started each day with the Pledge of Allegiance, a salute to the American flag, and a Bible reading, the Protestant version. As children, our criteria were very superficial—I still grin when I remember how the girls broke into school groups and Brownie Scout troops according to which Sunday school class they attended, even though Scouts was supposed to be secular. I was in the Methodist group, but I really didn't like anyone and felt like they didn't like me because they had real mothers and I didn't. The popular girls wore nice dresses bought at Thalhimers Department Store and leather buckle-up shoes. I believed that I had friends because I had even better clothes, ones that Aunt Beatrice and Uncle George bought in New York City when they would go there on business. The poor girls had homemade dresses or mail-order clothes from Sears Roebuck & Co., and old-fashioned tie shoes, so we always knew they didn't belong in our group.

Then when the racial difficulties began in earnest about four years later, I was transferred to the Catholic school. It was necessary to be driven each day, and Uncle George usually dropped me off on his way to the office. He was easy-going and became my ally as we talked about our more difficult encounters with Beatrice.

Aunt Beatrice was very strict with me, insisting that I must be a proper, young Southern lady. She made sure I followed the necessary social rules, learned all the popular sexual taboos, went to church every week, maintained traditions, and kept a rigid schedule with many lessons. I grew to believe that there was a powerful evil demon inside of me that, if not kept under control by these rules, would explode. Fortunately, most of the instructions were given to Martha, who often did not carry them out, and it seems to me that I survived in spite of Beatrice.

Good ol' Uncle George, his way was different. Every once in a while he had a treat hidden in a pocket, often a penny candy or a stick of gum, and he would make a show of looking for something that had been misplaced. When he finally "found" it and handed the treat to me, a mock seriousness darkened his face, and he would say, "Now see this here piece of Juicy Fruit? I'm thinkin' that this might be your prize for being good today and doin' all the things a nice little girl always does. I'm jus' not sure if I should give it to you now, or if I should wait until I get a report from your teacher." Well, of course I would promise to be good, even if he gave it to me early. He's been dead for four years and I still miss him.

I remember discussing the new school with him. I didn't understand why I had to change schools. For instance, in Sunday school, we faulted the Catholics for being the wrong religion and made fun of them, then suddenly I had to go to their school, learn their catechism, and hear criticisms about the Protestants. Uncle George told me it was a better school and I would learn more, and that I could ignore the religious lessons if I wanted. He told me to make a game out of it, and the game was to get a good grade without believing it and to trick the nuns into thinking I did. We often talked about how I was succeeding at the game, and his encouragement made it easier.

"Bucky," I suddenly come back to the present and turn to him as I recall the Catholic school, "I was just thinking about the old woman in the nursing home and trying to decide where I might know her from. I don't think it was from school. I'm thinking she might have been with my real mama and daddy."

"Sugar, that's foolish. How would she ever recognize you from when you was a li'l baby?"

"I don't know. I've thought and thought about it. She talked to me as if I was a child. She wasn't at Aunt Beatrice's, I know that almost for sure. She wasn't at school, I'm pretty certain, and she isn't anyone we've had in our home since we've been married. Where else could she be from?" I wonder if I should tell Bucky about the strange feeling I get when I think about her. It's a feeling of being safe and warm. I keep searching for a picture in my mind to go with the feeling, but nothing ever comes, and I'm frustrated because I can't find the clues that will tell me who she is. I also wonder why thoughts of my real mother seem to surface when I think about Emmaline.

"Why're you worryin' about that at all, baby doll? Sounds to me like you're chasing windmills. You plannin' on bein' Don Quixote an' savin' that ol' woman from herself?" He sounds annoyed, but his tone changes as the subject changes, "Let's talk about our trip this summer, instead. How you comin' on the plans? I really wish you hadn't let our passports expire. It's gonna to be a problem to get them reissued."

"Bucky, I'm very curious about her. It seems like a nice challenge, and I'm planning to figure this one out, somehow." But I allow him to change the subject. "Darling, we haven't needed them in years, but it'll be all right, don't worry. I'll get my birth certificate from Aunt Beatrice today so I can apply for another passport. Did you find your certificate yet?"

"Not yet. But I will. I think I know where it is, just haven't had time to look, I'm so busy nowadays, you know that. Maybe you could be a good wife and take care of that for me, honey bunch?"

"Darling, of course I would." As the rolling fields of northern Virginia pass, I ponder my life. *Always do what Aunt Beatrice says, that is the way I have lived most of my life, and now it's always do what Bucky says. I had a taste of freedom once and I felt strong and powerful for a little while. I wonder if I will ever feel like that again. I love Bucky dearly, and I want to be a good wife to him, but sometimes I wonder if I am someone who is more than just Bucky's wife.*

3. AUNT BEATRICE AND MARTHA

Even after all these years, I still feel a sense of apprehension as I approach Aunt Beatrice's house. Her two-story, Italian Renaissance house was built by a prosperous merchant in the 1820s and was later extensively decorated around the windows and verandas with black, ornamental iron from the famous Tredegar Iron Works of Richmond. It is set back from the street, nestled in a grove of tall, oak trees and surrounded by a cool, gray winter mist even in midday. Going to her house always causes me to reflect on the pain of growing up, feeling as if I was doing without something essential while living in the midst of abundance.

"After you, my dear." Bucky opens the gate and we follow the old brick sidewalk. Today, he is more elegantly dressed in a charcoal Armani suit and a light gray shirt that shows off his winter tan and the white hair at his temples. His style has always been to wear his coat casually over his shoulders, and it flares slightly in the winter wind of Virginia, drawing attention to his elegance. He had insisted that I wear the full-length leather and mink coat that he gave me for Christmas, and he is proud as he takes my arm. Instinctively, I stoop to pick up a fallen leaf from the impeccably manicured lawn.

"Why, look who's here, it's Miz Frances!" Martha throws open the white double doors of the red brick house and rushes out, "It's *sooo* nice to see you 'gain, dumplin'." She speaks excitedly with a warm drawl. Martha has on her finest white apron over a long, dark dress, and her robust body shakes as she gives Bucky and me warm hugs and takes our bags. Even though I am grown, she is taller, and I still feel like a child in her arms. I notice that her hair has become quite gray in the past year, and she limps a little. "It's so nice that you could make it down 'gain this year. We sure would like to see more of you." She turns and holds the door for Aunt Beatrice, "Lookie here, Miz Beatrice, look who's come to see us again, our dumplin's!"

"Bless the Lord, our prodigal child is here. How've you been, darlin'?" Aunt Beatrice comes out the front door. She is now the grande dame of Richmond culture and wears her role well, imbuing everyone in her presence with the significance and importance of gentility. Physically she is small, but she uses the steady tapping of her ivory cane to create a commanding aura. In her seventies, with a thin angular face, she wears wire-framed glasses perched on her prominent nose. I never considered her to be an attractive woman, but she maintains herself well. Her skin is powder white, set off by discreetly applied pastel makeup. Silver hair is piled high in a bun on top of her head, creating the illusion of height, with a few wisps trailing around the edge. A floor length hostess dress of muted blue and purple flowers ripples with her movements, and her traditional brooch is at the throat, with too much dangling jewelry on her arms. "Come here and let me see you." Her voice has a sharp edge, mitigated by a soft accent. After a quick hug and perfunctory cheek kiss, she holds me at arm's length. She still smells of expensive gardenia sachet, even after all these years. "Why, you're doin' just fine aren't you, darlin', and ..." turning to Bucky for a hug, "you, too, son?"

Bucky's charm never passes anyone by. "Thank you so much for askin'. You're lookin' jus' like a fine pearl yourself. How's our favorite relative?"

Her "Fine, dear, fine," is absentminded as she looks ahead to the next group opening the gate before turning back to us and pointing toward the door with the carved lion head of her cane. "Well, now, why don't you go on inside there and help yourself; there is so much fine food. As always, Martha outdid herself." She pats my forearm, "You'll excuse me, darlin', won't you? I see the governor coming up the walk here, and I must do my duty." She abruptly turns to greet her new guests, the first black governor of Virginia, Douglas Wilder, and his wife. Bucky notices, hesitates momentarily as if he wants to greet the governor himself, but decides against it and enters with me.

The house verges on being a mansion. The colonial architect who designed it also built the governor's mansion and several other prominent homes of the era. We enter through the classically designed, oval foyer where early callers were often seated. Beatrice only employs one full-time live-in, Martha, and a catering staff has been hired for the open house. A maid who has been assigned to handle the coats greets us, along with a waiter carrying a tray of champagne.

As we move into the larger, two-story entrance hall, my eyes are drawn to the focal point, which is a five-foot, white marble statue of a delicate blind girl. She is in an alcove with soft backlighting. I still remember Aunt Beatrice's pleasure in acquiring this statue at auction when I was a child. For her it seemed to be the air of owning something important, not the pleasure of enjoying fine artistry. The sculpture is by an early Virginian and its story is engraved on a brass plate at the base, which I have often read. In part, it says, "While visiting the Deaf, Dumb, and Blind School in Staunton, Virginia, Edward Valentine, a prominent artist in his day, was greatly affected by a young girl singing the 42nd Psalm. Later he sketched her and carved this statue, which was displayed at the 1893 World's Columbian Exposition in Chicago." The child is gracefully and wistfully immortalized at peace with her thoughts and feelings. Her head is lifted in prayer, her eyes are covered with a tie, her hands are clutched, and she is wearing a simple, flowing gown. She still captivates me ... I often wanted to be the blind girl, oblivious to the treachery and pain of the world around me. I pause for a moment and wonder, *Am I that way now?*

While Bucky greets an old friend, my eyes are drawn up the stairs in the direction of my old bedroom, and I recall living in this house and climbing these stairs. Then, as now, I see this house as a beautiful and pretentious mausoleum. I often see Aunt Beatrice only as her trappings and I place her friends and colleagues in this world of make-believe.

The graceful staircase risers follow the circular right wall of the two-story entrance hall. The staircase sets off the French crystal chandelier hanging on a long cord from the ceiling far above. Etched lines and patterns of ivory, very pale yellow, and federal blue follow the molding and trim along the edges of the wall. These designs are repeated in the tightly woven, colonial-patterned carpet and runner on the stairs. As beautiful as it is, I don't like being here and feel myself emotionally withdrawing from the festivities. Again my fear surfaces that I have become my aunt in many ways, but I can't tell this to anyone, even Bucky.

With his normal flair, Bucky introduces me to a friend who is in the Virginia legislature, and I follow them into the large front parlor to the left through the mahogany double doors. A pianist sits to one side, quietly playing the Steinway grand piano. Silver-framed pictures of Beatrice, George, and me reflect in the shimmering black of the instrument, and it occurs to me that she still pretends to be my mother. I wince, remembering all the times Bucky has chided me for criticizing her.

This room is so "Beatrice." She has spent her whole life cultivating an image of herself. Oil paintings of early Virginia hunting scenes hang along the walls, and the floor is covered with Oriental carpets in deep red patterns. The furniture and styles have been carefully selected to reflect colonial Virginia culture, its history, equestrian interests, and tobacco industry. Full-length, sash windows look out to the side veranda and formal garden. In the summer, these windows function as doors directly to the outside brick patio, and many large gatherings extend to the lawn.

Bucky becomes engrossed in discussing Virginia's strategies regarding the new NAFTA agreement, and I scan the room, recognizing many important political people in Virginia but no one I know well enough to approach. As I have always experienced in this house, I feel out of place. I watch a number of guests mingle, and settle on listening to two people, a man and woman, seated on the Edwardian settees flanking the fireplace, who are engaged in an animated conversation about Rush Limbaugh. Eavesdropping, I am distracted by the glow from the fireplace reflecting in their faces.

The magic of the fire seems to transform the woman into a ten-year-old child in a pink organza dress, sitting uncomfortably on the edge. I know this child … she is me at my birthday party. I watch her look around, staring at a much younger Beatrice, who is chatting gaily with several mothers while their daughters play tag. The sash doors are open to a yard full of balloons, and Beatrice gently teases the girls as she ushers them out. Just as Beatrice steps out, she turns as if she has forgotten something. "Mary Frances, come, dear, it's your birthday. Play with us." The girl who is me continues to watch the party from afar, and I quietly shudder, shaking loose the memory.

On each side of the fireplace, there are large, glass display cabinets that contain her precious collection of antique dog figurines and early bone china, including two place settings from Jefferson's White House. A large oil painting of Beatrice hanging above the fireplace draws my attention. It was painted when she was much younger and a belle of the old South. In the portrait, she wears a red velvet nineteenth-century ball gown complete with hoop skirt and cleavage. Her eager self-assurance glows as she dances with an unidentified escort. It is Beatrice's essence, the red velvet lady, who became the ghost that followed me around this house when I was a child, watching my every movement and making sure I didn't break anything.

I amuse myself by watching her, still the epitome of a gracious hostess, remain the star of her event. Her movement from one small gathering to another has the feel and tempo of a waltz and seems to be paced with the background music. Watching her, I realize that the cane isn't necessary. *What an actress*, I observe. But, I am also haunted by the public perception of how grateful I should be because she graciously took me in as an orphan and gave me every material advantage, introduced me to Bucky, provided a lavish wedding, and successfully guided my husband's career. As I observe her, I feel guilty and don't understand my lack of appreciation.

Beatrice is the Southern woman who always maintains a beautiful house of quiet ease and comfort, whose garden and vases are full of flowers, whose tables flow with superb food and drink, but who seems to always walk through life alone surrounded by a pervasive emptiness. She explained my behavior toward her as my lingering melancholy and grief over my parents' death. She valiantly told her friends that "the child" preferred being with Martha, and this was fine because it gave her more time to attend to her social responsibilities. She turned a blind eye when Uncle George spent time away and rumors floated back that he was with other women. It was as if these aching thorns continued to grow when the flowers died out, took hold, and pierced her heart.

Beatrice's events always bring out the chivalry of old Virginia, with all of its courtliness, pomp, and circumstance. Today many of the women have chosen floor-length daytime gowns and some of the men are in dress uniforms from the Southern military schools that they attended as youths. These folks who worked so hard to defeat Governor Wilder in the last election now graciously fawn over him.

As I watch, Beatrice finds opportunities to gently guide Bucky into the crowd by introducing him as her successor, and I realize that Bucky has replaced Uncle George in her eyes. Several times, she says that if Bucky ever wants to move back to Richmond, she could handle his career nicely. Bucky thanks her each time she suggests that we move back and reminds her that he will as soon he is ready. She also brags about the work he is doing with the Financial Control Board and his significant opportunity for advancement as a political appointee, and how she would use her influence any time he desires.

As Bucky and I mingle with the crowd, drinking mint juleps and champagne, he is distracted by people wanting to greet him, and I patiently stand in his shadow as the dutiful political wife and placidly notice how I seem to fit the stereotype so well. Eventually we gravitate through the doors leading to the dining room and the lavish buffet offerings. Beatrice's finest silver coffee service, a set once owned by an English duchess, sits on the table, competing with the overflow of my favorite childhood foods.

The aroma of the food floats in the air as I remember all of these, especially the pleasure Martha and I had pouring through cookbooks to find them, and giving each dish our own special name … the scalloped ham 'n' eggs, brandied chicken livers, Confederate black-eyed peas, and Mississippi-style stewed green tomatoes. Southern fruit fantasia, cinnamon twists, and Georgia peach chutney are the accents. The sideboard brims with our Old Richmond spice cake, little homemade brandied mincemeat tarts, delightful date cakes, and meringue kisses. As I think about Martha, I realize that she is the real mother image in my life, the one who nourished me, not my aunt who is the pretender to the throne.

As the day wears on, I sense that Aunt Beatrice's New Year's Day brunch is a great success, as usual. Bucky, of course, is in his element and becomes more of a Southern gentleman as the hours pass and the women become more flirtatious. One woman, someone I don't know, takes it a little beyond acceptable limits. While I chat with a group of old school friends, she links arms with Bucky and guides him away toward the library. I turn back in time to see the door close behind them.

Her image briefly flashes across my mind. She has taken care of herself and fits her attractive dress well, but so have I. Bucky compliments me often about my shape, and I have worn the same dress size for twenty years. Initially, I did not pay much attention to this woman, but now I see her face and sense that she is younger than my forty-five years, but not enough to be a serious threat. The lingering image of her brief presence gives off an impression of quiet desperation. I turn to my friends, "Who is the woman who just took my husband into the library?"

"Adrienne."

"And who is Adrienne?"

I notice a pause, a glance between two old friends, and a knowing tone in one voice, "She's recently divorced. I hear that she did not do all that well in the settlement." A second voice, speaking close to my ear, says, "Be forewarned. She's on the prowl."

"Ladies," I nod to them, taking a couple of hands in a casual goodbye, and giving one a cheek kiss, "I believe it's time for me to take my leave. It has been a pleasure to see you again. Do try to visit when you are next up in D.C."

Without being obvious, I move to the library door, pause, take a deep breath, and fling the door open with mocked gaiety. "Oh, Bucky, darling! I've been looking everywhere! Aunt Beatrice has been asking for you, and you do know how she gets ...." I catch my breath and turn to the woman, "I'm so sorry for interrupting your conversation. I don't believe we've met yet ... I'm Bucky's wife, Mary Frances." I extend my hand in a truly limp gesture.

Bucky is leaning against the back of an easy chair, and the woman is standing entirely too close to him. She has just taken a swallow and her glass is still at her lips. She chokes slightly and the champagne recedes back into the vessel while her face flushes and she takes a step backwards. She puts the glass down on a table and takes my hand with mock enthusiasm, "Of course, how nice to meet you!"

Bucky is grinning like a Cheshire cat. He straightens up, adjusts his tie, and addresses Adrienne, "I'm charmed to meet you, but it appears that duty calls. I hope you will forgive me." Bowing slightly, then turning to me with a wink, he says, "Darlin', Aunt Beatrice can be such a troublesome one, can't she?" He takes my elbow and guides me out of the room while speaking, "What is it this time? Surely she doesn't have her dander up ova' anythin' I did, does she?"

After we clear the room, he leans into my ear, "It was mighty nice of you to rescue me from that. Your timing was perfect, my dear." He plunks a kiss on my cheek.

I stop a waiter and take two glasses of champagne, handing one to Bucky with a caustic smile. "I'm sure you enjoyed it, but let's not get too carried away." He beams and kisses my cheek before melting into the crowd.

. . . .

I don't have a chance to talk with Beatrice until late afternoon, after the final guests leave and the cool winter air begins to set in. Sitting on the enclosed veranda, relaxing from the day, I notice streaks of sunlight finally escaping the clouds.

Beatrice has let her yappy little dog out now that the event is over. It's a purebred white Shih Tzu named Chinaberry, and she is brushing his long hair and fawning over him. It's clear from the way he majestically sits on her lap that he knows he is spoiled. Watching them, it occurs to me that she never brushed my hair.

After we discuss the who's who of guests at the brunch, I tell her about our plans to go to Europe for six weeks in the summer. I mention that we need to get new passports and ask if she has a copy of my birth certificate.

53

"Why sure, darlin', those kinda papers are in the big drawer in the secretary in the library. There's a whole file there 'bout your adoption." She pauses and beckons to Bucky as he wanders onto the veranda behind Martha. "Son, come sit down here with us. We were jus' talkin' 'bout Mary Frances' adoption. I can't tell you enough how much joy she has brought to me, coming like she did after her li'l tragedy, and I know she has been such a fine wife for you. This trip that you're takin' my little girl on sounds marvelous." She elongates the first syllable of the word "marvelous." Martha places a tray of iced tea and snacks on a small table while Beatrice is speaking.

Although I cringe momentarily at being referred to as her "little girl," my attention shifts to admiring Bucky, bourbon in one hand, cigar in the other, as he sits in the swing on the other side of Beatrice. Bucky was the most eligible bachelor in Richmond and the prize catch of the cotillion set. She was responsible for introducing us after my return from my "Northern mistake," as she always calls it. Winfred, or "Bucky" as we call him, is a true son of the old South and is schooled in its traditions. He comes from a long line of early plantation owners in Virginia, and graduated from Fork Union military school before attending the University of Virginia in Charlottesville. Beatrice created an opportunity for us to get to know each other by sponsoring Bucky's first run for political office, and sometimes it seemed that she courted him for me. Our wedding was her crowning achievement of the 1972 social season.

We continue to talk about the European trip, and then I decide to bring up the subject of meeting Emmaline. "Aunt Beatrice, something unusual happened last week, and you might have a better understanding than I. Bucky and I visited a nursing home on Christmas Day with our church group, and there was an old black woman there who seemed to recognize me. Her name was Emmaline ..." I pause, "... she called me 'Miz Fancy.'"

Beatrice's eyebrows narrow and her tone is hard, "Now, what's that suppose to mean?" Her body tenses just enough that Chinaberry jumps off and runs into the house.

"She seemed to know me, and I think she might have known me as a child. I was wondering if you might have any recollection of who she could be. Did I ever have a childhood name of 'Fancy' or a mammy by that name?"

The frown wrinkles in her forehead deepen. "Child, how'm I supposed to know? Besides, we don't keep track of the coloreds."

"Could you have had someone besides Martha for a while, or maybe in addition to Martha?" Martha has remained, and I turn to her. "Martha, does any of that ring a bell with you?"

The sunlight pours through the window onto the back of Martha's head, and she casts a shadow on Beatrice. Her hesitation is longer than usual, and she looks directly at her employer. These two women have known each other for many years, and I sense an unspoken communication between them. "Miz Beatrice ...."

"Martha, you mind yourself now, y'hear?" Beatrice's voice is harsh, and she looks at Martha intensely. "I know perfectly well that I'm not suppose to use the word 'colored,' and I'll thank you not to remind me. It was a slip, that's all. Now, you go on and get those dishes cleaned up." I sense the heat of anger rising in Martha and notice a fleeting glare at Beatrice, but she turns and leaves the room.

There is a pronounced softening in Beatrice's voice as she collects herself. "There have been a few blacks," she turns and pretends to shout after Martha, "hear that? I said 'blacks,'" then resumes in a quiet tone, "they came in to help now and again, but

55

there was no one of any consequence who would remember you, I'm sure." Her chin juts into the air with confidence.

"What about my parents? Could it be someone from then? Someone who was with us before they were killed?"

Beatrice hesitates, "Darlin', your parents certainly had household help, but I don't remember any of them. You probably had several." She pauses. "Can't count on good help, y'know, but household help's not folks that you remember ... and do keep in mind that was many years ago."

Bucky interjects, "There now, sugar plum. I didn't think your aunt would remember anyone. Are you satisfied now?"

I look at him, feeling annoyed. "Quite frankly, darling, I'm not. I think I will go back and visit her at the nursing home and see what I can find out. I'm very curious about this."

"Oh, Lordy, child." Beatrice is condescending as she reaches over and pats me on the knee. "It's not right to get involved in their lives, darlin'. They have their place, and we have ours. It's not the right thing to get too close. It causes too many problems."

"Aunt Beatrice, there is something about that woman that intrigues me."

"Let's not talk about it anymore. I know you'll do what is right for your station in life, now won't you?" She pauses and changes her tone to an enforced cheerfulness, "I'm gonna go find that birth certificate you'll be needin'."

"I'll come and help you."

"Don't you bother, child. Just sit here and keep your fine husband company. I'll go get it; I know exactly where it is." She rises with a slow elegance, positions her cane, and disappears into the house with a steady click on the floor. She returns a few minutes later with the document and hands it to me. Chinaberry trails behind at her heels. "Here 'tis, child."

I unfold the piece of paper and stare at it briefly before placing it in my pocketbook. It feels strange to see Beatrice's name listed as my mother.

"Darlin'," she says with uncommon warmth, "how's about we go for a drive this fine afternoon. Get the kinks outta our legs and have a good mother-daughter chat?"

"Now there, you see, Mary Frances?" says Bucky. "Beatrice wants to start the new year off right. That would be a grand thing to do! Want me to get your coat?" He doesn't wait for an answer before getting up and heading toward the coat closet.

Much more than Bucky, I understand the meaning of Aunt Beatrice's drives and her chats. Even when I was a child, when she wanted to have a very private talk, away from the "eavesdroppin' ears of my ungrateful help" as she called it, we would take the car out and have our conversation. I resent these drives, but I've never said no to her. I wish I could.

There are two parks that we have frequented, Bryan Park and Maymont Park, but her favorite spots are both cemeteries, one being the site surrounding old St. John's Church on Church Hill. Here, we would sit on a bench by the grave of Elizabeth Arnold Poe, the young actress who left Edgar Allen Poe an orphan. Beatrice would talk to her as if she were alive and representing the Ghost of Richmond Past. Miz Poe, as my aunt would say, always knew the proper way of behavin' like a true lady, and I would do well to learn it. St. John's Church was also my favorite, but for a different reason. As Aunt Beatrice talked to Miz Poe, I would imagine myself as Patrick Henry, who spoke his famous line, "Give me liberty … or give me death!" from this pulpit in 1775. As a teenager, I had secretly adapted this to "Give me liberty from Aunt Beatrice, or give me death!" But when my best friend from college was killed, it became too personal, and I couldn't say it, or even think it, anymore. Perhaps I also outgrew my intense bitterness toward her and settled into mere dislike.

Beatrice's other favorite spot is the Hollywood Cemetery, named after the abundance of holly trees and overlooking a rocky area of the James River. This has been the resting spot for Richmond's citizens and many prominent Virginians since 1847 and it is the final home for most of my relatives.

She pulls her old Cadillac out of the carriage house, and we head down Twelfth Street. When she turns right on Cary Street, I know it will be Hollywood Cemetery this time, portending a visit to the family plots and another lecture on familial loyalties. Our chatting stops as she turns through the crumbling stone gates next to the caretaker's slate gray Victorian house and onto the narrow, sloping drive winding through the graceful, old trees. The late afternoon sun pierces the clouds and glistens off the remaining light snow. We can already see many of the headstones that are marked with green wreaths and red Christmas bows. As the car crawls along the road on the slight decline, I feel as if we are once again descending into history.

I know her circuitous route by heart. We swerve to the left and follow the drive along the cliff above the James River. Along the road and in small semicircular alcoves, we pass numerous old family mausoleums that are built into the hillside. Finally arriving at the knell where Jefferson Davis continues to hold court, she stops in front of his life-size statue in the center of a small, grassy area, gets out of the car, and reverently leans against the front fender.

From my seat in the car, I patiently observe the pattern of light casting a shadow on the only president of the Confederacy. Two small Confederate flags flutter on each side of the concrete slabs, commemorating Davis and his wife. To his left is a sitting angel. Behind him, with her head bowed, a white alabaster, robed woman blesses the tombs. Beatrice knows the inscription on the statue's base by heart and whispers it reverently, "Oh Lord, in thee I have trusted. Let me never be confounded." She turns and whispers loud enough for me to hear, "He was a great man and did not deserve what happened."

"Mary Frances, dear child," she begins after seating herself in the car again. Her voice has an air of confusion and resignation. "I am confounded."

"Sorry?"

"I am confounded."

"In what way?"

She speaks as if talking to herself, looking straight ahead. "I never had my own children, although I always wanted them. A woman without a child is not complete." She is quiet. I sense the solitude of a confessional and wonder if she is on the verge of tears. Her head turns toward me. "When you came to me, I felt that my prayers had been answered. I was older than my sister, and the good Lord had finally given me a child to raise, a daughter as I had always wanted. You became my only chance to be a mother." She leans her forehead on the steering wheel. "I did what I thought was right. I tried … I tried to love you … Lord, how I tried. You needed me, and I needed you. We should have been able to find something to make us a family." She looks at me silently.

I can say nothing.

"I gave you everything you ever wanted … everything … the best education … a good husband … a fabulous wedding. I have the best connections Bucky could ever want. You asked, I gave." She sighs, "I have only asked one thing from you, ever. Only one thing."

The muscles in my face tense.

"I wanted to be your mother." Her voice cracks, "I wanted you to think of me as your mother. I have never understood why that was so hard for you." Her words are plaintive and wistful. She waits for a reply. Again, she seems to want me to speak the word.

I grasp for my reply. "A person only has one mother."

She sighs with a painful expression, her voice hardening as she speaks. "Why do you continue to punish me like this?" She sits silently. I do not reply. Finally, she mutters, "I'm sorry we haven't been closer." Slowly coming out of her mood, she starts the car, bearing to the right toward our family plot near the crypt of President James Monroe. Instead of stopping when we arrive, she keeps going until she turns left on a narrow road and parks in front of a one-hundred-foot-high stone monument. This pyramid, with a forty-by-forty base, is a collection of rough-hewn stones that looks as if it might tumble down at any minute.

"Sometimes," she says as we sit in the car, "I find it valuable to come here first. It gives me a sense of my history," and an afterthought, "and yours, too. See that monument?" She nods toward the pyramid. "The Daughters of the Confederacy erected that to honor the eighteen thousand young men who were buried here after the troubles. I'm a member, and you're eligible, too."

"Yes, I know." Her old self has returned. This has been a sore point between us for many years. I don't want to join.

"It's the only war that has ever been fought on American soil, but there isn't even a national display in the Smithsonian as recognition. There is no memorial in the District like the ones to the foreign wars. Something is wrong with that." Her voice hesitates. "It has been left to those of us whose families were desecrated to carry forward the memories and the recognition. These men also need to be respected and remembered. Look there ... do you see ...?" She points to a field of small, symmetrical, stone markers. "Many of them are only numbers. There are no names."

"I know. That's sad."

She is pensive and far away. "This is our history and the history of the South. Our family ancestors landed in Jamestown in 1642. We are the original citizens of this country." Pride rises as her tone becomes stronger. She lifts her chin. "We fought for our families, for our land, and for our way of life. We fought for the great cause of state's rights, as Jefferson Davis said in his memoirs, and the right to self-govern, the same cause as the American Revolution. The heroism of our men was extraordinary. This is who we are— good, brave, noble people. I love this countryside ... the beauty of it ... the family traditions ...."

"Aunt Beatrice ..." I speak gently, remaining true to my own sensibilities, "this culture had many fine attributes, and still does, but the economy in the old days was based on slavery and it was morally wrong. They should have found a better way to resolve the problem and treat all people with respect. These men should not have died. It's an ugly mark on our country that we ever allowed slavery. The Civil War was not about states' rights, it was about human rights." I am repeating words that I have spoken many times—and again to no avail.

"Societies evolve, but you don't throw your dignity away because times change. You were raised to be mindful that you have a different culture than the Negro race. A Southern white woman treats those less fortunate with respect, but she does not participate in their lives. If you mingle, you are considered to be in a much lower class, and the class that you maintain for yourself is important." She sighs deeply and, without another word, starts the car and drives back toward our family sites.

We stop first at Beatrice's family plot. It has a three-foot, ornate, black iron fence with a fleur-de-lis pattern and surrounds a rectangular plot about twenty by forty feet. A large elm tree grows along the outer edge, providing shade in the summer for a weatherworn, stone bench just inside the gate. She parks, gets out of the car, opens the gate, and quietly walks in, the dry leaves crackling under her feet. Light from the late afternoon sun casts long shadows on her from tall obelisks on a nearby hill, and the breeze is sharp and cool. I follow, already knowing her litany.

"See this monument?" She touches a twelve-foot-tall obelisk. It reads "In honor of Fairfax Montague, who died as a prisoner of the battle of Vicksburg in 1863, and who lies in an unknown grave." "This was my great-grandfather … his body was never found." Her voice shakes as she says words that I have often heard. "He owned a large plantation and left a wife with six children. He was a good man. He was fair with his slaves, too. My great-grandmother lost everything. Her gristmill was burned, her cotton gins were chopped up for firewood, her fences disappeared, and her animals were stolen. She became more destitute than the slaves ever were. She had to suffer the humiliation of standing in line with ex-slaves and sweaty drifters for meager handouts of bad food from the Union soldiers. She never recovered and died a broken woman." Again, there is a heavy sigh reflecting memories of painful stories. "My grandmother, Ethel Bertha, was her youngest child." She quivers and waves with her arm. "Look around at the children here. Notice how many of them died young. It was the children who suffered the most.

"This one is my father ..." she reads, turning to another marker, "Randolph Hunter Barksdale, 1887—1929, son of Osworth Barksdale, 1857—1922, and Minnie Hunter Barksdale, 1866—1941." Her voice is once again proud and assertive. "Our people worked hard to reconstruct their lives and their fortunes. They were honest and ethical, which is more than can be said for the carpetbaggers! Those damn Yankee scalawags were scoundrels, all of them! My father was not a wealthy man, but he provided for his family, and he was proud, dignified, and honest, even to the end. He was a Southern gentleman until the day he died." She wistfully turns to another. "This was my only brother. He was killed in France in 1945. He left no heirs."

She surveys the rest of the plot, sounding as if she is talking to herself. "I did well when I married George Tyler. Southern women learned to do that. We knew the stories our grandmothers told of life after the troubles and we were determined not to live like that ourselves." She pauses and looks at me. "My sister also married well. You are the only heir to this legacy. It is important for you to carry it on."

I lean against the inside of the iron gate, realizing that the Civil War is more sacred in the South than the invention of the cotton gin. "Aunt Beatrice, I can't live with the bony hands of my ancestors always on my shoulder."

She sits on the bench, wrapping her coat and scarf around her. "Mary Frances, you have a fine heritage that you should be proud of and understand better. The only thing we were left with was our culture and our manners, which are the finest in the world. You have a proud family and a lovely life." She sighs deeply, and her voice shifts slightly to a softer tone. "It's not necessary for you to concern yourself with people who are not of your culture. It's not a good idea for you to go outside of your own community." She turns, looking at me directly, her voice acquiring a slight sense of authority. "You do remember how you tried to do that once, and it caused you a great deal of pain? It caused you to forget who you were, and we had to work hard to bring you back to your sensibilities. I'm too old to do that again."

I can only stare at her. It's not the time or the place to tell her how I really feel, so I keep it to myself and silently think the words I wish I could speak. I have often wanted to say, "I have spent my entire adult life in retribution for what you believe are my sins. When I am alone and contemplate my life, I look back to the years that I was away from your influence, and cherish those moments. I felt like a whole person then. I gained a sense of humanity that I should have learned as a child, but didn't." Instead, I say, "Perhaps it's important to blend the past with the present, don't you think?"

She rises, "It is important for the present to respect the past." Her tone and body language imply that she has spoken her final words on the subject. She walks to the car and I follow. We drive in silence along the narrow, deserted cemetery roads, slowly winding our way up and down the slight hills, to my father's family plot. Again we stop and enter a small, gated enclosure with weathered stones and markers.

I only know my parents as grave markers. My father's stone says James Kerwin Roche, 1920—1954, son of Hubert Roche and Eugenie Clemens Roche. I smile at the tradition of also listing the parents' names on grave markers. My mother is Margaret Ann Barksdale Roche, 1922—1954, with a similar parentage designation. As I stand above the markers, my mind is awash with questions regarding my parents, questions that no one ever wanted to answer. I remember telling Martha made-up stories about my father who was always a famous hero in my eyes, and my mother, a beautiful misty lady who often came and talked to me in the night at Beatrice's house when it was dark and I was alone and afraid.

I recall some of the stories I have heard about the other people buried here. My grandfather had been a state senator and had groomed my father, his only child, to follow in his footsteps. He was heartbroken by my father's death and became a recluse in his later years. My grandmother suffered from Alzheimer's disease and grew to the point of not recognizing me the last ten years of her life.

Beatrice interrupts the silence as we stand viewing my parents' grave. Her voice has a subtle tone of manipulation. "Your father's insurance provided well for you, Mary Frances, but George and I have been your greatest benefactors. You do understand that, I hope?" She pauses for effect. "You also understand that you are designated to inherit my entire fortune, don't you?"

"I think you've mentioned it before."

"There are some responsibilities that come with it, of course."

"I can assure you that I am a responsible person."

"There will be some restrictions that you will need to understand when the time comes."

"Whatever you wish."

"I still have my health, so I don't plan to die soon, but I do expect a certain amount of loyalty and respect."

"Aunt Beatrice, I don't believe I've been disloyal or disrespectful. I trust that you will tell me if you view it differently."

She contemplates before replying. I sense that she is deciding how to proceed. "Mary Frances, it would be important not to meddle in the lives of people who are of no concern to you."

I'm puzzled. It finally dawns on me that she must be referring to the black woman in the nursing home, and I bristle with the thought. "I consider that most of my activities with those less fortunate are of a charitable nature."

"I don't think you should be high-headed with me." Her gaze is very direct and her tone curt. "You can be quite charitable by giving large donations. It is not necessary for you to spend your time meddling with unfortunate folks and their lives." This time she emphasizes the word "meddling."

"Why Aunt Beatrice, you've always supported my charitable work in the past. You've told me that it's good for Bucky's political ambitions."

"You might be inclined to go a little too far, as you have been known to do in the past. For your own good, you need to rein it in a bit." With an air of finality, she turns and walks out the gate. "Perhaps we have said enough, and it is time for us to get out of this decidedly chilly air." She opens the car door and gets in.

We drive back to the house slowly, talking about Beatrice's friends and her activities. When we arrive, she parks the car in the old carriage house, and we enter through the side door that was once designated for the household servants. She decides that a nap is in order after her strenuous day, goes to the entry hall, and graciously ascends the circular staircase. I smile, remembering that Beatrice never uses the steep, narrow staircase in the service hallway. I descend these stairs into the half-basement area that is now the kitchen.

The original colonial house had a small, separate kitchen house that no longer exists. About seventy-five years ago, the main house was upgraded with plumbing, electrical, and heating systems. At the same time, storage rooms and the household slaves' quarters were remodeled to provide for a modern kitchen, pantry, laundry, furnace, and hot-water heater. A three-story dumbwaiter was installed for easier access to the dining room and the upper floor. The original stone fireplace is still present in the kitchen along one wall and lends a feeling of antiquity to the room but cannot be used. High windows look out onto the formal rear yard. A back door directly to the outside leads to a few stairs and Martha's vegetable garden, now maintained by a gardener.

The present kitchen was remodeled in the early sixties, when Beatrice and George entertained extensively. It has a six-burner, restaurant-quality stove, a commercial refrigerator, and a large, wooden worktable in the center. For everyday cooking, Martha favors her microwave and seldom uses the old appliances and utensils, except during big gatherings. Late afternoon sun rays hit the collection of pots and pans hanging from hooks above the table that cast long shadows across the room, hitting the old wooden table by the fireplace, where I often ate meals alone and where Martha supervised my homework.

Martha is unloading the dishwasher. I open the old refrigerator, pour a large cup of milk, spoon in powdered Ovaltine, and put the cup in the microwave before taking a seat on a kitchen stool next to the counter. "Martha, when are you gonna talk Aunt Beatrice into getting you a new refrigerator?"

"After we get rid of that turquoise stool you're sittin' on."

I get off and look at it. "Lordy, this thing belongs in the Smithsonian."

"Just like your ol' aunt and me."

Sitting back down, I muse, "Martha, may I ask you a question?"

"Sure, dumplin'." She puts a leftover mincemeat tart in front of me.

"Why have you stayed with Beatrice all these years when she is so rude to you?"

"Dumplin', I'm sure I could have found something better, and there were times, believe you me. But, sometimes …" she stops and thinks, "sometimes it just gets easier to stay with what you've got. I ain't never been one for movin' around a lot." She lobs a dollop of whipped cream on the tart and washes the bowl in the sink.

"But the rudeness? She has never been nice to you, except when other people are around." Then staring at the dessert, "Martha, that's too much. How can I ever keep my figure if you keep feeding me?"

"Baby chile," she laughs, "you is too skinny for your own good. That pretty li'l blue dress can't be more'n a size five, and size five is for girls. And chile," her eyes twinkle, "your aunt and I done have an understandin'. I understand that she is gonna be the way she is," she pauses, "and she understands that I'm gonna have a talkin' to her about that rudeness after everyone is gone."

"Martha … really?" My eyes dance at the thought of Martha having her "understanding" with Aunt Beatrice. I remember many of Martha's "understandings" with me as a child when I misbehaved. I imagine Beatrice privately smarting from one of Martha's talking-to's, just as I did. Taking a bite of the tart, I comment, "Bucky wouldn't like it if I gained weight."

She frowns at me, "Don't you let that man keep you from eatin' proper, y'hear?" She begins to wrap other leftovers, talking as she works. "I've had to take some flack off of her, ain't no way around that. But, we's jus' two old ladies who have learned how to get along. She is the boss and she pays me my due. I done gets what I want, though. Once upon a time, I asks her to put me on that there social security an' I tol' her that if'n she didn't, I'd find me a job where they would. Well, she did, so's I have my pension now 'long with my wages. But," she opens the refrigerator, turning to me and grinning, "I sur' nuf tells her how to behave sometimes. I'm always polite to her, like a good Christian ought to be, but I do tell her when she misbehaves, like she did this afternoon."

"Martha, you're really something! How come you never had any kids of your own? You woulda been such a good mother."

"Dumplin', you done asks me that question every year since you've know'd me!"

"Now, now, it's only since I've been grown up, and I always like to hear what you say."

"I done tells you the best I can every year, too. Long befor' you was born, I done had me a husband an' when our li'l baby boy was born dead, an' the doctor tol' me I weren't never gonna have another chile, I just put it outta my mind. An' when Mr. Williams hisself ran off up to the north, I found me a job, which wasn't so easy to do in those days. Then, when you came along to live with us, I took it upon myself to raise you the way I woulda wanted to raise one of my own … you was jus' like having my own. Besides," she says, "I still has my relatives, an' I been able to help my nieces through their school and to college, so it ain't been all that bad."

"But with all the changes, you coulda gotten something better, more respectful of you."

"Mebbe. Most of the better education came for the younger ones, most of the better opportunity, too. But, lookee here, I had you as my charge, an' it was more important that you knows. I needed to stick by my li'l dumplin', 'cause you'd been through some bad times and needed lovin', and there weren't no one else to do it."

"Martha, you've certainly been good to me. I appreciate you so much." I feel enormous warmth as I reminisce about the way she has cared for me. "I don't know what I would have done without you." I lean across the counter and whisper for effect, "You and I know that ol' Aunt Beatrice has always been such a wicked ol' witch! That's what Betty Suzanne calls her."

She turns and glares, speaking with firmness in her voice. "Don't you go saying that about your aunt. She done the best she could, which may not have been much to you, but it was all she knowed how, and you need to think of it that way. You need to think kindly about her. An' that there daughter of yours needs her comeuppance, if you asks me. Calling her grandmama a wicked witch ain't right, and you tell her I said so."

All I could do was grin at the thought of Martha giving Betty Susanne a "comeuppance." My daughter lives a punk lifestyle. The last time she visited us in Georgetown, her hair was green. I roll my eyes and imagine what Martha would say if she knew.

I contemplate for a minute. "Martha, you heard me asking Aunt Beatrice about whether I had a mammy when I lived with my mama and daddy?"

"Yes'm." She concentrates intensely on the ham she is slicing and storing away.

"She sure didn't want to tell me anything, isn't that so?" I watch closely for an answer in her face. "You would know, wouldn't you?" I challenge her, "An' you always tell me straight on, don't you?"

"Yes'm." She slices several times.

"Well ...?"

"Well ...." She pauses. Her face wrinkles up as she thinks. It takes her a couple of minutes. "You did have a mammy, just like most white families like yours."

"Could she be the old woman I met in the nursing home? The woman's name is Emmaline."

A twitch on Martha's face catches my attention, and she seems to hesitate. "I don't think I remember her name, now that you mention it, but I do remember that she loved you a whole lot."

"What else do you remember about her?"

"Not so much." Martha answers too quickly and turns to the dishwasher, picking up a couple of baking pans. As she puts them in the cupboard, the clang seems louder than usual. "I can tell you this," she finally begins, "your mammy done have herself a chile, though. You might want to look for that chile of hers and see if you can find out some answers for yourself."

"Martha, the woman in the nursing home acted like she had lost a child, I think. If it is her, something happened to that child." I stop. "Wait a minute, how would I find a child born to someone forty or fifty years ago, when I don't even have the full name of the mama?"

"Dumplin', li'l black children has birth certificates just like li'l white ones. You go off an' find the whole name of that woman that you found in the nursing home and sees if you can find her baby an' you'll start to get your answers, I promise you."

"I wouldn't know where to even begin to find someone with nothing more than a name on a birth certificate." I'm exasperated.

"And what if something has happened to her child? What if she lost the child? What do I do then?"

"Miz Frances, you is a smart one. You'll understand when you find the answers."

I stare at her. "Martha, why don't you jus' tell me what I want to know?"

Her movement stops. Her large body faces me. She wipes her hands on a dishtowel and speaks slowly. "Evil travels in straight lines. You don't give it a straight line, an' it won't follow you." Her eyes penetrate and I feel the power of her personality telling me that I have asked enough. "Now, ol' Martha has said too much an' I need to get on with my work. You run along now."

She shoos me away with my unfinished Ovaltine and mincemeat tart and goes back to her work. "An', dumplin'," she turns her head back to me and says quietly, "this is just between you and me, okay? Don't you go tellin' your aunt what I just tol' you." Knowing Martha well, I sense that something is not being said that ought to be.

Sitting at the old oak table and slowly sipping, I ponder what Martha means. *She wants me to go in search of clues. Why couldn't she just come right out and tell me what she knows? Get Emmaline's full name, she said, find her child and search out this person. What is that going to say? How will this tell me who she is and if she was my mammy?*

As Bucky and I travel back to Georgetown, he asks if Aunt Beatrice and I straightened things out. I tell him about the drive to the cemetery, emphasizing the veiled threat.

"Don't you go messing with her, y'hear? Beatrice has been everythin' in the world to us, and we don't need to throw a wrench into that jus' 'cause you're curious about somethin'."

Just as Martha asked me not to mention our conversation to Aunt Beatrice, my intuition tells me not to divulge any more to Bucky. Martha's evasiveness has piqued my interest, but I feel that this is a project to be undertaken without Bucky's permission or his support, and perhaps even without his knowledge.

I have never before kept anything from him.

4. THE NEXT VISIT

Once a month I have lunch with my closest friends—Effi, Katherine, and Patricia. It's Katherine's turn to choose the location, and she picks the Palm Restaurant on Nineteenth Street near Dupont Circle. In her unique way of speaking, she describes the Palm as the best place to watch politicians and other wild animals in their natural habitat. A light snow is falling as we greet each other in the foyer with comments about the weather.

The purpose of our regular meeting is to provide emotional support for each other in our daily travails. It was originally Patricia's idea, which is natural for a therapist, and this month she has her hands full. Effi is dealing with the rapid disintegration of her marriage just as her husband plans to run for mayor again. Katherine is furious because she has just lost a sought-after journalism assignment, and Patricia bemoans the fact that her husband is a workaholic who loves what he does and travels too much for her comfort. I tell them about my conversation with Martha concerning Emmaline. My issue, as the girls decide, is that I am afraid to go against Bucky and pursue my fascination with this mystery. They chide me for being too much of an obedient wife.

"You go, girl, this isn't any of his business," Effi says. "You've got something here you want to do. It's important, I can tell by what Martha said. Don't you let him mess with your head on this one."

Katherine, in her terse way, advises, "Fuck Bucky, don't tell him."

Patricia understands my reluctance to incur my husband's displeasure. She suggests that perhaps I should take it one step at a time and see what each small step brings, and thinks that maybe Bucky might change his mind later. I could go for one more visit, she suggests, with no commitment to proceed thereafter. Katherine says this is a marvelous idea, hands me a quarter, and suggests that a phone call right now wouldn't do any harm.

"Oh Katherine, you always make me do things, don't you?" I pout in fun, then find the public phones in the restaurant, and make the call to Northwest Convalescent Home. "May I speak with an orderly named Benjamin Mitchell? I believe he works on the seventh floor."

I'm still feeling shy and for a moment hope he isn't there. The operator diligently tracks him down and I recognize his distinctive deep voice when he comes on. "Benjamin Mitchell here."

"Mr. Mitchell," I suddenly feel very foolish, "my name is Mary Frances Andrews. I was there with a group visiting on Christmas Day and met one of your residents, a woman named Emmaline. Do you remember me?"

I hear a smile in his voice. "Yes, ma'am, I sure do."

"I'm wondering if it would be all right for me to visit again."

"It would be fine, indeed. When would you like to come?"

"How about this afternoon?" I'm afraid to delay because I might back out.

Returning to the table, I'm elated about my appointment with Benjamin, but am very fearful about Bucky discovering my plans.

I arrive at Northwest at three in the afternoon and bring a gift from our church charity committee, a small basket of scented soaps wrapped in blue cellophane. Stepping off the elevator, I feel awkward as I brush a few snowflakes from the shoulders of my coat. I know nothing about this woman, and I'm afraid of being nosy, out of place, and unseemly, as Bucky said I would.

Benjamin's smile greets me. He is standing behind the nurse's station and speaks to me warmly. "Why, it's Miz Fancy … you know somethin'? I've been hearin' about you."

Feeling instantly better and welcomed, I'm curious. "What do you mean?"

"Our Miz Emmaline has been talking about you ever since you was here." He is distracted by a ringing telephone.

While he takes the call, I wander into the day room where the Christmas visit had been. The holiday decorations have been removed, and the room is less inviting. Perhaps it's also because the gray clouds visible through the windows have dulled the green walls with winter somberness. Perhaps it's the monotonous drone of the afternoon game show on TV. Perhaps it is the vacant stares of the three residents, sitting in front of the TV, who are ignoring the program. My eyes search the room, and I notice a small group sitting together around a coffee table. They seem to be talking but not really to each other. There are no visitors.

Standing near the doorway, I feel Emmaline's presence in the room again and visualize myself with her. I wonder if I'm doing the right thing by coming back to see her but feel driven by Martha's clues and my own curiosity.

Benjamin motions for a nurse to take his place and joins me at the entrance to the day room. His face beams and his eyes laugh. "Our Miz Emmaline has certainly come alive since you was here, an' we're real pleased to see it. You've had quite an effect on her. I'm certainly glad you came back."

Once again, I feel at ease with him. "Do you have any idea what the connection is? Has she said where she knows me from?"

"Well, now, I haven't picked that up, but I suppose you'll be able to figure that out by visitin' with her for a while."

"What has she said?"

"It's not so much what she says, but how she is," he shrugs. His accent is strong. "She's been here 'bout, oh, 'bout two years I'd say. Most of them, when they first come in, they don't like it much and have to be coaxed a lot. 'Course, it's like anyone whose movin'—its unfamiliar, an' it's a lot harder when you're older and incapacitated."

Looking at the people sitting around the room, I notice five of them in wheelchairs. "I wonder what it would be like living in an institution such as this...." My voice trails off and I think of my own parlor with its family pictures, antiques, and collected memories. Bucky and I are beginning to talk about retirement, and the stark contrast startles me. This is their living room, but there are no intimate home-like qualities, no familiar objects, and no family treasures. I shudder at the idea of ending my life in such surroundings, without my treasured mementos, close friends, and family.

He looks at me knowingly and continues, "Miz Emmaline, she didn't like us much either," he nods to the group at the coffee table. "Most of these folks, they make friends the best they can and they get along, but she ain't like that. She's always stayin' to herself." He turns, and we begin to walk down the hallway. "There's been a sadness about her."

"Do you know why?"

"No. She don't talk about herself. She don't talk much at all. Well, leastways, she didn't, but now, we're startin' to see a life inside of her." He looks at me with a grin. "She talks about you. She just says your name all the time, with a smile, and she's happier."

We enter her room on the left. It's semi-dark, illuminated only by the grayness from the window and light from the hall. The furniture and colors are the same as a hospital room: Two beds with pastel green bedspreads, both neatly made, two TV's hanging from mountings on the wall, neither one turned on. There are no photographs, personal objects, or mementos anywhere. I put my gloves, pocketbook, scarf, and coat on a straight-back chair near the door.

Benjamin goes toward her with a greeting, "Miz Emmaline, look who's come to see you!" She's in a wheelchair near the window. I notice her silhouette and the bend of her shoulders, heavy with age. He hurries to her, moves the wheelchair around slightly to face me, and turns on a lamp. She looks up at him with a blank stare as he cheerfully says, "It's Miz Fancy!" Her gaze turns to me, her eyes focus and light up.

I walk toward her and feel the same draw as before. Once again I feel that this woman has touched my life in some way but I don't know where or when. Seeing her face again, I remember the extraordinary dignity, but I recognize it more as a dignity born of pain. I sit on a chair next to her, reaching out with the package. "I brought you a little gift." I'm glad I have an icebreaker as she lifts her feeble hands slowly and takes it.

Benjamin and I wait patiently as she fumbles with the ribbon around the blue cellophane wrapping. He reaches over and helps her with the knot. Finally, she pulls the sides away, revealing the small basket of pastel soaps. Looking up she grins, her eyes sparkle, and she shyly says, "Thank you."

I lean closer to her. "How're you doing, Miz Emmaline?"

Her face glows. I see tears gathering as she looks directly at me and says with a quiet voice, "I'm so glad to see you again, li'l Miz Fancy." She draws a deep breath and speaks with quiet expectation in her voice, "Have you come to get me now?"

I look at Benjamin, who is standing behind her, and feel embarrassed. The expectation in her eyes changes. She turns to Benjamin with the look of a wounded child and a sense of confusion. Benjamin comes around to her side and squats down so that he can look at her directly. He speaks slowly and carefully, "Miz Emmaline, this is your home, and we like havin' you here." She looks back and forth from his face to mine, and her eyes cloud over.

I reach for her large, bony, and fragile hand. Her thumb begins to softly rub my fingers. I wait for her to speak. After a time she looks into her lap and says with a quivering voice, "I'm sorry, Fancy. I done thinks I was gonna lose you again."

I collect myself and shift the mood. "Would you like to tell me more about yourself? Perhaps you could tell me who you lost?"

She seems puzzled and stares at me as if she doesn't understand. A faraway look comes into her eyes as she turns back to the window. Her hands become motionless as her thoughts move into a different world and time. I watch her breathing become stronger and deeper. A long pause later, she speaks with a faraway, ethereal voice. "I done lost my babies, my two babies."

I speak, but it seems to be only an echo to her. "How did you lose them?"

Still seeming to look back in time, she says, "My one baby, she died, but the other one, they took from me."

"Who took your baby?"

"They did. They made me sign the papers."

"Who made you sign the papers?"

"The Missus." Her voice trembles, "The Missus made me sign the papers and took my baby girl, my other one. I weren't ever supposed to talk about it."

There is nothing I can say that would soften her feelings. She closes her eyes, squeezing them as she continues to feel the pain from long ago. Her large fingers hold mine tightly as she suffers.

Finally, her face turns to me, her eyes are wide open, and she seems to be with me again. Looking directly at me, she says, "Did the Missus send you for me? Is the Missus gonna give me back my baby now?" Emmaline's eyes are red and bulge with tears. One escapes and trickles down her cheek.

My heart aches for her, and I wish there was something I could do. I reach for a tissue, quietly wipe the tear away, and gently dab her eyes. My eyes are also wet, but I can't wipe my own tears. "Tell me about your babies. Tell me something good about your babies."

She breathes deeply several times before she speaks. "They was all I had, then they was both gone." Another pause. "They was Missy and Melody, my babies." Her voice hardens slightly but she continues looking into her past. "The Missus, she done took my baby and then got herself a white chile, good as you please, and I was her mammy. She was my charge, and I done takes care of her."

I try to make sense of this. "You were a mammy?"

"Yes'm, it was the li'l white chile."

"They took your child away and you had to raise someone else's child instead?"

Her voice is wistful and vacant. "They took her away." Sighing heavily, she turns to the window again. Propping her left elbow on the arm of the wheelchair, her chin sinks into her palm. Her right hand rises slowly and clutches a medallion hanging around her neck. Her eyes cloud over and she stares out the window into the gray nothingness. She seems to have once again entered her painful memories.

Benjamin and I remain quiet and still, waiting for her to come back. I don't know what to say. Once again, I feel bad because I have unwittingly caused this woman to remember her pain. For a long time, Emmaline continues to stay in her own world, a world where she has become numb to her grief.

My head swirls. Intuition tells me that this woman could have been my mammy when I was with my mama and daddy. Did my mother have something to do with taking Emmaline's baby away from her? I'm horrified by the thought.

Finally, Benjamin whispers to me as he gently takes the basket of soaps from Emmaline's lap and places it on her bedside table, "Perhaps we should go." He reaches for a shawl and puts it around her shoulders. She doesn't notice. Quietly, he gives me his hand. I get up from the chair, gather my things, and leave the room with him.

He whispers gently, "Miz Andrews, would you like to go down the hall for a cup of coffee?"

"Thank you. I'm feeling bad about this, and coffee would be an excellent idea."

Silently, we walk back down the hall. My head fills with images of my mother as I had imagined her as a child. In my young mind, she was a tall, thin woman, with the stateliness of a queen and the grace of a movie star. I always thought that I looked like her and often pretended to be her. I knew in my heart that she had loved me with unflinching kindness and patience. I'm overcome with the pain of realizing that she may have been cruel to this woman.

We go into the dining room. Benjamin suggests a table and indicates that he will fetch coffee from the kitchen. Momentarily, he returns with a tray bearing two cups, a small, glass coffee pot, cream, and sugar.

"Benjamin, I don't want to burden you with speculation but I would sure like to talk a little. She seems to be a prisoner of her pain, and I keep causing her to remember something really awful." I slowly stir in cream as I realize that he and I have become linked through Emmaline's personal tragedy, whatever it might be. "And please, would you call me Mary Frances?"

"Ma'am, I'm a li'l ol' Southern boy from South Carolina, and I spent twenty years in the army, so's I'm accustomed to bein' polite to everyone. But I tell you, you shur do seem more like Miz Fancy to me, not Mary Frances or Miz Andrews." His demeanor is warm and friendly. "I'm very sorry it's causin' a painful problem for her but, quite frankly, I hope we can get past that and find out more about our Miz Emmaline."

His warmth soothes me as I speak the words forming in my mind. "I came here with one thought about how we are connected, but if that thought is true, I'm horrified." Frowning, I take a sip.

"How's that, ma'am?"

"I am of the opinion that Emmaline might have been my nurse when I was a child, but if that's true, then I'm afraid it might have been my own mama who took her baby away from her."

He looks over his glasses at me, sipping from his cup. Finally, he says, "Would you be able to talk to your mama about this?"

I give him a brief personal history and tell him about my mysterious conversation with Martha. "My speculation is that Emmaline was my nurse and she recognizes me because I must look exactly like my mama. But I think that no one wants to tell me the truth because my mama did something awful in taking away her baby, and they're protecting her memory."

He scratches his head. "That'd be a can of worms, now wouldn't it?"

"I need to find her child and reconnect them. That would be a far better way of dealing with my mama's memory."

"Miz Fancy, that would be a mighty fine thing for you to do. Our Miz Emmaline would really appreciate it, I'm sure."

I sip my coffee contemplatively. "That's what Martha was trying to tell me, I'm sure. Beatrice and Bucky must know about it, too, and they want to protect me from finding out."

He contemplates for a brief minute then speaks slowly, "Now, you don't want to be causin' a problem in your family over this. It sounds to me like you might be climbin' into ol' Pandora's box all by yourself."

"I wonder ...." Speaking absently, I try to think it through as I pour another cup and help myself to cream and sugar. "I wonder how this should be handled .... I feel like it's the only thing to do ... I mean, to clear my mother's name ... or maybe to straighten out her bad behavior ...." My mind swirls as I stir. "Benjamin, remember how

83

I just told you that Martha said to find out her last name …? Tell me … what is Emmaline's last name?"

"Powers. It's Miz Emmaline Powers."

I stare at him realizing how foggy my ideas are. "Now, what do I do with that? How do I find out if a child was born to her about forty-five or fifty years ago? Well, in fact, there were two. So that's another complication. And … how would I ever find that child now?"

He shrugs. "Can't help you there."

"Perhaps you could keep listening to her, and if she says anything useful, you could call me?"

"I'd be pleased to do that."

From my pocketbook I take out paper and pen and write my information for him. "This is going to be an interesting mystery to solve, but I don't think it's a good idea to tell my aunt or my husband about it just yet. They're not gonna be too happy about me getting involved in this situation, I don't think."

He chuckles. "Miz Fancy, your family does seem to be good about keeping secrets. I'll jus' let you handle that business and I'll look forward to the day that child of Miz Emmaline's walks through the door and surprises her, how's that?"

"Benjamin," I smile, "I think we're gonna be a good team on this one." While he clears the coffee cups, I say goodbye, grab my coat, and head for the elevator.

· ·

In the evening, Bucky and I have a celebration planned. Many years ago, we decided to celebrate Valentine's Day every month on the fourteenth as a way of keeping romance alive in our relationship, and this is our special night in the month of January. We've had many ups and downs in our years, especially with his proclivity to enjoy the attention of women, and there are times when I feel like the long-suffering fool, but he never fails to come back around to make me feel special.

He had promised to be home by seven. The snow is beginning to stick to the ground, and ice is forming on the streets as the temperature drops. I breathe a sigh of relief when I hear the garage door opening. Bucky has been the center of my life for so long, I sometimes wonder what I would do with myself if something ever happened to him.

He greets me at the door with his open pocket watch in his hand, "I tol' you I'd be here on time. See how helpful my grandfather's watch is?" Carefully putting the watch away and taking my hand, he swings me around much like the final twirl of a dance, causing the skirt on my black cocktail dress to flare out, and whistles. "Don't you look fine tonight?" Bringing his other hand around from behind his back, he presents me with a crystal vase holding a single, red rose. "For my one and only true love," he says, kissing me lightly.

"Darling," I tease him with a demure gleam in my eye as I take the vase to the dimly lit dining room table, "you know I melt at the sight of flowers, and you certainly take advantage of that, don't you?"

He follows, playfully shrugging. "Hey, a fella's gotta do what he's gotta do."

I place the vase in the center among the fine china and crystal, and take up a small matchbox to light the candles. He notices the corkscrew and, reading the wine label with approval, uncorks the bottle and pours it into two large, bubble, wine glasses. Salads of sliced beefsteak tomato and mozzarella are already on the table, and we leisurely enjoy our first course.

85

"Sugar plum," he raises his glass of wine in salute, as I return from the kitchen with his favorite dinner of chateaubriand and asparagus, "you're one mighty fine wife. You take care of me better'n any woman I can imagine."

Placing the tray on the table and giving him a kiss on the forehead, I joke, "You mean to tell me that I've won out over all those women who flirt with you?"

"Why, darlin', I've never taken any of them serious, and you know that. You are my pride and joy, and the one I always come home to." He pauses for a minute and laughs. "Besides, you flirt better."

"You're sure, of course, that it has nothing to do with the fact that I have a nice trust fund?" Sometimes I tease him because Beatrice appointed him as the administrator of my funds. He has never abused his role, and I have certainly not complained.

He leans toward me, taking my hand and kissing it. "It has entirely to do with the fact that you are a superb woman in this age where women don't know how to be women anymore, and I enjoy that very much." Over dinner, we discuss Bucky's point of view about women in politics and business and how much he appreciates the way I have conducted myself in both, which is to say that I have stayed out of it and not had opinions on the topics that are important to menfolk. He concludes with, "Why sugar plum, I can see you, plain as day, bein' a fine lady just like your aunt when you get to be her age."

Bucky means this as a compliment, but I'm taken aback by the image, realizing that he has never understood my ill will toward Beatrice nor my fear of becoming her. I'm not sure I understand it either. As he talks, I give him a sly grin, remembering my plans to roll back the rug in the parlor, put on a Strauss waltz, and invite my husband for a slow, romantic dance after dinner.

The wall phone in the kitchen rings as Bucky and I are finishing our chocolate and crème dessert. Bucky casually gets up to answer it. "Hello … yes, it is … can I take a message?" There is a long pause. "Sure will … thank you much." He puts the phone back in its cradle, hesitates, then turns and speaks to me from the kitchen. His demeanor and body language change dramatically in that moment, but his tone is even and careful. "Mary Frances, what did y'all do today?"

"An assortment of things … was that for me?"

He comes back to the table, leans forward across the back of a chair, and looks directly at me. All flirtation is gone from his voice, and I'm alarmed by the tone. "Sugar plum, I'm interested in specifically what you did."

I gather the dishes, realizing that something is wrong and feeling the evening's magic disappear. "Ran some errands, bought groceries, did some visiting."

"Who did you visit?"

I've never lied to Bucky. I feel like it, but I suddenly feel like a child who has been caught and who dares not. Stalling for an answer, I take the dishes into the kitchen, refusing to look at him directly. I pretend to flirt. "Now, Bucky, why would you suddenly be interested in my visitin'?" Evasiveness shows in my voice, which takes on a more pronounced accent.

He moves to the doorway, his large body taking up most of the space. "You need to tell me." His tone is that of a stern parent trying to be patient.

I clean off the dishes and put them in the dishwasher, still avoiding a direct connection with him. "Just some lady friends."

"Which ones?"

I turn to him directly, knowing full well that I am being cross-examined. "Well, let's see … it was my regular monthly lunch with Effi, Katherine, and Patricia. Then I visited with a shut-in, someone who needs company."

"And who was that?"

"No one you know … just a kind ol' woman."

"Who was the woman?"

"No one you know … I was bein' charitable and visitin'."

"Mary Frances."

Taking a couple of pots off of the stove, I begin to clean them, ignoring him.

He becomes impatient and his face flushes. Finally he says, "Mary Frances, it was that old colored woman, wasn't it?"

"I believe the proper term is 'black,' even Aunt Beatrice knows that."

He leans against the doorway, his arms folded defiantly. "Black, colored, what difference does it make? I thought we decided you weren't going to do that."

"Did we?" I emphasize the 'did' as I put soap in the dishwasher and close it.

"You know perfectly well we did. Isn't it traditional when a man tells his wife not to do something, that she doesn't do it?"

I turn to face him, lowering my voice for emphasis and saying words that surprise me. "I'm not gonna make that comment legitimate by responding to it."

His face becomes red with anger, and his eyes narrow. "Even Beatrice told you it's not the proper thing for you to do."

"Aunt Beatrice has been telling me for years to be charitable, that it would help your career. Since when is visitin' an old woman in a nursin' home the wrong thing to do?" I dry my hands, hang up the towel, and lean against the counter, changing my tone from assertive to quizzical. "And by the way, who was on the phone?"

His tone is sarcastic. "It was the black guy from the nursing home." He pauses. "Seems you left your gloves there."

"Oh."

He stares directly at me. "Why did you give him your phone number?"

I hesitate, feeling defensive and knowing that my real reason is more personal. "You know that the church group likes to help folks in nursin' homes. We take things, little gifts, all the time. I told him that if she needed somethin', to give me a holler, and we would provide it. She doesn't have any relatives, y'know."

"It's not your place to take care of an old black woman. The blacks take care of the blacks, and the whites take care of the whites, and that's the way it is." Once again, he acquires a lawyer's tone and begins to pace the kitchen floor. "Why didn't you give him the number for the church? He could have called there."

"Darlin', it's my committee. The church would have told him to call me anyway."

"Mary Frances, sugar," there is a slightly softer tone, but it's still an instruction, "it's not appropriate for you to give your home phone number to a black man, a stranger."

I'm still leaning with my back against the counter, feeling like a witness on the stand, but I'm annoyed. "What in the world do you mean? All kinds of strangers have this phone number, and all kinds of strangers call here without any problem."

His arms gesture as he paces. "You don't know this man … he could harass you, he could be inappropriate with you … who knows? You have just made yourself wide open to anythin'."

"Bucky, that's the most absurd thing I have ever heard."

He turns to me with his hands on his hips. "Mary Frances, you're from the South. You were brought up with this; you should know better. Don't you know that a white woman neva gives her phone number to a black man?" He emphasizes "neva."

"Don't be ridiculous." Privately, I do remember being brought up with the warning that all little black boys want to rape all little white girls, and a white girl never went near a black boy, but I would never admit that to Bucky.

He shakes his head in disbelief. "You don't know the locker room talk, you just don't know, do you?"

"What do you mean?"

He tries to explain very matter-of-factly, but raises his voice a touch more than normal. "When black men get together and talk, all they talk about is gettin' white women." He reaches for a tumbler in the cupboard. "The main reason that a black man goes after a white woman is to ruin her for all white men so that she has to be with a black man. A white man won't have a woman afta' she's been with a black man, remember that."

"Slow down, Bucky. This is me you're talking to." My voice is slightly louder, and I point to myself. "I'm your wife. I'm a married woman. No one 'goes after me.' I'm not available."

Briskly, he opens the refrigerator, talking over the lower door. "Every black man considers every white woman available; it's a game with them."

My voice taunts, "Benjamin is an orderly in a nursing home. He is taking care of that old woman. I'm curious about her and I'm even more convinced now that there is a connection between us."

He abruptly stops, his eyes bulging as he turns. "Are we calling him by his first name now?" He slams the lower door and opens the freezer door.

"Certainly. What else would I call him?" I mock him. "You certainly don't expect me to call him 'boy' now do you? That's disrespectful and is not used anymore, and you know that."

He reaches for ice in the freezer, making a considerable amount of noise. "And what does he call you?"

Coldly, I reply, "Mrs. Andrews."

He's sarcastic. "Well, Mrs. Andrews," he slams the freezer door and his voice is hard, "remember, you make bad decisions about people. You've done it before with the coloreds, and your aunt won't let you forget it. Did you happen to think about what she will do with your money this time if you disobey her?" His stare is long and hard. "I just don't understand you. Don't you ever learn anythin'?" He points his finger at me and issues a command. "Don't you go doin' it again, y'hear?" Turning on his heels, he walks into the parlor, pours a bourbon, and lights a cigar.

I stand in the middle of the kitchen, watching him in the other room, shocked and astonished at how the evening has changed, my heart beating rapidly with anger. I cannot remember another time when he has been so rude to me. He has just adopted Beatrice's ultimate weapon—always it's the money. She placed him in charge of my trust funds because I was involved with the civil rights movement during college; she said she couldn't trust my judgment anymore.

I find a mug and teabag and set the microwave to heat water. I've never answered back when she reminds me of my past and I have struggled to be who she wanted me to be. But I must find my voice—he can't be allowed to carry on in her place! Pacing in the kitchen, I sip tea and decide to take a long, hot bubble bath to calm the rage rising inside of me.

With each step that I climb toward the upstairs bathroom, my resolution grows stronger. On the landing, I pause, take a deep breath, and whisper out loud, "How dare you, Bucky Andrews. How dare you stab me in the back with my painful memories! How dare you threaten me with my own money! I will do what I damn well please, whether it pleases you or not. Besides, you didn't bother asking, but I'm feeling compelled to clear my mother's name and that's more important than your silly prejudice. And, sweetie pie, I'm going to find Emmaline's child, whether you like it or not."

5. THE NORTHERN AWAKENING

I seek sanctuary in my old claw-foot bathtub. After starting the water and generously pouring in bubble bath, I light a candle in front of the vanity mirror, turn out the lights, and stare at myself in the dark. The flickering points of light in the mirror seem to hypnotize me as the subtle scent of vanilla fills the room. I step into the water and sink into the thick foam. It feels much like a safe womb.

The fire of Bucky's attack has seared my heart and confused my soul. I am surrounded by a twilight zone where nothing makes sense. I have shared with him all of my love, my pain, my need for closeness and intimacy, as well as the joys and rewards of our life together. I have been generous and have gone out of my way for others, especially for him. My unselfish love has been rewarded with demeaning emotional abuse, time and time again. I have always ignored this abuse and pretended that it wasn't real, but this time I can hold it in no longer.

Closing my eyes, I float in a sea of darkness, allowing thoughts to tear themselves away from their moorings. I become lost in the emotional pain that envelopes me like the water and feel the ache more than I have ever felt it before. Childhood feelings of unworthiness and grief overwhelm me. I feel as if the embryonic sac holding the fluid of my life is ripping apart. I tremble and cry, wanting Bucky's approval more than anything else. Bucky and Beatrice merge in my mind, and I realize that I also cry for Beatrice's approval.

I breathe in and out, over and over, and let the sobs flow. The turbulence of uncontrollable tears brings comfort. Much like a boat cast adrift and floating aimlessly in a storm, I begin to disengage from timid thinking, from fears, from low opinions of myself. Finally, a sense of calm emerges, and I sense that once again, I am in the eye of a hurricane.

My anger with Bucky slowly fades, my mind clears, and I feel an emerging sense of resolve. Words ring inside my head, and I hear an echo, *Look to who you are, look to who you are.* Boldness stirs in my heart, and memories emerge from many years ago when I chose actions because they were right, not because I needed someone's approval. These were intuitive actions that came from my heart and were neither logical nor objective. Once I had an inner power that guided me through an emotional labyrinth when there were no easy answers. I have been living for many years without this power, without knowing what my life is, without feeling it, without owning it. It's as if intuition wants to guide me again, and I must let it. I must find this power again if I am to solve the Emmaline mystery, and if I am to confront my fear of Bucky and Beatrice, as I know I must.

With a deep sigh and a longing to rediscover myself, I close my eyes and reach for the memory of my first experience when I felt this inner sense of knowing right from wrong, of feeling genuine humanity and personal strength. I remember that this sense of power began on my first day at Wellesley College in the fall of 1967.

It was my driving force for two years, until a painful tragedy caused me to wrap myself in a cocoon.

Growing up, I had led a sheltered life. The late fifties and early sixties were the golden years, when young women learned their preordained roles as the keepers of domesticity. As a Southern child, I also learned "charm." I was protected, cultivated, and formed. I was told what to do and I was molded with fear. Aunt Beatrice set the rules, Martha followed them for the most part, and Uncle George did his best to foil them and to spoil me, all in the name of raising me as a correct, li'l ol' Southern girlchild. Good ol' Uncle George was a fine ol' cigar-smoking gentleman, who treated women with a "never you mind" attitude. I successfully learned to smile sweetly, to be subtle, and to pout when I wanted something from him. This training became my guiding force as Bucky's wife.

Beatrice chose my college, just as she chose everything else in my life. In the early sixties, Wellesley women were described in *Time* magazine as "simply wholesome creatures, unencumbered by the world's woes, who make normal, well-adjusted housewives." Her own education had been cut short by the Depression, and Beatrice was determined that I should go to Wellesley because it was the finest women's finishing school on the East Coast. Although she married well, Beatrice always seemed to feel inferior to her social set, and it was important for her to have my education as an emancipation. I wonder if she will ever understand how much I resent the failures in her life that made her hold on to me so desperately.

In Beatrice's mind, choosing Wellesley College for Women was choosing my guarantee of success. She was sending me into pastoral quietude to be cultivated as a graceful wife, where I would patiently wait for my successful Ivy League prince. She expected me

95

to be instructed in wearing white gloves, keeping my figure shapely, and pouring tea. Passivity and domesticity were fundamental. Skirts were mandatory.

And so I remember that in the fall of 1967, Aunt Beatrice and Uncle George drove me up to the quiet, suburban Boston town of Wellesley with smug expectations for my domestic future and few worries that I would be caught up in the country's emerging social upheavals. Fall is barely a whispering breeze in the trees on the beautiful, old, gothic campus as we turn into the grounds. Hardly a leaf is on the stone stairs leading to the admissions office in Green Hall. Walking through its door feels like entering an old stone monastery with hushed hallways and interior arches that are flying buttresses, or more properly, it feels like a convent. I sit quietly on an overstuffed couch as Beatrice handles registration.

We unpack my belongings from the rented truck, and they install me in Severance Hall, my new home on campus. Beatrice and George return to the parking lot to prepare for the trip back to Virginia while I linger in my new room. We have just had an awkward moment with the girl who is assigned as my roommate, and I am contemplating what to do.

The housemother of the dorm, Mrs. Fitzgerald, appears at the door of my room. She is a matronly person in her fifties, has a clipped, New England style, speaks softly, and acts embarrassed. "Miss Tyler, may I speak with you for a minute." I step into the hall, and we walk slowly toward the window at the end, where she pulls aside the curtains and we silently gaze out onto Lake Waban. It's late in the day, and a brilliant afternoon sun shines on the still water and graceful old trees. "Your mother has just told me of the complication, and I do apologize."

"You mean my aunt."

"Oh, well, yes, of course, your aunt." She pauses. "And we will make the change immediately. I'll explain that there was a mix-up in the assignments."

"What are you talking about?"

"Your mother—excuse me, your aunt, explained that it would not be a good idea for you and the other young lady to be rooming together, especially with all of the tensions now. It will be sufficient exposure for both of you simply being in the same school."

I stare at her. An unknown urge gnawing away inside of me rises and becomes a feeling, a feeling that must escape. I have no words for it. It's the suffocating bear in my dreams that still smothers me. The feeling explodes and screams inside my head. The words in the scream tell me that I have no life unless Beatrice approves … I have no friends unless she approves … I do not exist unless she approves … I am nothing more than her life being lived again! I am expected to be the person she wanted to be, and I do not know who I am … I do not want to be her, I can't! Right now, I hate her more than I have ever hated, and by association, I hate everyone else who tries to control me. I need to scream aloud and can barely control myself. I walk a few steps away, turn, and face Mrs. Fitzgerald, speaking sarcastically. "Did she also tell you how much she has donated to this school, and how important she is?"

"Of course, your aunt is important. She is important to you and to this school. But that's not really necessary, my dear."

I breathe deeply, shaking. "Why don't you tell Aunt Beatrice that you're gonna make the change then conveniently forget about it? I won't tell if you won't." With no forewarning, I know that I have already decided not to be controlled anymore. I can't let her keep doing this to me. I have to make decisions for myself. I need my own life. I want to do something that she doesn't approve of. I have to!

"That's not ladylike behavior, now is it?" Mrs. Fitzgerald's voice is artificially sweet.

I walk over to another nearby window that faces the parking lot, pull the curtain aside, and watch Beatrice and George walk to the truck. "I believe Aunt Beatrice and Uncle George are fixin' to leave right about now." Turning and brushing past Mrs. Fitzgerald, "I need to say goodbye to them. I will speak to you about this later." I dart away, hurrying out to them.

Standing in the parking lot, Beatrice asks me if the dorm mother has spoken to me yet, and I truthfully reply yes, and that we will take care of things. I do not tell her any details or that I plan to pursue my own solution. The smug look on her face tells me that the situation is resolved for her and needs no further discussion.

Stopping to see Mrs. Fitzgerald, I tell her that I explained to Aunt Beatrice that I am looking forward to this new experience, and she is going to be fine with everything, including the new roommate … it was simply a small misunderstanding. After all, times are changing and not to worry. I don't give her a chance to reply, nor do I respond to the questioning look on her face. Rather, with feigned cheerfulness, I close her office door and go off to my room to unpack and begin creating a relationship with my new roommate, Susan, a black girl.

I have no idea how to begin my first act of defiance. The room is comfortably large enough for two girls, with twin beds, two wooden dressers, and two identical, small desks. Susan had arrived before me, selected one of the beds, and is in the midst of putting bedding on it. She has several trunks and boxes scattered around, and so do I. Standing inside the door, I look around. "Susan? You did say your name is Susan, didn't you?"

"Yes, Susan Devereaux." I sense that she feels uncomfortable with me as she snaps on the last corner of a crisp, white, fitted sheet. She is very pretty, with almond-shaped eyes, long lashes, and a medium complexion. Her willowy body is tall and thin, and her smooth hair is styled in a pageboy. She hums softly as she works.

"I'm Mary Frances Tyler. Oh, but I already told you that." I awkwardly gesture toward the door. "That was my aunt and uncle. I live with them. Uh … where are you from?"

"N'Orleans." She picks up a top sheet and tosses two pillows toward the head of the bed.

"I'm from Richmond, in Virginia."

"I know where Richmond is." With the precision of a surgeon, she centers the middle crease on the sheet and makes hospital corners at the foot end. She picks up a blue and red plaid bedspread and shakes it in the air before placing it carefully on her bed.

Wanting to ease the awkwardness, I look around, go to the window and open it, then walk over and open each of the doors on the two closets. I notice that her luggage has been placed in one of them. Glancing at both, I realize that the closet that she chose is larger. Without thinking, I blurt out, "Oh, Susan, it would be all right if I took this one, wouldn't it?"

The humming stops, her hands drop, and she stares at me. "I've already chosen it."

"But …" I stop myself. In my head, I finish the sentence, *…but, I'm the white. I get the better things.* For the first time in my life, I hear this unspoken assumption. The civil rights law had been passed three years before, and I am a Southern girl caught in the middle. I want to defy Beatrice. I want to rebel. I want to do everything a proper, Southern, white girl shouldn't do. I want to be part of the movement, part of the changes, but I don't have the faintest idea what that should be. My whole life has hung on my shoulders like a comfortable, old, Confederate flag. What do I do? How do I reach out to her? I feel frustrated and awkward because I've gotten off on the wrong foot.

"Susan, of course ...." I don't know what else to say, so I empty my suitcase in silence and begin hanging my clothes in the smaller closet. When Susan finishes her bed, she leaves the room.

I spend two hours unpacking and fixing up my own area. Finally finished and feeling discouraged, I sit on the edge of my bed. There is a knock on the door; it's the dorm housemother. She sits next to me and tells me that Susan has just asked to be moved to another room.

Mrs. Fitzgerald explains that she promised my aunt that a change would be made and a promise can't be broken, but she can't make any changes for a week until everyone has settled in and she can assess the situation with all of the girls. She understands that our diverse backgrounds might make it extremely difficult for us to continue as roommates. She asks if I would try very hard to make the situation tolerable for this one week. She has asked the same of Susan.

I see Susan at dinner in the dining hall, but we don't speak. She comes back to the room later that evening around ten and avoids eye contact as she flips on a radio and prepares for bed.

Sitting on my bed, I venture, "Could we talk?"

"Certainly." She chooses the wooden chair that is part of her desk area.

"Um ... I haven't been around Negroes, I mean black people much and I know there's a lot going on right now, so I'm feeling a little awkward."

She looks at me intensely but doesn't reply.

"I went to an all-white Catholic school in Richmond."

She stares at me. "I went to a Catholic school in N'Orleans. It was integrated in 1961, but it was mostly black."

"Was yours a girl's school?"

"Yeah."

"Mine, too." There is silence, as we both seem to be preoccupied with listening to the radio playing Mary Well's "My Guy."

"Susan ... look, I know you want to move from this room. I don't blame you. I'm one of those jerky people from the South who is awful."

"My family kept me away from it as much as possible. But I hear the stories other people tell. I watch the news."

"Could we try to make it through the next week, okay?"

"Yeah, I'm sure ... I want a black roommate anyway." She pauses and seems to want the last word. Her voice takes on an edge as she nods toward the better closet. "It's not right, you expectin' to get what I already had."

We have negotiated a peace, and we are able to make it through freshman week. Susan is assigned as a Little Sister to one of the two upper-class black women students, and I am assigned to a Jewish girl from New York named Katherine. We both become active in campus Welcome Week activities. Our Big Sisters guide us through initiation activities, take us to the traditional stepsinging on the first day of class, show us the hangouts and cheap food places, answer questions, and integrate us into college life.

101

By the end of the week, we learn that there are no other black women in our entering class available for Susan to room with. She and I agree to continue as roommates. We go to Mrs. Fitzgerald together and tell her, and she accepts our decision but refers the matter to the administration. Beatrice is told that a number of reassignments are being made to meet the needs of each student, and she assumes that I am one of them. She and I talk on the phone a few times as the semester begins, but I get the impression that she is relieved that I am away at school, and the topic never comes up again.

When classes start, Susan and I discover that we have three classes together, one of which is a yearlong Introductory Psychology class taught by Heinrich Helms.

. . . .

Professor Helms is a short, potbellied, balding man who wears a musty, tweed jacket with frayed buttonholes and leather elbow patches. He starts his first class with instructions on classroom decorum and a brief autobiography. He had been raised in a comfortable lifestyle in pre-Nazi Germany, but in the mid-thirties had been forced to flee because his mother was Jewish, and had come to America to live with relatives and attend university. All of his Jewish relatives in Europe perished during the Holocaust. He speaks about how it was necessary for him to work his way through college, toiling at menial tasks, and how he has suffered great humiliation in the process. He proudly considers himself to be an American, a Freudian psychologist, and a faithful Great Society Democrat, in that order.

Professor Helms continues, "I will teach you in the finest traditions of American learning and culture. I am proud to be one of the few men on the Wellesley faculty and I have great respect for the education of women. You should not see me as a father figure or as an oppressive male, but rather as someone who has suffered many of the indignities that women have suffered, and someone who has great sympathy and understanding for the role of women in society."

He points to a raised hand in the rear of the class. The student asks, "You use the singular of the word 'role.' Do you see that women have only one role in society?"

"Good question, young lady. There are men and there are women. Do you know of a third?" He pauses, chuckles at his joke, paces, and continues talking with his hands. "As women, you are unique and wonderful creatures, gifts to mankind. You have an ability that no man can ever duplicate. Do you know what it is?" He points to the one who asked the question, and she hesitatingly shakes her head no.

"You have the ability to give life ... to be mothers ... to perpetuate the species! Freud speaks of penis envy. How about womb envy? We men should be jealous of you, isn't that true?" His pointed finger is in the air, and his tone challenges us. "Speak up ladies! Ladies ... ladies ... this is not a course in learning how to be quiet!"

No one responds. I feel intimidated.

A hand is finally raised.

"Yes, yes, young lady, the pretty blonde in the lovely pink sweater."

A barely suppressed giggle sweeps the room. Sitting in the front row, Susan and I turn around and look at her. She's the cheerleader type.

"Professor Helms, how do you explain women who don't want children?"

"Ah, very good, we already begin to delve into our coursework, the abnormal woman." He picks up the text and flips to the table of contents. "We will study her in great detail as we progress through the year. First, you will learn about normalcy as established by the finest minds of psychoanalytic thought, the standard bearers ... Freud, Adler, Erickson, and the modern Fritz Perls." He flips to the center of the book. "Then we will begin to see the deviations ... the women who are abnormal because of their hormonal imbalances, who cry too much, who talk too much ... the women who are different." He puts the book down and walks around the podium, his hands sweeping the air, visually emphasizing his points. "You will learn to appreciate the inner flaws and psychological deficiencies that can be overcome simply with knowledge and training."

The cheerleader speaks again. "Are you saying that women who don't want children are abnormal?"

He bows his head to her slightly, almost as a mockery. "My dear, surely you are not thinking along those lines? With your magnificent looks, you will be wanting at least ten children, all girls, to follow in the footsteps of their beautiful mother." The class giggles; she is embarrassed and doesn't reply.

Another hand shoots up. "What do you think about careers for women?"

"Women are too irrational and moody to have careers, other than taking care of children. Why should you want to toil at men's work? Believe me, it's boring. Let your husbands do it. Take advantage of the special place you have in society as the *crème de la crème*, the cream of the crop for those who don't speak French. We will be teaching you the finest arts of womanhood, the pleasure of taking your rightful place in the world as wives of powerful and successful men."

He paces in front of the room while he talks, tapping his pointer periodically … first on a student's desk and then on a plaster bust of Freud that sits on a pedestal in the corner. "The working world must be able to depend on those who are hired. Women are fickle about their careers, always changing their minds and stopping to become mothers. We cannot run our businesses if executives are allowed to take six months off to have a baby, and then run home every time the baby sneezes."

The voice speaks again. "I want to become a doctor." Half of the class turns to look at her. She is a very small, dark-haired woman, possibly not even five feet tall.

"Why would you do that? Think of the math and science you will need to take. Think of the years of study. You will waste the most productive time of your life with your nose stuck in books. It will be difficult for you to find a husband if you are more educated than he is. And when you finally settle down and decide to have children, it may be too late for you."

She looks straight at him. "I enjoy science. I always get A's in math." She takes a breath. "Are you saying that if I define myself as a woman, then I am automatically less than an fully achieving individual, but if I define myself as an achieving individual, then I'm not a real woman?"

He ignores her and goes back to the podium, flipping his wrist to brush aside her question. "Okay, girls, let's not get on this track. According to Freud, career aspirations are unfeminine and unnatural. A woman with an impulse to succeed at a man's job has an unhealthy psyche. We want to study normalcy. We here at Wellesley want our girls to become normal, functioning women. We are not educating our women to be scholars. We are educating them to be wives and mothers. The motto of this school is *Non ministrari, sed mistrare*—'Not to be ministered to, but to minister to,' and it should be the motto of your lives."

A girl near the front of the class speaks up. "I agree with the professor. I love my femininity and look forward to being a Mrs. and changing my name and taking care of my children." She looks around, mindful that she is representing the popular cultural image. "If you don't want to get married, then don't. If you find that being a mother or a wife is burdensome, then don't. Just don't let this new women's liberation thing speak for all of us. Some of us will cherish the love we will give and receive in our future families." She folds her arms in satisfaction, her face glowing with pride and actively seeking approval.

"Bravo, my dear, bravo," he applauds her briefly. "This women's liberation thing that we are beginning to hear about is a small, lunatic, extremist fringe, and you would all do well to leave it alone." He continues in this fashion for the rest of the class. He struts. He intimidates. He flirts and cajoles. When challenged, with the inflection of his tone, he asserts the natural superiority of his own opinion.

Walking down the steps of Pendleton Hall after class, I ask Susan what she thinks of him.

"He reminds me of every white man who has ever told us what we could and could not do. He's a jerk."

"But haven't men always set the rules? Isn't that the way it is?"

"Yeah. That's the problem, isn't it?"

This is a new concept for me. It takes time for it to crystallize.

. . . .

Susan is the star of the freshman talent show, singing a soulful rendition of Billie Holiday's "Good Morning Heartache." With the first chord of her tape-recorded accompaniment, the lights go dark and a spotlight follows her slow, vampish walk onto the stage. Her tall, thin body is stunning in a low-cut, skin-tight, floor length red dress, black spike heels, long black gloves, and hair piled in shiny curls on top. Slowly catching her hand on a lamppost prop, she sensuously twirls halfway around, bringing the microphone up and beginning the melancholy song. The student audience loves her; teachers react with consternation at her boldness. At the cast party afterwards, she laughs about how her mama would "have a catfish" if she had seen her performance, because, after all, she is suppose to be a quiet, serious scholar who sings in church and is not a budding diva. "Times are changing," she says, "an' my mama lives in a diff'rent world."

She often entertains around the fireplace in the dorm with jazz and songs from the South. Her deep, resonating voice echoes against the walls, encouraging many voices to join in. Our group is eclectic in voice, style, and background, but the music brings us together. Some of the songs, such as "Cotton Fields" and "Mighty Mississippi" are recent hits of the New Christy Minstrels, and we know the words well enough to sing along. She teaches us other songs, many of them traditional Negro spirituals. One very playful evening, a conga line forms spontaneously, with Susan in the lead, and the line of boisterous girls snakes through the dorm singing "When the 'Girls' Go Marching In." Once, she comments to me that she never takes the lead singing if guys are around to do it, but since there aren't any, she has to step forward.

Life in the dorms and New England opens my eyes to a new world. I learn a lot by talking with new friends, women who have come to this campus from all over the world. Sometimes our conversations are deep, other times philosophical, and often light and playful. When the weather is good, we take walks along the lake, swing on the old wooden swing in the big tree near the chapel, or watch the squirrels play. Several times, we take the subway into Boston to see the sights, attend events, and mingle with students from other schools. Other times, we spend quiet Saturday afternoons exploring local museums that celebrate the birth of the American Revolution and New England's heritage.

Perhaps the most intriguing after-class topic is the new and emerging discussion of women's roles in society. Betty Friedan's book, *The Feminine Mystique*, becomes the underground rage. In the late fall, we hear about a Saturday luncheon at a hotel in Boston where she is the speaker, and several Wellesley students attend. It becomes a lively discussion about the frustrating lives of women who are expected to find fulfillment through the achievements of husbands and children. We all know these women—they are the generation that has just raised us. We seem to understand the problem and feel angry, but can't identify a solution.

After the luncheon, Katherine, Susan, and I are invited to join a small discussion group at a nearby apartment, referred to as a *consciousness-raising* experiment. Fifteen women from different ethnic backgrounds—college students in patched jeans and long hair, young working women in miniskirts, an older married woman or two—congregate in the living room of a large, old, Victorian flat, some sitting on a couch, others on floor cushions, and still others on straight-back chairs from the kitchen. Few of us know each other and none know what to expect.

Patty, the moderator, pulls the curtains shut, announcing that she wants the room to feel private. She lights three tall, fat candles on the coffee table, moves us around so that each woman is included in the circle, and asks us to hold hands. She speaks about how women's histories are secret, hidden behind doors that keep us feeling ashamed and afraid. We endure our hardships alone, she says, not knowing how much the same burden is repeated behind other closed doors. When women's issues are discussed in the media, she asserts that it is usually with hostility or unabashed humor and ridicule. When decisions affecting women are made, they are made by the men in our lives, the men in our churches, or the men in public life. Sometimes, she says, men don't understand; they have their own motives, and sometimes these motives are not in our best interests. She has invited us to experiment with sharing who we are … directly, openly, without judgment … and to simply talk together. She asks us to put aside all judgments about ourselves and the other people in the room, and to be willing to talk the way sisters would talk. "Imagine," she says, "that you have a very special, big sister, the very best friend you have ever had, and you are talking late at night in your bedroom."

Given this context, her first question is startling. "When you think about having a child, do you want a boy or a girl?" "Oh brother," someone says, "isn't this about being ourselves, not being mothers?" In spite of the reaction, Patty goes around the room with a sense of serenity, letting women answer or pass as they wish. The answers are short and the tone seems to be either resentful or questioning. Many in the group whisper to each other, shuffle noisily, or move around.

The seventh woman stares at Patty. In her quiet presence, noises fade, bodies cease moving, the energy in the room merges, and all attention settles on the speaker's face as we wait to hear from her. She unclasps her hands with the women next to her and drops them into her lap. "I've already had a child," she says softly, avoiding all eyes and staring straight ahead, "it was a beautiful little boy. He was born in a home for unwed girls, and I had to give him away. They wouldn't tell me where he was taken. It's been three years." Breathing in the room seems to stop. Patty watches the group's reaction. The speaker turns to the woman next to her, pain and embarrassment showing on her face. "You're my best friend, but I've never been able to tell you because I was too ashamed."

"How do you feel about giving your baby away?" Patty asks gently, leaning forward and making eye contact with the speaker that seems to exclude everyone else in the room.

"I feel a very painful knot here," she presses a hand against her heart and stares at the candles, "and it never goes away. I did something awful … I gave my child away." She looks up nervously. "I didn't want to marry the father. My parents tried to force it, but I refused. I wanted to go to college." Her friend reaches over and takes her free hand.

Another woman across the room picks it up, speaking with reverence, and all faces turn to her. "I've had two abortions. My uncle got me pregnant when I was sixteen. I couldn't tell anyone, not even my mother. The other time, my boyfriend told me he was sterile, but I got pregnant." Her pause reverberates like an echo. "One abortion was here in the States. It was illegal, and I almost died from the infection, but I couldn't seek any medical help. The other was in Puerto Rico." Tears fill her eyes. "I can't have children now, and it's my fault."

The women in the room seem stunned. We are witnessing strangers sharing their most private and painful agony. Patty speaks softly. "Feeling ashamed about sex and childbirth has been a very effective way of making women feel less than worthy … of making us bear all the responsibility." She pauses and carefully looks around. "I'm going to tell you my story," she begins, and the room becomes still. "When I discovered I was pregnant, I made a desperate trip to a Boston doctor for an illegal abortion. He quizzed me in a dark basement room for over an hour, trying to decide if I was a police informer, then he gave me a shot of sodium pentathol to make me tell the truth. When he finally believed me, he said he was going to do a saline injection. I knew that it would have killed me, and I ran from his house, and walked for miles because I couldn't flag down a taxi … it was late at night in a bad part of town. I was alone and scared." She pauses as if remembering. "I was beaten and gang-raped that night. I began to have a miscarriage there on the street before the cops found me."

The silence in the room is heavy. One woman speaks, and then another. Words begin to tumble out. "My sister's body was found in a run-down motel after an abortion went wrong." Another voice began, "My father …." Convulsing in tears, she buries her face and cannot go on.

The women tell similar stories. As one finishes, another story begins. We hear about women driven by desperation to clandestine rides late at night, with large cash payments and no names; coat hanger attempts; fast trips outside of the country, cloaked in secrecy; family incest. A horrible collective truth emerges over the evening, a truth about shame, humiliation, and lack of control over our bodies and our lives.

"You see, we are able talk about our pain," Patty says as the stories begin to wind down. "You have learned to be afraid of speaking up, you have been told a million times to be quiet. But we have a right to be angry and hurt. Sharing our pain gives us the opportunity to talk frankly and openly about how we are treated as

111

women, and it's the first step to making changes." Susan listens as if she is silently comparing these stories with ones she knows. I feel dumbfounded by what I have heard and fearful of what might happen as I become an adult.

Katherine has not yet spoken. She is studying each woman carefully, listening to the experience in a way that seems to make the speaker feel heard. As Patty finishes and the room absorbs her pain, Katherine speaks softly and reverently, looking directly at each woman who has spoken her dreadful truth. "I have profound respect for each of you. I can't image the pain that you have gone through. Today feels like a turning point for me. I haven't known what I wanted to write about as a journalist; you have given me the answer. I know that I must write about women like you. I must write about what can be done to stop these things from happening to other women, to other little girls. If I can do something to prevent other women from having the same experiences, it will be because you, each of you, was willing … brave enough … to talk about it. I can do nothing more than humbly express my appreciation to each of you."

Coming back to the campus late in the evening, we speak in hushed tones, moved by the experience of learning other women's hidden stories and feeling initiated into the powerful experience of talking openly and candidly, unafraid of what the world would think, unafraid of the rules that have been constructed to keep women quiet. Each of us, in our own way, expresses empowerment from the voices of women speaking out loud, their voices seeping like fog under the closed doors.

I react by joining with other girls on campus for regular consciousness-raising groups, where we begin to talk about ourselves as women, as separate human beings. Susan becomes a volunteer counselor at a rape crisis center in Boston, and Katherine begins investigations that she can turn into newspaper stories.

In a literature class, we are assigned J. D. Salinger's *Catcher In The Rye*, but informally we talk about Sylvia Plath's *The Bell Jar* and compare the two. Esther in *The Bell Jar* seems more relevant to our lives than Holden Caulfield, and the tragedy of Plath's suicide is still fresh. Talking late at night, shrouded by the mystery of candlelight and sharing a contraband bottle of wine, Susan and I worry about becoming Esther-like, or Plath-like, unable to fit into life and not knowing how to deal with men and sex. We see ourselves as becoming adult women who cannot find our ways in the world, and who are destined to go insane or end up as old maids. We wonder what "normal" really means, and whether it would be normal for us to have independent lives like men. We also fear that we will become dependent on psychologists to solve our problems and keep us normal in the eyes of the world, and wonder if all psychologists will be like Professor Helms, who becomes the focus of campus ridicule.

"But what if he's right?" someone says to a group early one afternoon at Café Hoop in the Schneider Center after a difficult class with the professor. She is a redhead from Kansas and has just arrived at the table with a hamburger.

"He's not right." It's Katherine, who had joined us moments before with a fresh cup of coffee.

"How do you know?" asks another, a quiet librarian type from Tennessee, who is eating a vegetable salad.

"Look at the women who have not fallen into the trap."

"Aren't they abnormal?" the redhead asks.

"What's abnormal?" Katherine questions. "Is it abnormal to be discontent and bored? Is it abnormal to want to be treated the same as men? No, it shows intelligence to think about your own needs. Look at it this way: Men fear that women will outshine them, so the only way to prevent that is to keep the shining women repressed." She shrugs her shoulders, "The law says we are equal now. President Johnson signed it. So instead of being better than them, we're equal. Live with it." She sips her coffee knowingly. Katherine is from New York City, I quietly chuckle to myself, and New Yorkers are arrogant, often speaking in hyperbole and displaying extreme confidence.

The redhead winces, "I don't want to be treated like a man. I don't want to be drafted and go to Vietnam to die ... that's horrible. I want to be taken care of, always. I want to be looked up to as a mother ... I want to be a good companion for my husband."

Katherine looks at her askance and pleasantly mocks, "'I want to be a good companion for my husband.' Sounds like Sleeping Beauty waiting for Prince Charming, doesn't it?" She slowly moves around the table and sits down, shrugging pleasantly to the redhead. "Maybe you ought to get a life."

The girl glares at Katherine and no one speaks. Someone from Chicago finally asks me, "What is your term paper for Helms going to be about?" She is one of the upper-class women who has already been through his class.

"I don't know. I think he wants us to follow some classic psychology theory about women. None of this new radical stuff will be acceptable."

The redhead muses, "There is no scientific basis for this new stuff anyway."

Turning to my friend, "Katherine, what did you write about when you were in his class?"

"I wrote a paper comparing McCarthyism with the way women are treated."

All eyes turn to her in amazement. Several people ask, almost in unison: "What happened?" "How did he take that?" What kind of grade did you get?"

She raises her hand to quiet the group. "The schmuck flunked me, of course."

"How are you going to graduate without that course?"

"You do whatever it takes. I went to the dean ... the dean is a friend of the family. She read my paper and changed the final grade to a C for me." Katherine turns to me. "So, little sister, what are you going to write about?"

"I don't know. This Freud stuff is really weird. What Friedan says about it makes more sense, but Helms would never go for a paper on that. How could a mere woman, much less me, presume to question a Freudian truth?"

"What does Friedan say?"

"She calls Freud's theories obsolete, an obstruction."

"Good, then do it." Katherine seems to always counsel us to go against the entrenched protocol.

"What?"

"Go ahead, question his authority."

"I couldn't do that."

"Sure you could ... it's fun. We should all do it once in a while. You know the old story ... the 'emperor's new clothes' concept. Freud was relevant in his own generation but he is wrong for this generation. You have a good enough basis to show that Helms is also wrong."

"You can't tell a teacher he's wrong."

"There are a lot of things wrong with the world right now, and you start by saying it. Lay it out … exposure starts the cure, even for Helms." She pauses. "Look, if you can, you put it in words that he can hear. Say it in his language, then do a bait-and-switch and prove he is wrong. I'll help you get started, if you want."

I take her offered assistance, and the next weekend we write a preliminary outline of an analysis that is contrary to everything that Helms has been teaching us, but it is carefully camouflaged in his perspective in order to get the topic approved.

The more Katherine leads me into the library stacks of psychology books and funnels the writing of feminist leaders to me, the more I ponder and discover new truths. Her guidance is an awakening. I diligently look for answers but I'm not satisfied with what I find in the textbooks. In the classical world of psychology, women are described as childish and helpless, with no possibility of happiness unless they adjust to being passive objects. The popular theory is that a woman's primary goal is to be attractive enough to allure the right man. By affirming her natural inferiority, they say, a woman becomes fulfilled in her relationship with the world and through her husband, fulfilled in her sexual development.

In secluded study carrels, on long walks through campus and around the lake, and through conversations late into the night, Katherine tears these theories to pieces, sometimes with extraordinarily logical reasoning, sometimes with caustic humor and playful sarcasm. I tell her that recognized experts talk of anatomy decreeing a woman's life and the natural need to seek approval and direction from others. Katherine points out the self-serving nature of these theories … men need women to bear and care for their children and keep their houses. *Voila,* she says, women must believe that they should be kept pregnant and barefoot. Business and commerce flourish on consumer goods. It stands to reason, she says, that if someone believes she must keep up appearances and have all the stuff, she will buy more. What if, she says, what if we did not buy into any of it? What if we decide that we are not passive, empty mirrors, reflecting the lives around us; that we are not frilly, useless decorations; that we are not mindless animals or something to be disposed of by others? What if we decide to have a voice in our own lives? What if we say "no" and mean it? What then?

Through the winter, I slog through snow for the first time in my life, and I slog through my term paper as it takes shape. I construct it in two parts: The Theories and The Responses. Each time I have to review my progress with Helms, I listen to his suggestions, show him my compilation of the theories, and tell him that I am still working on the responses. Then I write a responsive position that seems reasonable to me, but is the opposite of his point of view. Katherine cheers me on with each draft, encouraging me in my daring assertiveness.

When I finish the paper and turn it in, I am proud of the originality and boldness of my work. I have applied the major traditional psychological theories to women's personalities and I have concluded that they were developed without sufficient scientific method and control and are, therefore, unreliable and unsupportable. Helms is outraged, of course, and my report card at the end of the year has a failing grade for his class.

Meanwhile, the country is suffering excruciating social pains, and the virginal halls and hearts of Wellesley begin to absorb it. We closely follow the underground news reports from Washington on the opening day of Congress in January 1968. Five thousand radical women march in an antiwar rally. Thirty women from New

York break away and march with an empty coffin and signs urging women on: "The Death of Traditional Womanhood! We want our rights and we want them NOW!" Women in the anti–Vietnam War group are appalled ... stopping the war is their first priority, and they claim that demanding equality is petty, disloyal, and divisive. Campus women, caught in the sudden explosion of longhaired hippies, dope, hard rock music, and flower children, divide along these same lines. Increasingly, we gather in informal groups after class and in our dorms, arguing heatedly about emerging political issues. Each day starts fresh with new surprises and shocks as we suffer the awkward pains of our own growth.

One of the black students on campus writes a political editorial for the school newspaper based on Malcolm X's thoughts, but the editor refuses to print it. Instead, the student prints it herself, and a small group of black students, including Susan, passes it out on campus and through women's groups in Boston. "The average white man doesn't realize his basic assumption of superiority," it begins. "So, too, the average white woman finds it difficult to discuss women's issues because she also believes herself to be superior. Middle-class white women have no right to make demands for themselves without including the black woman's needs. It is the black woman who is shot down in every way. Unless this new women's liberation movement reaches out to poor and oppressed black women and forms meaningful alliances, it does not stand a chance."

A chasm develops between Susan and me as we individually sink deeper into discoveries about ourselves as women, initially and foremost. We begin to feel the seething anger of those who speak for the amorphous concept of women's liberation and the equal anger of those who oppose it, whatever "it" is. We join shaky alliances and struggle within the groups to define our causes and ourselves. My groups and alliances are populated with white women; hers are black.

. . . .

Bucky's knock on the bathroom door shakes my thoughts and brings me back to the present. "Mary Frances?"

"I'm here."

"May I come in?" He enters slowly without waiting for a reply and sits on the toilet seat. He is wearing boxer shorts, with a robe over his shoulders. The candle on the edge of the washbasin flickers with the air movement. In the shadow, his face shows weariness; it may even be slight intoxication. I guess that he has had time for two or three drinks and I wonder. Resting his elbows on his knees, he rubs his forehead and eyes, finally bringing his chin to rest in the palms of his hands. Watching him, I am reminded of a professional athlete after a grueling match, recuperating in the locker room and explaining his team's loss to the camera. His curly, black hair is mussed as if he has been running his fingers through it.

Settling my head on the bath pillow, I sink below the remaining cover of bubbles. I feel buoyed by my sense of resolve and my reminiscing, but also begin to feel my patterns of subservience slowly resurfacing. I wait for him to speak.

"Sugar plum," he starts and hesitates. His dark eyes look directly at me. I hear the pain in his voice. "Today is our special day, and I'm feelin' bad that we're endin' it this way."

I feel his power over me. Tiny invisible fingers pull on the muscles of my body and my whole self, once again, slowly and quietly wants to become the acquiescing wife. He has the face of an adorable child. I am unable to speak, and look away.

"I'm offerin' to talk about it so we can continue celebratin' the years that we've spent together." His eyes beseech. "We've always resolved our differences before going to bed."

I feel the defiance reluctantly seeping out of my skin, one pore at a time. I smooth over some of the bubbles before I speak, making shapes as a distraction. "The situation with Emmaline is important to me."

"I'm beginnin' to appreciate that. Would you tell me why?"

Hesitating and looking for words that would not be inflammatory, I sift my thoughts to frame them in a way that would appeal. "She said something today that concerns me and leads me to believe there's a wrong that needs to be righted."

"I cannot argue with wrongs that need to be righted." He is trying to be accommodating and conciliatory. "Would you tell me what it is and what your connection is?"

I fear that he might manipulate me into a verbal corner. I speak slowly and carefully. "I've told you that I believe there is a connection between Emmaline and me."

"Yes, I don't see that yet, but that's your assertion."

"I think she may have been my mammy when I lived with my mama and daddy."

"I'm not sure how you came up with that, but go ahead."

"She told me that she was a mammy, and that the mother of the child she cared for made her give up her own child."

"… and?"

"She said something about being forced to sign papers. It sounds to me like she had to give up her child in order to keep her job."

"Sugar, I don't mean to be argumentative, but women give up babies all the time. That's what adoption is all about, but no one is ever forced to. The law is explicit about that, and birth mothers are always protected. If she was your mammy, maybe she was an unwed mother and they felt she couldn't do an adequate job takin' care of two babies all the time. Maybe they simply gave her a reasonable choice."

I stare at him silently. "Bucky," anger seethes in that secret place where I sense right from wrong, "you attorneys like to hide behind your laws when you know that isn't the way things really are. This woman suffered through something that was either very wrong, or she had no control over, or didn't understand." I pick up a bar of soap and begin to use it on my arm. "Maybe she was frightened and intimidated. All I know is, it was a long time ago, there is a human side to whatever happened, an' it's not right to take babies away from their mothers. She still suffers immensely."

"… and tell me again what your connection is?"

Putting the soap down, I look directly at him. "If she was my mammy, then it was my mother who did this to her."

"… and where is the evidence that it was your mother?"

I know perfectly well that Bucky always needs hard facts, and I sound silly from his point of view. "Right now, it's my intuition. My gut tells me there is something important here. And I'm not going to be satisfied until I can find out for sure."

Bucky buries his face in his hands and tension quivers the muscles of his forearms. I know he wants to tell me that I am wrong, but for the sake of peace, he is forcing himself to stay silent.

I don't like the feeling in the air and try again. "Bucky, I don't remember my mama. Beatrice never wants to talk about her. When I was little, my mama was my fantasy. I talked to her at night. I made up stories about her and told them to Martha. I played dress-up and pretended to be her." I pick up a washcloth from the side of the tub, wet it, squeeze it out, and bury my face before continuing. "She was like a goddess in my eyes. I've protected her sacred memory for all these years."

He lifts his head and spreads his hands in supplication. His face is puzzled. "Why would you want to destroy your memories of her by finding out somethin' different?"

Burying my face again, I search for words, and speak slowly as I look up and the thoughts come. "Because … I can't go back now. I have information that could destroy those memories. Because … if I don't, I will always wonder, and it will eat away at me. Because … if she did take away that woman's child, and if I can reconnect them, I could right the wrong that she did." I look up at him. "I have to do it, that's all."

He stares at me, finally saying, "I suppose I'm gonna have to let you do this." I feel a twitch that tells me he has just assumed control of my project, but I also feel a sense of relief. He thinks for a minute and stands, propping himself against the wall with a hand. "Will you make me one promise, though?"

"Of course, what is it?"

He takes his robe off and tosses it across the toilet seat before he leans backwards against the washbasin, almost sitting, "Will you promise me that when you find out, you'll let it go, that you won't drag it on?"

"Of course."

"Another thing."

"What's that?"

"Keep your distance from that black man. That's only askin' for trouble."

I'm annoyed with this and retort. "Bucky, you have no cause to worry about me. I have always been appropriate around men, black or white. I am your wife, and I love you." Emphasizing the word "you," I lean back in the tub and decide to dismiss his last comment as male pride, realizing that I have won a major concession, even though it is not a complete victory. I begin to feel the tension between us dissipate much like the light from the candle disappears into the shadows of the room. As much as I have hated the fights over the years, I'm also grateful that we have always been able to reconcile.

"Just as long as you remember that," his tone changes. He is strong, but in our life together, he has invited me to be part of his world, which gives me a sense of belonging to someone very powerful. The look of control in his dark eyes changes to a look of desire, a desire for me. As our eyes connect, I see subtle shifts in his facial tension. The sternness around his mouth shifts to a softened desire to kiss. The flickering shadows make his body come alive, and I feel drawn to his physique, slowly shifting my attitude so that I begin to notice the effect of his taut muscles. I have always enjoyed being with this man and admiring his strength.

Bending over and kissing me lightly, he kneels alongside the tub and takes the washcloth from my hand. I know this signal and willingly bend forward over my legs, resting my forehead on my knees. He wets the cloth, holds it a few inches above my skin, and dribbles warm water on my back, starting at the nape of my neck. The water caresses my shoulders, speaking to each muscle as it trickles down. Many times he reaches into the bath and brings water up over areas of my body. Each drop falling from the tip of the cloth massages a nerve ending. When he has masterfully brought me to the point of complete relaxation, he reaches for my shampoo, pours a small amount in his hand, and lathers my hair. The fingertips of both hands lovingly massage my scalp. He fills a pitcher with warm water and rinses the shampoo out, starting with the crown of my head. Washing my hair is a cherished ritual in our foreplay. He is taking care of me, concerned about my pleasure.

After the rinse, he helps me stand, gently wipes the bubbles off, and wraps me in a large bath towel. Drawing me close, his strong arms envelope me. "All is forgiven?"

As his fingers touch my skin, I begin to feel the sacred excitement that he has always generated. I nuzzle my face in the comfort of his neck. "Darling, I'm not upset with you; you simply have to let me make peace with my past, whatever it is, and wherever it takes me."

He pulls away slightly and kisses my forehead. "Of course," he whispers, "it's just that I don't want to lose you in the process." His hand comes up to my face, gently touching my cheek and tracing the line of my jaw. As he moves, the towel drops to the floor. He reaches for his robe and places it around my shoulders, drawing me into a caress. We stand there together, silently hugging. Words are no longer necessary as the intensity of our feelings melt and mingle. He picks me up, tucks the robe around me, and carries me into the bedroom. Nuzzling against his shoulder, I smell the freshness of his skin and feel the excitement of anticipation.

He carries me to the bed, gently lying me down, and adjusts the pillows for my comfort. Although he is the only man I have ever slept with, I can't imagine how it could be better with someone else. Earlier in the evening before he came home, I had put champagne on ice in the bedroom, set up a fire in the fireplace, and closed the drapes against the outside world. Before coming into the bathroom, he had uncorked the bottle and lit the fire. The woodsy smell of hickory logs fills the room and the flames crackle softly in the background. Leaving me for a minute, he pours two flutes and brings them to the bed. Only the sound of the fire and the clicking of our glasses break the silence. He kisses me lightly before the first sip.

Putting his glass down beside the bed, he takes up a book of Shakespeare's sonnets and opens it to "Sonnet XVII," reading some favorite lines,

> "If I could write the beauty of your eyes,
> And in fresh numbers number all your graces,
> The age to come would say, this poet lies,
> Such heavenly touches ne'er touch'd earthly faces."

I recognize these lines from other evenings, and relish them. He is making love to me with words, and I respond by taking the book, gently putting it down, and touching his cheek. I am overcome with thoughts of our years together and the sense of intimacy that has grown out of our love of poetry. *How many times have we recited love poems to each other,* I silently wonder, and speak aloud,

> "Rough winds do not shake the darling buds of May,
> and our eternal summer shall not fade.
> So long as I can breathe, or my eyes can see,
> I give my life to thee."

His eyes dance in the darkness of the room, and he raises his glass. "I compliment your creativity. Shakespeare would approve." He reaches over and takes the glass from my hand and puts it on the nightstand.

He brushes a few strands of wet hair off of my forehead before sliding the robe off my shoulders. As he does this, he plants tiny kisses on my neck. I stretch to receive them, and feel the tingling of my body coming alive for him.

My husband knows me well. Sitting alongside me, his strong hands glide over my skin barely touching it, yet he masterfully arouses excitement with his light massage. His touch caresses my arms, my thighs, my stomach, and my breasts. His fingers rest on my nipples, encircling them lightly until the tips are hard. I reach for him with both arms, wanting to pull him close to me, to feel the warmth of his skin next to mine.

"Sugar plum, you like it best the longer I make you wait," he coos. His hand moves to the delicate skin on the inside of my thigh, and I melt in his arms.

My arms encircle his neck and pull him gently. "Sweetheart, I've waited long enough. I need you."

"You're sure?"

"Yes, darlin'," and I tease him with a touch of playful melodrama and flirtation, "I want you ..." I run my fingers through his hair, lightly grabbing small bunches, "I need you ..." I pull him closer, "I must have you."

His muscles twitch in the dancing firelight as he moves onto my body, his large frame covering me with warmth and excitement as we yield to the intimacy of our marriage, and I experience one of the pleasures that sustains me.

Lying awake in bed long after Bucky has fallen asleep, my thoughts go back to my friend, Susan. I wonder how she would have reconciled our feminism with my life as Bucky's wife. I also wonder how her political commitments and relationships with men would have evolved if fate had not intervened.

6. NEW CULTURES

Thinking about Susan brings back many memories, and over the next few days I continue to reminisce. I remember walking into the common room at the dorm after dinner on Thursday, April 4, 1968. Susan is sitting nearest the TV, crying. A number of other girls are somberly gathered around, sitting on the floor and on couches, eyes glued to the TV set. A news special is on, and the screen shows the Capitol in Washington, D.C., with smoke rising behind it. A reporter standing in front of police barricades comes on the screen.

"What happened?" I plop down next to Susan.

With tears in her voice, she says, "Martin Luther King was shot and killed in Memphis." Instinctively, I reach over and hug her shoulders. I have not followed Dr. King closely, but I know how much Susan respects him and supports his work.

Fear tenses my muscles as I watch the screen and feel bewildered at this act of violence. After a moment of silence I ask, "What's this?"

"Riots are breaking out everywhere. That's Washington. It's burning."

Shocked, I stare at the screen, feeling horror creep into my bones and unnerving my sense of well-being. The announcer speaks of an unconfirmed report that Stokely Carmichael, gun belted to his body and surrounded by vigilantes, has been seen walking through the shopping district of Washington, an area stretching north from Pennsylvania Avenue. He has been asking the shopkeepers, restaurants, and businesses to close their doors in homage and unsuccessfully urging his vengeful followers to disperse. The reporter, fear in his voice, speaks in front of live camera shots of solitary columns of smoke rising from fires.

"We've lost a leader. It's more than that … it's like … he was family." Susan indicates the screen with an uncertain wave and a shaking voice. "This will hurt what he tried so hard to bring about peacefully."

The other black girl in the group, Vivian, comes over and sits on the floor in front of Susan, leaning against her legs. They take each other's hands and silently cry together. She looks up at Susan, whispering hoarsely, "Everything will be destroyed." They melt into a hug of sorrow. I feel helplessly afraid of what I am watching.

For the next week, we are mesmerized with horror as the country convulses. Riots break out in Boston, Detroit, Chicago, Philadelphia, and several other major cities. President Johnson appeals for calm, asking citizens to reject retaliation and to respect Dr. King's life of non-violence, but the president is forced to sign an order calling up the army and National Guard. The looting and fires reach within two blocks of the White House, and by Saturday morning, soldiers in full combat gear with machine guns are guarding the steps of the Capitol. Thousands of people are arrested, and many deaths are reported. Roy Wilkins, the successor to Martin Luther King Jr. at the Southern Christian Leadership Conference, appeals to the crowds, speaking in tearful, disconnected thoughts about how King's memory is being desecrated by looting, instead of focusing on the sorrow and anger. Robert Kennedy, speaking from Indianapolis, asks the country to feel its pain but tame the savageness of man and make life more gentle.

Many campuses around the country shut down as fear spreads that a student reaction, already primed by unrest over the Vietnam War, would take up the black anger and explode out of control, adding to the nation's angst. Wellesley does not close completely, although activities are cancelled, and most people stay indoors out of fear and watch the coverage on TV.

Tributes pour in as the media recounts the years that Dr. King led the struggle for civil rights, from his beginnings as a minister and the yearlong 1955 Montgomery, Alabama, bus boycott, to his successful march on Washington and his strong influence on the passage of the Voting Rights Act of 1967. His appearance in Memphis was to have been a prelude to a new encampment planned for April to be known as the Poor People's Campaign for more economic and social legislation. His courage and his success as a bridge between cultures are extolled. He is eulogized as someone who was able to hear the anger of the poverty-stricken and link their demands and needs to the legislative and legal processes in order to accomplish change with dignity.

We watch the funeral in Atlanta a few days later. Lester Maddox, the racist Governor of Georgia, retreats into the state capitol, surrounded by troopers, fearful that the one hundred fifty thousand people who congregate for the funeral would, instead, storm the building. While he fumes his fear to the press, Jacqueline Kennedy and Betty Shabazz, the widow of Malcom X, comfort

Coretta Scott King at her home. The funeral is conducted like a state affair. There is no rioting.

A number of girls in the dorm make sure that Susan and Vivian are cared for in their time of grief. As the days wear on, I become more sensitive to the civil rights movement and aware of its difficulties. Others in the dorm talk in small groups, fearing black anger around the country and worried that violence will erupt in their hometowns. We watch with dread as students at nearby Columbia University explode with anger only three weeks after the King riots, sparking still more outbreaks. King's death seems to have opened a festering wound as campus unrest gains momentum around the country.

A new strain of thinking begins to emerge in our conversations. Those who had begun the year convinced that they would become housewives for wealthy and successful men express frustration with their presumed status quo. Discontent feels like a necessary issue. Morality questions gain urgency as campus discussion topics ranging from the new availability of birth control pills and abortion to the Vietnam War. The seething anger of blacks and the emerging stories of legally sanctioned atrocities prompt critical discussions of political allegiances in classrooms, in the school newspaper, and in impromptu debates. Much of what we have accepted as normal is wretchedly peeled away like an onionskin. The emerging fumes hurt our sensibilities, and the heart of the nation is found to be morally rotten.

Many of us feel helpless and wonder what can be done to change America. We are excited and certain that we, the younger generation, can find the answers to the mess our parents have made. As we talk among ourselves, one of the dorm seniors suggests that women from our school should join the growing groundswell of college students who are supporting the voter registration drives in the South, much like in the summer of 1964, when students everywhere congregated in support of the civil rights movement and finally succeeded in getting legislation signed into law. This time, she said, it will be easier because the laws have already been passed but they need real enforcement.

One afternoon about a month after the King assassination, Susan and I walk across campus from Clapp Library, slowly finding our way to the dorm. The air has the balmy coolness of a New England spring, tiny buds are appearing on many trees and flowers, classes are winding down, and summer plans fill our thoughts. I venture a question, wondering if the blacks in the South really want whites interfering with their cause.

After several careful steps while concentrating on avoiding the muddy water along the edge of Campus Drive, she replies, keeping her eyes focused forward and speaking to me thoughtfully, "Is it interference? Is this only our cause?"

"No, of course not. We want integration, too; that's the way it should be, but it seems like we can't work together anymore," I said, hearing the defensive tone in my voice. "All of this anger, all of these bad feelings should just go away, and things should be the way they are supposed to be."

She moves to let a car pass on the narrow roadway. I feel a chill in the air as the sun passes under a cloud, and she sighs. "Which is what?" She is now standing in the middle of the road, oblivious to the possibility of more traffic.

"Everything. Everything you want. There are so many white people who want to see it happen, who want the old ways to change, but the anger and hostility .... Susan, this anger is causing a backlash." Fear wells up inside me and I gush with frustration,

"Look what's happening ... look at the country falling apart. It scares us ... it scares me. The actions of the blacks are destroying everything that has been accomplished. If you would stop being angry and destructive, we would stop being afraid, and progress could finally be made."

Slowly, she turns her head and looks at me blankly. Sadness shows in her eyes. It's as if gloom has suddenly permeated the air, casting a shadow everywhere, and she is reminiscing about what has been, what could be, but what isn't. "How about, if the whites would stop being afraid of us, we would stop being angry? We have been afraid of you for a very long time."

"Is it fear that you feel toward us? We are the ones who are afraid ... look what's happening to the cities." The words come before I recognize that I seem to speak for the collective South, the indignant South that I both love and hate. "It's the blacks who are angry and rioting in the streets and destroying their own neighborhoods. Don't you understand why we are afraid of your people? Don't you understand the fear that grips America? We don't want our houses and businesses burned. We can't give you what you want now; it would seem to be a reward for lawlessness. This is not the way the world is supposed to be." It seems to me that I speak for all whites in America.

We walk again for a while before she speaks, her voice slowly swelling with her own emotions and the anger that I fear. We reach Academic Quad, but it's late afternoon, and few people are out. "For two hundred, maybe three hundred years, people were yanked out of their homes in Africa ... proud people ... they were put in chains ... treated even worse than animals ... killed ... forced to do backbreaking work as slaves ... forced to bow in shame ... forced to give up their culture and their history ... and now the ones who did it are afraid of retribution? They blame us for the lawlessness? They are afraid of being punished for their sinful ways? Don't you think it's about time?"

I have never seen her this way. She has always been controlled, careful, her every thought weighed. Now, it's as if the pain of thousands of people is throbbing in the veins of her temples, and she is someone completely different. I must calm her rage. "Susan, no, we didn't do it. Other people did ... a long time ago. That's all over. We're on your side. The laws have been passed to change things. It's not fair to take it out on us. It's time for your people to get past it and move on with their lives."

"Why are we 'those other people'? Why are we blacks first, and people second? Why does everyone in this school, even you, react to me first as a black person? Why is it that everything is defined first in racial terms?" Her voice changes from angry to frustrated. "It's so tiring, the constant wondering ... the vigilance. Why is this person condescending to me? What is that person really thinking when he treats me badly? Is it me, is it the color of my skin, or maybe, is this person just a slimy jerk to everyone? It has never been all right to be black in this country, even for fortunate people like me, and it still isn't."

"It can be better. We can make it better. You and me, others like us. We can change the way things are. We can be friends, we are friends, and like us, more and more people can start accepting it as the new way, and you can get over it."

"You rape our bodies, you rape our souls, and then you tell us to just get over it? It doesn't work like that! Humiliating someone over and over, for a lifetime, is an intrusion that requires the aggressor to experience agony, doubled-over agony, to fully feel it. The whites need to feel the same way we do." She emphasizes her point by clutching her books and bending over as if in pain. Straightening up, she continues. "It requires revenge, and no rape of the soul is ever completely forgiven." She looks at me pointedly, "It also requires retribution." She begins to walk without talking, tensely holding her books to her chest as anger emanates from the core of who she is.

Finally, more quietly, she begins to talk as she walks. "Sometimes when you talk to me, it feels more like pity. Something like, 'It's a pity you were born that way, poor dear.' I have ambitions just like you, just like all white kids. I want to be someone special, to rise above the ... oh, what would you call it ... rise above the clouds maybe. Stick my head out for the world to see. But," her face wrinkles in a frown of disturbed recognition, "every time I do something, every time I try, what do you see, what does the world see?"

I look at her blankly—I don't understand. We approach a bench, and I sit down, feeling a need to listen without distraction. She remains standing, balancing her books on a trash bin, and answers her own question. "You don't see a face, just the face of someone trying to better herself. You see a black face. And because of what you see, you, and I mean white people, you always see me as a black person first; you make decisions about me because of the color of my skin. And because of that, you will never let me belong; you will always put me over there." She sweeps her arm across her body and points away from us. "I have to stay away, stay out of the mainstream. I have to be the one who cleans your bathrooms, maybe tends your kids, or serves you food. I'll never be able to live in a nice house next door to you or get the same jobs that white folks get, or make the same kind of money." She sighs, "Will it ever be all right for me to just be someone who wants to accomplish the same things as you?"

I see a vision of her behind a podium speaking to a crowd, skillfully using body language to emphasize her points. I see her becoming a leader, speaking out for the dignity of the oppressed, making a difference. Feeling like her first audience, I am helpless to address her concerns, and I hear the limpness in my voice. "Susan, times are changing. You're doing well. You're going to a good school. You sing well, you dance well. You make good grades. You'll be able to graduate and do whatever you want. You could really make something of yourself, I know you can."

She looks at me fearlessly. Her stare is clear, her eyes piercing. "I will graduate and apply for a job somewhere, and if it's in a white company or if it's something mainstream, someone else will get it, I already know that. If I want to sing or dance, I'll be told there are no roles on major stages for a black woman. If I want to step forward anywhere, for any cause, I won't count, because I'm black and I'm female. Even if my opinions are right or my talent is the best, no one will hear them. I'll be told to disappear or go on the black circuit. They will never use those words, but that's what they will mean." She pauses and adopts a faraway look. "And what about all the sisters out there who aren't as fortunate as I have been? The ones who haven't been able to go to private school or who want to go to college but can't because they have to work to help the family? Or the ones who had ambitions at one time, but gave up because they couldn't see it happening for them? Or maybe, the ones who have been told from the time they were li'l babies that they had to act like ass kissers just because of who they are?" A fire glows in her eyes. "You have to be able to see it, to believe it can be true for you, before you can ever make anything happen, an' there is no one showing us that it can happen for us, too."

"Susan, you can't expect to be handed everything. I have ambitions, too. I'm excited about what I'm learning about women, the changes that I see in how we view ourselves. I'd like to study more psychology, maybe teach in a school like this. Wouldn't it be great to replace all of the professors like Helms with women professors who really understand how women are? Think of the concept … women could help women, and we could all be strong! But I don't expect someone to hire me just because I ask for a job, and I'm not going to blame it on something like my skin color if I don't. I'll just have to keep working hard to get what I want."

She shakes her head, not believing me. "You've never had the experience of being humiliated just because of who you are, something that you have no control over and can't change anyway." She mocks me gently, "You know as well as I do that your aunt will buy you any job you want. You won't ever have to struggle for something you want. And your aunt will do everything in her power to hold on to the racist past, to keep things the way they are with all of the hatred and injustice. It's that hatred that made her who she is, and she's not goin' to let it go easily … and she's powerful enough to keep it," she breathes deeply. "There are too many people out there like her who can't let go of their hatred and racism. People like her will remind me every day of my life that I need to stay in my place, whatever they decide it is." The bitterness in her voice lingers, and she picks up her books and begins to walk again. I follow.

"Susan, I'm with you. Times are changing, people are changing. Please give us a chance. What can we do to show you that not everyone is like that?"

She turns forcefully. "What about having sympathy? What about having enough sympathy to give your soul, to give enough of who you are to make other white people hear what is troubling America? Mary Frances, it's the silence of the good people who make us hear the voices of the bad ones."

I feel stymied by my inability to understand her, but my heart wants to reach out on a personal level. For several days, I ponder how to respond to her plea. In spite of our differences, she has become my friend, and in many ways, my confidante, much like Martha and Katherine. Finally, I ask if I can go home with her for the summer recess and work on the voter registration drive alongside her.

"Your aunt would never allow it."

"I won't tell her what I'm doing. I can just say that I'm going to New Orleans for the summer."

"She knows I'm from there."

"I don't think so. Besides, she still doesn't know we're roommates, and Eileen O'Connor is from there also. I'll say I'm staying with her."

Susan finally agrees, reluctantly, since there are several other girls from the school who are going to the South for the summer. Eileen agrees to participate in our plan, although she won't be able to work on the voter drive. In mid-May, Eileen calls Beatrice, pretending to be her own mother extending the invitation and assuring her that I will be safe and well cared for. Since Beatrice and George are going to Europe for the better part of the summer, Beatrice is relieved that I have made arrangements for myself.

A few days after the end of classes in late May 1968, Susan and I join Eileen and another girl, Lorraine, in Eileen's Volkswagen van for the drive to New Orleans from the Boston area.

Eileen is a tall, slender, auburn-haired senior from an Irish family in New Orleans, who has ambitions of becoming a lawyer; while Lorraine, a dishwater blonde from California, wants to marry one and jokes about wanting to hang out with young lawyers-in-the-making. Leaving Massachusetts and then New York, we connect with the New Jersey turnpike and the Delaware turnpike, and are near Baltimore, Maryland, for our first night on the road. Driving into Baltimore, we soon find a motel on Russell Street. All four of us climb out, glad to stretch our legs, and go in to register.

An overweight, middle-aged woman in a turquoise and purple bowling shirt is seated behind the counter, watching the Lawrence Welk Show. She does not turn around when the bell on the door tinkles.

Eileen takes the lead. "Excuse me. We'd like a room for four."

"Sure darlin'," the woman begins, slowing swiveling her chair around. She stops when she sees us. "Benny," she turns her head sideways, calling loudly into the back room, "come here … please." She stares at us. The moment is awkward as she yells back to him again. "Benny, we don't have any rooms, do we?"

"That's bullshit, Madge. What do you mean, we got all kinds." Benny walks through the door and stares at us. He wears a stained undershirt, is short and stocky, with a beer belly and thinning, frizzy, gray hair. "Guess you're right, Madge." He walks over to the counter pugnaciously.

Eileen continues. "Your sign says there's a vacancy."

Benny reaches over and turns off a switch on the wall. "Now it don't."

"Mister, what you're doing is against the law. You're required to accommodate us."

Benny reaches down under the counter with mock casualness. He is the caricature of every ugly, white Southerner known to man. Slowly he brings up a shotgun and lays it on the counter, casually resting his hand on the trigger. "Don't you be sassin' me, little girl. This here is my place and I rent to whoever I want, and I don't want to rent to niggers, or nigger lovers. Ain't nobody gonna make me," he stares hard at Susan, "an' in this state we can shoot trespassers, and I've decided you're trespassing. Y'all get outta here before I have to make you go."

I look at Susan, who says nothing, but her face shows terror. Slowly, we absorb the tension, file out of the lobby, and climb into the van. The silence is deadening. Eileen speaks first, lashing out about how she would like to do something about people like Benny. Susan is trembling, unable to speak. We drive until we get to College Park, Maryland, and find another motel. This time, Susan and I stay in the van while Eileen and Lorraine rent the room. Susan and I remain in the van each time for four more nights as we travel through the South to Louisiana. We buy food in grocery stores and eat in the van to avoid problems in restaurants. Susan never talks about our racial encounters, or the stares that we receive, but she begins to unwind and feel more comfortable the closer we get to New Orleans.

We arrive on Sunday evening, June 2nd, and Eileen follows Susan's directions to her home. Susan has already told me the basics about her family. Her father is a high school principal and was involved in developing the Louisiana school integration plan. He is now part of the team implementing the program. Her mother is a visiting nurse, who also takes in foster children for the Welfare Department on an emergency basis. The police and social workers come around at all hours with babies and little kids who have just been taken from their parents or found somewhere in a bad situation. Most of them have mothers who are on drugs. The foster kids usually stay a few weeks until they are returned to their parents or a permanent placement is found.

Two years before she was born, her parents had taken in one of their first foster children, Eric, and later adopted him. He is the only other child in the family. Susan told me that his birth mother had been heavily into drugs when he was born and had ended up in the state mental hospital, where he visited her a few times before her death. He never knew who his natural father was. She also told me that Eric attends Stanford University in California on a football scholarship, majoring in political science, and will be home for the summer, working as an intern on a city council campaign.

I feel petrified going to their home. At Wellesley, and driving from Boston to New Orleans, I was in a white environment where I felt comfortable and where I was the liberal white person embracing a new political cause; but as the van turns off of Highway 10, I become acutely aware that we are in a black neighborhood. As Susan guides Eileen through the maze of streets, I question the sanity of what I am doing and feel a knot in my stomach as we stop in front of her home. Why am I doing this? The voices from my childhood scream at me to run away, to back out of this commitment, to hide behind skirts and fearfully peer at people who are different from me. I don't belong here. Will everyone hate me? Will I be safe with all of the racial unrest? I bite my tongue and force myself to begin taking my suitcases from the van as Susan runs to her mother, who meets her halfway down the sidewalk with outstretched arms. Mrs. Devereaux is tall and fairly dark. She's an older version of Susan, rounded, but not plump, and attractive in a mature way.

The house is a large, older, plain, turn-of-the-century Victorian with a wide Southern porch in the front and along one side. The white paint is in good condition, the yard and fences are well kept, and the neighborhood is respectable. Two small black children on tricycles stop nearby and stare at us, and I smile at them nervously. An older black man and a teenage boy who are working under a car hood across the street stop and idly watch. Another car drives by, slowing down as the occupants stare at us.

Eileen, Lorraine, and I stand by the rear of the van, three naïve, white, college girls who believe in a political cause but who have little experience of the real world, waiting nervously in a black neighborhood in a very Southern city less than two months after the leader of the black movement has been slain by a white man. I realize that I expected to be in the middle of slums, and that I expected to be seen as the benevolent and unselfish white woman showing good will toward the less fortunate. In spite of the bountiful old oak trees, the summer sun beats down on us, and sweat appears on our brows. Eileen walks over to Mrs. Devereaux with an outstretched hand and introduces herself. I follow with mock cheerfulness. "I'm Mary Frances. I'm the one who is stayin' with Susan for the summer."

Mrs. Devereaux has a congenial presence about her but I can't read her face. Is she being gracious, is she privately checking me out, is she wondering what in the world I am doing, or do I see thinly masked black anger on her face? I don't know if I am welcomed or if a rush of racial resentment will swoop down on me, hold me accountable, and force me to run for my life. Standing in the hot sun, I suddenly feel at the mercy of all of the wrongs committed against all of these people. "Welcome to our home. I hope you will be comfortable here." She takes my outstretched hand, carefully watching me. "Have you been to N'Orleans before?"

"No."

She reaches down for the two suitcases. "I hope you enjoy yourself while you're here. Are these yours?"

I nod my head, not moving from my spot. She puts my bags down and moves to the open hatch door.

"Susan, which ones are yours? Oh, these two, I think. Oh, dear," she speaks to Eileen as she tries to lift one out, "would you help me with this? Very good, now this one. That's it. What a long journey you've had. Won't y'all come on in for some iced tea? You must be very tired. I prayed for you all the way and I'm so glad you made it without troubles. The good Lord hears us sometimes, doesn't he?" As she talks, she hands out suitcases until we each have one, as if it is the most natural act in the world, and we are welcomed company. Each of us complies, grabs one, and carries it in, thankful that she has taken charge of the situation.

Walking through the door, I realize that I have never been in a black household before, and it feels strange. In my upbringing, I had heard that these people were different, that they were inferior in some way. They were spoken about with derision, and jokes were made about how poorly they lived in their shantytowns. I remember comments about everyone spittin' watermelon seeds on the bare wooden floors. I heard about the welfare cheats and the lazy, shiftless folks who refused to work. I feel as if I am crossing into forbidden, enemy territory, entering the home of a stranger in a strange land where I do not know the rules and I am hated because of the color of my skin. I have a tremendous sense of the tables being turned and am thankful that I have friends to walk through the door with me.

"Jus' leave the bags in the hallway here. We'll take care of 'em in a minute. This way to the kitchen, girls." Susan had gone ahead, and Mrs. Devereaux deposits her daughter's bags on the rug in the hall and leads us around a formal table in the dining room and through a swinging kitchen door. We are greeted by the muted, summer sun pouring in through the kitchen windows facing the side porch.

The room is large, and the white cabinets on one side gleam in the sunshine. The bright yellow tile catches my eye, and I notice accents of light blue and yellow in the wallpaper and the accessories. Hanging copper molds glisten on the walls and a rack full of copper pots hangs above the stove.

She waves to a large, round, oak table in the corner. "Push some stuff aside and make yourselves at home." Picking up a chrome baby's high chair, she folds it and moves it into a utility room, "We won't be needin' this during the summer while you girls are here. I tol' them I won't be takin' any babies for a couple of months." At first I am puzzled but then I remember the foster children, and have a mental image of this very warm woman tending to sick babies and making them feel welcomed. "Sit down, y'hear? I've got some fresh tea brewing here." She picks up a child's booster seat from one of the chairs and tosses it on top of the high chair before pouring tea over ice cubes in tall glasses and asking about our trip.

Mrs. Devereaux inquires whether Susan had gone to Mass earlier in the day. I know that Susan has not been attending church while at Wellesley, but she has warned me not to tell her mother. She says, "No," and declines her mother's suggestion to go to Sunday evening Mass. Her mother seems slightly perturbed, but says nothing. For the first time, I see a similarity with my rebellion against my aunt and wonder if Susan's friendship with me is part of it.

When Eileen and Lorraine leave, I am caught off guard by a sense of panic at being left alone. I feel drained of my notion that I can arrive in New Orleans with a past that doesn't matter and I can start fresh with no racial baggage. Leaving little time for me to dwell on my thoughts, Mrs. Devereaux picks up my suitcases and shows me to my room. This is the room, she explains, casually beckoning to the crib in one corner, where the babies and li'l children stay. She points out Susan's room and the two other bedrooms on the other side of the upstairs hall.

I meet Mr. Devereaux and Eric late in the evening when they return, exhausted, from a political rally. Our introductions are brief. Mr. Devereaux is not a large man, but he is an inch or two taller than his wife and thickly built. His skin is a lighter color, his features are more Caucasian, and his hair is wavy instead of kinky. I wonder if the features and French name indicate a connection to the French Creole heritage that Louisiana is known for. He welcomes me graciously but seems more distant than his wife. Eric is hostile, or at least seems so, initially, because of the intensity in his dark eyes. Even though I know that Eric is adopted, I am surprised, because he is so much lighter than his family and he is physically larger than his parents. He is a well-conditioned athlete, and strength emanates from his every move.

On Monday, Susan and I sleep late and come downstairs after the others have gone. I had spent most of the night tossing and sweating as if I am sleeping in a tropical zone, and sensing an emotional discomfort that I can't identify. We spend the day unpacking and resting from our trip, and I wander around the house in an effort to feel more comfortable. A collection of family photos is displayed in the downstairs hallway next to a framed depiction of their family tree. Susan speaks of her father as the descendant of an early Creole Free Person of Color who settled in the Cane River area. A Free Person of Color, she explains, was the early Louisiana designation for blacks who were not slaves and who were often the mulatto children of plantation owners or early French settlers. She explains the family tree and shows me that his ties go back to French traders in the 1700s, to the Indians, and to slaves who came from the Sengambia region of Africa. She also tells me that her mother's family emigrated from Haiti after an uprising that killed the president in 1915 just before the American Marines occupied their country for twenty years. She has relatives who are still living under the dictatorship of "Papa Doc" in Haiti that she has never met.

Another group of family pictures shows Eric and Susan as they are growing up; one is of her riding a bicycle with training wheels, another shows a younger version of Eric in a football uniform. Susan picks up a framed photo. "Look, here's where it snowed in New Orleans … for about a day and a half on New Year's Day in 1964," she says, handing me the photo of Eric and her playfully standing next to a snowman in front of their house. "And this one, this is from Hurricane Betsy in 1965." The picture shows water flooding the neighborhood streets. "That was sure scary." Over lunch, we share our hurricane stories, and I tell her what little I know of my hurricane story from North Carolina.

Before leaving for work, Mrs. Devereaux had started a simmering Crock-Pot of jambalaya for dinner, and its tangy aroma fills the house and tempts us all day. I have never had this dish before and look forward to the heavily spiced chicken, sausage, and rice stew that Louisiana is famous for. That evening, as we sit down to dinner, Mr. Devereaux brags about the local cooking, saying that only God cooks good enough for the local palette and lightheartedly commenting, "There are two times of day in Lou'siana, mealtime and in-between, and now we're at the mealtime, which is like prayin' when the food is as good as this is." He continues to be generous with his praise for the dinner and for his wife's attentions as we sit down around the large, oak table in the kitchen.

The conversation initially seems more formal than I had expected, and I wonder if it is because I am a new guest or if it is because I am white and not really welcomed. Mrs. Devereaux shifts the tone, saying to her children, "Since both of you will be home for the summer, this would be a good time to work out who's goin' to do the chores ... setting the table, washing dishes, taking out the trash ... you remember those things, don't you, or has college spoiled both of you?"

Susan and Eric quickly exchange knowing looks, apparently sizing up who will volunteer for what. Susan goes first and claims her old job of setting the table. It's Eric's turn and he pauses for effect, intentionally glancing at each person, then flatly says, "Is Miz Scarlett goin' to be doin' chores, too?"

"Eric, mind your behavior," his father sharply rebuffs. "Miz Mary Frances is a guest in this house. She is not asked to do chores."

"Is she better'n us?"

Before he can reply, I realize that I'm being tested and respond, "I would be very glad to help. What could I do, maybe dishes?" In my whole life, I've never done the dishes and I'm not sure what I am volunteering for. I keep my eyes on Mrs. Devereaux, but Eric's stare is burning.

"That isn't necessary but it would be greatly appreciated." Her voice is kind and it becomes firmer when she turns to Eric.

"Sounds like taking out the trash is yours, but tonight I want your help with the dishes."

Eric looks at me intensely as if he has made his point and says nothing as he continues to eat. Both Mr. and Mrs. Devereaux and Susan have done their best to make me feel comfortable but Eric puzzles me. I've never been close to someone like him and he seems to be a mixture of good manners, intelligence, ambition, respect, and caustic, seething anger.

Dinner ends abruptly when Susan asks if she and I could have our dessert outside. She fixes a tray, pours iced tea, escorts me out the kitchen door to the breezy side porch, and sets the tray on a small table between two rattan chairs. She apologizes for her brother's rudeness and tells me that he has become interested in the Black Muslim movement and is sometimes too militant about black consciousness. She reminds me that her parents are followers of Dr. King's point of view instead and that they work hard to bring about changes through cooperative efforts.

Our conversation is cut short when I hear Eric's voice. "Mom, that white girl doesn't belong here."

"Hush now, son, she's Susan's friend from college. Susan invited her and she's welcome here." I realize that neither Eric nor his mother know that we can hear them on the porch while they clear the table and clean up the kitchen.

"White people seem to think that the black man is gonna rise up and shout 'hallelujah' when one of them patronizing liberals with a halo comes into our midst."

I hear the clatter of silverware. "Eric, you are being blasphemous of the Lord and disrespectful."

"You don't get it, do you ... some little white bitch is gonna come into our house, our home, our private space, and believe that she is absolved of the sins of the white man and call it integration." I feel my face flush and stare at my dessert, unable to eat any more.

"If you can't keep your words to yourself at least keep your tone down." Mrs. Devereaux walks over and closes the back door, not realizing that the window is also open. Susan is embarrassed.

Eric continues, his tone becoming louder and angrier instead of softer. "You know what all this integration shit is? It's a smoke screen designed to confuse us. They want us to say 'yassuh, we be good, you jus' give us a crumb or two, that's all we want, yassuh! Jus' a lit' ol' crumb and we keep on kissin' yo' ass.' They think we want to be like the white man. Civil rights? Man, that's nothing; we want human rights ... we want to be full-blooded human beings with our own lives!"

I hear Mr. Devereaux's stern voice as he seems to enter the kitchen. "Eric, son, we don't talk like that in this house. We do not harbor anger and bitterness. We are already human beings in this family and there is no 'wantin' to be,' we simply are, and we treat everyone with respect, regardless of what your personal feelings are."

"I don't see the white man respectin' you. They gave you the shittiest school in town and you did nothing more than say 'thank you, I appreciate what you done for me.'"

"I've done more for my school full of poor kids than this whole town did before I came along, an' it's because I treat my students with respect, both the black ones and the white ones, and I'm tellin' you that you're going to respect that young lady sittin' out there ...."

Susan takes one more bite of her dessert, gets up, and says, "Let's get outta here. It's time for a walk."

I follow, still feeling terrified about being in a black neighborhood and staying in a black house. "Susan ..." I start, but shake my head and drop it. I don't know how to react to Eric or to my fear. We walk away quickly.

Susan takes me to meet Helena, who lives two blocks away, explaining that I probably need to know her because she is a white woman that I could talk to when I need to.

Helena is reading on her front porch swing when we arrive. Susan introduces me and tells her that I will be visiting for the summer. She is a gentle-looking woman with dark hair, who seems to be in her forties. When she says, "Welcome to our neighborhood," I hear an accent and ask where she is from. She was born in Germany, she says, but her mother was Italian and she went to school in Switzerland during the war years.

"Miz Helena, I'm goin' to leave you two to talk, if that's all right," Susan says, slowly backing away, and turning to me as I take a seat on the steps and lean against the porch railing. "Come on back to the house when you're ready, okay?"

As we watch her walking away, Miz Helena speaks like a kindly aunt, telling me what a fine girl Susan is and how proud her mother is of her. She wants to know if I have ever heard her sing and agrees with me that Susan has a fine voice. I ask Helena if she has children and she wistfully says no, she and her husband decided not to have any. "It was painful for me, you know, because I wanted a child so much, but when we came here, to this country, it was a very difficult time, and our children would have been treated badly. I did not want that for them."

I look at her quizzically.

She gently rocks her chair a few times and gazes into the distance seeming to understand my look. "My husband is a Negro.

He was an American soldier in Europe after the war. I met him when we were both literature students at the Sorbonne in Paris, and we were married there. But in the end, he wanted to come back to his home, back to his old neighborhood."

I look around, contemplating the experience of an interracial marriage. "What's this like for you?"

"The country or the neighborhood, or the ... what should I call it ... my social situation?"

"Both I guess. Well, all three."

"My husband is a wonderful man, and our marriage has been a blessing for me." She looks at me kindly. "My father was a Nazi soldier. I was not welcomed anywhere in Europe after the war." Her tone and facial expression change. "My husband is now a professor of classical literature, and we still have a great love for books. But there has been much that is painful."

"How could it be painful to you? You're white and you're not even American?"

Helena looks at me gently and tells me that I would be welcomed in her home any time, and she will gladly tell me the story of her life, but it won't fit into a short telling. She asks questions of me and is very interested in the reasons why I came to New Orleans. She tells me about some of her activities with international political and peace groups. Best of all, I am able to tell her about my first moments of immersing myself in a black neighborhood, with all the racial turmoil in America and the fear that I feel. She assures me that I will be safe and that most folks don't react like Eric. Walking back to Susan's house two hours later, I feel more comfortable and quietly go upstairs, pleased to find a kindred soul.

The next morning at breakfast, Eric surprises Susan and me by politely asking if we would like to go sightseeing. The whole family suggests that we go on a cemetery tour, a favorite New Orleans pastime and the city's gleeful offering to timid tourists. Susan and I give each other thoughtful stares. Later, when we are in her room getting ready to go, we talk about Eric. Susan says that their father can sometimes be very stern and demanding, and we decide that he must have put Eric up to it.

We take the bus along North Broad Avenue and transfer to Canal Street. As we navigate the public transportation system, Eric explains that there is a unique sense of direction here in N'Orleans because the original city was built on a crescent shaped area of the Mississippi River. To create this off-center arc, the river abruptly turns southerly from its southeastern path and wanders a bit to the east before making a lazy arc back to the original path. This unusual shape created difficulty in laying out streets and explaining how to get anywhere using the traditional directions of north and south, east, and west, so a scheme evolved that used the large, swamp-like lake directly north of the river that creates the northern city boundary. Directions are given as "riverside" and "lakeside," meaning the river to the south and west and Lake Pontchartrain to the north and east, and "uptown" and "downtown," which are up the river, or down the river toward the Gulf of Mexico. So, when someone tells you to go to the riverside downtown corner at an intersection, it is the corner closest to the river, on the closest side to the Gulf. Makes sense, doesn't it? he says.

He also tells me the history of the aboveground crypts of New Orleans that we are going to see. Because the city is six feet below sea level, requiring a levee to separate it from the river, the water table is so high that nothing stays buried for very long, even caskets, and basements are impossible. Imagine, he says, going to a funeral and when they try to intern the casket, it floats back up to

151

the surface on the water that has seeped into the hole in the ground. He says that in the early days they tried filling caskets with rocks and drilling holes so the water would come in and weigh it down, but neither worked. Finally, they simply started burying people above the ground.

Eric seems like a different person today, playful, fun, and polite. Although we have not warmed up to each other, we are both careful to be respectful, each to the other. I begin to feel like a guest who is being escorted rather than a political enemy.

We leave the bus on Basin Street, uptown from the French Quarter, in order to see St. Louis Cemetery #1, probably the most famous of the New Orleans cemeteries. As we get off of the bus, he points out the beginnings of the Super Dome, which is under construction a few blocks away. "I came back for the very first Saints game of the season last year over at Tulane," he reminisces. "Man, you should've seen it: A 94-yard kickoff return by a rookie. I hope I can do that someday." His face is glowing but he grins sheepishly. "Sorry, girls just don't understand, do they?"

Although it's a humid and warm summer day, I feel a chill as we walk through the gates of the cemetery and sense the otherworldliness of the environment. Looking around, it seems like a morbid, child-size, haphazardly built concrete city, with angels, wrought-iron crosses, and dead and dying weeds decorating the little buildings and cluttering the street-like pathways. Coffins are built into a wall to the left of the entrance and all along the perimeter wall much like a large filing cabinet system with immense drawers.

"Tell her about them," Susan says. Eric once again adopts his air of a polite tour guide. "These are the wall vaults and they are usually owned by the benevolent societies for the families who can't afford to bury their dead. Please notice they are much longer than a normal casket, and there is a reason for this, and I'm about to tell you what it is." He grins at me. "After a respectable time has passed, the old remains are pushed to the back and a new corpse is slid into the same vault ... as you can see, we are very practical here."

He beckons, "Come ladies, let me take you on a guided tour ...." He begins to read names as we pick our way through the cluttered graveyard, sometimes implying a personal acquaintance, and always with a sense of fun. I do not recognize any of the names. "Ah, this one you should know, Susan, and even you, Mary Frances, must have heard of Homer Plessy of the *Plessy v. Ferguson* Supreme Court case fame. Brave man, he was. He intentionally climbed on a segregated train to get himself arrested so's to start that case. As you can see, he died in 1925 and never, ever got to ride that train. His was the first famous case askin' for an end to the Jim Crow laws and segregation. The Court turned him down jus' before the turn of the century."

I look at him puzzled, trying to remember this fact.

His voice is sarcastic. "You would have learned about it in the black studies section in your history class." His pause emphasizes his point.

"Eric, you don't have to be so political." Susan pushes us forward and guides us down another pathway and around several crumbled stone vaults.

We stop in front of one of the crypts and Eric continues. "So, we have here another piece of our fine Southern history. Ladies, say hello to Marie Laveau, the Voodoo Queen of N'Orleans." He gestures toward a large, weathered, house-like structure, much like many of the others, but covered with hundreds of hand-drawn red X's. In front is a small, concrete vase containing wilted, red carnations. Next to the carnations is a concrete bowl that holds a few coins, a rusty rosary, and a string of multicolored beads. Eric reaches to the side of the crypt and picks up a piece of broken red brick, handing it to me. "Want to bring yourself some good luck?"

"Oh no, Voodoo is wicked. It's devil worship. I can't do that."

"Are you kidding? It's gotten a bad rap. Voodoo grew out of the Catholics tryin' to convert the African slaves and the Africans holdin' onto some of their culture. It's no more superstitious than many other religions, if you really understand it. All they do is consult the wisdom of their ancestors, but their style is diff'rent and that is what makes 'em scary. Americans think that everythin' diff'rent is bad." He lightens up. "Hey, listen, there is also N'Orleans style Voodoo … snake charmers, witchcraft, and magical charms. It sells to the tourists.

"Here," he continues, "I'll do it. All you do is speak to her and ask for what you want. It's no different from all the people who go to shrines and pray for somethin'… or … like making the sign of the cross and praying to the saints, in fact." He makes three X's on the crypt with the piece of red brick, then covers them with his hand, rubs his right foot against the side three times, closes his eyes and whispers softly. When he finishes, he takes a few coins from his pocket and drops them into the bowl.

"Do you believe in that … do you stick pins in dolls to kill people?"

He laughs, mocking me with his fiery eyes. "You whites think we are all savages right out of the jungles, don't you? If you lower the black religions and cultural styles to lurid witchcraft and sorcery, it makes us less than human, doesn't it?"

"Eric! That's enough!" Susan deliberately walks away. Not knowing what to do, I follow, and Eric catches up, playfully grabbing Susan. "C'mon, li'l sister," he says, "let's go over to the Voodoo Museum and show her what it's all about." He turns to me and once again a sense of fun is in his voice. "Only in N'Orleans can you openly buy witchcraft items and Voodoo dolls." We walk down St. Louis Street, turn left on Bourbon Street, and detour half a block to the old Preservation Hall to see who is playing. Eric suggests that we come down sometime on a hot summer night to listen to jazz. As we continue to walk, the very old shotgun houses that make up the French Quarter fascinate me, and I keep slowing down to absorb the atmosphere.

The Voodoo Museum is a very old, nondescript, dark gray building on Rue Dumaine, two blocks away from Preservation Hall, with typical old shutters and a small stoop in front. An enveloping smell of incense dissipates out of the door as we enter the poorly lit room. "Hey, Mr. G," Eric greets the proprietor sitting behind a desk as we walk in.

Mr. G is a very old, dark-skinned black man, whose thick, white hair is slicked down and pulled back from his forehead. Dark-tinted glasses sit far down on his nose. I can see his large pupils and feel his penetrating gaze. He is wearing a wide, red-and-white striped tie with a blue plaid shirt. A pale yellow vest stretches across his belly as he slouches with age. "Son ... son. We haven't seen you here for a while, I don't think."

"Been away at school. Keepin' busy?"

"Oh, the usual." He raises his chin to point, "Who these young lady friends of your'n?"

155

"My li'l sister and her friend from up North. Just showin' 'em around. Maybe you can give 'em a spell to catch a man with, you know how the girls always want that."

He looks us over slowly, peering through the bifocal part of his glasses and seeming to stare through Susan. "Yep, that's what they want, ain't it? Git those men and hang on to 'em." He chuckles. "You have a good *ti-bon-anj* there, girl. We could do that for you, help you catch a man. Can't do it today, though; somethin's amiss out there." He shakes his head with frustration. "I have spoken with the *lwa*. The spirits are restless. There is a bad one loose and it will perform evil after the sun sets. I am very disturbed. The victim must fight back, but he's not a believer." He shakes his body visibly, as if shaking off something uncomfortable. "Come back again on St. John's Eve, at five in the evening. That's the right time for what you want, but go on in and take a look, if'n you want."

Susan and I follow Eric through the curtained entrance to the small museum and into a darkened hallway. The roughhewn walls are covered with African facial masks. One room is to the left, and a hall leads to the second room in the back of the small building. After becoming accustomed to the dark, I examine the eclectic assortment of talismans, drawings, masks, drums, charms, Voodoo dolls, candles, sequined pictures, and other artifacts with fascination, peering carefully into old display cases full of objects that are said to have magical or spiritual powers. Many Catholic ceremonial items and pictures of holy people are mixed in with the displays of African cultural items. Numerous small cards with handwritten explanations describe the name of a spirit or ancestor, and how this spirit is ranked and consulted. Each table has a candle surrounded by what look like offerings. Eric explains once in a while but mostly stays in the background. One display case built into the wall in the back room contains a large and very alive albino python snake that stares back at me with the same horror that I feel looking at him. I decide that I've seen enough and return to the entrance.

Behind Mr. G at the counter are rows and rows of small bottles of assorted oils, and a nearby shelf contains clear glass canisters of herbs. I watch him measure out herbs into a bag for a customer and fill her order for oils. A bookcase of reading material about Voodoo is nearby, and I browse some of its offerings, particularly a book about Haiti, where Voodoo originated and still flourishes, and another book that describes the history of the folk-like hoodoo of mostly rural blacks across the South. I have never been exposed to strong cultural differences and I am fascinated by what I see. Susan and I rummage through the case of merchandise available for sale and I buy a small charm to hang around my neck. On the way home, she makes a point of telling me that she doesn't believe in Voodoo, and that it's also foreign to her.

Wednesday morning, June 5, 1968, we awaken to the news that Robert Kennedy was fatally wounded just after winning the Democratic primary in Los Angeles the night before. The world is stunned because two national leaders have fallen to assassin's bullets within two months. Painful memories of John Kennedy's assassination are resurrected in the news coverage. I feel numb to the pain of the third major assassination in my young life. It's as if the nation has spent its ability to grieve and cannot bear any more, and the festering wounds of a disturbed country have no boundaries. Mrs. Devereaux, watching the news reports, painfully declares, "We have lost one of the few white people who cared, who really cared. Thank you, Jesus, it wasn't a black man who did the shootin' or there would be too much hell to pay."

We watch the televised reports of Kennedy's funeral Mass at St. Patrick's Cathedral in New York City and the cortege that carries him to the train. As his funeral train emerges on the other side of the Hudson River and carries him to be buried in Arlington Cemetery, Virginia, a panorama of Americans, old and young, black and white, rich and poor, unite to line the train route for the full two hundred twenty-five miles, waving flags in mourning. In Washington, as his casket is taken from the train and delivered to the cemetery, the quiet crowds light candles, matches, and lighters to create thousands of flickering lights to quietly speed his journey along. I attend Mass with the Devereauxes at their church in Corpus Christi Parish as part of the public mourning in New Orleans. Joining together to share the pain of Martin Luther King Jr.'s death, and now this national loss, has brought Susan and me closer as friends. In spite of our many differences, sharing this moment of public pain as part of a close-knit family is comforting.

Eric arranges for me to work with Susan on the voter registration drive sponsored by the local Democratic Party at their branch office on North Broad Street but he makes me stay home for the first few days while arrangements are made. He knows the people running the campaign and he's going to find something safe for me to do, he says. He also tells me it's gotten a little better than the summers of 1963 and 1964, but I still need to stay out of some parts of town and not let the whites see what I'm doing. When I ask why, he tells me that I will hear the stories soon enough. On my first day, there are three young and one middle-aged white women working for the campaign, and we are assigned to work in the back room, sorting records and preparing mailings. Susan is assigned to accompany people to the registrar's office, where they must fill out forms. I learn that many of the elderly blacks who come in have tried to register several times in their lives but have become confused or intimidated, have never succeeded, and have never voted.

I also get to know many of the local leaders, people like Reverend Alexander and A. L. Davis, who were both associated with Dr. King, and who are both vying for local political positions, and Dutch Morial, who worked hard to get the NFL franchise and is planning a run against the mayor. My co-workers tell inside stories about the civil rights activities in the South over the past five years, and I am both heartened by their commitment and horrified by some of the stories. My summer of work gives me a new perspective on the civil rights issue, valuable experience in the political trenches, and new friends. I hear another point of view about the old political fanatics of the sixties bent on preserving the traditions of the South, and oafish, hopelessly provincial, Southern white politicians who are treated as revered icons by the white population.

It becomes common for Eric, Susan, and me to sit on the porch, enjoying the humid Southern evenings after I help Mrs. Devereaux with the dinner dishes. Sometimes their parents or neighbors join us, and we tell jokes, sing, or Mr. Devereaux tells some of his favorite Louisiana tall tales and ghost stories. Sometimes we discuss political articles in the liberal Southern newspaper, the *Delta Democrat-Times*, and its editor, Hodding Carter III, who is advocating an alternative Mississippi caucus to the Democratic Convention that would represent both black and white voters.

One evening, Mrs. Devereaux mentions that she would like to call my aunt and assure her that all is well and that I am enjoying myself. I am glad that I can tell her that Aunt Beatrice and Uncle George are in Europe. Realizing that she probably needs a phone number, though, I give her our number in Richmond and tell her that if anything happens to me, she should call Martha. I shudder at the thought that Beatrice might learn the truth and I call Martha myself to assure her that everything is fine.

At the end of my first week in New Orleans, on a warm evening when Eric, Susan, and I are alone on the porch, Eric begins to talk about his previous political work. As a high school student, he had gone to Mississippi for Freedom Summer in 1964 when hundreds of black and white students congregated to register black voters amid a large backlash of angry white vigilantes. The mayor of Jackson, the capital of Mississippi, had hired an extra 200 policemen and had bought thousands of weapons and an armored tank in retaliation. Hundreds of black families who worked with the movement had their houses and businesses burned. White families that provided housing for the freedom workers had garbage thrown on their lawns, their windows shot out, and water pumped into their basements. Three of the volunteers that he worked with in Meridian, Mississippi, disappeared one night after investigating the bombing of a black church. Their bodies were later found in an earthen dam. The FBI was called in to investigate, and after a long, difficult investigation that commanded national attention, three whites were charged, including a sheriff and a deputy sheriff. "Those white kids came down from the North, full of their do-good visions, but not knowin' a thing about what was goin' on here," Eric concludes. "They got their eyes opened, for sure, and learned real fast that it was an exercise in living with fear every moment." He looks at me hard. "That's what it's like all the time being a black person in the South."

"Not all white people are like that."

"You couldn't prove it by me."

"Eric," Susan pleads, "Dr. King would have wanted us to use cooperation and non-violent protests. He wants our behavior to be better than the angry white people. We'll win in the end; we just have to be patient."

"You know what, li'l sister? I don't think you've ever seen what it's like out there. Before going to Mississippi, I had to go to a weeklong training session in Ohio to learn how to get beaten, how to check cars for dynamite before we got in them, and how to protect myself when the houses got bombed. That's how bad it was. Here in this neighborhood, we're all the same an' we never run into too much trouble, an' besides, you're a girl. I don't think you've ever really experienced what it's like to be treated like a criminal. White men carry guns so's they can aim them at black men, an' I know 'cause I'm one of 'em and I've been there."

I catch her eye as I start to tell about our experience in Baltimore, and she quietly shakes her head no.

He rises from his chair, takes a deep breath, and looks into the darkness of the night, angrily clutching his hands. His voice changes. "It gets to you ... sometimes I think we're treated like criminals so much that a lot of the brothers jus' begin to believe it. It does somethin' bad to your head to be treated that way all the time, especially when you're a li'l kid and you haven't done anythin'."

He turns around, leaning his body against the porch railing. "Let me tell you how it is ... how it always is for me ... it started eight or nine years ago. I was a really naïve little kid and I was interested in architecture, so I decided to go over to the Garden District and sketch some of those really fine houses over there, the old mansions. I was jus' this innocent li'l boy, maybe ten, eleven years old, who wanted to draw some pictures. So anyway, I took the St. Charles streetcar over there and I sat down on a bench at a bus stop and started drawing one of the places with big, white columns. Well, you know it wasn't ten minutes before this big ol' police car came up to me, an' these two big cops, white cops, got out, and asked me what I'm doing. I tol' them and showed them my drawin', but they thought I was casin' the joint or something."

He directs his question at me. "You know what they did? They came right up to me and harassed me ... they frisked me right there, with people gatherin' around. Made me spread my arms and legs against their car and checked my pockets, then they tol' me to leave, that I was a vagrant and they would run me in if I didn't. Man, I was ten years old and I was pushed around and treated like a criminal just waitin' to commit my first crime. Made me want to go out an' do something jus' to get back at 'em."

"What was their basis? You weren't doing anything," I said.

"The charges were N.I.N.N.Z."

"What's that?" Susan and I spoke together.

"Nigger in a no-nigger zone," he laughs with a bitterness born of humiliation. "You know what's the first thing a little black boy learns in this country ... it's the correct pronunciation of the word 'nigger' as spoken by a white cop."

Beginning to pace back and forth on the porch, he speaks to an unseen audience, becoming pensive and thoughtful. "My Pop made sure I never did anything wrong, and I've never gotten into trouble. Even when my friends did, I didn't because I was too afraid of him. He was *The Man* to me. I'm tellin' you, I should be able to live with the dignity and respect given to every other person and not be subject to insults or be wary or fearful all day long, but that's what I live with every day of my life." He paces a little faster, finally turning to me as if he wants me to understand him. "You know what, I feel safer in a barroom full of angry and drunk black ex-cons than I feel sittin' in a classroom at Stanford, and that ain't right."

He is upset, consumed by the frustration that he has just expressed, and goes inside. After the door slams, Susan quietly says, "Eric is a very smart person, but very few people see it because he is so angry all the time."

Another summer evening as Susan, Eric, and I listen to the crickets, Eric startles me by caustically remarking that white women usually mean death to black men.

"What do you mean?"

"You're a Southern girl, you know the stories … talkin' to you in the wrong part of town would make me bait for a hooded lynchin' mob in most parts of the South."

I do know the stories but don't want to admit it. "That doesn't happen anymore, does it?"

He continues, ignoring me. "White women have been gettin' involved in the civil rights work since 1960 and it's been makin' it tough. The white an' the black women are runnin' around, rebellin' against being kept in their place. We really don't have time for that right now, it's still too dangerous. They have to be more patient."

"Eric," Susan bristles, "women have a right to equality, too."

"Li'l sister, the mere sight of a white woman walkin' with a black man is still enough to make every Southern white man pull out his shotgun. An' we're the one's who get shot for it, or strung up. That Till boy lynching wasn't that long ago." He talks to Susan but gestures toward me. "There's no way I'm gonna be caught alone with her for any reason."

He looks at me. "No offense, but you understand, don't you? That's been the mainstay of Southern chivalry since the beginnin' … keepin' the white women under control, with white men holding the responsibility for all morals and protection from rape—well, rape by a black man, anyways."

"Eric, that's why those of us who are Southern white women want to rebel. We don't want to be treated like that anymore."

"You can't do it yet. There's a timing factor here that you women have to get ... an' you're not gettin' it."

Susan speaks up. "I think we've waited long enough, don't you, Mary Frances?"

I nod my head in agreement, and Eric shrugs. "Have it your way, just don't get me lynched while you're at it."

On June 23rd, as we promised old Mr. G, the three of us return to the Voodoo Museum at five in the evening. I notice that Eric doesn't tell his mother where we are going and wonder how she feels about his interest in Voodoo, but I also decide not to tell on him. Eric explains to me that this hour is considered to be especially good for casting love charms because of the angle of the sun and planetary arrangements. This day, St. John's Eve, honors St. John the Baptist, who is the patron saint of Voodoo. In the evening, we plan to watch a Voodoo dance ceremony in Congo Square, where the Voodoo Queen, Marie Laveau, once held her ritualistic ceremonies.

Old Mr. G is pleased to see us again and leads us through the museum and into a back room where he conducts private ceremonies. We sit on brightly colored floor cushions decorated with sequins and ribbons, each of us on one side of a low, square table that seems to be an altar. A single, white candle is in the middle next to a small vessel of water and a few feathers in a vase. On each corner is a small stone. Mr. G takes a deep breath, claps his hands once, then waits for each of us to become still. When he is sure of our attention, he lights the candle and places a stick of incense in the vase and lights it.

Watching the thin trail of smoke rising from the burning incense, a fog of confusion surrounds me, having been schooled to reject all religious practices and all cultures that are not my own. Yet, I have purposefully stepped into an abyss of suspended beliefs and opened my eyes to other ways of being and I have gone too far to be able to turn back.

"Voodoo," Mr. G. begins, speaking to the candle as if in a trance, "is an open religion of experience, not a religion of written words or an afterlife. We are one with the universe and welcome into our midst those whose ancestors have sent them here. We call upon all ancestors for guidance and wisdom to improve our lives and find happiness for those who seek it." He calls upon the spirits in our names. His tone and demeanor has changed much from the "aw shucks" old man who was at the front desk in the museum, and he takes on the air of an educated priest.

"As in all beliefs," he continues, raising his eyes and staring at each of us, one at a time, "the power of suggestion is the most potent ingredient. As in all remedies, the force of positive thinkin' is the greatest healer. And, as in all magic, it is the magical powers of the mind that accomplish true sorcery. I will use my power as someone who cultivates the ancestors for wisdom and I will ask for their services, but they may not wish to participate. It is you who must show respect to your ancestors and believe in their power before the magic works."

He takes a small box from his pocket and removes seven stones, laying each one on the table in a careful pattern and saying words under his breath. Next, he takes a little brown cloth bag from the same pocket and rolls seven small shells in Eric's direction, much like someone rolling dice. "I have asked them to cast your fortune in the realm of love. But I am told that your ancestors come from two different roads, and that you will journey down both before you find your lastin' happiness. Your ancestors are strugglin' now with who shall have influence over you. It will be one ancestor for a period of time, and then the other and each will bring you true love."

He asks Eric for his handkerchief. Folding it carefully so that it is one-fourth its original size, he lays it out on the table and smoothes it with both hands, chanting in a whisper before reaching under the table for three small bottles and pouring a drop of scented oil from each bottle onto the handkerchief. "I shall give this to you now, and you must carry it with you until you find your first true love. When you find her, hand her the handkerchief, so that she can smell the scent, and she will follow you. If she is the woman you wish to marry, print her name backwards on a piece of paper so that she is comin' toward you, and put the paper here." he places his hand in the center of the handkerchief, "then fold it toward you, like this, coverin' the paper completely, and place it close to your body for seven days, and she will be all yours." He makes the handkerchief into a small, folded square and carefully places it in Eric's hand.

He takes up the shells, puts them back in their bag, and rearranges the stones while repeating his meditative words. Taking a second small bag from his pocket, a red bag, he throws these shells in Susan's direction. "These shells are for the women and carry the power of menstrual blood." He stares at the shells, finally raising his eyes to somberly look at Susan. "You are descended from an ancestor who is angry with you. This ancestor is a very powerful *Iwa* who rules over the home and brings good fortune, love, and fertility. She has been your *mèt tèt,* but you have chosen to ignore her." His voice softens. "A *mèt tèt* is the master of your head. It is the principal ancestor who serves throughout your life and who acts as your primary guardian and patron. The one who is your *mèt tèt* can be jealous and spiteful and is prone to malicious fits of rage if she does not get the attention she deserves. She is capable of fulfillin' the greatest dreams but is also capable of severe punishment."

Susan stares at him, saying nothing.

"She will not respond because you are not willin' to hear. You have a nature that reveals itself in your dreams, that draws you to its bosom with longin'. You must hear that nature to be able to find your true love." He pauses, thoughtfully. "I will give you a powerful *gris-gris*. Perhaps the charm will prevail." He brings a little leather bag out from under the table and a small pair of scissors. "May I have a few of your hairs?"

Susan gives Eric a questioning stare, and he shrugs his shoulders. "Why not?" She allows Eric to use the scissors to cut a few hairs from her head and gives them to Mr. G, who places the hair in the little leather bag and continues. "These ingredients will mix with your hair and bring their power to you." He cups the bag in his hands, speaks quietly to it, then gives it to Susan. "It is up to you to hear the voice that speaks to you. When you are alone late at night and cannot sleep, you will hear it, and it will guide you. But you may wish to consult your *mèt tèt* sometime to discover the nature of her anger and pacify her. While she waits, I will attempt to keep her calm."

When he is finished with Susan, he turns to me and repeats the meditation over the stones and the throw of the shells. He looks up at me with a puzzled stare and repeats his catenation over the shells. His eyes show concern. "Who are you?"

"Me?"

"Yes, you. What is your name again?"

"Mary Frances Tyler."

"No, you have another name."

"I was Mary Frances Roche when I was born. My parents were killed, and I was adopted by my aunt and uncle."

He frowns. "Where are you from?"

"Richmond. Richmond, Virginia."

He looks at me with disbelief, averts his eyes, and stares at the wall behind me. His fingers tap on the table as he seems to be listening to a sound that we cannot hear. Suddenly he crosses his arms tightly across his chest, assumes a painful facial expression, and holds it for at least a minute. It is as if his mind is not present in the room, only his body. Finally, he shudders all over and returns his attention to our stares. Slowly he announces, "I have just avoided a dangerous possession." He stares at me; his face has a wildness that was not present before. "I cannot talk with the *Iwa* for you. There is an evil spirit that is in the way. I'm sorry. We must end this now." Abruptly, he blows the candle out, stands up, and leaves. We follow, puzzled, and say goodbye at the front desk. Even though he has returned to the persona of the laid-back old man, his eyes seem to follow me as we leave, and I feel uncomfortable.

We stop at a bar on Bourbon Street, where Eric knows the bartender and knows we won't be carded. Over beers, Eric asks us what we think. Susan is disturbed and says she isn't going to keep the *gris-gris* bag. "You know what Mom would say if she knew, don't you? We're Catholic and we don't believe in this. Eric, I also think that it is detrimental to the progress of black people for us to persist with this magic nonsense."

"It's a part of our history … it's our folklore really." He leans back in the booth, addressing her with a sense of seriousness. "The white man's history is not ours, and we shouldn't want to adopt it. Our history comes from the Dark Continent, and it's fascinatin' if you're ever of a mind to study it. Voodoo is where the slaves found a measure of personal power and where they maintained the history of their past." He does not wait for her reply and turns to me. "What did you think, Mary Frances?"

"I think it was my Aunt Beatrice's evil spirit that stumped that ol' guy. I just can't get away from her anywhere. Hey, can I smell that stuff he gave you? It may smell so bad that it drives women away."

They both laugh and the tension eases. He passes his handkerchief under my nose. I decide that the smell is tolerable and jokingly ask him how long it will take for him to learn to write backwards. "Eric," I ask in a more serious tone, "do you believe all that?"

"About as much as you believe in the magic of the U.S. Constitution."

"What do you mean? We're the best country in the world."

"Guess you might say I'm cynical right about now. This country isn't much to me. I'm old enough to be drafted an' sent to Vietnam an' get killed but I'm not old enough to vote the bastards out of office. Even if I were old enough to vote, I'd have a hard time registering. That doesn't make sense to me. If I've gotta go to war, I should be able to vote, don't you think?" He shakes his head. "A whole lot of things pass for somethin' we are told to believe in, but doesn't make sense. I could give you a good argument that justice in this country is a lot of hocus-pocus. The lawyers, judges, and politicians are an awful lot like the Voodoo priests." He becomes sarcastic as he imitates his composite character of the three. "'Here, we're not gonna do right by you, but if you mess up, or don't do as we want you to, we're gonna give you some of our black magic. It's called "jailtime," and you will keep doin' it until you's straighten out, an' if you's don't, we'll just keep throwin' it at you and beatin' you up until you do right by our terms or you die. Take your pick.'"

"Eric," I challenge him playfully, not wanting to be convinced that he's right, "you could become a politician or a lawyer and help change things."

We gather our stuff to leave as he scoffs, "If you can't beat the enemy, then join them, is that it?"

Over the summer, Susan and I visit sites around town where she introduces me to the local history of the European, Creole, Caribbean, and African cultures. I also take great pleasure in sampling the food for which New Orleans is famous, things like hot and spicy gumbo, crawfish etouffée, pralines, and beignets. Eric, Susan, and I, along with some of their friends, attend several local jazz fetes, including an impromptu jam session with Louis Armstrong, who is always welcomed in his hometown.

One afternoon, after watching a news story about them, we go down to Jackson Square in the French Quarter to see the hippies and flower children who have taken over the small park, openly camping and cooking in defiance of local ordinances. The police are not sure how to handle them because of the disastrous outcome of a confrontation at People's Park in Berkeley a month before. The cops skirt the edges of the park, merely containing the group rather than disbursing it. An impromptu stage is set up in front of St. Louis Cathedral and an antiwar demonstration is going on in the shadow of the stately old church. The pigeon-covered statue of Andrew "Old Hickory" Jackson, the hero of the Battle of New Orleans, seems to raise his horse in defiance of the scene almost as if he wants to lead another charge. Eric is interested in the message of the war protesters, and I feel jealous of the uninhibited atmosphere on the square, almost wishing that I could join them. The whole country seems to be alive with young people questioning the authority of their elders and optimistically talking about changing the accepted social values.

Susan's parents take us on a weekend trip into Cajun country, where we go on a swamp tour into the marshy land of tall cypress trees and swaying Spanish moss. The tour guide is a crusty ol' bearded, French-speaking, Cajun singer, who brings his motley dog and homemade banjo onto the swamp boat with him. As we pass under the narrow bridges leading to the swamp, he strums and sings the ballad, "Son of a gun, we're gonna have big fun on the Bayou …," and invites the tour group to join in for several stanzas. When we reach the swamp, he brings out a bag of raw chicken legs to feed to the alligators with a long pole and sharp tip. He has trained these big ugly animals to come right up to the boat and jump to grab their dinner from the long pole. We squeal as the open mouths of the alligators come within two or three feet of our hands and arms. As we travel along the gentle waterways, the guide points out great blue herons leaving their nests in flight, snowy white egrets, the abundance of water vegetation, and an old, abandoned, hunter's cabin on the edge of the water. On the drive back to New Orleans, I reminisce about my vacations with Beatrice and George in swanky hotels, and decide that riding around the marshes in a beat-up old swamp boat with a carefree Cajun 'gator man is much more fun.

Another weekend, we drive north to the Cane River area to visit Melrose Plantation, south of Natchitoches, a house built for and owned by a woman who was a former slave, Marie Therese Coincoin. Marie was born a slave in 1742, and at the age of twenty-five, she was purchased by a Frenchman who was taken with her beauty and intelligence. She served for many years as his common-law wife, bearing fourteen children, but the early laws did not allow him to marry her, or for her children to inherit, and the local clergy had great difficulty with their arrangement. Before the wealthy Frenchman finally left her to seek an heir, he granted her freedom and their children's freedom, and gave her substantial acreage and money. Through the hard work of her family and the community she gathered around her, she became a wealthy plantation owner and the owner of slaves herself. Some of her descendants now serve as guides on the plantation.

Over the summer, I occasionally visit with Helena, feeling both a need for a connection with a white woman and a fascination with someone whose past is very different from mine. Her life story weaves in and out of our conversations like a complicated melody. For many years, she tells me, she was unable to talk about her father's Nazi background and pretended to be from a German-speaking Austrian family. She also talks to me about the classical literature that she loves and occasionally lends books to me, and we later talk about the stories. Each time we meet, she asks me how I am adapting to my circumstances in New Orleans. I am able to tell her, quite honestly, that it is becoming easier and easier for me, and I feel like part of a family.

Eric continues to be very careful around me, never allowing us to be alone together. In spite of his aloofness, I prod him with questions and learn that his interest in Voodoo stems from a keen interest in both Southern black and African folklore. He occasionally gathers material for a book he would like to write some day as a sequel to Zora Neale Hurston's cultural anthropology work. I don't know who she is, and he explains that she spent a lifetime gathering the folklore of the Southern blacks, and using the material to write plays and stories. He also mentions another writer whom he admires, Richard Wright, a black man born in the South, who wrote *Native Son*, a well-received novel that was made into a successful Broadway play in the 40s. Wright, Eric explains, lived in Europe to escape segregation. Eric lends me copies of both Hurston's and Wright's works, and I read them on quiet, hot, New Orleans summer nights. Talking to Susan and Eric, and reading stories written by black authors, opens my eyes and my heart to the experience of being a black person in America, although I know I can never fully understand what it must be like.

One weekend in early August, Eric proposes that Susan and I go with him to visit someone he has heard about, an old woman quiltmaker who lives in the Louisiana countryside. He has heard that she knows the legends of the slave quiltmakers and the stories of hidden messages these quiltmakers wove into the patterns of their quilts. These messages, as the oral legend goes, helped to guide runaway slaves as they made their way up the Underground Railroad.

The two-hour drive finally takes us down a long dirt road that rises between marshy fields that are sometimes raised enough for a crop to grow, and we pass fields almost ready to harvest. Eric had borrowed an old car from a friend, a rusty, '57 Chevrolet, and asked us to dress very casually in old clothes because he didn't want us to set ourselves apart from these folks. The smell of saltwater lazily lingers in the hot air and mixes with the cloud of dust stirred up by the tires. When we reach the end of the road, we are in a shady dirt clearing where several weather-beaten shacks sit around the edge close to tall, old trees. Dark green Palmetto fronds soften the edges of the buildings, and the distant sound of swamp frogs mingles with the songs of the birds.

Five elderly black women sit around the steps of one house. Three are weaving reed baskets, while the others are stitching pieces of cloth. One woman has a large, white turban on her head and is seated on an old wooden chair, another turbaned woman is on the steps, and three sit on short stools in a patch of grass. Two dogs are sprawled out in the nearby shade. Everyone, including the dogs, raises their heads to stare at us as we drive up.

Eric assumes a gentle demeanor as he steps out of the car to speak with them. Holding his straw hat in his hands, he approaches timidly, acting almost as if he is reluctant to disturb their work. One of the dogs growls at him. A few feet from the group, he casually falls to his knees, sitting on his heels, and scratches the dog behind the ears before he addresses the women. I cannot hear him but it seems from his gestures as if he is asking about their work while he draws something in the dirt. At first, the women seem apprehensive, but they warm up to him as he talks, and the body language indicates that the conversation has become lively.

After a time, he comes back to the car. "These are the women I was looking for," he says as he climbs back into the driver's seat. "The old woman sitting in the chair is the one designated as the keeper of the stories, which is," he leans toward me, "a very sacred and special honor. She has been entrusted with the oral history of the slave quilts, and these are stories that have been passed down from her grandmother and her grandmother before that. And, by the way," he turns to me, "she continues to wear the turban formerly required of the Free People of Color because she is very proud of her heritage."

"What do we do now?" Susan asks.

"I told them my interest in their stories and my respect for them. Here," he hands a notebook to Susan, "you take notes. Mary

Frances, they aren't going to trust you much, but they will allow you to sit and listen. You need to keep quiet, though." We get out of the car and slowly approach the women and, following Eric's lead, we sit on the grass and dirt nearby.

"Mother, my friends and I have come to you seeking the knowledge that you carry for those of us who come after you," he begins with a gentle sweep of his hand after he introduces everyone. "We have heard that many years ago, when some of our ancestors were slaves, there was a powerful secret code hidden in the quilt designs that told the slaves how to escape their bondage, and it was brave women like you who made the code and kept the secret."

She looks hard at me, settles her body, then turns and speaks to Eric as if he is the one she trusts, with an occasional glance at Susan. "Dere was a time in dis land when de skies rolled wid thunder and fire and de mamas of dem babies, dey did cry the songs of death an' despar an' it still be happenin' some, but not for too long more. Dat ol' Mother Earth, she done provide for us in all our days dat have gone by, and she done still provide for us. An' de Lord does provide our strength. Dis freedom is ours an' it's a comin'." She pauses. "Dem ol' slaves, dey be braver dan all git out an' dey keep da secret so goods dat nobody knows how goods dey were."

Her face softens, and a glow comes over her as she begins to bring forth her memories. "Dem codes, dey be de real way de slaves talked. Dey ain't had no readin' and writin', but dey could read de pichers. Dem slaves made de quilts right under de eyes of de massah, and dem quilts tol' how to run away wid' de pichers." She slaps her knee and laughs. "Dem massahs who dinks dem so smart, dey neva knows. How you like dats?"

175

"It shows how really smart the slaves were, doesn't it?" His tone changes and he says gently, "May we write down your words?" indicating that Susan was waiting to take notes.

"Yessuh, you write dis down. Yessuh, dem slaves were a whole lot smarter den dey dinks. It's time folks knew about it."

Eric began to prod her gently, using his knowledge to elicit her oral history, and I listen with fascination, absorbing a piece of Southern history that I have never known. Eric had told us in the car coming down that secret codes were commonly found in old African cultures and they became part of the slave culture in America. Household slaves often knew much more than the plantation owners ever realized, and they passed this knowledge along through signals, and quilt patterns were sometimes used to convey these signals. The house slaves made the quilts and they made them with very specific meanings. A certain quilt was displayed on the fence for an airing at a certain time as a signal for the slaves fleeing through the Underground Railroad. The late afternoon flies buzz around us as the old woman describes the lives of the slaves in great detail, embellishing much of Eric's understanding, while Susan takes notes. Eric carefully guides her through the story, always making her feel at ease, and at the end asks, "Can you show us a sample? Do you still make these patterns?"

"Yessuh, I does. I done make me a sampler wif de codes." Slowly, she gets up, moves up the steps with the aid of one of the younger women, and goes inside the cabin, returning momentarily with a beautiful quilt in shades of browns, tans, and whites, containing thirty different squares. As she sits again, Eric helps her spread the quilt out around her lap, covering her legs. "See 'dis here?" she says, leaning over and pointing to the pattern in the upper left-hand corner. "'Dis here be de monkey wrench; it be de firs' one. When de monkey wrench quilt be hung out in de early spring, it be time for de ones who is leavin' to gadder up de tools and supplies needed. Ain't dat so?" She turns to the woman closest to her, who is sitting on the steps.

"Yes'm, it does." The younger woman takes up the story, and seems proud to tell her part of it. I feel honored sitting among these older women, listening to their stories and trying to understand the best I can. I also realize that I am witnessing the process of passing the story down to another generation. "De monkey wrench, it done turns the wagon wheel on a bear paw's trail to de crossroads." As she narrates, the younger woman points to three more of the squares with patterns of a wheel, a paw print, and a symbol for a crossroads. "Dey be five knots on each square and on de tenth knot on de tenth square, is dere day to leave."

The first woman continues, still pointing out pattern squares in the quilt. "Once dey gets to de crossroads, dey dug a log cabin in the ground, and Shoofly tol' 'em to dress in cotton and bow ties and go to de church and get married and exchange double weddin' rings. Den de flyin' geese takes de drunkard's path and follows de stars to Canada."

I watch Susan to see if she gets all of this down and wonder if Eric understands. Susan is drawing each of the pattern squares with its name. Eric goes back to each square and softly elicits an understanding of what the code means. As he quietly talks to the old woman and listens carefully, I also begin to understand that when the signal was given, the fugitives followed a bear trail through the Appalachian Mountains to a crossroads where they met a contact person designated as Shoofly. The secret signal between them was to draw a log cabin in the dirt. The fugitives were instructed to change into clothing that would blend them into the community and go to a church, where they would meet the contact who would remove the ankle chains and rings of bondage. Then, the fugitives would follow the geese or the stars to Canada, often doubling back much like a drunkard to avoid being caught. The codes in these quilts were like the old drum codes and they carried meanings and power that transcended the strictures of the plantation system and formed a common bond of communication.

We sit on our mounds of dirt and grass in the shade of the old trees of rural Louisiana, listening in awe to the women talk about the code structure of the Underground Railroad and the pride of the people who ran it. They talk about how the Africans, despite the horrors of the passage from their homelands and the abuses in their lives, maintained a sense of honor, a means of communication, and an expressive culture.

As the sun begins to wane and the day's heat settles in the marsh, Eric talks about leaving. One of the old women decides that we can't leave without having something to eat. She brings out hot mint tea and the sweetest honey oatcakes I have ever eaten. Another woman lights a pitch torch outside the door to the cabin. As we sit with our tea, the woman in the white turban stands once again and quietly surveys the group but ignores me and goes into her cabin. A few minutes later, she carries out a folded, ragged quilt, holding it as if the quilt contains something precious inside. She gently places it on the ground in the center of the group.

"See dis here?" she says reverently. Squatting down slowly with her massive body, she pulls a corner away with one hand, then the second corner, and the third. As the last corner is pulled away, we see an old, rusty piece of chain attached to a circular loop. A long thin bone is in the loop. "Dis here is a shackle dat we found out dere in dem fields a long time ago, and dat's de leg of de man who died out der. He done give his life and his blood to dis land. That's why it so rich now."

Eric stares at the bone from his spot on the grass and Susan backs away slightly.

"Go ahead, touch it, hol' it in your hands," she urges Eric. Her voice has an ethereal tone, and she speaks softly, keeping her eyes on the center of the quilt. "Dat man was a strong man, a powerful man, a proud man. It took a strong man to be snatch from his cradle in his African village, and make it cross that dere ocean to a land he don't know, where he neva sees his modder and fadder again an' maybe even de wife an' babies he lef' behin'. He done works hard here and he got hisself a fam'ly here and it shamed him to be whipped in fron' of his chillen. He is reachin' out to you. He wants you to feel his pain." She looks up at Eric. "Take what he gots to offer you."

Eric carefully raises his eyes to Susan and to me. He seems to want to refuse, but he doesn't. Moving to the other side of the quilt and squatting like the old woman with one knee on the ground, he picks up the bone. Slowly with his other hand, he brings the shackle and chain up to his chest.

The old woman watches him closely and whispers loudly in her deep, raspy voice, "Feel dere pain, feel dere hurt. Let it enter into yur heart. Only when you feel de pain can de healing start. We done took all da bad things and de pain and de sadness, and now all dat's lef is de healing."

Eric's hands tighten around the bone and shackle. His eyes close and his body tenses. Watching from only a few feet away, I imagine proud, defiant Eric as he might have been had he been born two hundred years ago. That shackle would have been on his leg. Susan rises and comes over, gently placing her hand on his shoulder. The old woman looks up at her, speaking gently much like an old grandmother, "Go on, girl. Let dem saltwater tears come for de sadness. Dem plantation slave women had lots to cry for, too."

The old woman reaches out and slowly takes one of Susan's hands in hers and with her other takes the shackle from Eric's hand and gives it to Susan. "Take it. Feel de ancestors. It don't hurt you to know who dey is. You be proud dat you come from such fine people."

Susan kneels beside Eric with the shackle in her hand. Light from the torch flickers eerily on the three figures hunched over the small quilt in the fading light of the day. I feel like an intruder, watching the silent connection that Eric and Susan are making with their past. As I watch, I quietly wish that I could also connect with my ancestors in a very meaningful way like this. The evening seems completely silent, even the sounds from the marshes have faded. I avert my eyes to watch the sliver of a moon hanging low in the sky, feeling that Eric and Susan's moment should be private.

Finally the old woman speaks. "You don'ts has to be angry to carry them shoulders high. Just be's someone your ancestors can be proud of." She reaches over and allows them to release the shackle and the bone into her hands and gently lays her treasure back on the quilt. She folds the quilt lengthwise first, then each end over to the middle, and finally rolls it up. Eric helps her to stand, and she carries her bundle back inside.

We say a warm goodbye and thank the women for their time and knowledge with hugs. Driving back to New Orleans, neither Eric nor Susan talk about the experience with the shackle and bone, and very little is said about the history of the slave quilts.

At the end of the summer, Susan and I return to Boston with Eileen and Lorraine in the Volkswagen van. I bid a warm farewell to Mr. and Mrs. Devereaux and Eric, realizing that the summer has opened my eyes to the world around me and given me experiences that I had never imagined. Mrs. Devereaux has treated me like another daughter, and I appreciate being included in their family for the summer.

As we drive, we listen to news from the explosive Democratic National Convention in Chicago and follow newspaper accounts of the alternative Mississippi delegation and their attempts to be seated. We are also horrified by the fierceness of the Chicago police against the war protesters.

Driving along the highways between New Orleans and Boston, I contemplate my summer experience and realize how my view of the world has changed. I have learned to understand and respect a culture that I did not know, that I was blindly taught to belittle and revile, and I have felt the pain that people feel when they are mistreated. I have seen the magic and meaning of family, of striving for a cause, and walking barefoot down the dusty dirt road of common memories that bind a culture.

I recall how I initially feared being surrounded by people whose lives are different from my world. Over the summer, I began to see beyond the differences that separate and learned to see and understand the spirit of people, regardless of their circumstances, and appreciate that there are histories and beliefs that should be respected.

Driving back, I sense that somewhere in my past I lost something of what life should be about. The magic in my childish soul was churched out, spanked out, scrubbed out as the tangles were combed out. I was told to act my age, told to grow up, told to be responsible and follow rules that were supposed to be correct, by people whose belief in the goodness of life had already been educated out of their souls and they were ashamed. It's as if my trip to Louisiana has been like walking into a darkened theater and seeing what life is supposed to be. When the silver screen lit up, I was once again young enough and innocent enough to see my destiny in the clouds, to sing with the birds, and to believe in the power of the soul.

But it didn't last, and I am once again standing on the sidewalk outside the theatre, with the hot sun beating down on me, and I have returned to a land with rules to follow, rules that I don't like.

7. THE MISSISSIPPI EXPERIENCE

I return to Wellesley with more refined opinions on political and racial issues, especially on the Vietnam War, and begin to find the magic of living in the present and believing in a cause. During the summer, Dr. Spock is convicted of aiding the draft evasion movement; a racial protest is staged at the Mexico City Olympics; and I notice behaviors in my daily life that seem to have unintended racial nuances. On our campus, student groups actively support the antiwar effort and the women's movement, and two of my classmates participate in a feminist protest at the Miss America pageant. In the winter, Katherine's family invites us to attend an antiwar rally where their friend, Bella Abzug, an emerging political activist from New York, is a featured speaker. Throughout the year, a swirl of excitement and strong conviction surrounds our campus activities, and questions are asked about what 'morally right' behavior really is. We sense that changes are happening and feel like a small part of history in the making.

Susan transforms. Born into her sheltered, Catholic, middle-class world, with many adopted white values, she has never overtly challenged the obstructionist nature of the white culture. She has an intellectual understanding of racial discrimination but not the gut-level experience that comes from a lifetime of facing it down on a day-to-day basis. In her second year away from home, she takes on the voice of an angry activist, adopting the experiences of others as her personal mantra, and becoming very active in the black political movement in the Boston area.

Shortly after starting the fall semester, through one of my feminist magazines, I discover that a paper has recently been published in a national scientific magazine that has a theme similar to the paper I had written the year before for Professor Helms. It rebukes the reliance on traditional personality theories to explain the behavior of women. The author, a female research psychologist, as well as a Wellesley graduate and former student of Professor Helms, concludes that the theories are wrong and the psychology profession does not really understand women. I take a copy of her report to Professor Helms and ask him to change my grade to a passing mark. He refuses. Katherine suggests that we protest to the administration. She gets the power of her family connections behind it, and I call Beatrice for assistance. By spring, the school administration changes my grade. Professor Helms is outraged that his wisdom would be questioned once again. He resigns in protest, and I become a folk heroine on campus for a short while.

. . . .

The summer of 1969, I return to New Orleans with Susan, using the same ruse with Beatrice that I had used the year before. I call her periodically to avoid receiving a call. Mr. and Mrs. Devereaux warmly welcome both of us. This year, I feel braver and more comfortable, even when I learn that we will not be protected by Eric, who has a summer job in Oakland, California. I realize how much I will miss his friendship and our conversations. The first week in town, Susan and I attend a Student Non-Violent Coordinating Committee meeting in order to help organize its summer activities.

The political mood of the group has changed from the previous summer. The idealism and optimism that we had found the summer before seems demoralized and cynical. In spite of the largest black voter turnout in history, Nixon was elected President in the fall of 1968, and a white backlash seems to be emerging. The civil rights leaders feel alienated from the political power structure and have a foreboding fear of failure because they no longer have Lyndon Johnson or the overall sympathy of the Democratic Party to support their cause.

Young black men and women in the group are difficult and impatient. Unaccustomed to working together as equals and awash with ideological disagreements, the women accuse the male leaders of oppression and they demand a right to take on leadership roles. The men accuse the women of wanting personal publicity and grandstanding. One woman states that she is no longer willing to do only paperwork and backroom organizing ... she demands to be on the front lines with the men and accuses them of blowing off their responsibilities and being at fault for losing the election. Susan, previously quiet and reflective in these meetings, also speaks strongly about wanting a greater voice in the group's decision-making and activities.

When the meeting finally gets down to business, the SNCC leadership announces that it has received a plea from Mississippi for more help in their voter registration efforts and asks for volunteers. Susan and I decide to be part of the group that will go, and we show up the next day for the chartered bus ride.

"Hey, white bitch. There ain't no way you gonna survive this hell." The woman who speaks to me as we board the bus is new to the group. She has a large, Afro hairdo and wears bright African-inspired clothes. She mocks me, "You too helpless and spoiled. You ain't neva felt god-awful fear and humiliation like we has, nor eva been abused like we has. We been treated like caged animals all our lives."

"Hush up. You get your act together, girl," Susan says sternly, stopping in the aisle. "She's my friend and she's okay. Don't mess with her, y'hear?"

"We don't want whites comin' down here and gettin' all the glory … them newspapers up north don't write about anyone 'cept the whites doin' all the work. We wants them to know it's us that's doin' it, not them whiteys. You got a problem with that? Maybe you an Oreo? Maybe you been sleepin' wit' her man or somethin'?'"

Susan pushes me in next to the window and takes the aisle seat. "Nobody's sleeping with anyone. We're here to get a job done and we're all in it together. Whatever publicity we get, however we get it, it's all good." She defiantly opens a book. The woman turns to rebuke the other three white students on the bus.

On the drive from New Orleans to Jackson, Mississippi, I learn that our chaperone is Ella Bates, the newspaperwoman who provided guidance and emotional support for the nine black students who integrated Little Rock High School in 1957 and later, was one of the founding members of SNCC. Sitting in one of the middle seats of the bus, surrounded by high school- and college-aged girls who only know about Little Rock through stories, she reflects on how she gathered her small group together every morning before school and in the evenings and talked to them about the historic role they were playing and how she kept them going when emotions got really rough. Even now, she encourages, we still can't count on the federal government to enforce the voting laws; that's why she's still in the thick of it. Each of us has to stand up and be counted, she says, and we must continue to encourage every person of voting age to do the same thing. She makes a point of talking gently to each person and calming the stress on the bus.

On the journey, when we aren't being prompted in our mission, Ella leads us in many of the popular protest songs of the day. The bus reverberates with "If I Had A Hammer," "Green Fields," "Blowing in the Wind," and popular civil rights songs like "We Shall Overcome," "Kumbaya," and "This Little Light of Mine." By the time we arrive, it seems more like a bunch of kids going off to summer camp.

Our bus arrives in Jackson moments after another busload of civil rights workers from another state. Peering out the windows as we wind our way through the streets to the terminal, we see what looks like a ghost town, but as the two buses disembark, people pour out of buildings and alleys much like puss oozing from a wound torn open by a clinging bandage. The mob angrily waves small Confederate flags. Men carry pipes and clubs. Women have chains, and children have baseball bats. The buses are surrounded. "Give them niggers hell!" can be heard as they descend on us, wild with hatred, lurching after each person who leaves the bus.

I panic when it's my turn. A dark hand reaches out and pulls me through the battering crowd. I reach back, grab Susan's hand, and pull her. We run as if our lives depend on it, finally ducking into a church for safety, where I discover that the woman who pulled me through the crowd was the one who had been angry when we first boarded the bus. It takes many phone calls to locate all of the bus riders and learn that no one is seriously hurt. Hours later, Susan and I are picked up by Fannie Lou Hamer, another seasoned veteran of the movement, who will be taking care of us while our group is in Jackson.

The next day, we go to another church where we are given a week of rudimentary training in voter registration procedures and self-defense, similar to what Eric had received when he went to Mississippi in the summer of 1964. We are told to memorize a central phone number and to check in every hour. If we aren't heard from, someone will come looking for us. Working on voter registration in Mississippi is still like being in a war zone, we are warned, and we must take care of ourselves and treat everyone as a potential enemy.

Once our training is complete, we trudge house to house in the black neighborhoods in teams of two, listening to stories of how people had paid their poll tax years before but had been turned down when they tried to register or vote. Literacy tests and citizenship tests had been developed to discourage registration and to find ways of not permitting blacks and other disenfranchised citizens to vote. The new federal law forbids these tests but the law is not being followed. We offer childcare, transportation to the registrar's office, training on how to respond to intimidation tactics, and words of encouragement when people are afraid.

Susan and I sleep in an iron bed on the screened-in back porch of Fanny Lou Hamer's old shotgun-style home, and two other student activists stay in her second bedroom. Fanny is a short, plump, middle-aged woman from a hardscrabble, sharecropping background in rural Mississippi, whose mesmerizing voice and gentle guidance keeps the group pulled together and organized. She often talks to us about her life as a civil rights worker, including the story of a brutal beating several years before by a group of small-town deputy sheriffs that almost killed her.

In the evenings, the civil rights team gathers together at the hosts' homes, laughing, singing, eating traditional Southern cooking, and always telling stories on the hot summer nights, often sitting outside, watching the sun go down and listening to the slowly rising symphony of night sounds. The effort in Mississippi had begun with the Freedom Riders in 1961 and has been kept alive by the continuously gallant efforts of many movement people, and Fannie knows them all and loves to repeat their stories. Many times the crowd is so big and the furnishings so poor that a pot of beans simmers on the stove, and people dip out a bowlful and sit around eating the humble meal oblivious to the circumstances. Some of the hostesses express concern that the white students, unfamiliar with the food and privations, would be uncomfortable, but no complaints are heard even when the privations include an outhouse. Although there is tension in the sometimes disorganized efforts, closeness develops as we share suffering and danger in an effort to transform the social structure of the country. I love the magic of the experience, the warmth of the culture, and the friendliness of the people.

By mid-July, word comes that Picayune, a small town in the Mississippi Delta near Louisiana, needs help, and Susan and I volunteer. At the last small-town bus stop before reaching Picayune, we disembark for a fifteen-minute break in the sultry heat and go into the air-conditioned café next to the waiting room. We call in to the central number in Jackson and sit at the counter, asking the waitress for sodas. Staring hard at both of us, the ends of her mouth curl into a frown, and she throws her towel down, saying, "Sorry, girls, I'm on a break." She picks up the phone in the kitchen.

About five minutes later, two police officers walk in, casually amble over, and one sits on either side of us. The one on my side says, "Look here, in Mississip' we don't want more trouble, you see, so we think it would be a good idea if y'all get back on that bus righ' about now."

I give him a once-over before speaking. He's a big guy, about forty, fleshy and paunchy, with a puffy face, sunburned ears, a butch haircut, and weathered skin. He wears aviator-style sunglasses, so I can't see his eyes but his face seems to have a permanent sneer. He smells of cigarette smoke and sweat. The nametag on his tan summer uniform says "Millard Jones" and he has a small Confederate flag pin on his shirt collar. I quietly put my hand on Susan's leg as a signal to let me do the talking. "This is a public place, and I believe we're entitled to sit here, even if we can't get served."

"Law's only as good as those who keep it. Ain't no damn law gonna protect you here."

"I imagine we can still sit here an' rest till the bus starts up."

He slowly scratches behind his ear. "Y'all is gonna be one of those li'l white troublemakers, aren't you?"

"No, sir, we're just passin' through. We'll be leavin' as soon as the bus loads up again."

"I believe you're resistin' an officer, ain't that so, Bubba?" He talks over me to his partner. His tone gives a sense that he has reached a conclusion, and Bubba doesn't need to answer. Bubba looks much like his partner, only a little heavier, and his hair is longer and combed straight back. Arrogantly, they stand in unison, and with no further words, Officer Jones takes me by the elbow and Bubba takes Susan's elbow. They push us from our seats and along, until we are out of the café and the bus station. We try to resist without making a big show, but we don't say anything either. The waitress comes out of the kitchen to watch, and two other passengers, who are sitting at a table, turn to stare. After getting us outside, Jones pushes me up against the outside wall, putting both of his hands on the bricks over my head, "You're kinda a cute li'l piece of white trash, now aren't you?"

"Leave her alone!" Susan loses control, trying to pull away from Bubba.

Bubba slaps Susan hard across the face. "You keep your trap shut, you black-assed nigger bitch, or you'll get the same thing, only worse." Blood trickles from her mouth.

I realize that we have to calm the situation down. "We haven't done anything. Look, we'll just get back on the bus, like you said, okay?"

"We've been hearing all about you son-of-a-bitch college kids raising all that hell up in Jackson and around, and we don't like it. You got plenty of book learnin' but you ain't got the sense that God gave a pissant. I think we better run you in first, just to make sure you don't eva forget that this town don't like troublemakers, how's that?"

"That's not necessary, really, we'll just go." I try to squirm out from under Jones, but he lowers his arms and doesn't let me. I realize how strong he is.

"I don't think so, little girl." Jones moves back and grabs me by the arm and shoves me toward the police car and Bubba does the same with Susan. We're both trying to remain calm but we're remembering stories of Southern police brutality toward the civil rights workers and we're frightened beyond belief. After handcuffing us with our hands behind our backs, they push us up against the car and make a big show of frisking us, with their hands lingering too long on our breasts and behinds. I squirm to get away, and Jones makes a point of cupping both hands over my breasts and holding them there while he snickers. We can see the people inside the café, watching.

They shove us into the back seat of their cruiser and drive two blocks to the storefront police station. "I'll write them up; you lock 'em." Jones tells Bubba as they pull us out of the car and Jones pushes me over to Bubba.

"Got a better idea," Bubba says to Jones.

"What's that?"

"Let's take 'em for a ride and show them some of our countryside."

Jones snickers, "I think you're right." He hitches up his belt buckle and holster. "'Bout time for some nice, Southern hospitality, don't you think, girls?" He grabs me by the arms again and pushes me in the car as Bubba pushes Susan in.

"We're entitled to make a phone call. Could we please make a call first?" Susan pleads.

"You can do all the bellyachin' you want later on, nigger, but right now you ain't gettin' nothin' before we get our somethin'." The two cops laugh as they peal out of the parking spot, drive back past the café to honk at the waitress, and careen recklessly down a country road, intentionally swerving now and again to make us roll back and forth on the back seat. We are unable to brace ourselves because of the handcuffs and bump into each other. The cops laugh heartily each time it happens. After entering a grove of trees somewhere about twenty minutes outside of town, they turn left through an open gate and drive down a path that is nothing more than ruts in the weeds.

"God help us, Mary, Jesus, Joseph, and all the saints, please help us." Susan closes her eyes and prays over and over under her breath as the car stops.

Climbing out of the front passenger side, Bubba opens the back door and yanks Susan out of the car. "No amount of prayin' is gonna make you any better a coon than what you are," he snickers. "Y'all is first, but you get this all the time don't you, nigger bitch? Ain't nothin' new to you." He pushes her over to a grassy spot.

"HELP! Help me! God, please help me!" Susan screams in terror in a frantic attempt to attract someone. "Please, I'm a virgin, don't do this!"

"A virgin nigger? Ain't no such thing." He roughly pushes her down on the grass and stands over her, unfastening his pants while continuing to make lewd comments to her as she struggles and kicks his legs. "You ain't one of those lezzies are you? Let me show you what a man is like, how's that for somethin' nice of me to do?"

Jones comes around and pulls me from the car. As soon as my feet hit the ground, I run toward the trees but he lunges and tackles, bringing me down near some fallen logs in a swampy area. He grabs a sleeve and tears my dress.

Susan squirms away and stumbles to her feet while Bubba is distracted with unhooking and removing his gun belt. She runs in my direction, hitting Jones with her body hard enough to knock him over.

Bubba drops his gun belt, runs after Susan, grabs her arm just as Jones goes down, and pushes her on top of Jones. Bubba loses his balance and falls on top of both of them. With the only weapon she has, Susan sinks her teeth into Bubba's exposed arm and bites as hard as she can. Bubba yells in pain. Jones crawls out from under, wraps his arm around Susan's neck, and pulls back hard. "If you know what's good for you bitch, let go!" he hoarsely screams at her. The veins in his forehead bulge as he applies a tourniquet hold.

Susan bends in half as she is squeezed between the two men, coughing hard with the pressure on her throat, and finally lets go of Bubba's skin. I come at them kicking. Jones lets go of Susan and manages to get up and grabs me around the waist from behind, immobilizing me as we squirm in a small pool of marshy water.

Bubba pushes Susan down on her back. He climbs on top of her, grabs her arms, and pushes them high above her head. She seems to have had the wind knocked out of her and barely resists. He grabs the front of her dress and pulls her face close to his. "Don't you eva do that ...," he stammers. "I'm gonna teach you to neva, eva do that again!" He shoves her back hard, and her head bangs loudly against a fallen log.

With Jones still struggling to hold me while I kick and twist, I helplessly watch in horror, desperately screaming as Bubba tears Susan's dress open, yanks her panties down her legs, pulls them off, drops his pants, and spreads her legs. I try to bite Jones' dirty hand as he covers my mouth and clutches my body close to his, one hand tight around my waist, and one leg wrapped around my legs to prevent kicking. The taste of his skin and the smell of his sweat repulse me. He begins rutting. I can feel his erect penis moving back and forth against the back of my body in anticipation, the friction causing him to become more excited. He whispers hoarsely, "Watch them and enjoy it, because you're next, white trash. Get those juices flowing for me."

Bubba mounts and penetrates the motionless Susan as she lies in the mud and weeds. He talks dirty to her as his movement becomes faster. He reaches over to massage her bare breast and pinch her nipple. "Come on, cunt. Show me some action. Do what you do for the others." Her body remains limp. He slaps her. "Open your eyes," he finally demands.

He looks down at himself and discovers that his penis is covered with blood. Looking back at Susan's face, he slowly pulls out, wiping himself with her dress. "Somethin's wrong here," he mutters as he backs away and awkwardly gets up and pulls on his soiled trousers.

"What's that, Bubba?"

"Look at the bitch. Somethin's wrong with her." His voice sounds nervous. "This was suppos' to be jus' a li'l fun. Jus' some trashy ass." Bubba and Jones, both of their uniforms wet and splattered with mud, look at each other.

"Let's git outta here. We don't want anyone to know 'bout this. I'll git my belt. You take those handcuff off'n that one, I'll get this one. We don't want anythin' left behind." The two men begin to move lethargically in the mud and water, then faster as they realize how quickly they want to leave. After removing my handcuffs, Jones shoves me down next to Susan. The consternation in their eyes and the tone of Bubba's voice cause me to panic.

I reach for her limp body, gently holding her head in my lap. "What about us?" I call furtively as they hurry away. Neither one responds and they are quickly out of earshot and speeding away in their cruiser.

I stroke Susan's gentle face, speaking soothing words to her, my eyes desperate to find a spark of life. A mild shudder passes over her, and she becomes ghostlike. Taking her wrist, I feel for a pulse, but cannot find one, and bend over her body, hugging her, too shocked to know what to do. Sitting in the mud and water, with her body cradled in my arms, I suffer tumultuous grief, waves of pain, bewilderment, and unfathomable shock.

Slowly raising my head, I notice the swarm of gnats rising from the disturbed water and the quiet summer sounds of frogs croaking in the swamp. Gaining a sense of the surroundings, I feel cold and clammy. The late afternoon sun is much lower in the sky and steals its way in through the eerie hanging moss on the trees. The air is sticky with humidity, and nothing moves because there is no breeze.

I fear that we will not be found. Struggling to my feet, I am overcome with helplessness as I survey the situation. We are both covered with mud. My shoes are gone. I try to lift Susan's body but am only able to slowly drag her, and finally reach the grassy, drier ground, where I lay her out carefully, attempting to cover her with the remains of her bloody dress. I lie next to her for some time, my arms wrapped around her body, absorbing the horror, hearing her voice again back at school, talking about the rape victims that she has counseled. "Susan, Susan ...." I don't know what to say.

My thoughts go back to the day we met, and I begin to cry. I think about the closet in the dorm and our struggle to get beyond stereotypes. I recall her ability to entertain and bring people together. I remember her decision to become a volunteer rape counselor and our struggles with feminism. I remember admiring her as a young leader who had found a cause that pleased her and our summer in New Orleans when I began to feel like her sister. My sobs ache for the strength that I saw in her and my vision of her future.

Groping for a sense of sanity and still stunned, I rise, recognize where the police car had been parked, and stumble out toward the gate. I listen hard for the sound of vehicles, try to ascertain the closest roadway, and turn in that direction, still barefoot. The narrow dirt path in the weeds takes me to a larger dirt road and finally I hear an engine. When I see a vehicle in the distance, I wave my arms frantically. It's a vintage black pickup, weather-beaten and dusty. Coming to a halt, a stout, bushy-bearded man, probably in his forties, with a full head of curly, dark brown hair and dressed in overalls, leans out of the window. "Somethin' wrong, li'l girl?"

"I need help. My friend was raped and I think she's dead. Please, could you …?"

"Raped? Dead? That's not good." He turns to the woman next to him. "Mother, what say we do somethin' here?"

"Whatever's right, father." She is very thin and plain in a gingham housedress, with straw-colored hair pulled into a bun. She speaks with concern, "Come 'round here, young'un, and climb in." Moving a beat-up old accordion on the seat between them, she slides over. As we drive, I tell them what happened. I realize that I might be with similar kinds of folks and end with a hopeful plea, desperately searching their faces for a response. "My friend is black. That's not gonna matter to you, is it?"

"No, ma'm," the man says, "that ain't nobody's business but the Lord's. Not everyone is like the two you ran into. We're here to he'p you, and we're mighty sorry that you've been mistreated."

He pulls the truck in past the open gate and parks where the police cruiser had been. Rummaging in the truck bed, he pulls a dirty old blanket out from a wooden toolbox. "This comes in handy now an a'gin." We walk across the clearing to where I left Susan. Seeing her, he shakes his head. "Mighty sorry sight." He stoops and puts his head to her chest, listening for a heartbeat. "Nope, she ain't with us no more. Done gone to her maker and glory be." He stands and matter-of-factly begins the process of rolling her onto the blanket and removing her to the bed of the truck. The woman takes me aside, encircles me with her arms, keeps me from watching, and lets me sob on her shoulder. In spite of her thinness, she seems robust and warm, motherly. The sun goes down while we are there, and Susan is carried out in the arms of the backwoods farmer in the glow of the lights from his truck.

At their home, which isn't much more than a shack, the woman is gentle as she helps me bathe, gives me an old housedress to wear, and feeds me a simple meal of grits and eggs. She takes pleasure in gently brushing my hair while I talk to her. Their cat jumps up on my lap and begins to purr. They don't have a telephone, but the man writes down the central number in Jackson and goes to call from a friend's. Covered by a homemade quilt, I curl up on their battered old sofa and am asleep when he returns.

The next day, someone from Jackson drives down and picks me up and takes charge of Susan's body. The couple refuses any money for their help, claiming that they "were just doin' the Christian thing and they're mighty sorry for what happened." We retrieve our luggage at the bus station in Picayune before driving back to Jackson, where we file a complaint with the local police department. The next week is a blur. I am interrogated several times by white police officers, and they want every embarrassing detail of everything that was said and done, until I tire of repeating it. Every time questions are asked of them regarding an arrest, the answers are mired in bureaucracy.

Fannie Lou Hamer has the awful task of calling Susan's parents. An autopsy is performed before the body is released. Arrangements are made for me to accompany Susan's body back to New Orleans. The Devereauxes meet me at the train station in tears. Eric has come from his summer job in Oakland and is with them. We melt into hugs as I come off the train. Everyone is silent in the car on the way to their home.

The house is filled with flowers and food brought by concerned neighbors. Mrs. Devereaux heats up one of the casseroles for dinner, and we each take a plate to the side porch but little is eaten. Susan's favorite chair is left empty.

I finally break the silence. "I'm so sorry for what happened. I would give anything if … if it could have been me."

Eric is bent over with his elbows on his knees. He looks up. His face is a mixture of anger and sorrow and his voice is filled with pain. "I tried to tell you, both of you, that it wasn't safe. I told you that whites rape and kill and get away with it. Why wouldn't you listen?"

Mr. Devereaux speaks quietly. "Eric, anger won't bring her back." He slowly rocks in an old, wooden rocking chair, saying nothing more.

"It's hard on you, too, isn't it, my dear?" Mrs. Devereaux speaks to me softly, putting her hand on my knee.

Staring into the yard, I visualize the rape and murder again and shudder. "It was the most horrible thing I have ever been through. I can barely talk about it." Tears well up in my eyes. "I want to tell you everything, but right now I can't."

Eric stands and paces, abruptly turning to his father. "Isn't it about time for a lynching party where white deputies are hanged?" His voice is filled with malice. "I have enough friends here, and we aren't that far away. We could find those crackers and get it over with before anyone knew."

His mother pleads, "They would find you eventually and then I would lose both of my children. I would rather keep you."

Mr. Devereaux rises from his chair, goes to Eric, and puts his arm around his son's shoulder, both facing the yard. "I understand how you feel, son." They stand together, heads bent in pain, their silence speaking for them.

Mrs. Devereaux turns to me. "We would be honored if you would say a few words tomorrow at the funeral. You were her best friend for two years."

"I … I can't. They will blame me."

"No one blames you. This type of thing happens too often for it to be any one person's fault. It's a failure in the way we live."

"What can I say?"

"Whatever comes from your heart."

I excuse myself and go to my room, unable to go to the viewing and needing to be alone as I listen to my feelings, search for words, and prepare to face Susan's family and friends.

The next morning, I attend the funeral Mass with the Devereauxes at their parish church. More than two hundred people are in the sanctuary. A soloist sings "Ave Maria" during the processional when Susan's casket is brought in. Eric gives both of the readings during the funeral Mass. During the homily, the priest talks about knowing Susan, baptizing her, serving her first communion, and raising her in the church and nearby school. After Mass is concluded, Mr. Devereaux rises to give the eulogy. He talks about the unbelievable pain of a parent burying a child and how she is still with us through her voice. He announces that a recording of Susan singing "Swing Low, Sweet Chariot" will be played and asks the congregation to stand silently. Hearing the purity of her voice again brings tears to my eyes. When she reaches the second verse, he asks the congregation to join in, and we all sing through our tears.

Mr. Devereaux introduces me and I rise to haltingly read the poem that I had put together the night before. It's a simple expression of praise and respect for my friend, asking why the angels came so soon to carry her away. It ends with the lines,

... be happy that you had this time to spend here with our friend.

She touched our lives, enriched us, showed courage in the end.

If we look to one another and search deep down inside,

To our amazement, that's where we'll find her spirit lies.

Afterwards, many in the congregation express their thanks for my participation.

I walk with Eric in the New Orleans–style funeral parade behind a brass jazz band. My friends from the summer before, Helena and her husband, are in the large crowd of friends and students from Mr. Devereaux's school who offer hugs and who fall in behind the band and walk to the cemetery as they share their grief. On the way, the music is grave and somber, much like a dirge with muffled drums. At the cemetery, more comforting words are spoken. The jazz band music on the return is much livelier, celebrating Susan's entry into heaven and her joy in meeting her savior.

Before I leave, I frame my poem and give it to Mrs. Devereaux as a gift. She hangs it on the wall in Susan's room. Saying goodbye to Susan and her family seems like leaving my family.

8. NEW BEGINNINGS

Fall semester of my junior year doesn't start for three weeks, so I go back to Richmond after the funeral. Beatrice and George are surprised when I call but don't give a reason for my sudden return.

Boarding the plane in New Orleans, I'm still shocked and dazed. I feel safe only when I see Uncle George waiting for me at the gate of National Airport near Washington. As we drive back to Richmond, he notices that I seem sullen and asks why. During the two-hour trip, I confess to him the true nature of my trips to Louisiana and end with the horror of Susan's rape and murder. He doesn't answer right away but pulls the Cadillac over to the side of the highway. "My little pun'kin, I'm so sorry for what you went through," he says sincerely. He looks at me, frowning intensely. "Were you violated by those men?" When I tell him no, not in the way he means, he is relieved, starts the car again, and switches to a more contemplative tone. "You know, we can't tell your aunt about this; she would not take it too well. It's best left between you and me. I think I'll make a few inquiries to be sure that it didn't make the newspaper here. Was there anythin' in the paper out there, bein' a nigger girl an' all?"

"Uncle George, she was my friend. Please don't call her a nigger."

"Sure, pun'kin. But you'll have to realize how things are." His tired, suntanned old face turns to me, and I notice that his hair is much whiter than I remember. His voice is full of soft-spoken, Southern charm. "It's still pretty raw here, and if you don't use the local language, folks'll think somethin' is up. You're still expected to act white here, darlin' child."

Yes, our sacred way of life requires absolute conformity, I think bitterly.

"I'm not so sure it's a good idea for you to have been mixin' with 'em. You gotta understand that it's neva been a good idea to intertangle the races, because, inevitably, it leads to mulatto children. You know how those black boys are, don't you, and we don't want that happenin' to our women."

Uncle George continues in his gently philosophical way, "If God had wanted us to all be equal and alike, he would have made us that way. The Bible makes it clear that those people are meant to have a separate society ... you remember the mark of Cain don't you? Besides, this country just isn't ready for mixin'," he declares, "and that's evident with all the strife going on. That's why ..." he muses as he drives, "... I've been actively campaignin' to annex Chesterfield County into the City of Richmond. Those additional white votes will keep the balance of power the same as it's always been, which is only right."

Years of unconfirmed stories about his philandering haunt me. "Uncle George, we already have mulatto children. We have all those white men who go to colored town and leave their wives feelin' like fools." I've never before been so blunt with him, but my nerves are too tense to accommodate his rationalizations.

He ignores the poignancy of my comment. "You can't turn the South upside down like this and not expect problems. I agree with you that the lot of the Negro needs to be improved, but it must be done in a law abidin' way and within the system we already have, which is the way God intended it to be. These young folks who are breakin' the law aren't any better than anyone who's in jail already, and you don't belong with 'em. I'm glad to get you outta that mess."

"Uncle George, the mistake was in taking away their right to vote a long time ago. You can't be messin' around with giving it back. It's just plain wrong." I spend the rest of the trip brooding and looking out the window, ignoring his justifications. At times, I shiver with the fresh memory of the deputy, still holding me from behind with his smelly hand over my mouth, but don't mention it. Uncle George wouldn't understand that my dignity was violated.

Reaching Richmond and pulling in our driveway, we concoct a reason why I had to come home: Because my friend's mother became ill. Nothing more is said. By the second day, I am exploding with the need for a sympathetic ear, so I walk to the grocery store with Martha and slowly tell her the truth about my stay in Louisiana and my Mississippi experience. Martha and I are taking turns pulling the full shopping cart home when I get to the part about Susan's death. She stops in the shade of a tall, old tree, her eyes fill with tears, and she quietly hugs me for a long time. Her instinctive acceptance of me, her pliant human spirit, and the warmth and softness of her fleshy arms and bosom allow me the freedom to cry until the pain once again subsides.

We take the groceries directly into the kitchen through the back door. Beatrice hears us come in and calls down the stairs, "Mary Frances, I need to speak with you." Her voice is hard.

"I'll be up in a second. I'm helpin' Martha with the groceries."

"Immediately." Her tone is icy and hard, and I hear the rapid click-click of her heels as she moves away, unwilling to discuss her command. Martha shoos me up the stairs, and I find Beatrice in the library. The smallness of her body is stark against the dark green, leather, wingback chair next to the library telephone table. The afternoon light falls through the blinds and across her face and makes a pattern of light and shade.

Walking into the room, I am stopped short by the atmosphere. Beatrice's back is rigid, her arms are firmly arranged on the chair, and her lips are tightly drawn. Her face is ashen, and her steel gray eyes stare at me with bitter coldness, seething with anger. "Sit down," she commands.

I take a straight-back chair from a table near her and sit like a schoolgirl in front of a stern headmistress and feel the cutting edge of her venom. Memories of other times that I sat in this chair facing her wrath haunt me, and I await my sentence, not knowing what my crime is.

Slowly she places her right hand on the telephone and pronounces her words carefully. "I just received a telephone call from a Mrs. Devereaux in New Orleans."

My heart stops. The blood drains from my face.

"Mrs. Devereaux," she repeats in a stiffly modulated tone, "called to express her appreciation for your recent kindnesses and thanked me for allowin' you to visit with them for the last two summers." She stares at me. "Would you like to tell me about your recent kindnesses?" she sneers.

I have no clue what to say. Tears well up in my eyes and I shiver. It's the middle of August but the room feels cold.

"Suit yourself, young lady. Shall I tell you? What Mrs. Devereaux told me is that you are a liar. I sat here feelin' like a fool, because I could do nothin' but listen. I didn't know what she was talkin' about. Don't you think it's time for you to tell me the truth? Don't you think you owe me that much?"

"She would not have said that."

"Of course not, she was gracious and I certainly was also. But ..." she pauses, "... this was not the voice of the woman who called me a year ago or at the beginning of this summer. This time, I heard the voice of a Negress. The grammar and pronunciation were good, but they were unmistakable. I am assumin' that these were the people you were really staying with in New Orleans. Please tell me that I'm wrong."

"Susan was my friend. I was staying with her family."

"And her family ... is Negro, isn't that true?"

"Yes."

"Isn't it a basic truth of our culture that the Negroes and whites don't mix? We don't break our bread with them. We don't use the same restrooms or water fountains. We don't live with them as equals either in the same house or the same neighborhood." She sighs deeply, "For many generations, this city has had a successful program of cultural exchanges and shared values while maintainin' an appropriate sense of separateness. We plan to continue in spite of pressures from those damn Northerners who simply don't understand the acceptable Southern lifestyle."

With a heavy sigh, she continues. "You have disgraced me. You have disgraced your Uncle George. You have disgraced this family, and everythin' that we stand for. There is not a decent white man or white woman who believes in social equality among whites and blacks, and it will never happen."

"This is 1969. It's not the old South anymore. Times are changin', and these people have a right to vote. I was workin' on voter registration with my friend Susan, that's all."

"You're not in a position to answer back to me. Your culture has not changed. Negroes don't have enough sense to vote properly and you should not be encouragin' it. They are uneducated and don't understand politics or economic reality. They will destroy this county if that is allowed. What is happenin' in the world is madness and hysteria brought about by the Communist instigators. Those fanatics you are associatin' with are pawns for the Communists who are trying to take over the world, and you are helpin' them. You are actin' like a Communist yourself, y'hear?" Each time she uses the word "communist," her tone is louder. She seems to realize that she has gone too far and softens to sarcasm. "If you want to be one of them or if you want to be a goody-two-shoes missionary, and God help you if you do, go to Africa. Those heathens need people like you."

"Aunt Beatrice," I blurt out, feeling more anguish and pain than I can bear, "my friend was raped and murdered by sheriff's deputies. I had to watch, and they weren't even arrested."

"Any girl who is raped is askin' for it. What was she doing out there? What did she think was goin' to happen to her? Those Negro girls do it all the time for a livin', and for one of them to suddenly call it rape is beyond me. You were actin' just like her. What happened to your upbringin'? We certainly did not raise you to behave like this. You don't put yourself out there with poor white trash sheriff's deputies and not expect them to do their business."

"How can you be so heartless?" I can't believe the difference between what happened and her interpretation. I can't believe how Susan is being insulted without Beatrice even knowing her.

To survive her onslaught, I quickly imagine myself surrounded by Martha's warm arms.

"You're actin' like white trash yourself, disgracin' this family an' then callin' me heartless!" Her voice becomes shrill. "I took you in as an orphan. I gave you everything you wanted. I have done my best to protect you and make you into a respectable person. I've seen to your Christian education and I've given you all the trappin's that will get you into the best families, and this is how you thank me?"

She stops as I bound from my chair toward the door unable to listen anymore. "George is not the one who is making you who you are and neither is Martha," her voice has risen to a scream, "it is me … me … and some day you will have *me* to thank!"

Reaching the door, I turn and shout, "Your Southern white Christians are lemmings, and you are a pretentious ol' biddy! I don't like your trappin's. I wish you had left me alone to die or be adopted by someone nice. I wish that I had died instead of Susan!"

Pulling the door open, I head for the staircase but she follows, holding on to the newel post and calling after me as I climb the stairs. "I'll tell you what I ought to do … I ought to take you out of that school up north that is causin' this. It was a mistake for me to send you up there! I ought to bring you down here and put you in a school nearby where I can keep an eye on you, where they have enough sense to keep your culture and your sensibilities the way they are supposed to be."

I hear nothing more as I slam the door to my room and throw myself on my bed to sob. The next three weeks are miserable as the fire in my soul drains out. Most of the time, I stay in my room venturing out only for the most necessary events and needs. Martha makes every effort to talk to me, but I lock her out of my life. Instead,

I spend sleepless nights reliving the rape and cringing with renewed fear each time the memories surface. Beatrice requires me to have dinner with them but my "Northern mistake," as she now calls it, is not spoken about directly, only with innuendos.

Beatrice relents on Wellesley because a last-minute placement can't be found for me in one of her chosen Southern schools. Using her influence, however, she tightens the reins and pays an additional amount for me to have a private room in the dorm. Her contacts with the school administration result in weekly sessions for me with a traditional psychologist, who carefully doles out tranquilizers. I say nothing to the psychologist that I would not want repeated to Beatrice and tell him that I am dutifully taking my pills.

The next two years become a robotic-like blur. I switch to a major in English literature, where I find solace in the misery of characters and begin to write poetry and stories that express my deep depression. The essence of my wounds speaks through my writing. My poetry reflects the value of having known Susan and how I had become an honest and caring person under her tutelage. The characters in my stories are punished for exploring natural curiosities about life and the magic of other cultures. All of them suffer the disastrous results of what society considers treasonous living.

My room becomes a dungeon and it becomes my only world. My life is bereft of social functions and friends. Solitude wraps its arms around me, and I confide in no one, and no one is able to draw me away from the enveloping pain. As I write, I realize that I have become a tragic character, lost between the freedoms that I long for and the culture that enslaves me. I wonder what will become of me and periodically I wonder if life is worth living.

Katherine becomes my only connection with the outside world and she worries about me. She had graduated at the end of my sophomore year and now has a newspaper job in Boston but comes out once a month to see me. We spend lazy Sunday afternoons talking in my room, walking the campus, or curling up in front of a fireplace, talking about my quiet life and her antics in Boston. A time or two, she tries to get me to talk about the murder and rape but I say little. She offers to read my stories and poetry, but I refuse.

In the early spring of 1970, Katherine unexpectedly shows up late one Saturday morning with a car, a recently purchased shiny, black, English sports car, a 1959 Triumph TR-3. "Come," she says, gently taking my hand, and leading me to the parking lot, "I had a feeling about you this morning … like you needed to see me. Or maybe I just needed to show you my new car. Come, come, come … I want you to feel the wind in your hair. It's wonderful!"

"Oh, no, I can't do that. Your car looks dangerous."

"It's okay, really it is. You would only be taking a very small risk. You know that I will take care of you … here, I have a scarf for you." She doesn't let me protest any further and gently guides me out of the dorm and down to the parking lot. When we reach the car, she hands me a long, bright red scarf with a fringe at the end and drapes a similar one around her head and neck with the ends dangling down her back. "We'll be the Red Baronesses," she laughs. "Help me take the top down … see over there … pull that latch … pull it up and out, that's it … now fold it neatly … good girl." She continues, showing me how to snap the white leather protective cover over the folded convertible top. "This is the way to get in," she says as she adroitly climbs over the tiny door and slides down into the driver's bucket seat. Feeling far less adventuresome,

I use the miniscule door on the passenger's side. Settling in, I'm uncomfortable with how small and old-fashioned the car is and how low to the ground. I feel like I'm sitting on top of a roller skate.

She turns to me, "I want to see Walden Pond again … would you be up for that?" I barely have time to agree before she pulls out the choke knob, pushes the starter button, jams it into gear, and peals out of the lot. Within minutes, we are on Highway 126 searching for Walden Pond, the wind quickly making the scarves flutter.

With no one else in sight and few cars in the parking lot next to the pond, Katherine pulls in, climbs out, stretches her arms wide, closes her eyes, breathes deeply, and recites, "I went to the woods because I wished to live deliberately, to see only the essential facts of life and see if I could learn what it had to teach, and not, when I die, to discover that I had not lived." She turns to me. "Did I get Thoreau right?"

Her efforts are not effective. I feel morose and unable to see the beauty that she breathes in. Knowing that I cannot share her enthusiasm, I walk over to a large tree stump, sit, and respond, "Thoreau never had anyone die in his arms."

She comes and sits quietly next to me, her arm around my shoulder and her head leaning against mine. "Mary Frances, my sweet dear friend, you have such a beautiful innocent spirit. I'm sorry that you are so troubled."

"I cannot forget the horror …." My voice trails off. I look around at the deep green forest and the distant trees surrounding the pond. Quickly, she takes my hand and we cross the road, descend the pathway to the beach area, and take the trail leading to the right, slowly following the edge of the water in single file, sometimes climbing over remnants of the past winter's damage, sometimes avoiding muddy spring puddles, and often brushing aside tree limbs.

After a time, we reach the cove just below the site of Thoreau's cabin. The water is high with spring runoff and the sand is sometimes muddy as we circumvent the water's edge. This is where he came down to the water and perhaps sat on the sand and mused ... where he thought of the quietly desperate lives that most men lead.

Katherine ascends the slight incline to the cabin site, but I remain near the water and find a fallen log to sit on. There are no signs of civilization anywhere, and for a very brief moment, I wonder where I am and what century I am in. Even with the sun high in the sky, the shadows are deep and the air is misty like a foggy day. Vapor rises from the water and I see the Mississippi swamp again, feel the stickiness of its air, and hear the country noises. I am afraid to look down, fearing that I will see Susan's head in my lap again.

Looking around and still feeling dazed, I am startled to see someone far away in the shadows of the trees that skirt the water's edge. It is a woman dressed in buckskins, sitting among the fallen logs and weeping over an outstretched body. She is the vision of a character from one of my stories, and the written words echo in my mind. I hear the cry of someone suffering with no one to hear the pain. I ache to comfort her but I was unable to do so in the story, and still can't.

Instead, I turn away and deny the apparition, quietly rising and walking up to where Katherine is. A rectangle of upright logs outlines the foundation where Thoreau's cabin once stood. A noticeable pile of rocks is nearby. "The stones are a tradition," she speaks quietly. "Look, there is the one I put on the pile last year."

I ignore her and morosely lean against a tree, speaking to the air, to my memories, to all of those who seem to accuse me. "Susan was so much better than me. She had a great future, so much promise. I am nothing more than Beatrice's shadow and I'll never be anything else. I tried, but having a life to call my own is too difficult. I should have been the one to die."

Katherine's voice is soft. She casually wraps an arm around another tree and leans her head on the bark. "Oh, how I wish I could be in your body and see the world that you have seen and feel the pain that you have felt. It would make it easier for me to understand. All I can do is be your friend and I feel helpless at that right now."

"I know everyone is blaming me but they're just too nice to say anything. I know it from the way they look at me, the way they avoid me. They know I killed her. I should have been able to stop it. I shouldn't have been so sarcastic to that cop."

"Those cops would have done what they did if you were the Queen of England. They were bullies who have been getting away with beating up on people all their lives. It wasn't anything you did. It's just something horrible that happened, that's all."

"They should have been arrested for murder."

"I know," she speaks quietly, "but it's important to remember Susan and what she stood for. I hope someday you will be able to focus on the good that came from knowing her and make the impact of those deputies irrelevant."

We lean against our trees in silence, staring into the distant pond while squirrels scamper near the edge and rays of light steal their way through the mist. Every few minutes I look up to watch the weeping woman in the shadows near the water. Because she is the woman in my story, I know what will happen. She reaches over and pulls a knife from the supine body of her lover, who is from another

Indian tribe, a tribe that is enemies with hers. She rises and I gasp quietly as she quickly plunges the knife into her own chest and collapses.

While I am lost in my visions, Katherine walks to the water's edge and starts picking up pebbles and tossing them into the pond one at a time, making the minnows scatter. "Let's walk," she says. She puts her arm around my shoulder, I hold her at the waist, and we continue walking along the dirt path that hugs the bank of the pond. The ethereal quality of Walden Pond and her quiet presence finally allow me to talk. Nervously, and sometimes hesitantly, I speak of my memories from the Mississippi Delta. Sometimes I shake with pain. Katherine listens carefully, sometimes asking questions about what happened, sometimes asking how I feel, but never, ever judging me. Occasionally, we stop for a quiet hug. I describe each detail, each lingering moment. Tears flow. Sometimes we stop to listen to a bird or watch a squirrel in silence. The walk takes more than two hours.

As we come back around by the beach and cross the road to where the car is parked, she brings us back to the present and changes the mood by reaching up for a tree limb, examining the tiny green leaves. "Look at the new growth. I love it in the spring!" We slowly meander back to the car and stop for pizza on the way back to the campus. When she drops me off, I quickly go to my room because I don't wanting to speak to anyone and need to bring closure to my suffering.

Shutting the door behind me, I go to my bathroom and reach for the supply of tranquilizers on the glass shelf above the basin. Rather than taking them as prescribed, I have horded them, anticipating that a day would come when I would take them all at once. When I awoke this morning, I counted them out and knew that my day had come. I had decided that my life would end this evening when I went to bed. I stare at myself in the mirror, still feeling the tear stains on my cheeks and the burning in my eyes.

Leaning my forehead against the glass shelf as the waning daylight quietly filters into the room, I agonize over my decision, still aching with the fresh memory of the vulgar deputy sheriff pressed against me. I hear his harsh voice ringing in my ears and smell the sweat of his body. My arms feel Susan's limp body even though I cling to the fresh memories of Katherine's hugs. Vividly, I see the apparition in the forest and feel my shock at the Indian maiden's decision. In my imagination, I hear Katherine's voice screaming at her, "No, no!" I lift the bottle of pills and pour them into my waiting palm. Slowly, one by one, I drop the pills into the toilet and flush.

I graduate from Wellesley in the spring of 1971. Beatrice insists that I return to Richmond. I have not attempted to find work or enter graduate school and return to Richmond, where I blend into a blur of Southern traditions that blot out my feelings and my need for introspection, and learn to blend into the collected traditions.

. . . .

In June I attend a grandiose Southern wedding with Beatrice and George. The bride is the daughter of one of Beatrice's influential friends from her exclusive Garden Club of Virginia set, and the groom is a local high school football hero who has recently graduated from Virginia Military Institute. The event is a three-day affair, beginning with luncheons, showers, and brunches, all held in the best places in town. I decline to attend anything except the reception, which is held at the historic Jefferson Hotel in downtown Richmond, where the main lobby has been commandeered. It's obvious that the bride has chosen peach and pale blue as her theme colors … swirls of blue ribbons and bows decorate the thirty-two, beaux-art marble columns in the two-story rotunda, accenting their rich, rust coloring and the hotel's maroon tapestries. Table linens and covers on the rented chairs alternate the blue and peach theme, and countless commodious vases of peach-colored flowers fill the room and the mezzanines.

Even though the ceremony has just been held at a nearby Baptist church, the procession is held again, with the ten attendants slowly making their way down the thirty-six-step marble staircase as a small string orchestra plays. Their long peach dresses and wide-brimmed hats, hairstyles, shoes, and nail polish all match, and they look hideous to me. The ring bearer, made to look like a young prince in a costume of blue satin, carries an empty satin cushion, and the flower girl is barely old enough to understand that her role is to scatter peach-colored petals on the blue carpet runner in the center of the majestic stairway. The bride and groom enter together, their first appearance in Richmond society as a couple. He is in the full military dress of VMI; she looks and acts like a reigning princess in a pearl-studded, formal gown and train. The intimate crowd of seven hundred cheers as the couple descends. Beatrice is beside herself with compliments for the mother of the bride, who has been planning this event for more than a year. I stand nearby, watching the whole affair with the scornful eye of a reformed pretender. I notice that there is not one black face in the crowd, except for the waiters.

Several women congregate around the glowing mother, including a mature woman who seems to seek Beatrice's attention. Beatrice makes a point of introducing me to her, Mrs. Andrews, a friend from the Garden Club, who gushes, "Mary Frances, darlin', I haven't seen you since you graduated from high school. What a lovely young lady you have become. I would love to introduce you to my son this evening. I don't believe the two of you have ever met." She gestures toward a tall, handsome, young man standing near the statue of Thomas Jefferson in the Palm Court. He is exquisitely dressed in striking formal attire and is surrounded by five flirtatious young ladies. He seems to be carrying on an animated conversation with each of them simultaneously but is still able to look up and wave to his mother.

"That's very kind of you, but it's not necessary. He doesn't look to be in need of introductions."

"Don't be fussin' about those girls. They are chasin' afta' him, he is so well liked in these parts, but he isn't the least bit interested in any o' them."

Beatrice interjects, "Mary Frances, he'd be a fine catch for you. I understand he is aimin' for a career in politics, which might suit you nicely."

"Aunt Beatrice, I suppose I'll worry about that later." I concentrate on admiring the Tiffany window in the hotel lobby.

"Child, you just turned twenty-three years old. It's high time you started thinkin' about who you want to marry, an' Bucky over there would be a good one."

"I'll think about it when the time is right." I turn away from them abruptly, make my way to a buffet table resplendent with the offerings of an amazing Southern wedding, and quietly watch preparations for the cutting of the wedding cake that has just been wheeled to the center of the room. A few minutes later, I feel a light tap on my shoulder.

"Excuse me, Miss," it's a waiter, "the gentleman over there asked me to give you this card." He hands me a calling card. Reading it, I look up, puzzled. Mrs. Andrew's son, who is walking in my direction, raises a hand in a polite salute.

"You and I probably need to get this out of the way before our mothers explode," he grins as he approaches, nodding his head in a bow. "My name is Winfred Andrews. However, my family has called me 'Bucky' since I was knee-high to a June bug, and that'll do just fine. If you will be polite to me for a minute or two, I'll not bother you again." Up close, he is exceedingly handsome and debonair, but I don't let my expression show it.

"Yes, this is awkward, Mr. Andrews. I don't wish to take you away from your admiring public."

"I admit I've not always been so well admired and don't know how to handle unwanted attention very well. You seem to be a safe harbor in this storm."

"It's not personal, Mr. Andrews. I'm simply not seeking male companionship right now. I've just returned from college and I must decide which direction I wish my life to go in."

"I fully appreciate your situation. I've only very recently completed a master's degree myself."

"I understand, though, that you have plans already made and that you will be enjoyin' a political career."

"That's my father's wish. It takes many years and much work to succeed, though. I have recently been appointed to fill out the seat of a local politician who passed on, and I am about to face my first election, with mild trepidation I must say."

"I wish you luck." We both turn as the orchestra signals the cutting of the cake and the best man begins a toast to the new couple. The ceremony is completed and cake is passed out. We continue our politenesses to each other as the floor is cleared for dancing. The bride steps out triumphantly with her new husband, and they dance to "We've Only Just Begun," sung as a duet with soft strings in the background. When the time comes for the general crowd to join in, Bucky invites me to dance with him, but I decline and excuse myself from his company.

The following week, Beatrice informs me that Mr. and Mrs. Andrews and their son have been invited for dinner. Bucky has asked Aunt Beatrice for political advice, and she announces triumphantly that she and George intend to help him with his career, which will assure his success, she comments wryly.

Our dinner guests rave at Martha's cooking. Beatrice makes a point of telling Bucky that I have an interest in Shakespeare and reminds him that a Shakespeare company from up north will be coming to town soon. In his favor, Bucky notices how I roll my eyes with embarrassment at this obvious attempt and he changes the conversation to the upcoming political campaign. However, I grin when I notice that he intentionally weaves two of Shakespeare's political observations into the conversation. He notices that I notice and winks.

Bucky becomes a regular visitor over the balance of the summer. Each time the meeting is for his campaign and it is an opportunity for Beatrice to introduce him to other important people in local and state politics, including senators, representatives, and the governor. In his appointed position as the county assessor, Bucky is involved in the rezoning and reappraisal of properties, and I discover that he is working closely with Henry Marsh, a rising star in the black political caucus. Without saying anything to him, I privately admire Bucky's efforts to solicit and accommodate the views of the black citizens.

Local politics are currently very lively as a result of the new registrations brought about by the Voter Registration Act of 1967, and all local political races are fought intensely. In 1970, Uncle George's project of annexing Chesterfield County, an affluent white suburb, was successfully completed and it increased the white voter base in the at-large elections, but this action was immediately challenged through a lawsuit brought by black citizens. Additional controversy swelled around major economic revitalization programs and urban renewal projects and their effect on the black population. Large sections of town, mostly blighted black neighborhoods, had been torn down by the previous administration and moderately priced replacement housing has been a hot issue.

Slowly, I develop an interest in Bucky's work with the black population and appreciate his call to develop a black middle class and better housing for the working class, both black and white. In his campaigning, he sympathizes with those who wish to preserve traditions but acknowledges that the laws have changed, and the challenges to these new laws have not only failed but have wreaked havoc on the city. He talks about how it is important to come together to recreate a healthy local economy. Bucky speaks both publicly and privately with a glowing romanticism about the South, its quintessential goodness and ability to rebound with grace, and asks the good citizens, both black and white, to trust him to resolve many of the current problems in a fair and honorable fashion.

He downplays his invitation for me to join him for the final production of Shakespeare's *Macbeth* by saying that I should not consider it a true date, only a request from someone who knows that I have an interest in seeing the play, and he is offering to escort me. To emphasize his point, he invites Beatrice, George, and his parents. The six of us have a grand night on the town, and I don't feel any romantic pressures.

As the election nears, I become involved in his political campaign based upon my organizing experience in New Orleans, and supervise a cadre of zealous, sweet young things, ostensibly campaign volunteers, who vie for Bucky's constant attention, each trying to outdo the other with tales of Bucky's favors toward her. It becomes a guessing game as to which one he is really interested in or actually spends time with. On election day I work a precinct for him, and join in the celebration when his victory is announced. In the excitement he kisses me but I consider it only in a congratulatory manner.

Beatrice backs off considerably in her efforts to create a romance between Bucky and me, but she rejoices when he invites me to join him soon after the election in a victory appearance at his high school homecoming weekend. The event is held at Fork Union Military Academy, the cherished, private boys' school that is the mainstay of Fork Union, a small town in north central Virginia. Although it is the second weekend in November, the weather is pleasant and many of the trees still hold their autumn splendor.

We join with an old school chum of Bucky's and his date who also live in Richmond and arrive in the late morning to check into our motel rooms, one for the women and one for the men. The four of us join the crowd for the late-morning exhibition of precision marching on the parade ground, where Bucky makes an orchestrated entrance to the tent area that is set up for visiting dignitaries and illustrious alumni. He glows in the attention from his alumni friends. "Have you saved your Confederate money, boys?" he jokes with some of his classmates. "The new South is rising up and I aim to be part of it."

I can't help but notice that I am introduced as "the daughter of my dear friends, George and Beatrice Tyler. They helped me so much with my campaign." I begin to feel that my own efforts are being ignored and on the third introduction, I step forward and remind everyone that I was also quite involved in the campaign and did much myself. Bucky grins broadly as he catches my eye and winks.

After the marching and on our way to the football field, Bucky escorts us around the campus, pointing out the barracks where he lived, the buildings where he attended classes, and relating stories of his life as a fun-loving academy student and athlete. Several passions are important to Southern men and most important is their love of football. Southern regional rivalries fight themselves out in bloodless battles on football fields every Saturday as the weather changes from sultry humidity to sleet and bone-chilling rain. Although I have very little interest in the sport, I cheer for the correct team and join in the revelry when they win. Later in the evening, we attend a dressy dinner-dance, and this time I consent to dancing with him.

"My dear Miz Tyler," he whispers, gazing at me softly as he skillfully maneuvers a turn, "your waltz is superb."

"That's very kind of you, Mr. Andrews. Aunt Beatrice was careful to see that I had all the lessons that a young woman in the South should have."

"I will thank her the next time I see her." We are at the edge of the dance floor when he stops intentionally and gazes at me with glowing eyes. "You're different than most of the girls in town, you know … much more worldly, more serious about life."

"Me?" I say this just as the music ends. Taking my elbow, he guides us toward two comfortable chairs away from the crowd.

"Yes, my dear, you," he says, "the charming, lovely lady who hides behind mysterious dark eyes … the one who thinks deeply … but never tells her thoughts … the one whose face explodes with emotions that we never seem to hear." After helping me to my chair, he takes a seat and continues, casually taking my hand and leaning toward me. "Your face reads like the plot of a mystery novel with a surprise ending ... who are you and why do you fascinate me?"

"Quite frankly, I've never been described that way."

"You impress me as being a diamond in the rough ... a jewel in a pot of gold at the end of a rainbow."

"Careful, you are sounding too much like a politician. Remember, the campaign is over."

He gives me a long, careful look with his twinkling eyes. "I believe my campaigning has just begun." His smile is very understanding. Actually, it's much more ... it's reassuring, as if he is no longer smiling at the world, but at me, knowing me, understanding me in a way that I have never felt understood.

I realize that I have let my guard down. "I don't believe I'm voting in your district, sir. You have a whole bevy of sweet young things that you've won with your charm, and I hear there are others."

He doesn't answer but rises and walks through an open French door onto a terrace and stares into the distance. I am confused by his departure and feel a momentary sense of abandonment. I stare after him, then rise and follow. Quietly, I approach him from behind and try to understand what he sees through the darkness.

"Mary Frances," he acknowledges my presence without turning, "I don't like to borrow this phrase unceremoniously, but I also have a dream. I have a dream for a better Virginia, maybe even a better country. Many things are wrong now and they need to be made right again. Those of us who can see above the problems that this country has, have an obligation to assume the leadership. The fanatics on either side of the issues cannot govern this country. I don't know yet what my contribution will be but I want to make it. I must give to my country as Kennedy once asked us to. I want this war in Vietnam to end and our boys to come home. I want this racial strife to end. I want to see all people treating each other fairly and honestly. We are the largest generation that this country has ever had and we can make a contribution not only to our country, but also to the world. I want to be part of that and to give something toward making it happen."

He turns around, folding his arms gently across his chest, leaning against the stone railing, and maintaining a sense of looking into the future, with occasional glances in my direction. "But I can't do it alone. I must be part of the right groups. There is a flight of Southern Democrats to the Republican Party over this civil rights issue. I think that's wrong. The Democrats are the right party to be with and I'm staying. But, I need good people around me ... the right staff members. I need to find fellow politicians who feel the same sense of obligation that I do. I need to link into the existing power structure and take advantage of the opportunities, but I don't have to buy into their way of playing the game. In fact, I won't." His gaze drops to the flagstones on the terrace. "I also need to find the right woman to be my wife and my partner in this quest. Those sweet young things see the personality ... the outward images ... the appearances ... the flirting ... whatever. They don't see me. They don't understand me the way I think you do ... you might."

I'm completely off guard. For two years I have managed to stay withdrawn and simmer in the pain of my experience in Mississippi. For two years I have felt no attractions, no longings, not for life, not for love, not for ambition. "Mr. Andrews, I'm not seeking a husband."

"Yes, I know. I wish you were, though. I have heard about your sadness. I see it in your very lovely face. I have been told that you had a very bad experience in Mississippi."

I turn away. "I was forced to watch a man rape and kill my best friend. She died in my arms. It's hard to forget but it's not something I wish to discuss."

"Quite naturally. It's not my desire to intrude on painful memories. You are very unattainable, but a man can dream, can't he, once he sees something that he wants?" His gaze makes me uncomfortable and I walk away, stepping down onto a walkway through a flowerbed that leads me a few feet away to a grove of small trees with a secluded fountain and a stone bench. The plants along the path and around the fountain have lost their summer spirit and are limp with winter scorn. Light from the ballroom barely filters through the trees.

Staring at the dead and dying plants, I realize how alive I had been my first two years at Wellesley and in New Orleans and how my soul had died in the aftermath of my Mississippi experience. I remember my near miss with suicide and shiver once again with the loneliness and pain. I know that I discovered the cost of living, of being alive and striving, and I retreated because I could not handle it, and I am only the shell of the person I wanted to be.

Bucky gives me time alone and then slowly ambles down the pathway, his hands in the pockets of his school's dress uniform. He casually leans against a tree, speaking softly. "If I promise not to pursue you romantically, will you be my friend?"

"Being friends would be nice."

"Good. Now, if we're goin' to be friends, just friends mind you, wouldn't you like to know more about me?"

I grin, feel a little foolish for my melancholy, and move over on the bench allowing him to sit. "Okay, friend, your life history then."

"I was born." He turns to me with an impish grin. "My mother was a mere waif of twenty, my father had been dead six months, and my Aunt Betsey showed up for the first time ...."

I laugh out loud.

"You don't believe me? Try this ... I was born in a workhouse and my mother died almost immediately afterwards. I was a starving orphan for nine years and then I was sold to an undertaker who made me sleep in a coffin."

"Nope, not that one either. You don't have an English accent." By this time, however, my fear has dissipated and I listen attentively as Bucky tells me about being the only child in his family. At one time, his family had been well connected, prosperous, and respectable, but they had barely held on to a dilapidated plantation house outside of Richmond for many years, selling off most of the fields and working the remaining land for a livelihood. It was only when his father inherited some stocks and bonds from a bachelor uncle that they were able to sell the house, move into the city, develop the social relationships that his mother felt were important, enroll him in Fork Union Academy, and later, send him to the University of Virginia in Charlottesville. "I've sown a few wild oats, but haven't we all with everything that is going on in the world?" he concludes, reaching up to scratch his head. "So, you see, I'm jus' a li'l ol' hayseed compared to the fine and respected Miz Tyler."

"I suspect that your background has probably given you a sense of ambition, now hasn't it?"

"Yes'm." He's still acting playfully contrite. "But a fine lady like you would neva be interested in a country bumpkin like me, even as a friend."

"Enough of this foolishness, we've agreed to be friends, so let's go dance some more, just as friends." I jump up, energized because I no longer have to be wary of his attentions, grab his hand, and gently lead him back to the dance floor.

Time passes and I don't realize how close my friendship with Bucky has developed until one day several months later, when I casually run into one of the sweet young things in a dress shop. "Why Mary Frances," she says, "you're the talk of the town, gettin' Bucky Andrews the way you did. You jus' know he's gonna be gov'nor some day."

"I beg your pardon?"

"You know what I'm sayin'. Bucky is tellin' everyone he wants to marry you, an' we're jus' waitin' to see how big the rock is gonna be."

I have to leave the shop and stand on the street in amazement, finally coming to the realization that Bucky has been wooing and spending time with me without ever saying anything about romance, all the while, just acting like we're the best of friends. Through him, I've become engrossed in the texture and complexity of the society in which I was raised. I understand my alienation from this culture, yet find pride in the accomplishments of the charities where Bucky is on the board of directors. I have attended countless political dinners with him as my escort and we regularly discuss social issues when he attends dinners at our house. I have learned to appreciate his thoughtfully progressive political leadership and integrity and admire the way he often disagrees with Beatrice without incurring her ire. I have never encouraged his affections, and he has never breached our agreement.

Being near the courthouse, I walk over. All of the clerks in the assessor's office know me and they wave as I go toward his office. The door is open and he rises to greet me.

"That's all right, Winfred. Sit down," I motion to him, taking a chair in front of his desk.

"Uh, oh. What have I done to upset you?"

"Mr. Andrews."

"Yes, Miz Tyler."

"I have just heard that you are talkin' all over town that you intend to marry me. Is that true?"

He chuckles. "I told you that several months ago up in Fork Union. Remember?"

"You neva said any such thing."

"I may not have used that exact word but the meaning was clear as day."

"It was clear as mud to me, sir. It's no wonder that no one in this town is askin' me out on a date. You're tellin' them not to."

"I'm doing no such thing." He gets up and ambles over to the door, gently closes it, and returns to his chair.

"You're conniving to get me to work on all of your political committees and your charities, and coming ova to our house all the time, it's no wonder I don't have time for anything that girls my age normally do. I should be going to garden parties and off to the country an' the ocean, an' chaperonin' at cotillions, an' all sorts of other things ...."

"Miz Tyler, if I may be so bold as to interrupt your tirade, you'd be mighty bored with those things, I believe. Let me suggest that you have become involved in political and social issues because that's what you like to do."

I ignore his assertion, get up from my chair, and walk back and forth, becoming more agitated as I speak. "Don't you think that it's more than a little bit outrageous that you are tellin' everyone in town that you want to marry me?"

He puts his feet up on the corner of his desk and quietly folds his arms across his lap. "Can't be outrageous. It's the God's honest truth. Cross my heart and hope to die."

I keep moving, pointing my finger at him. "Don't you think that you make me look a little bit ridiculous when you tell everyone this foolishness and they come an' tell me, an' all I do is work for you as a volunteer?"

He waits for a long pause and speaks gently. "I beg your forgiveness."

I stop behind a chair, place my hands firmly on its back, and stare at him. "Don't you think you ought to be talkin' to me about this before you blab it, so I can say no and hush you up once and for all?"

His feet come down from the desk and he sits upright, leaning on his elbows with his chin resting in his palm. "I will give you that opportunity right now, if you would like for me to. Miz Tyler, I would like to marry you. Would you like to marry me?"

I speak without thinking and am stunned with my answer. "Yes ...." My voice trails off weakly while a blush of embarrassment overwhelms me. I cling to the chair. "No. I mean no, I don't want to marry you. I said yes to the first question ... did I want you to ... I said no to the second question."

He stares at me for a very long time, his chin resting on his palms. The grin on his face becomes serious and his eyes sparkle at my confusion and confession. He speaks slowly. "Let's try it one more time. Miz Tyler, will you marry me?"

I am speechless. A gate opens and a flood of feelings tumbles out. I wonder if he sees me shaking. I realize how aligned our lives are and how he has brought me back to life. With more than a minute of hesitation and a heavy sigh, I finally admit, "Yes, Mr. Andrews, I believe I will."

Beatrice and George are extremely pleased, although it slowly dawns on me that everyone in town seems to have been in on the scheme except me. I try to insist on a small, informal event but both Beatrice and Bucky claim that it would be important for Bucky's career if the event were a traditional, grandiose event with all of the right people invited. Within a week, in spite of my initial protests and efforts to have my own way, I give in to everything Beatrice wants, including the colors, which are to be lavender and deep purple.

More and more the affair becomes a blur to me as Beatrice takes over its planning and management. Since I was a child, she has envisioned me descending the grand staircase at our house in a bridal gown and has planned to have the ceremony in the living room in front of the fireplace, with a reception in the garden. When I become especially agitated or get in the way of all the chaos, Beatrice sends me on an errand or I find refuge in Martha's kitchen, where I am soothed with kindness and gentle admonitions that it will all work out fine and not to worry. At times even Martha, with the menu under her charge, seems caught up in the excitement.

The week before the event, gifts begin to arrive, and the library becomes the viewing room where all the finery is laid out. Gifts from the two bridal showers, one with a kitchen theme, the other with a lingerie theme, are displayed. Several luncheons and brunches are held, and Bucky's parents host the rehearsal dinner the evening before the big event.

Katherine, who is my maid of honor, is my one island of calmness. She's in town for the week, and each night we stay up late talking about our college years. I introduce her to Bucky her first evening in town and each night she insists on knowing more about him. She is very happy for me, especially knowing that I seem to have finally resolved the Mississippi experience.

The evening before the ceremony, as we privately say goodnight, Bucky gives me a gold bracelet with our wedding date inscribed on it and the phrase, "Together, we shall soar with the eagles." Slipping my hand through the band, I promise to never take it off.

September 17, 1972, arrives bright and warm. Beatrice is calm as she checks and rechecks her list and is assured that everything will go as planned. Her close women friends and many of my old schoolmates arrive throughout the morning eager to help with last minute preparations. Beatrice is at her gracious best and makes each arriving guest feel special and personally welcomed.

The old grandfather clock in the upstairs hall tolls four o'clock. Ushers in cutaway, afternoon coats and white gloves are downstairs seating the final guests. Most of the regular furniture has been removed from the living room, the rugs have been rolled up, and rows of rented chairs fan out around the fireplace. The room is filled with lavender, deep purple, and white flowers and large ribbons in elaborate vases. During the reception in the garden, the chairs will be removed, and later on this room will be used for dancing. The signal is given by the string quartet and the lookout at the top of the stairs runs into my room. "They're ready!"

My personal feeling is that the attendants' dresses of purple satin are preposterous, but not one of the five has complained. We line up for our descent down the grand circular stairway into the entrance hall. Just before taking her place, Katherine takes off the tinted pumps that Beatrice bought and puts on her own shoes. Closing the door behind me, I realize that I will not return, that I am closing the door on my childhood and that I will never sleep in this room again. Coming down the stairs slowly, I touch the statue of the blind girl who has been my friend, and say a silent goodbye. George is waiting for me at the bottom of the stairs, his hand reaching out for mine, his face beaming. "You are beautiful, my little pun'kin," he murmurs as the photographer catches him kissing me. Martha is next to him. Tears of joy run down her cheek as she hugs me, quietly whispering, "Honey chile, your real mama would be so proud of you. I wish she could see you now."

The wide, mahogany doors have been thrown wide open, and the crowd strains to watch us enter behind the attendants. My dress is copied from a wedding costume from the nineteenth century, with rows and row of lace, appliqué, hand-sewn pearls, and tiny, off-the-shoulder, cap sleeves. I can imagine all the commentary silently registering under the gray hair of the society matrons as Beatrice quietly thinks to herself, *Is it good enough? Is everything fancy enough? Did I spend enough money? How does it compare to last month's wedding? Have I outdone everyone?*

I feel like a marionette on a stage, void of feelings and operating mechanically. This is not my event, it is an event put on by someone else, and I am only the central prop in a theatrical production. It will all be over soon, I remind myself, and I will be out of here forever with a husband who will make me happy and protect me. My bags are packed, and the taming of my inner pain has overshadowed all of the difficulties of the last few months of planning. I leave behind the awkwardness and uncertainty of my childhood and the misadventures of my adolescence and step forth as an adult in a culture that respects and admires me, where I fit in.

I watch Bucky take his place next to the minister. He is splendid in his cutaway coat, white vest, brocade cravat, and shining hair. His dark eyes watch me intently, and I feel a surge of love for him. All of my initial trepidation fades and I look forward with excitement to a life with this man. He is a new Southerner, a man of honor and bold ambition who can bridge the old and the new, and I will be his wife.

The attendants begin to step onto the white runner and move in time to the music, each person in the pageant playing the role that is assigned, each knowing his or her place. A slender, female arm links with the stronger arm of an usher, each as it should be. A young boy carries the jewels. A father escorts his daughter and safely turns her over to the man who will care for her the rest of her life.

The minister begins to chant the age-old words that bind people together with faith in the future: "Love ... honor ... cherish ... obey ... forsaking all others ... in sickness and in health ... for richer or poorer ... till death do we part." Bucky slips the golden ring on my finger. The service is over and the minister is saying, "Ladies and gentlemen, may I introduce to you Mr. and Mrs. Bucky Andrews." The crowd stands and applauds.

Mary Frances Andrews, I think the words to myself with a sense of reality for the first time. *I am a new person with a new role that will comfort and protect me, one that I can understand and participate in without questioning its values.*

9. VISITS

"Sugar plum, why don't y'all come on down to the office? We'll get you fixed up with someone who will find that ol' woman at the nursing home," Bucky says about a week after he agrees to let me continue with my quest to resolve the Emmaline mystery, and I make plans for an afternoon visit.

Entering the reception area at his office, I run into Beaux Leander, a local basketball hero who started one of the foundations where Bucky serves as the board president. "Hey, Miz Andrews … nice to see you again!" Beaux extends a friendly hand. "Are you here for the press conference, too?"

"No." I'm puzzled as I look around at several reporters with cameras, who stand in an attempt to get his attention. I am the titular secretary-treasurer of the group, but don't actively participate. Instead, Bucky brings papers home when he needs a signature and occasionally tells me that everything is fine with the organization.

"Gentlemen … gentlemen, I'll be right with you." He escorts me into the conference room and tells me that the foundation is about to announce a large purchase of baseball equipment for the local Police Athletic League, which will allow them to sponsor a summer league. Bucky joins us and jokingly apologizes for not mentioning it to me but he knows I have no interest in baseball. "Hey, man," Beaux claps him on the back, "don't overlook the ladies—we need them to come out and sell the peanuts and Cokes. We may even need you as an umpire, 'cause you like to call the shots!"

I stand in the background as arrangements are made to meet the press. Three young athletes, two police officers, and a representative from the equipment company are brought in along with samples of the new equipment. Two more reporters arrive, including my friend Katherine, and everyone is escorted into the conference room.

"Ladies and gentlemen," Beaux begins and explains the plans for the sponsorship. "… and let me conclude with an acknowledgment of Mr. Bucky Andrews, our board president. The organization bears my name, but it's Bucky who is responsible for the funds that have been raised and the effort that it has taken to bring this together." Cameras catch Beaux shaking hands with Bucky and one of the young athletes.

"See, Bucky isn't so bad," I whisper to Katherine as we stand in the back of the room. "His heart is in the right place … he has a very strong interest in this city." She smiles knowingly as she quickly takes notes.

"Sugar plum," Bucky says as the reporters pack up and leave, "let me set you up with Grace in my office." He introduces me to a young associate at his firm, Grace Ngyuen. Grace is tall, slender, and exotic looking. She has strong Asian features and dark hair pulled into a severe bun at the nape of her neck. She seems to be around thirty and is dressed in a conservative, dark suit with a delicate, white silk blouse.

Grace listens patiently and takes notes as Bucky lays the groundwork for our project before leaving the room. After the door closes, she turns to me and politely begins. "Mrs. Andrews, would you fill me in on the details?"

"Please, call me Mary Frances." I'm not comfortable with her business-like coolness and try to establish a connection. "You're new at the firm, aren't you?"

"I've been here almost a year." She poises her pen over the yellow pad with a very professional air. "When did you meet this woman?"

"I don't remember seeing you at the Christmas party."

"My daughter was ill that night. I didn't go."

Her coolness dissuades me from pursuing the small talk. "May I call you Grace?"

"Certainly."

I allow her to question me. She is very businesslike, almost curt, and takes copious notes. Although she seems thorough, I don't get a sense that she is genuinely interested and feel an uncomfortable distance. Finally, I decide to try again for a more personal connection. I sit quietly and carefully modulate my tone. "Grace, which projects have you been working on since you've been with the firm? Bucky tells me about most of the major work that the firm does."

She gives me a long, thoughtful stare. "I've been doing background on some of the Hill projects, but I've been hoping to get more challenging work." She pauses. "I also manage some trust funds for Mr. Andrews and handle all of his non-profit board activities."

"Oh, do you take care of my trust fund?"

"Yes, I do."

"I should get to know you better. I probably should know more about my money. I'm sure it's not very challenging to you, though." She smiles politely, and I return to our project. "What do you think we should do next on the Emmaline mystery?"

"I think we should go visit. I would like to meet her and the man who cares for her."

"Good idea." We take out our calendars and find an acceptable date, then call Benjamin.

. . . .

On the appointed day, Grace and I go to the nursing home. On the way, I gently ask personal questions and learn that Grace went to Georgetown Law School on a scholarship, that she was raised in a Catholic orphanage in Philadelphia, and that she went to Villanova.

We meet Benjamin in the seventh-floor cafeteria for a brief cup of coffee, and I introduce Grace as a lawyer in my husband's office who has been assigned to help find Emmaline's missing child.

Benjamin tells us that Emmaline has begun to sing a little song, and he has written down the words:

> "I am a fancy melody,
> I am you, and you are me,
> All together we are three.
> One, two, three."

"What do you make of it?" I ask. "Does she do anything when she sings it? It sounds like it goes with something."

"Well, I don't really have a good guess about it. When she sings, I get the feelin' that it's like that little dance that my grandchil'en does—'ring around a rosie, somethin' about a posie ....'"

I laugh at his hand gestures. "... They all fall down, right?"

"Yes, that's the one." He slowly rises from his chair. "So let's go on in and see if she'll sing it for y'all." He directs us to the day room where we wait while he brings Emmaline in a wheelchair. Her face lights up as he pushes her over to our sofa. I'm closest to her and Grace is next to me. Benjamin stays nearby.

"Miz Emmaline ... this is my friend, Grace, who has come to meet you."

"It's so nice to meet Fancy's friends." She smiles shyly and politely, extending her hand.

Grace gently takes her hand. "It's nice to meet you, too, Miz Emmaline." Grace seems to be silently evaluating Emmaline and thoughtfully glances over to me as she leans into the background and watches our interaction.

"Benjamin tells me you've been singing a song."

"It was the li'l chil'en's song. Y'all liked it. We made it up. Ain't nobody else sings it."

"Would you sing it for me?"

"Oh chile, that's so nice of you to want that ...." She sings the words in an animated, child-like voice, her face beaming with pleasure and her fingers keeping time to the rhythm. Her gestures indicate that the people in her imagination all happily fall down at the end. "The babies loved that song so much, they did, and they liked it best when we all fell down in a tumble on the grass."

I lean forward, catching her eye as if only the two of us are in the room. "One of your children was named Melody, wasn't she?"

She nods her head yes, her eyes glistening with pride.

"Is the song about Melody?"

She nods yes again.

"Was my name 'Fancy' when I was little?"

Again there is a gentle nod, her face alive with a broad smile.

"Was that song about both of us?"

238

"Yes'm, it was."

"Was I your charge … were you my mammy?"

She nods, slowly, like a child playing a game. "I was your manny, that's what you called me. It done be both names."

"Did Melody and I sing this song with you?"

Her eyes sparkle. "Yes'm."

"I'd like to see Melody again. Do you know where she lives?"

Her face clouds over. She frowns and looks puzzled. "We done left her."

"We left her? Where did we leave her?"

"There."

"Do you know the name of the place where we left her?"

She slowly shakes her head no. "I ain't never been able to go back like I said I would. I tol' Melody I'd come back an' I never did."

Grace speaks up. "Could we go back for you?"

Emmaline turns to her. "Chile. That'd be so nice of you but I sure's don't know how to tell you to get there."

Grace continues slowly, trying not to confuse Emmaline. "Tell us about the place … where is it … what does it look like … what do you remember?"

"Oh, it's way out in the country. Down there in 'nother state, Carolina I think it was. We left her at the ol' house, the tore-up ol' house back in the countryside."

"Do you know where Melody is now?"

She's perplexed. Her eyes cloud over. Her head shakes awkwardly and she has a hard time with her answer. "She's still there, far as I know."

Grace and I sense that we have probably reached our limit and silently agree to change the subject. Grace asks about her life at the nursing home and I follow her lead. In time, we realize that Emmaline is tired. Benjamin suggests that it's time for a nap and takes her back to her room.

Waiting by the elevator, I tell Grace that I'm still puzzled by how she was able to recognize me. Grace comments with a polite graciousness, "Miss Emmaline is very attached to you, I'm sure we'll get there, perhaps the next visit." Grace gazes out the window pensively. "She's challenging. There is something about this case that I don't have words for yet."

"What do you mean?"

"I don't know. It's only a feeling right now."

We silently wait for Benjamin to return, each of us lost in our impressions and reaching for words to explain. I am elated at Emmaline's clear memory that she was my mammy and wonder whether this will be enough to convince Bucky. I'm also curious about Grace's reaction, but she seems unapproachable.

When he returns to say goodbye, I ask Benjamin if we could find out more about Emmaline's background. He suggests that we talk to the nursing home administrator and takes us to her office. I tell her what I believe the connection is, and she reviews Emmaline's records for us. She also reminisces about the intake interview when Emmaline identified that she had an adult daughter and a grandchild. The administrator remembers trying to coax her but Emmaline would not give names or contact information. The administrator decided there was some difficulty in the family and didn't press the issue. There were no other relatives listed, but she gives us the name of the woman who first brought Emmaline to the home, her former employer, Mrs. Stanton.

The next morning, we visit with Mrs. Stanton at her stately home in the Cleveland Park area of Washington, north and slightly east of Georgetown. Emmaline had been in her employment since the late seventies and had been very competent for twenty-five years before becoming too frail to work.

"Tell me something, if you don't mind," I finally say, "do you recall if Emmaline ever spoke about her children?"

"She had a child, I remember," Mrs. Stanton muses, "and a grandchild, but I never met them. Once in a while, she would ask for time off to go to a school event. I remember a graduation that she went to shortly before she went to the nursing home."

"Do you know which school? Was it a local school?"

"I don't know, she wouldn't talk about it. I don't recall ever seeing pictures, either."

"But it was a local school?" Grace asks.

"Yes. I don't recall any trips that she took out of the city. She led a quiet life ... she had her church and some social activities and this grandchild that she would visit."

"This grandchild, was it a boy or a girl?" Grace continues.

"I don't recall; she was very private." Mrs. Stanton sips her tea carefully. "Emmaline had a sadness about her, and I didn't probe."

"I've seen the sadness also," I acknowledge. "Do you have any idea what caused it?"

"No," she says thoughtfully, and directs us to the pastor of the church that Emmaline attended in a neighborhood near Sixteenth Street and Meridian Hill. The pastor remembers Emmaline and tells us that she had a small photo album of the children that she occasionally showed him. He didn't remember any other details.

Back at the office, Grace and I tell Bucky what we have discovered. He shows an interest, but is annoyed because Grace is spending too much time with me and is needed on other cases. With a tone of mild defiance, Grace turns to me and suggests that I ask Emmaline about the small photo album the next time I visit.

Bucky surprises me by being visibly annoyed with Grace over this.

. . . .

"There's a new school superintendent," I read aloud from the *Washington Post* one morning over breakfast.

"I know," Bucky responds absentmindedly, drinking his coffee. "Hope he can turn things around. It's pretty bad over there. They just reported another big deficit that no one was expectin'."

I study the picture of the new superintendent. His name is Dr. Samuel Devereaux and he has come to Washington from Louisiana, where he was an assistant state superintendent. Could it be, I wonder? I haven't had contact with Susan's parents for more than twenty years but it's the same name and her father was in the school system when I knew him. I almost mention my thoughts, then reconsider. Bucky has always found fault with my brief spurt of activism and it might be better not to say anything. He has counseled me not to talk about my Mississippi experience to anyone, saying that if I leave it buried, it will eventually go away as just another memory of bad adolescent behavior.

After Bucky leaves for work, I reread the article and ponder whether I should try to contact them. Effi Barry calls while I'm on my second cup of coffee. She is calling her friends before the latest saga of the Marion Barry scandals hits the newspapers. "Mary Frances," she says, "I've decided to leave him. I've finally had enough." She will be visiting relatives out of town for a month as breathing space while the initial court documents are filed. We spend time talking about her difficulties and I sympathize with her, already knowing much about her struggles.

Effi invites me to a luncheon sponsored by the League of Women Voters at the Mayflower Hotel the day before she leaves. I ask if she has met the new school superintendent and tell her about my Louisiana experience and the possibility that I might know Mr. and Mrs. Devereaux. She volunteers to use her connections to contact Mrs. Devereaux and extend an invitation for the same event.

The day of the luncheon, Effi picks me up and tells me that she has arranged to meet Mrs. Devereaux in the lobby. I'm very excited and fervently hope that this is Susan's mother. Entering the hotel lobby, we glance around and spot an older black woman sitting alone next to a fireplace. "Mrs. Devereaux?" Effi graciously extends her hand.

"Yes?" She rises. I recognize the face of the woman that I knew many years ago … elegant, urbane in a gentle way, with high cheekbones, aging skin, and the same kindness in her eyes. Her hair is grayer and shorter than she used to wear it. The fullness of her years shows slightly in a soft yellow suit.

Effi introduces herself and turns to me. "And this is my friend, Mary Frances Andrews …."

"No, Mrs. Devereaux, I'm Mary Frances Tyler." I grasp her hand with both of mine. "I'm Susan's friend from college. Remember me?"

"Mary Frances? Mary Frances! What a surprise … what a delightful surprise." We hug warmly.

I turn to Effi, "Mrs. Devereaux is the mother of my college roommate …."

"Please, call me Renee. Both of you."

"... I think I have told you about Susan ... she and I worked on a voter registration drive and she was killed ...."

"... and Mary Frances brought her back home to me so that I could properly bury my daughter. She was very comforting to us."

"That sounds like Mary Frances, Renee." Effi, pleased with her role in connecting us, glances around and notices a group of women heading toward the luncheon. "This way, I think. We need to be in our seats soon. She guides us into the room just as the program begins.

During the meal, I congratulate Renee on their move to D.C. and her husband's new position, and we catch up with each other's history. She had become more involved in helping disadvantaged children after Susan's death and was a long-term foster parent for several children that she now considers her own. She also took a permanent position when they moved to Baton Rouge and rose to be the head pediatric nurse at Children's Hospital while her husband was the assistant state superintendent. Eric was elected as a congressman from Louisiana in the last election and lives part-time in a suburb in Northern Virginia, a town called Rosslyn, she says. I tell her about my marriage and my daughter. Just before the main speaker is introduced, Renee invites Bucky and me to have dinner with them.

Before I can answer, I realize that I must confront Bucky's racial attitudes. He is always publicly and politically gracious and I'm sure that he would not embarrass me in front of them. He seeks out political alliances with black organizations and knows that he needs the black vote and would welcome another opportunity for a connection with black Washington officials. He talks in terms of providing meaningful assistance to the poor and serves on a task force studying welfare reform. Yet, and this looms large for me, I know that his soul is still tainted with Southern racism and bigotry, and I do not trust his motives.

Before we married, he welcomed my assistance with his campaigns and seemed genuinely interested in improving the racial strife of the early seventies, but his attitude has shifted since we left local politics and moved to Washington. He now tells me that I have no real understanding of issues and the workings of government, and it's best if I limit myself to charitable work. For a number of years, he has privately made fun of my short foray into political activism and support of voting rights in the South. His recent expressions of disdain regarding Benjamin and Emmaline concern me. If I invite him to meet the Devereauxes, I fear that he will ridicule me for yet another link that is too close for his comfort, and that he will use the Devereauxes to scold me even more. I fear exposing this special friendship to that possibility.

"Would Wednesday night work for you?" I suggest, knowing that Bucky has a meeting on that night and would not be able to join us.

"Yes, I think so. I'd like to invite Eric also, if you don't mind."

"That would be wonderful, let's do it then. I'll check it out with Bucky. I know he will be pleased to meet you, but if he can't make it, I'll come alone and you can meet him another time." I feel a twinge of guilt at the sleight of hand that I have just planned. The speaker begins and we firm up arrangements later.

The Devereauxes are staying in a high-rise apartment near Scott Circle while they look for a place in Washington, and Renee has a New Orleans–style meal brought in. Eric is already there when I arrive and the four of us melt into hugs and exclamations. Eric is still tall, handsome, and muscular, and he carries himself with an air of authority. And Sam, as he insists on being called, is portly and dignified.

I look around the room and address Eric. "Is your wife here? Surely the Voodoo man found you a wife with those good smells, didn't he?" I laugh, reminding him of our summer in New Orleans.

He becomes sadly serious. "My wife and son died in a car accident in Louisiana a couple of years ago."

Renee quickly takes a picture from a table next to the TV. "Here they are. When we travel, we always take pictures of our family." I spend a moment examining the picture of Eric with a lovely woman and a child about nine.

"I'm very sorry, Eric, my sincerest condolences." I thoughtfully place it back with the picture of Susan and several young families. "I still miss Susan and think about her often. In fact, I named my daughter after her." Silence fills the room as I remember never telling Bucky the real reason why I picked the name "Susanne" for our daughter. "Renee, are these your foster children?"

"Yes." Picking up the pictures one by one, she talks about how she and Sam have helped them through difficulties and watched the growth of their families. "All these little ones are my grandchildren now."

Moving to the table, she lights the candles for dinner. "We're sorry we lost touch with you after you went back to Richmond, Mary Frances," Sam says with his booming voice as he sits, "but we are very pleased to see you now and to know that you are doing well. Here you go." He picks up a large platter. "N'Orleans-style seafood, best there is."

Much of the lively dinner conversation centers on the extended Devereaux family and their active involvement in Louisiana politics, law, and education. Some of the people I met during my summer in New Orleans are mentioned along with their successes over the years as local and state politicians. With great warmth and charm, Sam describes the political life in Louisiana as a living mosaic of black and brown and white and red and yellow, competing and allying with each other to achieve common purposes, realizing that sometimes it's hard to understand the accents both figuratively and literally.

Eric tells me that he went to law school after graduating from Stanford and moved back to Louisiana as a federal prosecutor, working primarily on the political graft accusations against Governor Edwards of Louisiana. When Eric entered politics, he says, it was on a platform fighting against the tradition of local corruption and the problems of the new offshore gambling casinos.

"Did you ever write that book?" I ask him gently as Renee serves pecan pie.

"No, I've never had the time. But I still have the materials and the research and I'm still adding to them. Cultures don't go away ... someday," he laughs, "when I finally lose an election and need something to do, I'll get it done." He pauses as he takes his first bite. "I understand you're married to someone involved in local politics?"

"Yes, my husband is Bucky Andrews. He's an attorney who works on a number of political issues and he's on the boards of several charities. Right now, he's quite involved with the D.C. Financial Control Board."

"I've heard his name," Eric says. "He's quite prominent in the local Democratic Party, isn't he?"

"Yes."

Renee gathers the dishes as we finish our wine and the group moves to the living room. Eric asks, "Haven't I heard rumors that he might be a challenger to the mayor in the next election?"

"I don't think he's decided yet."

Sam joins in. "It would be good to have a progressive person heading up this city … someone who understands both the black and the white issues. Do you think the city would elect a white who has a good civil rights background?"

I hesitate, silently thinking about Bucky's true attitude toward racial issues.

Eric continues, not noticing that I don't answer the question, "Did you meet him through some of your political work in the seventies?"

"Well," I stop, realizing that I ended up on a different political spectrum than the one Eric assumes, "I went back to Richmond after I graduated from Wellesley. I met him there, where he was involved in local politics. Later, he went to law school at Georgetown, and we ended up here."

"I'm sorry I didn't have a chance to meet him tonight," Sam says. "He would be a good person to know. There must have been some good fights in Richmond back in those days, what with all the resistance to civil rights. It's good to know that someone with a righteous head came out of it unscathed. You have yourself a real winner there, Mary Frances. We're real proud of you."

"I'm proud of him, too. He's been a good husband and provider."

"Mary Frances," Renee comes into the room with fresh drinks, "I've always been pleased that your aunt allowed you to come to Louisiana back then. She must have been a remarkable woman during those times. I still remember calling her to express my appreciation. Now that we've moved closer, I would enjoy meeting her. Is she still alive?"

I gulp as I remember Beatrice's reaction to that phone call and guiltily roll my eyes. "Oh, Renee, if you only knew!"

"Knew what?"

"My aunt didn't know the reason I went to Louisiana. She's actually a very traditional Southerner."

"She didn't know you were working in civil rights?" Renee's voice is concerned.

"No."

Eric bursts out laughing, joined by Sam. "Your folks didn't know you were staying with a black family? You were one of those rich white girls who came out to do good, and your traditional Southern family didn't even know, am I right?"

"Yes." I slowly nod my head, feeling a blush rise.

Renee sits next to me on the sofa. "Dear, I wish I had known. What happened when I called? Did she realize what you had been up to?"

"Yes. She wasn't any too pleased with me. It caused some problems then, but it's way behind us now."

"What did she think when you married a progressive like Bucky?" Eric asks.

I eye him quietly, not quite knowing how to describe Bucky. In recent years, Bucky's fanfare efforts have had little real energy and less long-term effect. "He seems to be able to keep both sides relatively content."

"Mary Frances," Renee asks gently, "if your family has a traditional background, have you been able to keep up your interests in social causes?"

"I've spent my time raising my daughter, Betty Susanne. She's in college now."

"And with your free time …?"

"Well … I do charity work."

"That's marvelous," she says. "Washington is such a great place for non-profits. Which boards do you sit on? Have you been able to stay active with some of the feminist issues that you and Susan loved?"

"I'm not on any governing boards. I work more with the church committees. Bucky doesn't like for me to get involved in politics or women's issues."

Eric says, "I remember how you and Susan couldn't leave it alone. Don't tell me you've come full circle?"

"My life seems to be very traditional now. I suppose that most political wives are traditional, don't you think?"

"Not the ones I'm getting to know. I've always heard that Washington's political women were arm candy with beaming smiles. The ones I'm meeting aren't like that. They seem to be pretty involved, although they have to be careful in their selection of issues."

We continue a lively discussion of Washington social and political relationships until it's time to leave. Eric volunteers to walk me to my car, and I offer him a ride over to Rosslyn, which is just across the river from Georgetown.

"Remember how you used to be afraid to be alone with me?" I tease Eric as we get to the car. "Things have certainly changed, haven't they?"

"Yes they have, but it's taking too long. An awful lot of people became complacent or gave up after the worst of it was over."

I recognize myself as one of these people. I'm thankful that I can distract myself with starting the car and pulling into the busy traffic on Sixteenth Street.

He's pensive, much like I remember him in New Orleans, as he continues. "Forgive me, but I'm still the consummate crusader. Martin Luther King Jr.'s dream isn't a reality for a lot of people, and I don't know if it will be in my lifetime. There are still a lot who are more comfortable under the old ways ... knowing the rules and staying within the boundaries is sometimes easier than learning something new. You can achieve desegregation with laws but you can't legislate integration."

"What's the difference? There are no vestiges of segregation anymore, and affirmative action has made the workplace very colorblind. Even the Christian Coalition has acknowledged that they were originally on the wrong side."

"Desegregation is passing laws that open doors or at least it prevents the doors from closing. Laws don't necessarily change attitudes. Integration is about behavior ... the way people act, what's in their hearts. It's the way we appreciate both the similarities and the differences ... living in the same neighborhoods ... socializing as friends ... having a life where skin color really doesn't matter ... honoring the heroes from all cultures."

"Isn't that the way it is now?"

"Ah, Mary Frances, it may be different here in this town but out there in the heartlands, what people say and what they do is a lot different. When too many black families move into a neighborhood, the whites start to move out. They still take their kids out of the schools when the school gets too black. The law may bring people together, but when people make choices in their own behavior and those choices are color-based, not much has changed. They just

251

don't talk about it. That's a lot of what keeps me in politics. I haven't finished what I started a long time ago."

I remember the same sentiment, the same passion for social change. "After Susan's death, I think I gave up a lot of what I cared about."

He turns his head gently. "As hard as it was on all of us, you were the one who watched her die. I imagine it was very difficult to get over."

"It was. I'm not sure I've ever really recovered." I turn left off of M Street onto Key Bridge and go into Rosslyn, where we quickly find Eric's apartment. We say a warm goodbye and I head for home, energized by Eric's passion for his cause. I'm also hoping that I will get home before Bucky returns from his meeting because I didn't tell him about my plans for the evening.

Without intending to, the Devereauxes have reminded me that I have lost the magic that my life once was … the magic of knowing that I cared about something that was morally important, that I believed in myself and felt a sense of responsibility, and that I believed I could make a difference in the lives of other people.

Sipping a cup of tea as I wait for Bucky, I feel uneasy about the life we lead in Washington. I have watched Bucky become consumed with politics and the secrets behind the official stories, and listened to many unworthy stories of political arrogance and greed. I wonder how Eric will attune himself to Washington, where deal making and tradeoffs run this morally relative climate that seems to willfully disconnect from humanity.

When he comes in, I ask about his board meeting. "I won a major concession," was the only comment he would make. "…'course, I usually do, don't I?" He grins and doesn't ask about my evening. I don't offer any comments.

10. INVESTIGATIONS

"The birth certificate!" I exclaim one morning in early February, realizing that I had forgotten about Bucky's passport application and that time is getting short for our trip to Europe. I haven't been able to find the copy of his certificate, and we surmise that I will need to go to Richmond for another one. I also know that I want to look up the names of Emmaline's children for Grace's project, hoping that we might find a clue. I mention the passport issue to Bucky in the evening and plan a trip to Richmond the next morning. Bucky and I seem to have a truce on the Emmaline mystery—he disposed of it by assigning Grace to work with me, and I don't talk to him about it.

I have no trouble finding the Department of Vital Records located on Willow Lawn Drive in Richmond and reach it in two hours, arriving around ten-thirty. Computers are available in the public room for general lookup, along with instruction cards for novices like me. I've learned to use Bucky's computer for letter writing, but I feel helpless much beyond that. I try the instruction card, get confused, ask for help from one of the younger people, and finally get the hang of it.

The first screen indicates that the computer gives me access to birth, death, adoption, marriage, and divorce records in Virginia. It states that the present database was started in 1978 using some existing records and that previous manual records from 1963 back to 1924 have been automated. Converting the records prior to that date is still in process and the information won't be available online until early 1995. Patrons needing information prior to 1920 should seek assistance directly from a clerk, the screen says. It also states that certain records relating to births, deaths, adoptions, marriages, and divorces have been sealed by court order, that this requirement will be indicated if it's the case, and that access to sealed records is available only through an additional court order.

"Well, business first," I mutter and select the screen for inquiries and type in Bucky's name, "Winfred Scott Andrews." The next question gives me the option of selecting whether I want a specific document or whether I want all database information under this name. I select "specific document" and choose birth certificate, then type in his birth date and hit the search button. Success! His parents' names, address, and the hospital where he was born come up on a screen. *I can't believe it! It works! Now, I wonder how to get a copy?*

I scurry over to a middle-aged clerk and pose my question. She responds with a bureaucratic scowl as if she has heard this question many times. Rolling her eyes, she looks at me like I am unable to comprehend the basics of life, like reading, and points to a large instruction sign above a table holding several piles of forms. I smile at her nicely and walk over to the sign, take a form back to the terminal, and fill it out. *Oops, I was away too long and the screen automatically closed me out.* I feel more confident as I type Bucky's name in again.

I hit the search button before realizing that I forgot to select "specific document" and everything in the database will come up, but I assume this will be a minor inconvenience. After a few seconds, a screen shows a number of entries and I idly read them, calling up some of the detailed screens to see how it works.

It begins with Winfred Andrews, no middle initial, born in Virginia Beach County in 1925. He married in 1945 and had four children; a son born in 1947, another son in 1952, and twin girls in 1953. *Good grief, four children in six years, poor woman.* He died in 1989, still in Virginia Beach County. *Hmmm, sixty-four years old was too young.*

Then there is Winfred Allen Andrews who died in 1937. No other information.

Then it is Winfred George Andrews. Then Winfred Henry Andrews.

Finally, I see Winfred Scott Andrews. *Here's my Bucky! Let's see if they got it all correct.* The screen shows a summary of the available documents:

Birth certificate, July 16, 1944.

I click and copy down the information that I still need for the form, then scan the screen again.

Birth certificate, March 25, 1970.

Marriage certificate, September 17, 1972.

I click and read the statistics regarding my marriage to Bucky, and fill out a form. *Might as well,* I think.

Birth certificate, November 3, 1973.

I click and read Betty Susanne's birth certificate and fill out a form.

Wait a minute. I scroll back. March 25, 1970. *This must be an error. Perhaps I should report it so that someone can fix it.* I click and the screen fills with data about a child named Corinne Witherspoon born on March 25, 1970. *This was a year before I met Bucky.* A knot forms in my stomach as I read on. The knot hardens. *The mother is Angela Thornton Witherspoon. The father is listed as Winfred Scott Andrews. It has Bucky's social security number, his birth date, and the address where his parents lived until they died.* I shake inside.

I read the birth certificate over and over with disbelief. The mother is listed as being of the Negro race. Her date of birth is March 30, 1946. The child is listed as a mixed race. I'm stunned. I'm more than stunned, I'm shocked. I don't know what to do. Mechanically, I write down the information on another form. My hand shakes. I know nothing about this.

When I finish, I hold my head with my hands, absorbing the shock of discovery but unable to show any feelings because I am in a public place. My face feels ashen. My heart beats awkwardly, its scared rhythms pound in my eardrums … Bucky has another child that he never told me about.

Slowly, with leaden actions, I take the forms to the clerk, pay the fees, tell her that I will pick up the certified copies in an hour, and walk out the door into the early spring day. The sunshine warms me even as I continue to shake.

I am barely able to walk to a coffee shop, purchase a cup, and find a bench at a bus stop. I watch traffic as I drink my coffee and contemplate what might have happened and why Bucky never told me, but come up with no answers. My body is becoming consumed with anger. I want to scream. I begin to feel the pain of realizing that he has never trusted me, if the facts turn out as they seem to be.

March 1970. Where was I? I graduated from Wellesley in June of '71. I met Bucky a month after I moved back to Virginia. Images of Bucky as a debonair twenty-six-year-old who is surreptitiously courting me in the grand ol' Southern style cloud my thoughts. *The old style often involved indiscretions that were treated nonchalantly by the men.*

After what seems like eternity, I finish my coffee and walk back into the building and spot a bank of telephones along a wall in the main lobby. I notice the telephone books and head toward them. I'm not sure what I want to look for but I need to do something, to find an answer, any answer. Lifting up the white pages, I look for the name "Witherspoon." It's there. Witherspoon, Angela Thornton. Underneath is the name, Witherspoon, Corinne. My heart stops. *These are real people. They're here in Richmond. They are still here in Richmond.* My hand rests on the page under their names. Frozen. It feels like eternity.

I reach into my pocketbook for a quarter. I must find out for sure, but I do not know what to say and anticipate that no one will be home. A constricting knot blocks my throat. I dial the mother's number and contemplate hanging up if she answers. It rings twice, then there is a click similar to a transfer and it begins to ring again. A voice answers. "Hello, Angela here." It's businesslike. I hesitate. "Hello … hello?" she says.

It seems too late to hang up. "Is this Angela Thornton Witherspoon?"

"Yes, it is. May I help you with something?"

"Ms. Witherspoon. I need to ask you a question. This is a little embarrassing, so please forgive me if I offend." I pause. She waits. "Do you … did you … know someone named Bucky Andrews?"

"Who is this?"

"My name is Mary Frances Andrews. I'm Bucky's wife."

"Why are you calling me?"

"I've just found some information that indicates that you knew Bucky about twenty-four, maybe twenty-five years ago. It's something that I would like to talk to you about."

"Are you here in Richmond?"

"Yes."

"Do you know Sine's Restaurant in Shockoe Slip?"

"Yes."

"Would you be able to meet me there at one o'clock?"

"Yes."

"I'll see you there. I can't discuss this any further right now. Goodbye." She has been polite, but hangs up quickly.

My hand lingers on the telephone. I'm feeling rage, anger, hurt. *Bucky has kept this secret from me for twenty-two years. Who is this woman and what happened?*

My watch tells me that I have another hour and a half. I go back to the Department of Vital Records, still in shock, but realize that I have not accomplished all that I came here to do. I sit down at the computer terminal with a new respect for the impact of information.

I log on again and type in the names "Angela Thornton Witherspoon" and "Corinne Witherspoon." The entries that appear match the information that I have already found. There are no marriage certificates, no other children, nothing more. Finally, I recognize that I must finish the searches that I came here to do.

I put Bucky, Angela, and Corinne aside and type in "Emmaline Powers." This time, I ask for all information in the database. The name is common enough that there is data about several people. I find an Emmaline Powers, whose life appears similar, but she was born in 1936 and seems too young. I am able to match a marriage license and five children to the 1936 Emmaline, beginning in 1955. There is another record, a sealed record in 1949 that probably applies to her also. I find one entry that seems right for my Emmaline, a birth certificate dated 1922. The 1922 birth certificate is for a child born to a woman living in the ghetto area of Richmond. This is probably the right one, I realize.

A birth certificate listed for a child born in November 1950 matches with the 1922 Emmaline as a parent. I click and read about a female child named Melody Powers born to Emmaline and Charles Edward Givens. She told me that her children's names were Melody and Missy. This is one of them. No address is listed for the father, and Emmaline's address is the same as my old family home. I write down the data on Melody and continue looking for Emmaline's other child but find nothing, no other birth certificates, no death certificates, and no marriages. I decide that the second child must have been born after she moved to Washington, D.C., and a separate search will be needed. I fill out forms to get copies of Melody's birth certificate and Emmaline's.

I perform a general search under the name "Melody Powers," born in 1950, but find no records indicating a marriage, births of children, or a death. Again, I locate a Richmond telephone book at a phone booth, this time inside the Department of Vital Records, and search for the name, hoping for another miracle but with no results. I feel the flush of success but also feel frustration because the answer is not complete and I still don't know how to find Melody.

Glancing at my watch, I still have more than an hour. My feeling of shock has lightened up enough that I'm curious. I decide to run a few family names, starting with my own. I type in "Mary Frances Andrews." The name is common enough, and the data is confusing, so I switch to "Mary Frances Tyler," my maiden name. I'm amazed at how many other women in Virginia have the same name but finally find a record that pertains to me, a birth certificate for Mary Frances Tyler, June 22, 1949. Clicking on this, I read the certificate with George and Beatrice's names. I also find my marriage certificate to Bucky and the birth certificate for my daughter. I surmise that a birth certificate exists under my original name and that it is sealed as a result of my adoption. I try the name "Mary Frances Roche," which was my original name, and find a listing for a sealed record. I suddenly decide that I want a copy of this birth certificate and wonder how I can get it.

I try my parents' names to see what happens. I type in "James Kerwin Roche" and ask for all database information. I find his birth certificate in 1920, his marriage certificate, and a sealed record that seems to correspond to my sealed record. There is no death certificate because he died in North Carolina.

I encounter more difficulty with my mother's name. I type in "Margaret Barksdale" and find her birth certificate and marriage certificate, but there is no sealed record that would correspond to my birth certificate. I also try "Margaret Roche" and "Margaret Barksdale Roche." Then I try "Margaret Ann Barksdale," "Margaret Roche," "Ann Barksdale," and "Ann Roche." I know the document is there because it shows up for both my father and me but I can't figure out which name she used, and feel frustrated.

I approach the same clerk that I dealt with before, collect the birth certificates that I had ordered, and ask how to notify the department of an error that needs correction. She tells me that their records are never wrong. I explain to her that it appears that something happened when my birth records were converted to the computer and I would appreciate it very much if the situation could be fixed. I show her the list where I had written down the names for my parents and me as I used them. I explain to her that I was adopted by my aunt and uncle and that I know who my real parents are, and that my birth certificate is in the system correctly but it is not showing a sealed record under my mother's name and for the sake of accuracy, I'd like this changed. She explains that she is sorry but she can't do it on my word alone and she would need something more. She also suggests that I contact the Department of Social Services, Report of Adoption Unit, on East Broad Street.

I ask how I could go about speaking with someone who could fix it. She hands me a business card for her department supervisor, and I ask to speak to this person. She politely tells me that he isn't available at the moment but I could write a letter explaining my concerns.

I ask if she really wouldn't mind just looking it up herself to be sure that she understands what I am saying, and to see if I am making a simple mistake that might be causing the problem. I tell her that I am such a novice at these computer things that I really think I have missed something, and it would certainly save her supervisor a whole mess of trouble if we could just figure it out ourselves. I also imagine out loud that she is so much better at these things than me and most likely has much better access.

She looks at me with controlled smugness but takes my list and disappears into a back room. A few minutes later, she returns. The look on her face has changed but I can't read it. She stares at me strangely and says that the information I am seeking is restricted by a court order. She pushes my paper across the counter to me, tells me very flatly that she is sorry but she can't help me, and tells me that I need to write a letter. I explain to her that I already know what the court order says and it has to do with my adoption, and I know all the people involved and I tell her the names again. She looks at me blankly and says very rudely, "I can't help you."

Abruptly, she leaves her post and returns to the back room, leaving other customers waiting. I puzzle at her reaction and the business card and notes go into my pocketbook for future reference.

It is time to leave for the restaurant. It's not far away, located in a fashionably converted old warehouse section of town. Sine's (pronounced "Shinaes") is a very popular, upscale, Irish bar and grill. I intentionally arrive ten minutes early and wait in a comfortable seat by the door. Precisely at one o'clock, a tall, thin, attractive black woman, probably in her mid- to late forties, comes in alone and looks for someone. She is dressed in a very stylish, pale orange suit that complements her medium brown complexion. Her hair is closely cropped and she wears large, gold earrings.

She approaches and asks if I am Mrs. Andrews. I'm apprehensive as reality begins to settle in. We introduce ourselves and shake hands awkwardly. She has a very professional demeanor and takes control of the situation, asking for one of the small booths along the window side. I notice that she chooses one where no one else is sitting nearby. The conversation is small talk until we order. We both decide on wine with lunch.

"Mrs. Andrews," she begins after the waiter leaves, "I don't want to seem rude but could you show me some ID that indicates you are Bucky's wife?"

I show her my driver's license, and she seems to relax a little and hands me a business card indicating that she is a real-estate broker. She apologies for the formality, but indicates that we will be talking about a sensitive subject and in the wrong hands, it could be used inappropriately. She tells me that she works in commercial properties, primarily in Richmond. She explains that her home phone is automatically forwarded to her private line at the office.

I tell her that Bucky and I have been married for over twenty-one years, live in D.C., and have a daughter who attends Columbia University. I give her a very brief synopsis of Bucky's career. She remembers seeing the announcement of Bucky's wedding in the papers many years ago and knows of his connection with Beatrice.

The waiter brings our wine. She picks up her glass, contemplates it, and then continues in a professional tone. "I signed documents saying that I would never talk about this, and every effort has been made to keep it confidential. I understood then that Becky planned a political career and it was necessary to keep certain things quiet. It's not my desire to harm him in any way." She breathes deeply. Her voice softens and the conversation becomes two women talking to each other. "I don't know how you came upon your information but it's something that you have a right to know."

"Then it's true." I don't wait for her answer because I know it is. Rather, I switch to explaining how I had come to Richmond to get Bucky's birth certificate for his passport and how the birth record came up at Vital Records.

When I finish, she says blankly, "The birth certificate was supposed to be sealed. There is a court order to that effect."

"I found another error myself, relating to my own birth certificate. I think it might have something to do with the conversion of old records to the computer. Someone goofed."

"We'll have to check on it."

I pause and look at her, realizing that this woman bore a child that my husband fathered. I feel an awkward connection but I also feel the sense of two mothers simply talking about their children. My voice quivers. "Tell me about her, your daughter."

"Well, let's see. Corinne is now almost twenty-four. My mother helped raise her. She did very well in school, she sings, she swims competitively. She's in law school here in Richmond and works part-time as a legislative aide. She's interested in a career working with domestic violence and child abuse."

"Does your daughter know who her father is?"

"No," she looks directly at me, "she knows that I never married, and she believes that I used a sperm bank in New York City. She believes that she is light-skinned because her unnamed father is light, not because he's white. She has a strong identification as an African American and in her religion and would not be comfortable with the circumstances of her birth."

It seems strange to realize that Corinne would be embarrassed having Bucky as a father. Angela's face clouds. She looks pensive and addresses her concern with a softer voice. "What is your motivation in contacting me?"

"Needless to say, I'm shocked. It's hard for a wife to discover that her husband has another child, one that he has never told her about. It's also hard to find out this way."

"Why don't you thrash it out with him? This is really between you and him, isn't it?"

I think about her questions and feel painfully honest when I reply. "Right now, I know that I won't trust what he tells me. I need corroboration. I need to be absolutely sure so that he can't talk his way out of it." I realize that I'm only concerned about myself and that I've not considered her. "I'm sorry if I'm bringing up painful memories for you."

Our salads arrive and the conversation pauses. Both of us seem to be absorbing this meeting moment by moment. She also seems to be confronting long-buried emotions, even though they are much different from mine. By the time the meal is finished, the wine glasses have been refilled.

Finally and with much hesitation, I say, "Would you mind telling me the circumstances of her birth?"

She looks over my shoulders pensively, hesitates, and smiles to herself. She removes her suit jacket slowly, revealing a flowered blouse in soft tones of orange and tan, and leans back into the corner of the booth, taking her wine glass in hand. She has mellowed substantially since the initial phone call, and I sense she has a better understanding of my situation.

"Let's see," she begins to reminisce. "It's a lot about me, really." Her eyes have a faraway look. "Bucky and I met at UVA, Charlottesville, fall semester, 1966. I was very proud to be in the first group of five blacks who registered there. If you're from around here, you probably remember the difficulty in integrating the Southern universities in the sixties." She pauses, glancing at me. "Do you remember James Meredith?"

"Sounds familiar, but I can't place him."

"He was the first black at Ole Miss in 1962, and there was huge press coverage. He was my hero; I wanted to be like him. I was raised in Richmond and my whole childhood was surrounded by political tension. My parents were people who didn't just talk about it, they stepped out and did what needed to be done. My uncle, William Thornton, led the Richmond Crusade for Voters for many years. My mother was the legal secretary for Oliver Hill. He's famous in some circles. You don't know that name, do you?"

"No."

"He was a Richmond lawyer. *Brown v. Board of Education* was really four cases that were consolidated by the Supreme Court. They came from different parts of the country, but the name and the fame went to the Kansas case. One of the other cases was from Richmond. It concerned a school district in Prince Edward County. It was Oliver Hill's case. My mom typed it."

She takes a breath. "Even after the *Brown* decision, integration in Richmond was stopped by massive resistance, a couple of Jim Crow newspapers, and more lawsuits. All I can say is, it was an ugly time. The Pupil Placement Board illegally prevented integration until the courts finally declared the board illegal in 1963. I grew up anticipating that I would be one of the first to go to a white high school. Well, that didn't happen, so I wanted to be one of the first at the university and I was."

She stops and breathes deeply. I feel no racial barrier between us. She talks to me as a woman who is proud of her past and who is a hero in her own mind. "My parents are the reason I wanted to be there. They were very clear about the fact that my worst enemy was fear. I lived each day of my life taking one small step toward my goal, whatever my goal was, and never giving up, never, ever giving up. 'Walk tall,' mama would say, 'take the risk, we ain't got nothing to lose 'cept our pain.'"

I notice my reaction. No one ever counseled me to take a risk. I have been controlled with fear my whole life. I have lived with it all day long, every day ... fear of this, fear of that, fears I never knew existed. I didn't have goals, real goals that gave my life meaning, like this woman had.

"There were five of us who entered the university that year ... three brothers and two sisters. What we lived in 1966 was total isolation, and none of us were used to it. People didn't talk to us. No one wanted to be the first to befriend the 'niggers.'" She winces as she uses the word. "We were excluded from all of the clubs and activities. No one would sit next to us in class, if they could help it. I had been a leader in my high school and I was protected from racism in my daily life. I didn't know how to take it."

I tried to imagine the horror of being in her place and how different her experience was from mine. I remember being back in college with Susan and was thankful that I had not caused her to have the same experience.

Angela stops to eat a few bites. "So I became a militant; Black Power and all that, Stokely Carmichael and his gang. I was one of them. Since we were not accepted as equal citizens, we talked about defining our own group realities, writing our own history, and creating our own culture. We decided to antagonize virtually every white opinion. It was our way of becoming distinctive, breaking out of the stereotype."

She continues to tell her story. "Well, Bucky was a sophomore that year as I recall. He was in a biology class that I took, second semester. I was the only black student in the class, and he was assigned as my lab partner. He was a jerk, a real college-age, redneck bastard and I was a militant. That combination would be called a volatile mix in a chemistry class." She laughs to herself. "Bucky was out to prove that I was too dumb to take college biology. I was out to prove I was better'n him. We made lousy lab partners because I intentionally messed with his stuff and he messed with mine. He had a heyday when the discussions were on genetics and heredity. He taunted me by calling me 'monkey-lady.' I really hated him. Badly! God, did I hate him then! An' he got away with it! That's what really got to me. The time finally came when I couldn't take it anymore and I asked the brothers to stand up to him for me."

She takes a long sip of wine. "So one afternoon after class, we got a group together and the brothers ganged up on him. Just like that! Must have been at least ten or twelve of 'em ... didn't do anything, just surrounded him when he came out of the lab building by himself … forced him to go where they wanted him to go," she laughs, "… and girl, it scared the pants off of him, too! I watched from a distance.

"They pushed him down out there in the bushes where no one could see. An' when he was sitting there in the mud, scared that he was gonna lose his manhood, they laughed at him. They taunted him … called him 'fat white boy,' and 'honkie,' and 'po' white trash,' and 'mama's boy,' and everything else they could think of. They finally told him that if he was ever rude to their sister again, he was gonna get the real treatment, only the next time it would be worse, and he had better look out for his own sister, if he had one. Then they let him go and you've never seen a skunk run faster." She chuckles, "I'm sorry to have to tell you this, but it's still funny!"

I react with astonishment, trying to picture Bucky and the comical scene of him running away. This is not the Bucky that I have known, and in spite of myself, I laugh with her.

"He reported the brothers to the admin, but no one admitted to it, and he couldn't identify any of them, because to him they all looked the same. The political tension was so high, no one wanted to touch a simple hazing." Her eyes twinkle. "But he changed. Maybe I changed, too. We stopped fighting and started working together, he and I, and we did good! We did real good, and we both ended up getting A's in the class and we took the next class together.

"Well, it took a while but we started being friends. I was careful about him because I didn't trust him, you know, being a redneck honkie and all." She eyes me to see my reaction. "We talked between classes and did homework at the library. That was all for a long time."

268

She stops to break apart a leftover piece of bread. "One of the things I eventually learned about him was that he was still a virgin, and he wanted bragging rights real bad," she laughs at her thoughts, "and his mama kept picking out his girlfriends for him, and they were all wantin' to be virgins on their wedding night." She eyed me curiously as if I were one of them.

"Well, you probably remember how college was, especially then. It was the late sixties and free love was everyone's motto. Experimentation, throwing off the shackles of the fifties and all that. By the time he was a senior, we were together pretty regular. Very few people knew about it 'cause I was still involved in the Black Panther movement and no way was I gonna tell them I had a white man in my bed. It was my trip as much as his … I'd never had a white boyfriend and he'd never had a black girlfriend.

"He graduated a year ahead of me and moved back to Richmond. I probably got pregnant the last time we were together, a month or so after his graduation. I didn't tell him. Abortion wasn't legal then, not here in Virginia. I suppose I could have gone somewhere but I didn't. Anyway, I had religious reasons for not doing it. So when he called me the next year at my graduation, I told him we had a two-month-old baby." Her face is very matter-of-fact. "That's what happened."

Another sip of wine and she continues. "He never came to see her. I got a phone call from his daddy's lawyer. His family wanted to do right by the child but they also wanted his name protected, so we made a deal. They paid me a substantial amount to cover her care. Basically, it was child support for twenty years in one check. And the record was sealed, or was supposed to be."

"Does it bother you that he has never seen his child?"

"It's probably been for the best the way I've handled it. She never had to feel rejected. She was taken care of in my family by my father and my uncles. She has a clear understanding of her identity and she is proud."

I think about her parents ... they step up and do what needs to be done. No judgments. No shame. They aren't afraid. They simply take care of each other. Even a simple statement like this has more family feeling than I ever felt. What would Beatrice have done if I had become pregnant?

"I used the money to get started in real estate. I don't know if you remember, but in the early seventies there was a huge uproar over the annexation of Chesterfield County into Richmond. We saw it as an effort to dilute the black vote in the face of the voter registration drive. I got involved after I graduated from UVA and worked on the annexation lawsuit that eventually went to the Supreme Court. The annexation was upheld in 1975, but the Court required that the at-large voting for city council be changed to ward voting. We crusaded hard and the blacks won the majority in the next election and elected the first black mayor. It was easy for me to see the future for more black-owned real estate, especially in Jackson Ward, and well, the rest is history as they say."

She stops and places her empty wine glass on the table. I feel humbled by how much Angela has accomplished with her life and awed by her frankness. I also appreciate that she doesn't have bad feelings toward Bucky. Her description of politics in Richmond also brings back fond memories of our early married years before Bucky decided to move to Washington to go to law school.

She looks at her watch carefully. Raising her face, a look in her eyes seems to say something. "Would you like to meet Corinne?

Anonymously? She will be dropping by the office in about half an hour."

I hesitate briefly. "Yes."

"I don't want to reveal any of this to her. I will introduce you as a client, if needed."

"That's fine with me."

We leave taking her car, a dark green, late-model Mercedes, to a nearby office building. She is part of a large real-estate group. The office is sleek and well-appointed. Several clerical employees greet us as we enter. Angela's office is situated so that the main entrance to the office suite can be seen as I sit in one of her guest chairs.

A high school graduation picture is prominently displayed on Angela's dark mahogany desk. I stare at it, comparing the child's features with her mother's and looking for signs of Bucky's genes. Corinne's coloring is lighter than Angela's and her eyes are different. I think I see Bucky's eyes and I suspect that she would have his smile in a less formal picture.

I recognize Corinne immediately when she walks in the main door. She is taller than her mother and has Bucky's way of walking. Dressed casually in jeans and a black sweatshirt, her body is muscular but trim. "Hey, Sam, how's doin'?" She waves and calls to an employee as she heads for Angela's office. "Mom ... oh, excuse me."

"That's okay, dear, come in. This is Mrs. Andrews."

She extends a hand in greeting. I rise and shake her hand, observing her broad smile. Of course she is Bucky's child. She exudes a warmth and friendliness just like him. She has his way of being. And she is beautiful, simply ... beautiful.

Corinne tosses her car keys on the desk, and Angela passes her own keys back while Corinne jokes with me. "Just borrowin' mom's car. Gotta play the game and impress someone tonight." And to her mother, "Thanks, see ya later." As she leaves, I realize that Corinne and Betty Suzanne are half sisters and wonder how they would get along.

Angela and I wrap up our conversation with genuine pleasure in having met, and I express my gratitude for her forthrightness. I tell her that Corinne is a child she can be proud of and I'm honored to have met her. I wish them both the best. I have no expectation that we will see each other again.

Driving back to Georgetown I rehearse, with great trepidation, all the different ways I could confront Bucky. I have always believed strongly in my marriage vows and I grapple with my sense of the totally shattered trust between us. I would prefer to pretend that I didn't know but I can't pull that off, not now. This situation pales any of the other difficulties we have had in our marriage.

By the time I arrive home, I have reached an intense state of anxiety. His car is already in the garage.

. . . .

Bucky is in the dining room when I open the back door. His voice is cheerful but he is concentrating on his pocket watch and seems to be concerned. "Hey, sugar plum, are you just now gettin' back from Richmond?" He walks through the kitchen door and sees my face. "Mary Frances?" He puts the watch back in his pocket. "What's wrong?"

I say nothing and do not look at him. Instead, I push past him and go through the doorway and take a seat at the dining table, staring straight ahead. I can't bring myself to say any of the words that I rehearsed in the car.

Bucky pulls out another chair and sits down, watching me closely. I open my pocketbook and take out the certified copies of the birth certificates. I look at each until I find the one I want. Without a word, I hand him Corinne's birth certificate.

He reads it. His face flushes. He mutters under his breath, "That damn nigger." He looks at me, his eyes bulging. "That goddamn fucking nigger bitch." His voice quivers with rage, "She wasn't supposed to say anything to anybody. How did you get this?"

"Don't you ever talk that way! Don't you ever use that language around me! Ever again!" I have raised my voice in anger and now take a deep breath, collect myself, look at him intently and feel the intensity in my eyes. "It's true, isn't it?"

He jumps up from his chair, waving the birth certificate. "This was supposed to be sealed. We made a deal with her and she didn't keep her bargain. She'll pay for giving you this!"

He paces. Back and forth. Back and forth. He breathes deeply, trying to regain control. Finally, he throws the certificate on the table, muttering the same expletives under his breath.

His anger calms me down. "No, she won't. She was also surprised. She thought it was sealed also." I reach over and pick up the document. "I found it at the Department of Vital Records when I searched for your birth certificate. It's a public record."

Realizing what I have just said, he stops suddenly and frowns, the veins of his temples throbbing and his voice seething. "You … you talked to her? Angela?"

"Yes." I fold the certificate and put it back in my pocketbook. "She's not at fault. I think there was an error when the computer records were converted to a new system."

He glares at me, wrath raging in his voice. "How did you find her?"

I realize that I am in control of this conversation and this gives me power as I stare straight at him. "The phone book. She lives in Richmond. She never married."

"What else did she tell you?"

My mind races back to my lunch with Angela. "Bucky, I want to hear it from you. This is the type of thing a husband tells his wife …" I wait, not taking my eyes off of him, "… before they get married." A power that I have never experienced before seems to drive me. It has no definition, no words, but I can feel it. It is the power of honesty.

He leans against the doorway to the kitchen. He takes the watch out of his pocket again, holding it carefully and turning it over to examine it. His demeanor changes and I see the excessive contriteness of a politician caught in a lie as he becomes evasive. "There is great value to traditions … to knowing what is expected of you and knowing who you are and what your place is in society." His voice becomes whiny. "She didn't tell me until after it was born." He sounds like a victim. "She wasn't fair with me. She should have gotten an abortion but she was trying to shake me down. You know how they are."

"Bucky, it's a girl named Corinne not an 'it.'" I decide that he is testing how much I know, and I'm not going to buy into his story. "And my understanding is that Angela did not contact you at all … you called her, and that's when she told you, and then your attorney voluntarily showed up with a checkbook." I feel like a defense attorney who has just forced the chief prosecution witness to confess in the style of Perry Mason.

"Is that what she told you?" He raises his tone as he places the watch in his pocket and walks back into the dining room. "Did she also tell you why she didn't get rid of it?" His voice quivers. He sounds unsure of himself, like he has just been disarmed. "They do it for the money. Black girls have babies as an easy way to get money." He is being Bucky again and he is on the offensive.

"I really doubt that; the money is never enough." I hesitate and decide to confront him with more of the truth. "And you've never seen your child, but I have. I met Corinne today. She's a lovely girl, someone to be proud of." I feel strange, like a hunter going in for the kill.

"You ... you met her?" He stammers in shock then reverts back to his victim approach as he begins to pace. "Everybody makes mistakes. I was sowing wild oats, that's all. Young men do that." He seems to be shaking inside. "And we did the responsible thing. We paid her off."

"I grant you that. At least you did that. It's the least that a gentleman does." How did I bring him to this so easily? What is it that he likes to say when he has scored a political victory? "Checkmate" seems to be the word.

"She is black and belongs in the black community," he speaks almost to himself, "and it's best not to have that as part of my family." He goes to the liquor cabinet. Taking out a tumbler, he pours bourbon and drinks it in one gulp and pours a second. Still facing the cabinet, he sighs heavily. "So, it's finally out." Returning, he bends down and leans across a chair back. His back is arched slightly and his arms extend over the chair, glass in hand. Sweat is on his brow. He takes a sip then speaks with an air of confidence. "So, what are you going to do?"

"Bucky, that's not the right question. The correct question is what should *you* do?"

He looks at me, trying to judge what I will ask of him and finally responds, "I'm not going to meet her."

"Why?"

"They'll be after more money."

Emphasizing each word, I speak slowly with an even tone. "I don't think so. Anyway, they don't want to see you."

In spite of himself, he is offended. "Well then, what *do* they want now?"

"Nothing. They didn't come looking for you, remember? I found them. Angela was very gracious, and Corinne was charming. But, I'm more than a little angry with you because you never told me. You lied to me."

"Mary Frances … you never asked. You simply made an assumption about me." He begins to find his old style. "And boys will be boys, you know." He finishes his drink and firmly puts the glass on the table. "Looks like this was all for nothing then. Didn't make any sense for you to contact them, I guess." His eyes mock me. "So, why'd you go do a fool thing like that? Why didn't you talk to me first?" He tries his standard line, "What's the matter with you, Mary Frances? You're not acting like you should."

This time, I don't buy into it. Slowly rising, I face him directly across the table. "Is it a wife's responsibility to ask her husband if he has fathered any other children? Bucky, what do you think I should have done?" I exaggerate a shrug. "I ran across a birth certificate with my husband's name on it and it's not my child."

"You could have talked to me first. You don't go blabbing it all over, trying to find out everything you can. This is Washington, you know."

"I think the right order would have been for you to tell me about it a long time ago so that this conversation would never have happened."

He is sarcastic as he stands erect on his side of the table and faces me. "Okay, so let's say that it's a long time ago, and I come to you and say 'Mary Frances, somethin' I gotta tell you.'" He throws his hands up in the air and pretends to be confessing. "I fathered a black bastard before we met." His tone changes. "Now, exactly what are you gonna do?" He points his finger. "I'll tell you what you would do, you'd kick me outta here on my nice little behind faster than water runnin' downhill, we would have never gotten where we are now, and you woulda missed out on all of this."

"You don't give me very much credit do you? I'm married to you, remember? We are in this for better or for worse." I raise my arm with the bracelet. "'Together, we will soar with the eagles' … is this what you had in mind?" I gather up my pocketbook with the prize evidence now inside. His paranoia strikes me as absurd.

Starting to walk out of the room, I face him. "We'll never really know how I would have handled it, will we? I wasn't respected. My right to make my own decision about this wasn't respected. You took it upon yourself to do my thinking for me. I'll thank you not to do that again."

I turn my back to him.

11. BETTY SUZANNE

"Katherine, I need help. I need to talk." It's the next day and Bucky and I are avoiding each other. We went to bed with hardly a word between us, and in the morning he tells me that he has an early meeting and will catch breakfast downtown.

"What's the schmuck done now?"

"Please, I'm serious. It's not something I want to talk about over the phone."

Her tone changes. "Okay, you're on. What are you doing right now?"

"I'm available. Can we meet somewhere?"

"I'm attending the opening of a new art exhibit at the National Gallery for Women in the Arts, Thirteenth and New York Avenue. Meet me there in an hour. We can have lunch at the Willard Hotel."

"This has to be as friends, best friends. You can't be a reporter."

"It's that good, is it? Okay, you have my word. You can trust me."

Katherine is waiting for me at the front door. The Women's Museum is housed in a wedge-shaped, 1905 building that was once an elegant theater. I have not been there since the restoration and

278

opening of the museum in 1987. Standing at the ticket window, I act as if nothing is wrong. "Tell me about the exhibit."

Katherine seems to understand. "I've seen the exhibit book. It's a little known Spanish woman from Mexico who did fantastic surreal work, Remedios Varo. She died about thirty years ago, and this is the first major tour of her work. She's fantastic, but has never received her just due. You'll like it, I think."

Although the lobby is impressive with its pale yellow, gray, and cream-colored, turn-of-the-century elegance and grand staircases, I barely see it as we walk toward the elevators at the narrow end of the wedge. After the door closes, Katherine says, "My notebook and pencil are put away. I'll be ready to listen when you're ready to talk."

Katherine has always been my closest friend and confidant and for all of her New York brashness and Washington cynicism, she is still very genuine and the only person I can turn to now, but I still can't put my feelings about the Richmond discovery into words. "Let's see the artwork first. I've never been a great fan of surrealism."

The doors open on the third-floor special exhibit hall. I'm immediately captivated by a large and very magical visual image entitled *To Be Reborn* in shades of browns and oranges, showing a nude woman emerging through torn wallpaper into a small, mystical room deep within a forest. Looking into a chalice, she sees a reflection of the crescent moon. A placard next to the painting describes Varo as a painter of intense metaphorical imagination whose paintings tell of women gaining lightness and wisdom in their mystical journeys of self-discovery.

A good turnout for the exhibit, mostly women, mingles in the room but it doesn't feel crowded. In the background, several musicians play gentle classical music for the opening. Soft lights and the quiet mood soothe me. Moving from one astonishing painting to another, we blend with the crowd and comment on the central themes of women's mysticism, emotional movement, and self-discovery. The vivid colors, evocative, dreamlike images, fantasy, and attention to minute detail suggest a powerful imagination unbridled by normalcy. I am fascinated with this unexpected escape from my concerns and at times, feel myself blending into the pictures and becoming the adventuresome, seeking women on the canvases. "I thought you would like this ... I'm glad I had the opportunity to invite you," Katherine says after we have absorbed several of the paintings.

Feeling lifted from my troubles, it seems easier to talk about them. I find a bench in the middle of the room and sit, withdrawing from the crowd. Katherine follows and sits next to me and turns slightly, folding one leg under the other in a casual manner. She is offhandedly holding her museum brochure and looking at me. Emotionally and physically, I feel slightly apart.

Looking straight ahead, once again I focus on my troubles and feel the tension in my shoulders. "I went to Richmond yesterday."

Katherine says nothing.

"I went to get a copy of Bucky's birth certificate for his passport application."

Katherine's head tenses slightly and she pays more attention. I've talked about our trip over the months.

"I ran across something else."

"Which was ...?"

I reach into my pocketbook and take out a sheet of paper and hand it to her. "Another birth certificate. Bucky fathered a child when he was in college."

She takes it almost unconsciously and reaches over and hugs me. "Oh, Mary Frances." A moment later she studies the document, "Are you surprised?" Her tone is soft and gentle.

"I thought he would have told me."

"Does he know that you found out?"

"Yes, I couldn't keep it a secret."

"What did he say?"

"He thinks it's unimportant because the child is black."

She turns back to the document. "So, a shvartzeh? Our Bucky had an affair with a black woman?"

"Yes." I pause for effect. "In fact, I met her."

"You did what?"

"I called her up and had lunch with her."

"Good girl, I'm proud of you." She has a questioning tone. "Did this little affair happen before you were married?"

"Yes, while he was in college. I also met the child."

"You did?" She's amazed.

"She's a girl. In law school, very beautiful."

She whistles under her breath. "Way to go." Grabbing my arm in a chummy way, she says, "Okay, champ. Tell me everything you did."

"Walk with me." I get up from the bench and examine the paintings again, but this time I barely see them. Katherine links arms and we slowly walk the rest of the exhibit, talking in hushed tones about Bucky, Angela, and Corinne. I am reminded of the many times in my life that Katherine has walked with me and we have talked. My heart is heavy as I tell her the story, but it lightens as I share my burden.

Finally, we leave the museum and walk three blocks to Lafayette Park across from the White House. The sun warms us, there is no breeze, and the air is crisp. Few tourists are around. A group of protesters with signs chants in a circle near a guard post, and several homeless people with their shopping carts have congregated under a tree. We buy hot dogs from a street vendor for lunch and continue to walk until we reach the Bernard Baruch bench near the statue of General Lafayette. Our conversation is mostly about my reaction to Bucky's past, but I also tell her about meeting the Devereauxes again. She is pleased that I have reconnected with them.

Sitting on the bench, Katherine's mood changes from her softness in the museum. Once again, she adopts the tone of a big sister. "My dearest friend, if I held a mirror up to his face, would you really see Bucky?"

"What do you mean?"

"Would you see who he really is, or would you see the person that you think he is? This may be your rude awakening to a different side of Bucky. Look," she says, "he's a fallible human being, he's male, and he's a politician. That's three strikes right there. He grew up in the South, always striving to be the privileged rich kid that he wasn't, but he was also a spoiled only child. He has been coddled and comforted all his life and has gotten his way, no matter what."

"Yes, but ...."

"Mary Frances," she leans forward, intently, "in spite of the fact that I am a Washington journalist, I am not always cold and arrogant. I understand these people here in Emerald City. In my profession, we make politicians into mystical wizards then send Toto in to pull back the curtain and reveal them for who they really are." She laughs at herself. "My difficulty with Bucky is that he was once a very decent person with great and honorable ambitions, but he has adopted a public identity that he now believes to be real; he has fallen for the common deceit that is Washington and he has lost his sense of what is right and wrong. He's your husband and I love you as my dearest friend, but ...."

"Katherine, what's happened to my marriage? What should I do?"

She is pensive for a few seconds. "I can't answer that question. It's your decision."

"Renee Devereaux asked me questions the other day about my life and I didn't like my answers. There were so many things that were important to me when I was younger. I haven't lived the life I wanted to live or accomplished what I wanted to do."

"You're still young." Katherine's eyes twinkle. She shrugs, "You can't do them now?"

"I'm Bucky's wife. My whole life revolves around him and his career. I can't do what I want to do if it conflicts with his needs and his ambitions."

"You're sure?"

"Katherine, how could I? I'm not me anymore. I'm not the decent and honorable person that I was when I went to New Orleans. Besides, I did something horrible that makes me as bad as Bucky."

She looks at me with wide eyes, waiting for an answer.

"When Renee Devereaux invited me for dinner, she really invited us, Bucky and me." I gulp, and continue. "Bucky has been very racist lately. He really doesn't like it that I am pursuing my interest in Emmaline, so I was afraid. I knew he would be polite to the Devereauxes, but I was afraid that he would be angry with me for rekindling my past. It's a connection that he doesn't like. So I, well, I made excuses for him and never even told him. I just went by myself. What I did was just as wrong as the way he has been behaving. I accommodated his racism. That's what I've become, too."

She looks at me thoughtfully. "How do you feel about it?"

"I didn't have room in my heart to be bigger than Bucky. I made a judgment about the Devereauxes based on the color of their skin. I hate myself now."

"You're still dear, noble, idealist Mary Frances, aren't you? And I still love you for it, by the way." She puts her arm around my shoulder and looks across at the White House. "I think your vision of an ideal, color-blind society still sluggishly lingers out there somewhere on the edge of never-never land. Maybe it will happen; maybe it will just end up as something polymorphous." She chuckles and stands up, taking my hand and gently tugging. "But, you're still Pollyanna, and you will always be Pollyanna. Come on. Where should we go next?"

We begin to walk again. "I don't know what to do. My marriage is too important to me to just throw it away. Katherine," I stop and turn to her, "how important can I make this?" I answer my own question, "I have to change things. Bucky has to change, too."

"How?"

"Well, first, we have to start being more honest."

"That's a good start. So, what's the first thing to be honest about?" She thinks for a minute. "Has Betty Susanne been told about her sister?"

"No. I don't know how."

"Still taking care of him, aren't you? Telling Betty Susanne is Bucky's job. It's time for him to grow up and be responsible for his actions."

"You think he should tell her?"

"Absolutely, and soon."

"She's coming home for spring break next week."

"There's his window of opportunity."

We walk along New York Avenue to our cars as we continue to examine my options and opportunities.

· ·

As a result of my discovery, the tension between Bucky and me remains strained. He works late several days in a row and I don't have an opportunity to talk to him. When he comes home the evening before Betty Susanne is due, I stay up and catch him as he walks in the kitchen door. "Bucky, we need to talk."

"What now? You been snooping around and discovered something else about my past?" He walks past me and heads toward the library.

"No." I follow closely behind.

He angrily switches on a light, throws his briefcase on his desk, and turns around abruptly. "Then what?"

"Betty Susanne needs to be told about Angela's child." I lean against the doorway, intentionally forming a barrier.

"Why?" He stands erect, tense with anger. "What concern is it of hers?"

"They're sisters, whether you like it or not."

He ignores me, reaches for a cigar, and lights it. As he exhales, he says, "No fucking way. If every time this kind of thing happened they called a family reunion, no one would know what family really is." He stops to take out his pocket watch. He opens and closes the gold cover twice without looking at the face. "You and Boopsie and I are a family. Period. That's it. No black bastards."

"Bucky, people don't think of children that way anymore." I look him squarely in the eye, slowly walking toward him with my

285

arms crossed in front of me. "Think about the situation. Someday someone somewhere will find out, and you don't want a reporter to be the one to tell Betty Susanne about her sister, do you?"

His hooded eyes glare. "You been talkin' to that bitch Katherine again? You keep your goddamn mouth shut around her, y'hear?"

"That's not the real point. The real point is that you have another child and your daughter has a sister."

"I don't know why she has to know. I don't know why anyone has to know. It stayed a secret for twenty-four years. Besides, a whole mess of black kids have white fathers. It's not such a big deal." He brushes past me, goes into the parlor, and picks up the newspaper, turning sarcastically, "But we'll get the damn record sealed again if it'll make you happy."

"Face the facts, Bucky, I found it. Someone else could easily find it. And, for someone with your ambitions, it could make a difference. It's not the racial mix of the child … it's the existence of the child and the fact that you concealed her. It's better to tell the truth now than to have secrets. You should never give someone something they could use against you. You want to rise politically, don't you?"

He rolls the newspaper and pounds it against the fireplace mantel. "Woman, don't lecture me about politics. I know how to play this game. There are more secrets in this town than you will ever want to know. And, they are far worse that this little situation."

"I don't doubt you for a minute. But think of it this way: In the end, who should be the one to tell our daughter?" I look at him squarely. "I will, if you won't."

He pounds the newspaper two more times as if he is striking someone. "The fuck you will," he shouts. "If you are going to force my hand, I will, but I will in my own way and in my own time." He turns and glares. "By the way, we had to put Grace on a big case today. You're so good at snooping, you don't need her." He turns and points the newspaper at me. "And, Mary Frances, I won't forget this. This is not how to treat a husband!"

I ignore his threat. "Will you tell Betty Susanne when she is here?"

"When the moment is right, and not before."

· · · · · · · · · · · · · · · · · · · ·

The next evening, we go in silence to the train station and wait on the platform for her.

"Boopsie, baby, you've added something!" Bucky tries to touch the ring in her eyebrow before taking her luggage as she gets off of the train. She pulls away as we walk down the outside platform and into the lobby of Union Station. I silently roll my eyes when I notice that her long, straight hair is now purple. She is wearing a leather collar with large rings on it, a black, mesh blouse over a black teddy, a leather mini skirt, mesh stockings, and clunky boots with thick soles that make her look much taller than she is.

"Daddy, don't call me that. I'm not a kid anymore. I'm called B. S. now, you know, like people who are called by their initials?" She turns to me, with attitude. "Hello, M. F."

"I'm not M. F., Betty Susanne. I'm your mother." I notice her black nail polish and lipstick but say nothing. I cringe because my daughter's awful appearance is a bad reflection on me.

"Oh God, not that mother thing again. That's so gauche."

Bucky playfully interjects, "We're not gonna worry about what you call us, we're jus' glad to have you come home." He moves in between us and gently links arms. "How about if I take my two favorite ladies to dinner?"

"Great idea, Dad. I'm dying for a beer."

"Betty Susanne, you know you're not old enough." I'm still the mother.

"Oh, you have no idea. You are so passé." She turns from me to Bucky and grabs his hand in a childlike manner and heads toward the elevated restaurant in the middle of the lobby. "This one, Daddy."

We ascend the circular stairs to the restaurant area and choose a table. Bucky and I each have a glass of wine with dinner, and I insist, over her objections, that Betty Suzanne have a soft drink. Partway through the meal, she suddenly reaches over and takes her father's wine glass and has a sip.

"Bucky ...."

"Oh, Mary Frances, lighten up. It's only a sip of wine." He turns to Betty Suzanne, almost joking, "Boopsie, you know you aren't supposed to do that."

She gloats at me while she takes another sip, puts the glass down, and turns to Bucky. "Yes, Daddy."

The rest of the evening is uneventful. When we go to bed, I suggest to Bucky that he say goodnight to Betty Susanne, hoping that he will keep the promise he made to me.

When he comes to bed, I look at him, "Well?"

"It wasn't the right time yet." He pauses with a long look. "It's not a good idea to push me."

I wonder when the right time will be.

Betty Susanne sleeps until noon then disappears and comes in late on Saturday night. We're surprised when she pushes open the kitchen door early the next morning.

"Mornin', Boopsie," Bucky says, "you look like you had a rough night last night."

She trudges in, wearing a long, black T-shirt, and collapses into her chair. "Oh God, Daddy." She turns to me, raises her eyebrows, and changes her tone to one of disdain. "Coffee?"

"Whose picture is that on your shirt?" I try to be pleasant as I get up to pour the coffee.

"Where have you been, don't you know anything?"

"Boopsie, show your mother a little more respect."

"Yes, Daddy." She makes a point of standing up, stretching out the shirt and saying, "It's only Sid Vicious—one of the most famous punk rockers ever." She sits down with her coffee and stirs it with great intention.

"That thing on your eyebrow comes out doesn't it? You won't be needin' to wear it to church," Bucky says.

"Oh, the public thing again." She looks directly at me. "The ladies social club meeting on Sunday morning." She mimics with an accent, "'Good morning, Miz Jones, how are you this fine mornin'? Who shall we gossip about today? Whose reputation shall we destroy because her daughter is wearing a ring in her eyebrow?'"

Bucky chuckles quietly, "Little girl, you go on upstairs and put on somethin' decent and take that thing off of your face."

She gets up to go, sarcastically turning at the door. "Can I bring a book? We take our Bibles don't we? How about *Life, the Universe, and Everything*? Doug Adams is my Jesus." She doesn't wait for a reply and the door slams behind her.

"Your daughter is such a brat." I try to ease the tension with Bucky.

He makes an exaggerated shrug, "Moi? She's just like you were. Isn't it the same as your 'little Northern mistake' attitude?"

I go cold and stare at him, saying flatly, "You're the one with the Southern mistake, aren't you? Betty Susanne has a sister walking around out there that she needs to know about."

He stands up and walks to the coffee pot with his back toward me. Turning, he points to me and his tone is firm. "She's not family, y'hear? Gettin' a little African poontang doesn't make it family. I told you, don't push me. I'll decide when the time is right." He takes his coffee and leaves.

Staring in the direction of the door as it closes, I say aloud, "Fathering a child makes it family." I finish my coffee, wondering how I could possibly connect with Betty Susanne during this visit, given her attitude.

When I go upstairs to get ready for church, I am surprised when she borrows a black dress from me. Bucky grimaces at her final outfit but doesn't say anything. She still wears the mesh stockings and thick-soled shoes but she has taken the ring out of her eyebrow. I don't think he notices the skull on the long necklace, and I decide to leave it be.

Sunday services go well and our neighbors pleasantly greet Betty Susanne as we arrive. Bucky's approach is tolerance and forbearance rather than anger when he realizes that Betty Susanne is reading her book in church. Afterwards, we decide to go to an Andy Warhol exhibit at the Corcoran Gallery and have dinner at Georgia Brown's. Betty Susanne continues to play off of her father and treat me badly and I have to bite my tongue often.

Monday, she disappears with a friend and we don't see her until late.

Tuesday morning she comes downstairs after Bucky has left for work. Still groggy, she silently falls into her chair. "Morning, Mom."

It's the first time she has called me "Mom" since she arrived, and I'm pleasantly surprised as I look up from my coffee. "Morning, dear. What would you like for breakfast?"

She mumbles, "I don't care, anything."

"How about your favorite, apple pancakes?"

"Sure." She gets up and goes to the sink, takes a bottle of aspirin from the cupboard, and pours a glass of water.

"Don't you feel well, honey?"

She's a little surly. "Oh ... it's nothing."

I reach for the Bisquick and spoon out enough for the batter, grab an apple out of the fruit basket, and begin to chop. While the griddle is heating, I pour orange juice for her, take syrup, milk, and an egg from the refrigerator, and ponder what to say as I begin to beat the mixture. "How's school going?"

"Oh, man, it's a bitch." She says nothing more while holding her head in her hands, elbows sprawled on the table.

"It would have been nice if you had brought a friend home with you. We would enjoy having company." The griddle is hot enough, and I pour the batter.

"You wouldn't want my friends here."

"Darling, any of your friends would be welcomed here."

She looks straight at me, pausing for effect. "You're sure Daddy would let the black guy with the pierced tongue sleep with me?"

"Betty Suzanne Andrews!" My spatula clanks on the edge of the stove as it drops. My first thought is of Bucky sleeping with a black woman, but I can't say anything as I regain my composure and distract myself by lifting off the first pancake. "I don't think your daddy would let anyone sleep with you in this house." Putting breakfast on the table for her, I pour more coffee, leaning against the counter as we talk.

"That's so fifties." She butters them and cuts off a big bite with her fork.

"I'm not exactly fifties and I realize that things do happen. Whatever you do, I hope you are being responsible about it. It's still the woman who ends up having the baby, so she's the one who has to look out for these things."

She stares at me, takes a couple more forkfuls, and says, "In some kinds of sex you don't need to worry about getting pregnant."

I have to stop and think about what she is implying and mentally shift to a very uncomfortable subject for me. "Are you talking about homosexuals? Those men get AIDS. That's punishment for their behavior. It certainly does not apply to you."

"Mother. I don't think you really know what you're talking about. It's a disease that is killing a whole lot of good folks. I personally know people who have died." She stops suddenly. I see tears swell in her eyes and a blank stare come over her face. "My roommate's sister died two weeks ago. She got it from a blood transfusion." A tear leaves her eye. She wipes it away. "It's not a punishment. There's nothing morally wrong about getting AIDS. Even if being gay is something that you can't abide, other people don't live by your standards. They live by what's right for them, not you." Her face falls into her hands and she sighs heavily with her pain.

Reaching over, I touch her on the shoulder. "I'm sorry darlin'." Her hand comes up and grabs mine. Her sarcastic shell falls away and a hurt child emerges. I put my cup down and hug her while she cries for her lost friend. While she is crying, I remember my tears and grief for Susan, and accept a hug back from her.

She finally resumes eating her pancakes. I clear the other dishes and begin to put them in the dishwasher. When her sensitive moment seems to be over, I begin, "I had an interesting thing happen a couple of months ago."

"What's that?"

"I met an old woman in a nursing home and I believe she was my mammy when I was little and lived with my real mama and daddy." I tell her about meeting Emmaline on Christmas Day and the subsequent visits. I tell her that I believe my real mother was responsible for taking Emmaline's child away from her and how I am trying to find the child. I talk about my trip to Richmond and the confirmation of Emmaline's address on Melody's birth certificate, but do not mention Angela and Corinne because of my promise to Bucky. I conclude with my feeling of frustration about how to find the living daughter, the one I believe is Melody.

Betty Suzanne wipes her remaining tears with a napkin. "Do you really think your mother would have done that? The ol' wicked witch maybe would have, but do you think your mother was like her?"

"I hope not but this makes me wonder, and by the way, don't talk about your grandmother that way." I pour more coffee. "Bad things like that did happen back then. I want to find Melody so I can reunite them and make up for whatever my mother did." I walk back and forth as we talk, cleaning up the kitchen.

She stares at me, wincing. "That would have been really cruel of your mother. Reuniting them won't make up for forty years."

"An apology, even a late one, is better than nothing. A lot of cruel things happened in the South before the civil rights movement. I never told you how I was involved in civil rights, did I? Times have changed a lot but I'm still proud of my small part in it."

She asks warily, "I can't see you involved in that. What did you do ... does Daddy know?"

"Yes, Daddy knows. He still teases me about it. He thinks it's a joke, a Southern white girl working on a black issue. My best friend in college, Susan, well, in fact, she was my roommate, she was black ..."

"So ... what's the big deal about having a black friend?"

"Well, it was significant then. That didn't happen much in the sixties. So, anyway, my first summer at college I went to Louisiana with her and worked on a voter registration drive."

"That sounds like a League of Women Voters thing. That's not a big civil rights issue."

"It was then. A lot of things were done to prevent blacks from voting, and they had to fight hard just to register. It was an amazing experience for me."

"That's ancient history."

"It doesn't feel like ancient history to me ... Susan was killed the second summer we worked on the voter registration drives. I was there and it was a very personal loss for me."

She stares at me. "You've never talked about that before."

"I know. I couldn't talk about it. I came home and became what Aunt Beatrice wanted me to be. Then Bucky and I got married, and these aren't stories that your dad likes to hear." I pause. "Daddy doesn't know this yet, but I saw Susan's parents a couple of weeks ago. They've moved to Washington, and I saw his name in the paper and contacted them."

"Cool. Keeping secrets, are we?"

"Under these circumstances, yes, at least for now. I'm sure it will come up soon enough." As the conversation and morning wears on, Betty Susanne and I decide to go shopping in the Georgetown Park shops on M Street a few blocks away.

We are unable to agree on any clothing purchases, either for her or for me. I begin to count the number of times I hear, "Oh, Mom, puh-lease, not that!" and she laughs when I tease her about it. Interspersed with the shopping is more discussion about Emmaline and Melody, as well as questions about my involvement in the civil rights movement. Our afternoon reminds me of when Betty Susanne was younger and we would designate a "girls day" and spend the whole day having manicures, getting our hair done, and doing other feminine things. It's the first time in several years that we have been able to meander together and keep pleasant company.

On the way home, we walk past a row of shops on a small side street. "Hey, look," Betty Susanne says, "why don't you hire them to find Melody?"

I look back to where she is pointing. It's a glass door leading to a staircase sandwiched in between two shops in an old two-story building. The name on the door in old-fashioned script is "Marco and Daniel Perelli, Private Investigators." Pausing, I respond, "I like that idea. Let me think about it."

"Don't think, do," she says, turning around and opening the door.

I follow mechanically. We walk up the narrow staircase to the second-floor office. It smells musty and the walls are gray. The carpeting on the stairs is threadbare and the stair risers creak. The light fixture on the landing is missing two of its three globes.

Betty Susanne enters the office first. A middle-aged woman sits at an old, wooden, secretary's desk staring at a computer screen. The glow from the screen lightens up the dark room and shines into the woman's face.

"Need something?" she says curtly. Her dark beady eyes flick between the screen and us. A large, Italian nose dominates her face and is emphasized by the smooth starkness of her pulled-back, salt and pepper hair. Her mouth is stern and her lips thin.

"My mom wants an appointment."

"Does your mother speak for herself?"

"Sometimes." She turns to me. "Mom?" I step around her and face the receptionist.

"Yes, I want to hire someone."

"The boys are out now. Come back Thursday at ten." She turns back to her intense scrutiny of the screen, oblivious to our presence. When we don't move immediately, she turns back. "Well?"

"Oh, nothing." I turn and leave behind Betty Susanne.

. . . .

I return to the detective's office at the appointed time. It feels strange to me to be doing this, and I realize that I have two topics to discuss with him. On the one hand, I have no idea how to find Melody Powers and it seems logical to hire a detective, but I feel totally out of my culture and upbringing to be dealing this way. My second topic scares me. I no longer trust my husband to be truthful with me and need to find out more about his past.

Mr. Perelli ushers me into his office and offers coffee, which I refuse. I'm not sure what to think of him and feel apprehensive. He is taller than I am but not as tall as Bucky. His build is heavier, his complexion is southern European, and he walks with a slight limp. His suit is rumpled. Not too much, not sloppy, but he reminds me of Colombo on the TV show, without the trench coat. There are two chairs in front of his desk. The entire office is perfunctory, non-descript, colorless—not fancy, not trashy, just perfunctory. He directs me to a very businesslike, beige, upholstered chair where I sit, stiffly.

He leans forward, puts his left elbow on the desk, and rests his chin in the palm of his hand, observing me during a long pause. His expression is slightly sarcastic. "What can I do for you, Mrs. Andrews?"

"I need to hire a detective."

"You've come to the right place." He searches my face. "Planning a divorce? Need some evidence?"

"No, no, nothing like that."

"Well then, why don't you tell me?"

"I need to locate someone and all I know is her name and date of birth." I reach into my pocketbook and pull out Melody's birth certificate and hand it to him.

"Why are you looking for this ... um ..." he refers to the certificate, "... this young lady known as Melody Powers?"

"Let's see, how do I explain this to a stranger?" Hesitating, I feel nervous and know that my story will sound strange. I speak rapidly. "I met this old woman in a nursing home a couple of months ago, her name is Emmaline Powers. I believe she was my mammy when I was a child. She had two children, Melody and another one named Missy. One of them died, I'm not sure which one, probably Missy, and that might have happened somewhere in the Carolinas, and the other one was taken away from her. Emmaline's a little incoherent and I've had a hard time understanding everything exactly, but she told me that someone took one of her children away and made her sign some papers. I think it was my mother who made her give up her child. After all these years, Emmaline is still very upset about it, and I want to try to find that child if I can." I say everything almost in one breath, and stop to see his reaction.

"Okay, and by the way, you can take it a little slower." He gives me a toothy grin, hoping I will relax, then takes out a yellow legal pad and begins to write. "Missing person. Good place to start, the mother is guilty of doing a bad deed, daughter wants to make amends. Tell me everything else that you know and why you aren't talking to your mother."

I tell him my history. I tell him what I know about my early life, about my parents, the hurricane, and my adoption. I tell him about meeting Emmaline and how she recognized me, what she has said, about Martha's hints, and about the song that Emmaline sings. I tell him that Beatrice might know something but won't talk about it, and how I got the birth certificate. He takes notes.

When I finally stop, he has three pages. He leans back in his chair and flips the pages back and forth as he asks questions: "Did you search for Melody Powers here in D.C.? Did you search for Missy Powers anywhere? What makes you think Missy is the one who died? Tell me everything, every single thing you have done to find Melody Powers?" I answer his questions.

"Okay," he finally says, "here's what I can do for you. I'm an ex-cop, got injured on the job. I have more resources than you and I can use my connections. I can tap into a lot more than you can but I can't guarantee anything. It's a crapshoot, plain and simple. For all you know, Melody is the one who died or she lives someplace far away, or maybe she moved, got married, and changed her name. Who knows? You also have the situation that papers were signed. Sounds like an adoption to me, so the kid, whoever it was, has a new name. Adoptions are often sealed. There are ways around that, but that takes time."

"Sounds a bit foolish doesn't it?"

"Not necessarily, but it's not a cakewalk. There are some agencies that we can check for adoption information. I can do an investigation and either find her or give you a good report telling you why I can't." He thinks a minute. "But we're going to start with a couple of assumptions. They may be wrong but we have to start somewhere."

He makes notes as he continues. "Assumption One. Two babies … one birth certificate. Poor black woman living in Richmond who says one kid died. Kid could have been born dead or she had a miscarriage but in her mind it's still a child to her. Or it was born at home, died, and was never reported. That's only speculation."

He makes a two and circles it. "Your mammy had a child with her at some point when she was taking care of you, one kid was alive then. You were big enough to play ring-around-the-rosie with her … maybe two, three years old."

He makes a three and underlines it. "Your parents died in a hurricane when you were five, so this incident of taking the child away happened sometime between, say, your third birthday and before the hurricane."

He makes a four then a dash. "Next question—were there any stories written about your parents when they died, newspaper articles, stuff like that, something that might give a clue about their lives? Some major change in their situation maybe?" He makes a question mark.

"No. I've never seen their obituaries. Beatrice doesn't like to talk about them."

He stares, his eyes gleam. "I wonder why? Are there any family secrets?"

"No. I'm not aware of any, nothing that would apply to this."

"Your father was a lawyer ... any unsavory clients, any questionable practices?"

"I don't know anything about my parents."

"Think about it ... maybe start by digging up their obituary or get me something about them."

"Okay."

When it feels like we have finished discussing the Melody Powers case, he looks at me as if he is drilling holes. He says nothing. I don't get up to leave. Finally, "Is there something else?"

"Uh, yes."

"... and ...."

"I have another situation ... this embarrasses me a little."

He flips the paper on his legal pad. "Lady, I've heard them all, nothing surprises me." A callous grin comes across his face and his eyes gleam. "Husband has a mistress? You want to know who she is?"

"No ...." I hesitate, not knowing how to delve into my private life with this stranger, "... well, it's a little along that line. When I was in Richmond looking for Melody Powers' birth certificate, I discovered something about my husband's past that is upsetting." I tell him how I discovered Angela and Corinne and about meeting them.

His demeanor changes and he softens. "Mrs. Andrews, may I call you Mary Frances?" I nod. "And I'm Marco. Does he know you found this out?"

"Oh yes, I confronted him when I came back. He didn't deny it. He couldn't. He just considers it old history." I sigh deeply and look up to the ceiling. "I've never discovered anything like this before. I didn't think he had ever lied to me. He claims it wasn't a lie, that it was my fault for not asking."

"Ah yes, the error of omission. Husbands love that one."

"My problem is that I now feel a lack of trust. When the trust goes, the marriage is the next thing to go. I still consider that I am married for life, but I have to deal with this. I need to find out if I can trust him again."

"Mary Frances, very few husbands are trustworthy. I know."

I notice that he is not wearing a wedding band and wonder if he is one of them. Privately, I wonder if he will tell me the truth or if he will protect Bucky. "I want to know if there is anything else. I want to know if there are any more skeletons in the closet. How do I find this out?"

"We start with a background check."

"Okay." I feel horrible. My hands are clammy and I'm sweating.

"You need to tell me the basic facts, and I will check them out. I can check all my sources on this one, too. Public records, criminal records, school records, stuff like that. Maybe we go to several surrounding states and see what we dig up."

"Will he know I am doing this?"

"No. A basic background check is relatively easy. If we end up expanding it, maybe he will find out some day, but you will already know everything you want to know by then."

I have to ask the obvious question. "Can we keep this very private … no reports, no phone calls except me calling you? I will pay you in cash?" I feel like I'm in a sleazy Hollywood movie.

"We can do it any way you want."

I gulp. I can't believe I'm contemplating investigating my husband. I can't believe that I don't trust him anymore. My heart aches. He waits. I breathe deeply then say, "Okay, what do you want to know?"

He asks about Bucky. I tell him Bucky's given name, birth date, social security number, place of birth, his parents, and his schools. I tell him about Bucky's career and political connections. Marco knows who Bucky is but assures me that it will not affect his investigation. In fact, he may be able to socialize with him through his political connections and get a better sense of what should be addressed.

I leave the office two hours later with a heavy heart. I had thought that turning Emmaline's situation over to a detective would give me a sense of relief, but that sense is overwhelmed by the agony of needing to investigate my husband, thoughts about his infidelities, and questions about his past.

On the morning after the visit, I go to the Vital Records Department for the District of Columbia and perform a search under Emmaline's name for the birth of her second child, Missy. I also check the records under the name of Melody Powers, hoping to find a marriage or children. I find nothing and feel discouraged when I report back to Marco.

. . . .

The week is reasonably successful, especially the times that Betty Susanne and I are alone without Bucky, but Bucky never talks to Betty Susanne about Corinne. On Friday, we have a family dinner because she is returning to New York on Saturday, and I make her favorite Southern meal ... Virginia ham, redeye gravy, grits and cornbread with honey, along with a favorite dessert.

As I'm serving the peach pie, Betty Susanne asks, "So, Mom, what did the detective say?"

Bucky interjects before I have a chance to reply, "Detective? What detective?" He stares at me, his eyes glaring.

I am dumbfounded and feel like a doe caught in headlights. My mind flashes on the investigation of Bucky and I wonder how Betty Susanne found out, then I remember that I also hired him to find Melody. Before I can collect my thoughts coherently, I am interrupted.

"Mom's got a secret?" The expression on Betty Susanne's face is puckish and sly as she carefully lays down her fork and turns to me. "You didn't tell Dad?"

"Tell me what? What's this all about?"

She turns to him, her eyes glistening. "Mommy hired a detective to find her old mammy's child." She sounds like a child who is tattling.

"What the hell you want to go and do that for?" His silverware bangs on the table and his voice is raised. "This nonsense is gettin' way out of hand."

"It's not nonsense and it's not getting out of hand," I address him directly, not minding that I have also raised my voice. "It's important to me and you know it. I want to find her daughter. It's the least I can do since you haven't been very helpful."

Betty Susanne mimics, "It's the least she can do, Daddy. She thinks she's being noble."

Bucky is angry, glaring at me but talking to her. "She's sticking her nose where it doesn't belong."

"I am not. I'm doing the right thing. I'm treating her with respect." I bite my tongue, trying to ignore all of the times Betty Susanne has played her parents against each other, and expecting the worse.

"No you're not, Mom," Betty Susanne is sarcastic. "That's not being respectful, that's you looking out for yourself. That's all you're doing. You want to find your ol' mammy's child because you want to feel good about yourself and you want to exonerate your dead mama. You're not interested in that ol' woman for who she is."

"What are you talking about? I most certainly am too interested in her." After our long conversation and mother-daughter closeness earlier in the week, I am astonished. Flashbacks of the times that Bucky has insulted me in front of her crowd my thoughts, and I cringe at her learned behavior.

"No you're not. You're only interest is in what she can do for you. How she can clear up your feelings about your mama. You're just as bigoted and narrow-minded and intolerant as Daddy. At least he's honest about it."

"I am not bigoted." I'm insulted. "I am one of the most tolerant people I know. I work alongside black folks all the time. I have friends who are black. I invite them to my house."

"Tolerant? Mommy dearest, you use them to make you look good. It's Daddy's politics; it's your charity case. It's the same thing. Throw them a crumb, keep 'em happy. You're both so goddamn transparent ... the great plastic politician and his plastic wife. You still harbor ill will against people who are different from you. You don't really care about them as people. Look at the way you feel about people with AIDS!"

"What's all this about a detective?" Bucky has been left out in the sudden tirade.

I ignore him. "Betty Susanne, you've got no reason to talk to me this way. I changed along with the times. I am not bigoted anymore."

"The hell you're not. You think it's the superficial stuff ... who you are seen with, who you invite to your house .... Bigotry is what you feel about all kinds of people who are different from you.

It's all the same … like how you feel about gays … and lesbians … and old people … and people who don't look the way you think they should. You're bigoted if you judge anyone by superficial stuff!"

Bucky slams his fist on the table and stands up. "Goddammit, tell me about the detective!"

"Oh Daddy, shut up," Betty Susanne condescends, then angrily turns back to me. "… and you," she blurts, "you think you are so full of charity. You're a hypocrite, and I am so utterly tired of all you hypocrites here. Washington sucks."

Betty Susanne and I are so full of anger that we can no longer speak to each other, and I turn to Bucky, strongly asserting my position both in tone and in voice. "I hired a detective to find Emmaline's daughter because I couldn't figure out what to do next," I turn to Betty Susanne, softening my voice while still feeling angry, "… and Betty Susanne, I'll start with you. I believe I accept you in spite of the way you make yourself look. And I would accept your friends if you were to bring them on down here."

"Oh yeah?" She becomes testy. "How much would you accept them if they were gays and lesbians?" Suddenly she jumps up from her chair and paces to the other side of the dining room. "How much would you accept me if I told you I was a lesbian and slept with a black woman? You'd shit and you know it."

Bucky sits down. "Boopsie, cut out that nonsense. Faggots are sick people, and you aren't one of them." Bucky turns to me, angrily. "I thought I told you to stay out of that ol' woman's life."

Betty Susanne defiantly stands against the wall with her arms folded. My attention stays with her and I ignore Bucky.

"You'd be surprised to know how many of your fine, upstanding citizens are what you call 'faggots,'" Betty Susanne yells at her father. "Who's to say what's normal?"

Defiantly glaring at Bucky, I respond, "If you brought your gay and lesbian friends here, they would, of course, be welcomed as your friends." I pause and look directly at her with a softer tone and a questioning attitude. "Darling, are you trying to tell us something?"

"What I'm telling you is that you would tolerate them as my friends but you would never see them as people, just plain ol' people who do it a little bit different, and that's the same way you see blacks. You'll be bigoted until the day you die, and you can't help it. You have no idea what the real world is like outside of your goddamn elite circle."

Using his hands to push against the table, Bucky gets up from his chair again. He has gained control of his demeanor somewhat. He shows political savvy as he calms down and gently walks over to Betty Susanne. "Come here, Boopsie." He puts his arm around her and slowly leads her back to her chair. "This country is made up of lots of different people, and we each have our own society. The blacks have theirs, the gays and lesbians have theirs, every other group has its niche, and we have ours. Some folks think assimilation is not a good idea." He holds the chair while she sits again.

I think of Corinne and speak firmly. "And some folks assimilate and don't like to admit to it."

Bucky knows what I am talking about and glares. "And some folks don't know when to leave well enough alone."

Betty Susanne turns around and stares at Bucky, noticeably picking up his intensity. She turns to me, realizing that Bucky and I are in the middle of a non-verbal communication that she doesn't understand. Our eyes remain locked as she resumes her childish sarcasm. "Is there some assimilation I should know about?"

"Bucky, it's your turn."

His eyes gather a dark cloud. He deliberately backs away and walks to the door. When his hand is on the doorknob, he turns to me, ignoring Betty Susanne. His voice deepens into a threat. "Mary Frances, I'm warning you for the last time, let it go." He opens the door and leaves.

"Mom, does Daddy have a little secret, too?"

"Right now, darling, this is something between us and it's something we have to handle ourselves."

Betty Suzanne leaves the next morning, not knowing about her sister.

12.   A JOURNEY BACK

"Bucky, I'm going to take a short trip." I place Bucky's sausage, eggs, and grits on the table in front of him, pour coffee for both of us, and put bread in the toaster.

"Where do you wanna go, sugar plum?" It's been a few days since Betty Susanne has gone back to Columbia University and we have resigned ourselves to a polite distance between us.

"I'm going to the place in North Carolina where my mama and daddy died in the hurricane. I want to see where it happened and find their obituary." I've decided to follow the detective's directive.

"Why would you want to do somethin' like that? That hurricane was a long time ago. All you're gonna see is a sleepy little town on an island somewhere. There won't be anythin' for you to find, and obituaries don't tell you a thing." He unfolds the *Washington Post* and hands me the style section.

"That's not the point. I feel like I need to go there, that's all."

"Well, I don't have time to take you. It'll have to wait." He folds the sports section and picks up the front page.

"I'm going by myself."

He stops, looks at me, and puts down the newspaper. "Mary Frances, you've never gone anywhere by yourself. I don't think it would be a good idea."

"Then this is going to be a first." The courage in my voice amazes me. "I've thought about it a lot and I'm leaving this morning. I expect to be gone two or three days." I butter the toast and give him a slice. "I believe you have a dinner meeting tonight and a couple of fundraisers over the next day or two, so you'll be fine."

"Is this about that girl, Corinne? You goin' lookin' for more about her?"

"No, I've put that behind me. I'm still very disappointed with you, and I'm going to insist that you do right by her when the time comes, but this is something different."

"Is it about that old woman, the nursing home one?"

"No, this is about me, who I am, what happened to me. I need to reconnect with my past."

He stares at me, puzzled. "You know what happened to you." He is matter-of-fact, but doesn't say anything else and goes back to his newspaper. Munching on his toast, he finally says with amusement, "You mean to say you're gonna depend on the kindness of strangers to take care of you? That's not very wise. You'll call me when you run into trouble, won't you?"

"Of course." In my mind, I am sarcastic, but I play the role for him.

I pack a small bag after he leaves for work. It's true that I have never gone on a trip alone. I realize that it's a scary thought for me, but I'm not about to tell him that. I'm forty-five years old and feel embarrassed that I haven't stepped out and taken any risks since college. Walking over to Borders Bookstore on M Street, I buy a map of North Carolina and a tourist guidebook and study them over a café au lait in their coffee shop. I began to wonder myself what is driving me. Maybe he's right; maybe it's foolishness. But then I remember that Angela's parents always encouraged her to face her fear and I know that I have decided to face my fears and the ghosts of my past. Right now I don't care what Bucky thinks, being foolish is sometimes okay. Besides, I was brash enough to announce my intentions, so now I have to go through with it.

By eleven o'clock, I'm backing my car out of the garage.

I also know that I want to find some kind of tangible evidence about my parents, such as an obituary in the local newspaper archives. I want to walk on the ground where they last walked and see the island where I survived for three days alone.

Driving across the Key Bridge into Rosslyn, I pick up the GW Parkway to Highway 395 and then Interstate 95 heading toward Richmond. This part of the trip is very familiar to me; it's the drive after Richmond that still seems frightening. Just north of Richmond, I stop at a gas station because it occurs to me that I should have the car checked, but I'm not sure what to tell the mechanic because Bucky always handles the cars. Feeling at a loss for the right words, I finally convince the station attendant to take a general look under the hood. My car, a Pontiac, is only two years old so I'm certain that I shouldn't worry, but I know this is a ritual before leaving on a road trip.

Interstate 95 is the main route to Florida going all the way through Virginia and North Carolina as it heads south. As I pass the turnoff to Richmond and take the bypass, I begin to have thoughts about what I might discover on my journey. Initially, as I drive, I watch the spring growth along the highway and notice the advertisements, but as I contemplate the issues stirring inside my head, the road becomes more of a tunnel, leading me into a different consciousness. I wonder what will emerge at the other end. I feel moments of exhilaration, and in between, I am frozen with fear and dread as I seem to take a risk for the first time in many, many years.

I contemplate what I really know about my parents. Hurricane Hazel happened in August 1954 while we were vacationing on Goose Creek Island, a remote area along the inner central coast of North Carolina. A bridge was washed out while we were attempting to flee, and our car was wrecked. My parents' bodies were found washed ashore. Somehow I survived for three days. What I really lost is what every other child takes for granted ... the security and knowledge of knowing my parents. Beatrice's childhood stories were always centered on her, not my mama or daddy. She never wanted to talk about them, and they still loom as mysterious shadows to me.

As I drive, I realize that I have given my right to make decisions for myself over to Bucky and, indeed, I am the complacent wife that Katherine, Patricia, and Effi describe. I have played the fool for Bucky's amusement, and I have not seen myself as worthy of respect. Perhaps discovering Bucky's other child is forcing me to see my reflection as it really is. Where I once sought refuge in my role and it protected me, being a passive wife now feels like an unwanted crutch.

Who am I? What change must be made? What do I want? become my internal mantras reverberating from the road as the wheels turn. *There is something I must know, something missing, and I don't know how to find it.* There is a big crack in my crutch now and I have nothing to lean on. As I drive down the Interstate in Virginia, I feel that I am indeed falling down without a safety net, falling apart. At times, my body shudders with these thoughts, and

I feel exhausted with their weight, but the tears appear and they trickle down my cheeks as the heaviness is carried away, drop by drop. For miles, I feel as if I am crossing an emotional frontier.

My husband is not the person I have always thought him to be. I envisioned him as the perfect spouse because I loved him, and he is not. I wanted to see him as courageous, brave, and independent, but instead, he has become a student of greed. He has become an opportunist, using popular words and efforts to further his own selfish interests. Where once I believed in his integrity and desire for justice, I now discern someone who plays only to win and to win at all costs. Instead of having a driving passion for leadership, I see him as someone who merely positions himself for power and control. I become weak with the weight of this realization and park for a time in a rest stop so that I can cry with no restraint.

By late afternoon, I reach the turnoff on Interstate 95 in North Carolina that takes me east on Route 64 to the small town of Washington on the north side of Pamlico River. The road becomes a two-lane country road, shaded by tall trees just beginning to show new growth, with occasional potholes from the previous winter that haven't been fixed. I begin to notice old farmhouses, modest newer buildings, and deserted produce stands. I think about the last trip my parents took down this road and try to resurrect memories of my life with them, but nothing comes to me. I wonder what it was like on that trip, how many times they drove down this road, and why they came here during hurricane season. I arrive in Washington two hours after leaving Interstate 95.

Driving into town, I don't know where to go. I stay on the state road, follow the signs to the visitor's center, and wonder what to do next. I don't know how to find a respectable place to stay at the last minute. Bucky and I always made hotel reservations through a travel agent, and we have never taken a trip that was not prearranged and highly scheduled. Gazing around, I panic. I worry that everything will be booked even though it is early April and traffic on the road is sparse. Alternatively, I fear that I will not find a place where I will be comfortable and will feel secure.

Suddenly, I notice that I am about to cross the bridge over the Tar-Pamlico River and that it will take me beyond the town. Quickly, I turn left at the last intersection onto an old-fashioned Main Street. The street is lined with traditional, old, brick commercial buildings that look largely deserted. Several blocks further down, the buildings turn into Victorian houses with wide front porches, crisply manicured lawns, and shuttered windows. Early spring daffodils and late crocuses fill the window planter boxes and garden flowerbeds.

A quiet dusk has fallen, and I need to eat dinner. I spot a restaurant sign pointing to an elegant old house on my right and pull into the parking lot next to it. Drinks are being served to several people at outside tables on the wide veranda of a traditional, white, turn-of-the-century home with thick porch columns. I go inside and request a table.

The restaurant is nearly empty. The hostess is also the waitress. She is a short, plump woman with short, white hair, and friendly smile wrinkles around her clear, button-like, blue eyes. As she seats me near a gun collection on the wall of the parlor, I quietly mention my plight as a visitor to her area and ask if she might recommend a place to stay.

"I'd be pleased." She breaks into a broad smile, speaking slowly with a melodious accent that is very kind to vowels. "Why don't you enjoy your dinner, and we'll take care of you jus' fine."

313

Her voice is soothing. "It's always nice to have stranger stoppin' by, 'specially this time of year."

I enjoy a meal of the freshest shrimp I have ever tasted. Later, when she brings my check, she tells me about two possibilities. "The first is a bed and breakfast inn a short distance into the country, run by a widow friend of mine from the church. It's a nice, old plantation home, and she'll cook you a good breakfast. T'other is a very small hotel on the water's edge along the esplanade, an' you can come on back up here for your breakfast. You take your pick, both'll be right happy to have you."

I tell her that the bed and breakfast place sounds wonderful and ask for directions. She goes to the phone and makes a reservation, then comes back and pours another cup of coffee and one for herself. Sitting at my table, she draws a map for me. For the first time, I notice a plastic nametag that says "Maybelle."

I sense that she is curious about me but is too polite to ask. I decide to tell her about my connection with the area and relate the story of how I survived a hurricane here in this neighborhood, and how I am on a quest to visit the place where my parents died. She was born and raised here, she says, and remembers Hurricane Hazel as a young woman, as well as several others. I ask her why she has remained in the area if it is so prone to hurricanes.

"Why, we wouldn't think of leavin'. This is our home and we like to brag about it." She sparkles and speaks with the tenderness of true conviction. "Besides all of that, we kinda like being isolated. This is our enclave where time has stood still. Ours was the first town in the country named Washington an' we aim to keep it alive. 'Bout every five years, that ol' Tar River down there gets backed up and floods at least to Second Street yonder," she gestures away from the river, "an' we jus' mop up and keep on a goin'. These here old houses on Main Street have seen it all. Some of the old ones've survived clear from before when them Yankees burnt down the town in '63."

"'63?"

"1863. Them hoodlum Yankees came in an' took over the town and looted it, and then burned it down when they left. There's quite a story about it in our little museum. We've very keen about our past here, y'know." She gets up and finds a brochure espousing the local tourist attractions. The brochure focuses on local folklore and speaks about the town's history. She talks about how Cecil B. DeMille and his brother were from Washington, then she tells the story of Edna Ferber, the novelist, who came to the area in 1925 to research a local vaudeville company that traveled the waterways throughout the southeastern coastal region. Her research became the musical *Showboat*.

My new friend, who is in high spirits by this time, pours more coffee and begins to talk about Roanoke Island, slightly to the north, which was the site of the very first English attempt to settle in 1585. She is a natural storyteller and is so enthusiastic about her stories that I can't help but catch her fever. "For four consecutive years, Sir Walter Raleigh tried to establish a settlement, and each time his English ship returned with more people and supplies the previous settlers had disappeared. There is a ghost story about them," she says. "In fact, there are lots of ghost stories about the early colonies, but this here is one of the best ...."

She retrieves a small book on local ghost stories from near the cash register, flips to the right page and continues. "So, the story goes like this ..." and begins to relive the plight of a pilot flying an ol' biplane in the winter of 1919, who thought he saw the ghosts of Raleigh's settlers, and they ended up saving his life. She stops

315

to catch her breath. "So," she says in a very convincing manner, looking me straight in the eye, "he was either in a time warp or the ghosts of the lost colony of Roanoke Island did, in fact, rescue him," she ends with emphasis, "an' he swore by that for the rest of his life."

She gets up to take a check from her last customer and joins me again. Her favorite stories, she says, are about Blackbeard the pirate. "You know who that is, don't you?"

I nodded a hesitant yes.

She must have decided that my knowledge wasn't sufficient, so she proceeds to tell me all about the pirate who carried on his terrorism from the lower end of the North Carolina Outer Banks clear up to the northern part of the state in the early 1700s. He owned several houses in the vicinity with secret passages and tunnels, and there were many rumors about buried treasure. And, of course, she tells me about Blackbeard's fourteen wives and how he hanged one of them from a tree that still stands, and if you get too close to it, you can still hear her screams!

I laugh at her animation of the screaming bride. I am delighted to have found such a charming hostess.

"Oh, he was a sight, too. They say that he was a monster of a man, with real long, black hair and a big, black beard." She uses her hands to emphasize the size of the beard. "They say he was crazy, too, that he would take fuses from his cannons and soak them so that they would burn real slow, and then he would braid them into his hair and beard. So when he attacked a ship and demanded that it surrender, he would stand on the deck with knives and guns strapped to his body and in his belts, and he would light the fuses and would be surrounded by smoke and look like the devil himself! They say that everyone was so frightened of him that they just surrendered and never fought."

"Amazing!" I sip my coffee slowly, totally engrossed.

"But they finally did kill him out on Ocracoke Island, beheaded him, too." With a sense of finality, she gently slaps the table with both palms, saying, "And the lore is that his headless body swam around the ship seven times before it finally died."

My impromptu evening's entertainment has raised my spirits. It is almost nine o'clock when I say goodbye and climb into my car, directions in hand.

My car won't start. It's completely dead. I panic and wonder what to do.

I go back to Maybelle, distressed. "I need to call AAA."

"Why darlin', what's happened?" I explain my predicament. I also think about calling Bucky but hate to be so helpless. "Now, never you mind. We got ways of taking care of folks in this town. It's not called Southern hospitality for nothin'—you know, don't you, that people are kinder here than they are up north." She pokes her head into the kitchen and calls, "Charlie, I've got somethin' to do, so we're closing up." Without waiting for a reply, she goes to the phone and dials. "Cecil, son, it's Maybelle. Hope I didn't get you outta bed … well, that's all right dear, you'll catch it up tomorrow night. How y'all doin'?… an' your mama, how's she?… that's just fine … now, listen here, I have a customer, a visitor from up north, who is having a bit of trouble with her car. I'm fixin' to take her over to Jimmie Sue's place directly, and I was wonderin' if you might could stop by in the mornin' and take a look … no, we're gonna leave it here at the restaurant … that'd be real nice of you. I'll leave the keys behind the counter, just ask the mornin' girl for them. I think that young'un Crystal's on duty for breakfast. Thank you much. I'll check in with you in the mornin'." Turning to me, she says with a twinkle, "I'd be most pleased to carry you up there and pick you up tomorrow."

We transfer my belongings to her car before I have a chance to even think about all the logical reasons why I shouldn't be doing this and leave my car keys behind the counter with a note for the unknown folks named Crystal and Cecil. Driving up the winding country road to Jimmie Sue's place takes about ten minutes. Turning into a circular, gravel driveway, Maybelle slows down and parks under the portico of a two-story, antebellum house with grand columns along the front. By this time, the moon is rising, and Spanish moss hanging from cypress and oak trees casts deep shadows across the lawn. The smell of jasmine lingers in the air and the rasp of a cricket breaks the silence. When she answers the door, Jimmie Sue has a freshly picked vase of spring tulips in her hand. Younger than Maybelle by a few years, she exudes a warm charm as she tells us that I will be the only guest for the evening, and she has just finished dusting the best room for me.

Maybelle bounces in when the door opens, introduces me, and explains all of my circumstances, including the reason for my trip. She amuses me, and I grin at the thought that most of the town will know about me before the next day is over. It makes me feel very accepted and special. The three of us bring in my luggage and belongings. Climbing the stairs, she whispers to me that Jimmie Sue is definitely giving me a good discount because it's the off-season, and she is also not charging me the rate for the best room.

"Isn't this charming!" Maybelle exclaims as we are led into the room. The Queen Anne-styled, antique cherry canopy bed has a matching dresser and armoire along the walls. The bed is draped in shiny, white cotton with big lace ruffles. The featherbed is also covered in white and there are six pillows. The bed is high off the floor, and a small, cherry wood stepstool graciously invites someone to climb into bed. The walls are covered with cornflower blue–striped wallpaper that matches the thick, blue carpeting. The room is filled with small antiques, artifacts, and collectibles.

Maybelle and I drop my belongings onto one of the two white, wicker chairs. Jimmie Sue places the vase of tulips on a small table between the chairs that fill out a corner conversation area. Everywhere there are pillows in a floral print against a blue background. Drapes are made of the same floral fabric and a dressing table has the same fabric for a skirt. I notice a door into an adjoining bathroom that has a matching decor.

"Now Jimmie Sue," Maybelle says, "let's just all scoot on downstairs and have a cup of tea before I leave." The teakettle is already whistling as we sit down. I explain to them that I would like to look up old newspaper records of the hurricane, and they direct me to the largest newspaper in the area, the *Sun Journal*, in the town of New Bern, south of Washington about an hour. As she departs, I convince Maybelle to let me walk down to the restaurant in the morning because I need a good stretch for my legs.

Early in the morning, Jimmie Sue brings me a sumptuous breakfast on a tray and pours coffee. I feast on orange juice, oatmeal pancakes, biscuits with gravy, sausage, scrambled eggs, and grits. Finally, I put on walking shoes, pack my map and guidebook, and set off down the road.

The clouds have settled into billowy, white clusters, the early morning sun is bright, and the air is crisp. Light green new growth graces the trees, and squirrels scamper energetically along the low-lying branches. A country stillness permeates the tranquility as I stretch and take a deep breath of clean air. As I begin to walk along the road, heading toward town, I am alive with enthusiasm for the day's plans.

I reflect on how good it feels to take risks, trust strangers, and have it all work out. I also imagine telling Bucky about my adventure so far and realize that he would be upset because of my rash behavior. I hear him telling me that it's not a good idea to trust folks I don't know, and I should never have let my car out of sight. I sigh and breathe a short prayer, hoping that the car will be all right.

I'm close enough to the lush growth along the road to examine the flowers beginning to bloom and watch tiny creatures going about their short lives. I stop to watch spiders in the dew and a creeping caterpillar on a leaf stem. I put my finger up and he crawls onto my skin. I talk to him gently. "Soon you will spin a flaxen shell and hide away from the world, much like I have. Do you always come out of your cocoon? Are there caterpillars who don't come out?" I gently stroke his back. "Could I come out of my cocoon? Am I a beautiful butterfly?" Gently, I place him back on the stem and continue my walk, musing about the caterpillar and his cocoon. Walking along, breathing in the fresh air, and hearing the quiet of the country, I am lost in a flight of fantasy words and an ethereal image of a butterfly woman rising from a cocoon. I find great pleasure in the simple act of walking along a narrow country road by myself.

Reaching town takes no more than thirty minutes, and I have no trouble finding the restaurant. True to his word, Cecil is bending over the engine of my car. "Mornin', ma'am." He lifts his head up and touches the dirty baseball cap twisted sideways on his head of straw-colored hair. It's just enough to imitate lifting his hat as a courtesy. From the looks of him, he's probably the last person in the world that I would trust with my car. He's a tall scarecrow, barely old enough to be called a man, with a fair complexion, freckled face, and a protruding Adam's apple. He has on the dirtiest coveralls I've ever seen. My heart skips a beat. How could he possibly know enough about cars?

"Uh, ma'am ...."

"Yes?"

"Would you mind doin' somethin' for me?" He sounds as if his words are strained through a bowl of stone-ground grits.

"Not at all, what do you need?" In fact, I am scared to death of having him touch my car and am wondering how to get out of this predicament. How can I call AAA without seeming rude?

"I'm too dirty to sit in there and try the key. Would you mind?" He hands me the keys.

Thankful for the opportunity, I climb into the driver's side and place the key in the ignition. This is my chance—it won't work and that will be my excuse. I'll just thank him kindly for his trouble and pay him a few dollars before he messes things up too much. I quickly turn the key.

The engine turns over smoothly.

"That's what I thought." His thin, angular face has a very broad grin and his pale blue eyes shine. "It was just a loose connection to the battery. You must hav' come on down some of our fine country roads. Shook you up a bit didn't they?" I'm stunned and I'm also very thankful that I didn't act on my first impression of the boy. As he puts his tools away and lowers the hood, I ask how much I owe him. "Shucks, ma'am, I ain't been here long 'nough for two fleas to spit at each other. Besides, my Aunt 'Belle said not to take any money off of you. It's just a kindness. All you have to do is pass it along."

"Pass it along?"

He places his tools in the back of a very old pickup. "Yes'm." Pausing as he opens the door, he says, "You pay me by doin' somethin' nice for the next person you see who needs help." He swings his lanky body in, touches his hat again, and starts his engine.

"I'll remember that." I feel slightly awkward, but pleased, and wave as I remember this as a version of Martha's old rule on being charitable and kind. "Thank you ever so much." As he drives away, I go into the restaurant, seeking Maybelle. She isn't there, so I leave a message that I will be back in the evening.

Pulling out my map once more, I determine that the easiest way to get to New Bern is the two-lane U.S. 17 going south, and head in that direction, crossing the old drawbridge into town well within an hour. New Bern is a larger river town, located on the Neuse River. My guidebook tells me that the town was settled in 1710 by Swiss and German immigrants, became a thriving port for the nearby plantations, and was the first colonial capital of the Carolinas. Equally important, I suppose, it was the birthplace of Pepsi Cola. Stopping at a gas station, I ask directions to the newspaper office and find it on Wellons Boulevard without trouble.

The newspaper, the *Sun Journal*, is housed in a modernized old brick warehouse with three stories and a large attic. I stop to read a brass placard near the main entrance indicating that the building, known as Havens Warehouse, was built in 1830 and served as a main waterfront storehouse for a thriving trade with the West Indies prior to the War Between the States. It was here in New Bern, the placard says, that the first state printing press was set up and the first book and newspapers were published in the Carolinas. Inside the front lobby, I find a display of newspapers from the 30s and

40s, describing the heyday of the New Bern Bears of the coastal, semi-pro baseball league. Babe Ruth's visit to the area for a hunting expedition captured a front page that is now displayed in a case on the wall, and the baseball that he autographed for one of the local boys is prominently encased in glass.

Sheepishly, I ask the young receptionist how I would go about researching the hurricane of August 1954. He explains how old newspapers are transferred to microfiche film and directs me to a librarian in the archives department. The librarian patiently listens to my request, goes to a tall metal cabinet with many drawers, searches the labels until he finds the right date, opens the drawer, and pulls out two small square canisters. "It'll be one of these here," he says with a quiet drawl, hands them to me, and points to the microfiche machine on a nearby table. "Use the one on the right, it works better. There's an instruction card if y'all needs it."

I stare at the contraption. It looks like a cross between a large computer screen and an old-fashioned film projector. The screen hangs suspended over an area that seems to be for the film and there are gadgets on each side, but I haven't the foggiest idea how it works. Standing there, canisters in hand, I wonder if I should ask for help. No, I decide, I can figure this out and resolutely walk over, read the instructions, then pull the film lead out from the first canister and attempt to thread it through, imitating the pictured instructions. When I turn on the machine, the canister spins and the lead wraps back up inside. I try again, comparing it carefully with the sketch. Same thing happens.

The librarian has been watching me. He walks over, smiles down at me, and tells me that I have the canister on the spool backwards and it would work better if I reversed it. He asks if he can show me how, and I gladly move my chair aside to let him. I watch in awe as he expertly threads the film. Newspaper pages from early August 1954 begin to appear across the screen. He shows me how to push the film around to get an image of the article I want and how to focus with the levers and dials.

The first article is a front-page discussion of the anticipated impact on the local schools of the new *Brown v. Board of Education* decision that was handed down by the Supreme Court barely a month before. The headlines are clearly biased toward a Southern white point of view. The librarian is a young black man in his twenties. The article interests me because I grew up in that time period and it affected me personally, but I'm embarrassed to read it because I think it might seem racist on my part. I wonder what he feels about reading articles like this. I wonder if I should say something like, "Gosh, you weren't even born then" or "My, how times have changed ...."

Instead, I say, "I think the hurricane was about the twentieth."

"In that case, we need the second canister. Do you want to try doin' it, ma'am?"

"Uh, sure." I remove the first, pick up the second, thread it correctly, and begin to search the pages for the date. "Amazing! I think I have it now. Thank you for your help." He walks back to his post.

I feel eerie as I get closer to the story. The front-page articles talk about the approaching storm that is traveling up the coast of Florida. The weather service forecasts that the tropical storm will dissipate by the time it reaches South Carolina. The next headline is "Without Warning, Storm Gains Momentum." Then another, "Tropical Storm Declared a Hurricane!" And finally, "Hurricane Heads This Way!" A photograph shows people fleeing from the

Outer Banks, and the front page is covered with information about routes to shelters. "Hurricane Hits!" The pictures show houses torn from their foundations, uprooted trees, stranded people. I read these stories as if I was there and feel the tension.

Finally, I find a story about the death of my parents, along with a photo of the wrecked car. It reads:

> PROMINENT VIRGINIANS KILLED IN STORM
> James Kerwin Roche, along with his wife, Margaret Barksdale Roche, prominent citizens of Richmond, Virginia and the only son of a Virginia legislator, were duck hunting on Goose Neck Island and were unable to leave as Hurricane Hazel suddenly approached. Mr. Roche was a partner in the law firm of Roche & Heath and comes from a long established family in the Richmond area. As the Roches attempted to flee the storm, their car was blown into a telephone pole at the same time that the drawbridge was washed out. James and Margaret were thrown out of the car and swept away by the 120 mph winds. His body was found about a mile up Goose Neck Creek on the north coast of the island, and her body was found nearby. The Roches' only child, a daughter, who was small enough that she was not thrown out of the car, survived them. Red Cross volunteers found her wandering on the island three days after the storm subsided. She was placed in the care of an aunt after being examined by a physician, who declared her to be none the worse for the experience.

I am in awe because I've never seen their obituary before. I read the story three times and stare at the black-and-white photograph of the remains of the car. It looks like an old Cadillac from the first year they appeared with tailfins. The car had hit the telephone pole on the right side by the rear passenger seat, causing an ugly vertical crease. Pieces of grotesquely twisted chrome jut into the air around the crease. The windshield is shattered. Both the driver's door and the rear door on the left side hang ajar. *I was in that car*, keeps reverberating in my mind. Closing my eyes, I shiver and hear hurricane-force winds whirling around. I imagine my parents in the front seat at the moment of impact. I try to see myself alone in the back seat.

Then it strikes me: *Something is missing. Something is wrong with this story.* I ponder my life as a child with Beatrice and George. *Families like ours didn't go on vacation without a mammy to tend the children. My mammy would have been with us on this trip. Where was she? Why wasn't she with us? Was she left behind in Richmond? Why? Could she have been Emmaline? I was five years old. How could I have survived for three days? Did anyone ever ask that question? Something is missing from everything I have ever heard about the hurricane story.*

The librarian must have noticed my lengthy stare. He comes over again and sits on the chair next to me. "Is anythin' wrong?"

I point to the article. "I'm the little girl in that story."

He takes off his glasses, peers closely at the screen, and reads the obituary. "Wow! That must have been something, being in a hurricane. I bet that story brings back some memories, don't it?"

"I don't remember any of it." My voice is flat as I blink back a vague sensation of being in the storm. "I came here because I'm trying to reconstruct what happened." I take a breath and point out the obvious. "My parents died there."

A respectful silence interrupts our conversation. "Ma'am, I'm sorry for your loss." Then he quietly says, "Is there anything else I can help you with?"

"Uh ... can you make a copy of this for me?"

He gladly does it. I thank him and slowly walk out of the building.

It's lunchtime, but I have no appetite. I had thought to drive over to Goose Creek Island in the afternoon, but the reality of my parents' death drains me. I decide to simply drive around New Bern while my emotions dissipate. I am enticed to stop when I smell freshly baked bread and notice a crowd gathered around a bakery. The place is packed, and the inventory of pastries, cookies, and muffins is extensive. I select two and order coffee to go. Driving around, I read several small historical markers and observe a number of colonial-era homes. From a distance, I glimpse an elegant, brick, Georgian-style mansion surrounded by formal gardens. The signs point to "Tryon Historic Palace, Museum and Gardens." Normally, I love touring traditional sites such as this, but today my heart is not into it.

A few blocks further on, I spot an old cemetery. It suits my mood. The clouds have become gray, and a steady breeze blows. The name Cedar Grove Cemetery is carved into the distinctive, marl gate which circles above the entrance. Parking the car, I take my pastries and coffee with me.

A short, marl fence follows the perimeter of the cemetery, and a profusion of Spanish moss–covered cedars mingles with the monuments and statuary. Just inside the gate, I can barely read the statistics on a headstone for a revolutionary war captain. As I walk, fungus-covered headstones and statuary emerge from the overgrowth of shrubbery, vines, and weeds. Some headstones are no longer standing. Others are worn to the point of being almost or completely unreadable. I pick my way along a dirt path down the center. I feel a sense of serenity that soothes the shock of finding the newspaper article and seeing the crashed automobile. Many of the inscriptions mark the resting places of children, young children, who are mute testimony to the harshness of life. I stop to read a small obelisk with the names of nine children in one family that all died within a two-year span. Behind this simple inscription, I realize, is the story of a mother who suffered more than I could ever bear. My heart melts with compassion.

I find a raised slab under a tree and rest, pulling out the newspaper account and photograph and staring at it. Aloud, I read my parents' names from the article and talk to them the way I did as a child. "James Kerwin Roche and Margaret Barksdale Roche." I pause. "Who were you? Were you like Beatrice and George? Would my life have been different if you had lived? Are you out there in the ether somewhere, looking down on me ... would I please you if you knew me now? Could you tell me who Emmaline is and what she means to me?" I close my eyes and try to imagine being in the old 1954 Cadillac when it hit the tree and shudder with the image it conjures in my head. "We were a family. You left me, and I had to struggle too much. I never found your kind of love again. Wouldn't it have been better if I had died with you?"

My imagination ruminates on my childhood trauma and the tenuous memories of my real parents. If Beatrice and George had been willing to talk to me about my parents, I wonder if it would it have lessened the pain and the searching, or if it would have intensified. A melancholy cloud settles over me, and I sense the mustiness and patina of the precious mythology of who I am. My beginning has always been a mystery for me, much like a spiritual quest that I cannot answer. In spite of the harshness of being raised by Beatrice, I was nourished and cared for by my parents' spirits, which were kept alive by my imagination.

With a deep sigh, the time comes for me to continue my journey along the path. I come across a grassy, circular area with a monument to the soldiers from New Bern. Reading the inscription, I discover that sixty-eight of the Confederate casualties of a battle in March of 1862 are buried here. It's difficult to imagine these men as soldiers. Instead, I wonder about them as local men with devastated families, families who tried to rebuild their lives. I try to imagine myself as one of the widows left behind.

"Which one you kin to?" a voice asks.

I'm startled because I haven't seen anyone, and it feels like a nearby tree is talking to me. I turn and see a craggy old man sitting on a stone bench near the Confederate monument, partially hidden by the tree, both hands resting on top of his cane. He wears a faded old Confederate cap. The face under it looks ethereal, and I can't imagine his age, but his eyes have a clarity and a sharpness that penetrates. He is small and thin, with hunched shoulders jutting out from his faded overalls. He blends into the shadow of the tree and the overgrown foliage.

"Oh, none." I feel a sense of relief finding someone to talk to. "Are you related?"

"Yep."

I wait for the next question. Nothing happens. I find a grassy spot in the weeds and sit down near his feet to finish my coffee.

He raises his shaky right hand in a salute, staring at the monument, not at me. After a long reverent pause, he says, "Confederate Memorial Day is a comin' soon, and I'm here to honor these here men." He points to a crumbling headstone off to the side and speaks with pride. "My grandpappy lies right there. See that name—William Henry Benton? That's my name, too, 'cept I'm a third, William Henry Benton III." His pronunciation is slow and deliberate, and then his tone changes to sadness. "I never knew him. He left a babe in arms, who was my pappy. I come visit whenever I can." He raises his voice. "These here were the truest Americans, let me tell you, and God bless 'em all."

"Why do you say that?" I feel a need to be gentle and compassionate in a way that I was never able to be with Aunt Beatrice. I also feel the kinship of someone who knows his relatives only by a grave marker. "Would you like some muffin?"

He takes the offered half of a muffin, holding it while beginning a proud liturgy that he has apparently spoken often. "This here country was found on the principle of resistin' a central authority." He pronounces "au-tho-ri-ty" slowly with emphasis. "It happened all the time back then, and that there American Revolution was exactly that ... George Washington, he was a Southerner who didn't want to take no crap from the King of England. If'n he knew what happened a hundred years later, he'd roll over in his grave, he'd be so ashamed of them Yankees."

He takes a bite of the muffin and waves to the graves, "That's what these here boys did. They didn't want to take no crap from powerful Northerners who wanted to change the way this country was formed. It's in the Constitution, you know, slavery was. Them Yankees invaded us and murdered our men and raped our women. Then they pillaged our land because they wanted it for themselves. Yes siree. Our way was the American way o' bein', an' I'm still proud to be a fightin' Confederate."

"My great-grandpa was in the war too."

"An' I imagine he gave his life for the sake of defendin' his rights."

"Yes, he did."

"There ain't nothin' better'n that. Robert E. Lee and Stonewall Jackson, them men w'ar outmanned and outgunned, but they still almos' pulled it off. Them's the finest heroes there ever was. They was bold and flamboyant an' a damn sight braver, too."

I sigh at the myth that has grown into a sacred truth and speak carefully. "Slavery was a difficult issue."

"You know somethin'?" He points his finger at me. "It would've changed on its own; it w'ar headed in that direction anyhows. An' it woulda been better that way. It was our right to govern ourselves, and we had them damn Yankees come down here and tell us what to do, jes' like ol' King George tried to do. They weren't no better'n him, 'cept they won where we lost. What happened after the war made things worse. We had a right to make changes in our own way and in our own time."

I knew I would never permeate his point of view. He is in a time warp dealing with a new world that he doesn't comprehend and can't accept, and like so many Southerners, his world is peopled with baffling ghosts from a country that broke away and lasted for only four years. "You know what I think?"

"What's that, young lady?" He seems guarded and defensive.

"I think that if women had been involved in making the political decisions back then, we probably wouldn't have had a war." I pause to observe the surprise effect. "Men have a hankerin' to fight all the time. Women have a different way about them. Most of them, anyways. They're much more prone to workin' things out for the best without causin' a fight."

He is caught off guard and chuckles condescendingly. "Well now, young'un, you jus' may be right. Too bad we didn't have you around back then. We could've elected you president. A pretty little thing like you issuin' the orders woulda kept all those boys in line, wouldn't it?"

Smiling to myself, I drain my coffee, get up from the grass, and bid him farewell. *Well, you almost got it right,* I thought.

Driving back, I reminisce about the old man, Maybelle, Cecil, and Jimmie Sue. The Southerner is an imperfect, conflicted character, but there is a spirit in this land that I love ... a spirit of unique strength and character. It's not the lush, red soil or the fresh, country air. It's not the scent of the trees or the warm sun that sustains. It's a sense of community, a sense of family, a sense of pride in a shared way of thinking, a shared experience, or a shared behavior. We are proud people. Losing the war and being treated badly afterwards intensified our wounded pride. There were big mistakes on both sides. But times have changed, the wrongs have been righted, or nearly so. We're beginning to include all people in our history as they should have been all along, and a sense of loyalty to our enlarged community heritage lingers. Some of us who live here have embraced the changes. Others, like Bucky, still harbor resentment and bigotry in their hearts, even though acceptance of everyone would demonstrate the true fiber of our Christian beliefs.

Feeling a renewed sense of belonging, I stop at Maybelle's for dinner and more charming stories of local color and legends, and later I go up to Jimmie Sue's for a restful evening. As the sunlight fades into night, Jimmie Sue and I sit outside in rocking chairs sharing the warm spring air, a glass of wine, and tales about our lives. I am exhausted from my day's explorations when I finally ascend the wide staircase to my room and gratefully snuggle down into the featherbed and between the crisp sheets.

I awaken suddenly in the middle of the night and need to use the bathroom. The room is very chilly. On my way back to bed,

I am startled by a woman sitting in one of the wicker chairs. I stop, alarmed, and, clinging to one of the bedposts, frightfully ask, "Who are you?"

She says nothing. She is in a shadow, lit only by moonlight filtering through lace curtains. She seems to be tall, young, and is dressed casually in loose slacks and a jacket. She has dark hair cut in an old-fashioned, long pageboy style. She watches me intently, saying nothing.

"Who are you? Why are you here?" My heart pounds. I am frozen with fear.

"You asked me to come." Her voice is quiet but it echoes in the room. "It's been many years since you talked to me."

"What do you mean?"

"We are proud of you," her tone is gentle, "but you couldn't have joined us. It was not your time."

My God! My supplication in the graveyard today ... am I dreaming? Is this my mother? Has the unseen ghost of my past become a reality?

"Mary Frances, I did what was best for you." She closes her eyes and then opens them again, speaking apologetically. "When you know everything, I hope you will forgive me ... forgive us." As her voice fades, so does her image.

"No, don't go." I move around the bedpost closer to her. "Talk to me more. Tell me what I need to know." She disappears. The chill in the room also leaves. I sit in the chair where I saw her image, try to absorb the last remaining rays of her presence, and ponder the meaning of her words. I am unable to sleep again and, wrapped in a blanket, watch the dawn rise from the wicker chair.

In the morning, I am still haunted as I prepare to drive to Goose Creek Island. It is further down on the south side of the Pamlico River just as it empties into the sound, perhaps thirty minutes across the bridge from the town of Washington. I understand that there are two small villages on the island, havens for duck hunters.

As I get close to the island, I discover a modern bridge that rises high above the narrow river that separates it from the mainland. Circling around the exit from the main road heading toward the bridge, I watch a graceful sailboat maneuver under it and realize the reason for the height. Even though this is not the old bridge that I am seeking, my nerves flutter as I begin to cross over it. After cresting the bridge and reaching the land, I see a street sign indicating "Old Drawbridge Road." This has to be it. I turn down the narrow old road to the right, feeling very strange. I am retracing my own history. I am on land that is sacred to me.

A dead end sign begins my passage down this forgotten road, overgrown with neglect and weeds. A few hundred feet further is an old wooden footbridge spanning a small inlet. Rotting logs are strewn around. An old road barrier is straight ahead of me, perhaps another five hundred feet. It has two large, red stop signs and several reflectors. On the other side of the barrier, the ancient asphalt crumbles and drops off along the edge of the water. On the other side of the water, I see where the bridge once ended and the road continued. The remains of a very old filling station are to my left, its roof long missing. Along both sides of the road are a few remaining telephone poles with no wires connected. Some of them are in advanced stages of rotting.

I stop and get out of the car. *It has been forty years since I was here. This is where my parents were swept away and died.* I walk over and touch one of the old poles near the barrier. *Was it this one?* I peer up the shoreline and wonder how far their bodies traveled.

I imagine myself as a five-year-old on this very spot and wonder how I felt. *How long did I stay in the car by myself? Was I frightened? I must have been. How did I get out of the car? Where did I go? How was I rescued? What did I do for three days?* I walk around, feeling dazed, trying to understand. Finally, with reluctance, I return to my car and drive further into the small island town and stop for gas before the drive back to Jimmie Sue's to collect my belongings. Standing by my car at the gas station, I wonder if I came this far when I was five, or did I stay by the old Cadillac and wait for the whole time. *I must have cried a lot. I must have been very cold and wet. I must have had a tremendous amount of courage.*

The newspaper story and my mother's ghost haunt me on the return drive. Being on the island today, and long ago as a child, lingers with me. I have come face to face with the death of my parents. Beatrice and Bucky have always avoided the subject and steered me away from any talk about "the sad, unfortunate event of my life" and always told me to think about the good things, not the bad. Perhaps they were right.

On the drive back to Georgetown, I mull over the experience of visiting the island. I know that much is missing and I need to know more. I decide that I will talk to my friend Patricia, the therapist, tomorrow. She always knows what to do.

· ·

I arrive home in time to fix dinner, but Bucky isn't home and I am unable to reach him by phone. I eat dinner alone and am soaking in the bathtub when he gets in around eleven in the evening.

He comes into the bathroom with a glass in his hand. He has obviously been drinking, probably all evening. He looks down at me, puts his glass down, and intentionally pulls out his pocket watch.

With a mock smile, he opens the cover and stares at the face. "Well, it's about goddamn time you figured out where you live."

I beam at him, ignoring his tone. "I had a really fine trip, and I'm looking forward to telling you about it."

"Where the hell you been?" He puts the watch back in his pocket and picks up the drink.

"Now, Bucky, you're being silly, you know where I was."

"Did you call me? Did you tell me where you were? You coulda been dead for all I knew. At the dinner tonight, everyone was asking where you were, and I was embarrassed that my wife wasn't with me. I couldn't even tell them where the fuck you were." He sounds accusing and awkwardly tries to point with the same hand holding the glass. "Remember, you had a ticket to the dinner, too. I had to sit next to an empty chair. People are gonna start wonderin' if we're havin' problems." He starts to pace in the small space of the bathroom. "A politician's wife always has to be by his side. It's a fine thing when my wife spends more time chasing after old colored people than she spends with her husband."

"I don't know what you mean. I told you I needed to go for myself and not for anyone else, and you coulda told folks that I was out of town, which was true. I needed to see where my parents died." I feel excited again and try to enlist him in my adventure. "I found the story of the hurricane in an old newspaper, and I found my parents' obituary. I went to the island." I stop to digest what he had said. "And besides, there's only been one old woman, and she was my mammy." I sigh, feeling tired of his tirade. "I have a request, dear."

"What's that?"

"I'm finding it offensive for you to keep calling her 'colored.' I think the correct word now is 'black.'"

"Black, African American, nigger, nigra, I don't give a shit. I don't see you calling yourself Irish American just because your daddy was from Ireland. When you and I was growing up, 'colored' was the better word. Now it's 'black' or 'African American' … means the same thing. I don't know why I have to change what I learned jus' to suit them. They're neither black nor are they from Africa. They are colored brown. If anythin', they should be called 'browns' like we are called 'whites.'" He extends his arm as if showing me his skin color. "They're as American as you and me and they don't get it. They live by our rules. This is America."

"Then why don't you treat them like just other Americans?"

"I do."

"I beg your pardon?"

He raises his voice. "I do. They are part of the mainstream, aren't they? The South is the most integrated part of this country and the most racially peaceful. It's not here where they're havin' race riots anymore … it's other places. An' there's no place in America that I know of that makes people ride in the back of the bus, or use a separate bathroom, or drink at a separate water fountain anymore."

"Bucky, it's a lot more than that, more than the symbolism stuff. I fully accept that you know all the socially acceptable behavior, but it's how you really feel that counts. Quite frankly, you're only two shakes away from old-fashioned racism yourself. You're actually a modern-day, two-faced, old-fashioned, bigoted politician, who barely hides behind being civil to folks." I give him an understated grin to tone down my bluntness, trying to flirt as I talk. "You're all smiles and handshaking when you want someone's vote or when you want their money, but you insult these people behind their backs and find fault with them unnecessarily."

He swings around. "And who appointed you as their caretaker?"

Stopping and staring at him, I finally respond. "I'm not goin' to fight with you." I feign cheerfulness. "I'd really rather tell you about my trip."

"Did you run into Benjamin down there?" His tone is sarcastic.

"What?"

"You're a nigger lover. I imagine he would follow you anywhere."

"Bucky, you're drunk. You don't know what you're saying."

"I may be drunk but I know what I'm saying. Any white woman who starts chasing around with a black man is asking for trouble. You know better."

"Who's chasing around with anyone? And even if I were, what difference does it make what color his skin is? And didn't you 'chase around' with a black woman once upon a time? Isn't that what you're really talking about?"

"That's different. I'm a man, some things are expected. Besides, that was her fault. Black girls are like that. They want to get pregnant by a white man, gives them status."

"Bucky, I'm sorry. I don't buy into that. That's the most ludicrous thing I have ever heard. That's old 'Bubba' stuff from a long time ago. When did you ever let a woman be in control and make decisions about anything? Even gettin' pregnant?"

His lower lip pushes out and he pouts. "Why are you doing this to me?"

"Doing what?"

"Goddammit, Mary Frances. You're cuttin' my balls off. You're running all around doin' as you please, not payin' me any mind, making me look like a fool in front of my own constituents."

"Bucky, you're the one who's making yourself look like a fool. You weren't even man enough to tell your daughter about her sister."

He glares at me. His eyes become hateful. "I'll show you what I'm man enough to do. Get your ass outta that bathtub and come to bed. You need to make up for this."

Something shifts deep inside of me. My memory of the rape in Mississippi flashes vividly across my mind. I feel thoughts forming, thoughts that don't have a sound yet, thoughts that I have never reduced to words. For a split second, I see him as the sheriff's deputy, standing above Susan's body, and I feel the paralyzing fright that I felt then.

For the first time in my life, I know that I must say no to him.

Slowly, I sit up in the tub and purposefully reach over to let the water out, brushing the bubbles from my arms, and avoiding his stare. My legs move, almost mechanically, so that I am kneeling. I turn on the tap for fresh water to rinse the conditioner out of my hair. My movement is robot-like. I have done this a thousand times, but it feels like the fibers in my muscles are moving for the first time. My new thoughts are telling me who I am, who I really am. I feel the tingle of warm water splashing, caressing, washing away old pains, old ways of being. My fingers feel my hair and massage my squeaky-clean scalp. I feel a sense of respect for my body, for my self as a person. It's a feeling I have never experienced before.

In slow motion, I rise and thoughts rise with me and form an intention. I feel the intention giving me strength. The thoughts find a voice and begin to silently speak to me, "Be who you are," "Find your strength." Without looking at Bucky, I reach for a large towel and wrap myself, carefully tucking the corner in alongside my left breast. Ignoring him, I brush past and go into the bedroom. Pulling out a dresser drawer, I take out a fresh nightgown.

He sits on the toilet seat watching me move. His eyes have a triumphant glare. "You won't be needin' one of those."

With careful pronunciation and an intentionally even tone, the words in my head speak aloud. "I'm going to be sleeping in the guest room tonight." I feel utterly, completely, and openly vulnerable, but stronger than I have ever been.

He stands and slowly walks into the bedroom. Anger swells inside of him, causing his chest to expand and his skin to flush. It pierces the air. His whole body tenses. He stares at the white satin nightgown in my hands. His arm movements check themselves, and I sense a constrained impulse to fling the nightgown aside and force me into bed. I know that he is almost out of control.

He looks around the room, wild-eyed, taking in the impact of my words. The veins on his neck protrude and throb. His hand clenches the half-filled glass. Beads of sweat appear on his forehead. His right hand slowly rises, and I feel him ready to strike me.

Instead, he flings the glass into the bedroom fireplace, where it explodes. Shards and liquid reverberate back into the room. "You'll do no such thing. You are my wife and you will sleep in my bed."

The moment hangs heavy in the air. For the first time ever, deep within me, I realize how much I am afraid of him. I have lived with the fear of seeing his anger, of having his anger turn against me, much like the deputy sheriff who almost attacked me. I am a peacekeeper because I am fearful. I calm situations down by giving in to forcefulness. I consider backing off. *I must take care of myself.*

I must protect myself. I cannot antagonize him. How bad would it be for me to sleep with him tonight? I have always slept with him. I have always had sex when he wanted it. Wouldn't sex calm him down? Wouldn't it be better to deal with this tomorrow? To talk about it later when he is sober? I am motionless.

His eyes meet mine. The cold, dark gray penetrates. I sense his bigness, his strength, the power of his muscles. I sense his ability to physically force me. But, behind his anger, I also sense fear. *He fears me. How can that be? What am I to him? Really? Who am I in this relationship?*

My thoughts speak to me. They give me an insight that I have never known and I understand Bucky in a different way. *He needs to control me, to be in charge. He is subtle. He is charming and flirtatious. But, he always maintains control. Being in charge, making someone else powerless, is the source of his strength. I have given control to him. I have given him the right to make my decisions, to order me around. I have given myself away.* The voice in my head asks, *Can I change this?* My whole sense of myself is riding on this moment.

For all of his drunken blustering, does Bucky have it within himself to force me into bed? Would he do it, would he damage our marriage that much, or is he bluffing?

I decide to take the risk. "Not tonight." I walk out of the room, turning just before I close the door behind me, feeling my voice quivering, "Goodnight, Bucky."

13. HURRICANE MEMORIES

Early the next morning, Bucky knocks on the door of the guest room and waits for me to invite him in. He carries a breakfast tray covered with a large, white, damask napkin and waits for me while I sit up. Setting the tray down in front of me, he whisks the cloth off with a flourish and reveals two poached eggs on an English muffin and apricot preserves on homemade biscuits. Next to the two coffee cups is a small bud vase with a single, red rose almost ready to bloom. As he gently spreads the napkin over the folds of my nightgown, I can tell that he is freshly showered and can smell the subtle aroma of his cologne. He steps back and performs a theatrical bow. "O' Lady Fair, I should not presume too much upon thy love. I have done that for which I shall forever be sorry. Please forgive this errant knight."

I remain silent. I have seen this before.

He stands, waiting for my reply. With downcast eyes, he fidgets with the fringed end of the tie to his bathrobe. "I don't know anymore Shakespeare right now." He looks up from the corner of his eyes, much like a child. "I'm trying to say I'm sorry."

"Yes, I know."

"What do I have to do to win your forgiveness?"

I look at him pensively, sadly remembering the previous night. "I didn't realize how much of the old South you still had in you."

"Neither did I."

"This is important."

"I know it is."

"I feel betrayed. I always thought you were more progressive. You were supposed to be someone else. Why didn't I see this a long time ago?"

"You're disappointed in me, aren't you?"

"Yes."

"What can we do?"

"I don't know what we can do, Bucky. I think it's something that you have to do."

"I will do whatever you want me to. I love you. You're my wife."

I sigh heavily. "Yes, I know, for better or for worse." I don't know what to say to him as I fidget with my gold bracelet. "Let's think about it." I hand him his coffee cup. "Here, drink your coffee before it gets cold."

He takes it slowly, lingering as his hand touches mine. He takes a sip, puts the cup down, and, sitting on the edge of the bed, breaks a biscuit and lifts a bite to my mouth. His finger stays on my lips.

I feel the electricity between us and the longing. He cups my face and begins to bend down for a kiss. I stop him. "Bucky, no, not now."

"But, sugar plum, I love you."

"I know you do. I appreciate your efforts to make amends. I will give it a great deal of thought, and we will work something out. But now is too soon." I gently remove his hands from my face. "I need to be alone with my thoughts. We have to work things out first."

"As you say, m'lady. I will await your decision." There is a gleam in his eyes, but as he gently backs away, I sense a feeling of confusion. For both of us, the rules have changed and neither of us knows how to play.

. . . .

I arrange lunch with Patricia. We meet at a small deli near my home and buy sandwiches, juice, and yogurt, then walk the few blocks to Dumbarton Oaks Garden, one of my favorite places. Patricia, tall and thin, with her prematurely white hair arranged in a high, loose knot on her head, is dressed in a casual jumper of woven, muted blues. Wisps of hair blow across her face, and she routinely brushes them aside.

Dumbarton is ten acres of thickly grown, formal gardens on the hilly, northern side of Georgetown that was once a private estate and is now a beautiful, formal park surrounding the mansion. Puddles dot the circular, brick driveway and the moisture in the grass is refreshing. Bright pink and red tulips are the first brushstrokes in the living artwork of the landscape. The humidity is high but a slight breeze keeps the air comfortable. It had rained the night before and the early spring buds on the cherry and magnolia trees are swollen with moisture and new life. Few people are in the park, and a feeling of quiet solitude lends itself to introspective conversation and thoughtful moments as we stroll through each garden and along terraces, talking about our lives. I tell her about discovering Corinne and hiring the detective to find Emmaline's daughter. I express my frustrations with Bucky and his anger at the trip I took. We find a stone bench in the rose garden that is perfect for our picnic lunch.

After we eat, I ask the question that is on my mind and the reason for the meeting. "Patricia, you know I don't think much of hypnotism, but do you think it would help me remember something from my past?"

"Hypnotism is very good for that. It would definitely help you remember what your conscious mind wants to forget. Is there something specific that you want to look for?" We have known each other since we were neighbors in Richmond, and I have always trusted her judgment on personal matters. During the seventies, she went to the University of California at Berkeley, became involved with several self-awareness groups in the San Francisco area, and is still avant-garde with her lifestyle. These involvements led to becoming a psychologist and using hypnotism in her practice.

I tell her the details about my trip to North Carolina and show her the obituary. "I don't understand how I survived on the island. I wish I could let it go at that, but I'm bothered by something I can't explain. I can't put my finger on it, and I'm wondering if there is more that I can't remember."

"Hypnotism would help, if you're willing, but I can't promise anything. It's a matter of how much you are willing to delve into your subconscious."

"Will it hurt me? Will I do crazy things afterwards?"

"No, absolutely not. The worst that will happen is that painful memories may surface."

"After the hypnotism, will I still remember them?"

"If you want to."

"Can we try it?" She agrees and we make arrangements for the next day. I spend the night in the guest room again, but this time Bucky respects my decision with no drama.

The next morning, I go to Patricia's home directly across the Potomac River in Arlington, Virginia. We quickly move into her small office adjoining the living room. The room fits her personality, with soft tones of blues and greens, comfortable furniture, several bookcases, and numerous framed pictures of her family interspersed with professional certificates. She motions for me to sit in a reclining chair near the middle of the room. Bright sunlight filters through white lace curtains. Pink and purple azaleas are beginning to bloom just beyond the window. She says gently, "I know the flowers are beautiful, but I'm going to close the drapes to make the light softer." She adjusts the window and sits comfortably in an upholstered chair next to me. "Are you okay?"

"I think so. I'm not sure."

Although I feel great trepidation about the process I am about to experience, a sense of determination keeps me going. We talk about what I want to accomplish with the hypnotism. I tell her that I want to uncover more than what I already know about the accident and how I managed to survive three days on the island. I want to confirm that Emmaline was my mammy. I also want to know more about my real parents.

"We'll take all the time you need; it may not all happen in this session." She is gentle. "Would it be all right for me to play some soft music in the background?"

"Sure."

"I have some very nice nature sounds ...." She rummages through a small stack of CD's. "A waterfall, a rolling sea maybe, here's a rainstorm ... ah, what about songbirds?"

"Songbirds are fine."

Patricia puts the CD in the player, listens for the background music to begin, then adjusts my chair so that I am in a reclining position with a raised footrest. She puts a light blanket over me and tucks it in around my feet. "Most people get chills when they are in a trance."

I begin to hear the chirping birds on the CD.

She continues. "There are three different levels of hypnotic trances. In the first level, you will stay conscious and will remember everything. In the second level, your consciousness lets go and your subconscious takes over, and in the third level, we go deeper into your subconscious."

"How will I know where I am?"

"You don't control it. It's a matter of how much you are willing to get out of the way and let us explore what is underneath. We will begin with relaxing techniques, and I will do a counting process that will take you into a trance. Then it's up to you."

"But I want to remember this. I want to stay awake."

"I always record the sessions, so you can listen as often as you want afterwards. You don't need to be concerned about staying awake. It's more important for you to get to the subconscious levels." She inserts a tape and presses a button on the recorder. "From this point on, everything will be recorded."

"This is it?"

"I'm ready to begin, if you are."

I shift my body in the chair, feeling a womb-like sensation from the warmth and closeness of the blanket. I focus on the songs of the birds and realize that my mental image is the accident scene on Goose Creek Island. I notice that I trust Patricia completely.

"Okay."

She begins. "Close your eyes." Her voice is soft and harmonious. She speaks with an even cadence, "Now that you are in a safe, comfortable position, I want you to take a deep breath."

Her tone is soothing. "Hold that breath and let it out very, very slowly. Once all that air is out, I want you to take another very deep breath, fill your lower and upper lungs, and hold that breath. Now let that breath out very, very slowly, and once all that air is completely out, I want you to take one more very deep and very comfortable breath, and hold that breath. Now, let that breath out very, very slowly, and as you do, you will feel your body begin to relax." She allows her words to sink in.

"Let that feeling of relaxation flow all the way down to your feet. Feel your feet becoming very comfortable and very relaxed. Now, imagine a soft, warm, liquid, white light surrounding your feet. This light penetrates your feet and goes deep into the muscle, deep into the bone. The light brings warmth. The warmth brings relaxation."

I allow her guided imagery to take hold of me. She pauses at the end of each sentence and allows me to hear the music and chirping birds in the background. Each time she uses the word "relax," I feel tension drain from my muscles.

"That wonderful, comfortable feeling of relaxation begins to flow from your feet up to your ankles. From your ankles, the light flows up the muscles of your calves and into your knees, then into your thighs. From your thighs, the light travels up to your hips then to your back, bringing relaxation to all of your muscles. With each and every breath that you exhale, your body relaxes even more, and you feel your body sinking down, deeper and deeper. This wonderful comfortable feeling flows right up over your shoulders and deep into your chest. Your body keeps on relaxing, and you begin to go deeper and deeper into another state of being."

She carries the white light to each part of my body, bringing relaxation and warmth to my arms, my fingertips, up the back of my spine, and over my head and down onto my face. She describes this sensation as letting my body feel like a rag doll. As she utters the words, I feel it. I have never before experienced such a state of complete and total physical well-being. At one point she asks if I am able to lift my arm. I try, but I cannot; I do not have enough tension in my muscles.

"Drift down now, sink down, go deeper and deeper with each breath that you exhale, with each thought that you think, with each sensation that you feel. Even the beat of your heart guides you deeper. Float down to a wonderful, relaxed state. I am now going to count from one down to three. With each number that I say, I want you to allow your body to relax even more. One … relaxing deeper. Two … more and more relaxed. Three … very deep, very comfortable. Your whole body is giving in, letting go, loosening up. Drift down. You feel safe. Peaceful."

She continues to instruct me to go deeper, and she counts again, this time down to five. I still hear the birds chirping. I float in time and space. My fear evaporates, I feel content.

"I'm going to take you back five years at a time. I'm going to ask you to think about events that happened and have you think about people that you knew then. When we get back to when you were six years old, we will go one year at a time until we can find the mammy you are looking for. Are you ready?"

I am barely able to nod my head yes.

"Remember when you were forty. Think about something that happened. Think about a person who was close to you then. Remember what he or she looked like, things that were said to you. Do you have someone?"

"Yes."

"Who is it?"

349

"Bucky."

"What is he saying to you?"

"He is telling me that he has been having an affair and wants my forgiveness."

"Do you forgive him?"

"Yes. I always do."

"How does it feel?"

"I'm very, very hurt. I don't want to forgive him. I want to hurt him, too."

"I think you have been hurt more than you have admitted. We can talk about that sometime soon. Let's go to thirty-five. Find something that happened in your life then."

"Okay, do you want to know?"

"No. Just think of the event and the person. Do you have it?"

"Yes."

"Now let's go to thirty." We continue the progression until we reach age six.

"Mary Frances, we are now back into your childhood. Think of someone you knew when you were six."

"My Aunt Beatrice and Uncle George."

"What are they saying to you?"

"They are trying to be kind, but they are very smothering. I need to run away and hide from them."

"Okay. Let's try just before that. Go back to when you were with your parents...."

I let out an agonizing scream. "Mommy ... Mommy! *Mommy! Daddy!*" My body stiffens. I am overcome with fright.

"Stay with it for a minute, just let it happen, it's okay. I believe it's the hurricane. You can feel this now if you want, or we'll come back to that. Right now, we are looking for your mammy." She speaks very softly.

"My Manny is holding me!!! My Manny is holding me, and I'm watching my mommy and daddy get blown away by the winds!" I scream and take a breath before talking again. "The front window is broken and the car doors are open. They're shouting and trying to hold on … she pushes me down behind the back seat … *Manny is holding me down so I can't see!"*

My body shudders and my voice quivers as I talk. I keep my eyes closed as I see the scene. "She's saying 'hush now, baby, hush now, it's okay, your Manny's here, it just got a little windy. They'll be back after the storm.'"

"Your mammy is with you?"

"She's Manny. My mother is mommy, and she is Manny. The car is broken and we are squished. It's raining, and blowing very hard." I shudder. "The wind is really bad. It hurts and I'm cold."

"What hurts?"

"She's hurting me. I want my mommy! Manny's on top of me, making me stay down on the floor of the broken car." I pause and feel myself as a small child. "I'm crying. I finally cry myself to sleep."

"Let's stay with this and keep your eyes closed. What happens next?"

"I'm waking up. Manny is holding me in her arms and rocking me and singing to me, 'Hush little baby don't you cry, Manny's gonna sing you a lullaby ….' The winds have stopped and it isn't raining anymore. We're sitting in the back seat of the car. Melody is there, too, but she is still asleep."

"Who is Melody?"

"Manny's little girl. She's my friend. I reach over to tell Melody it's time to wake up, but she doesn't want to wake up. Manny tells me Melody is gonna sleep a bit longer, but I say she has to wake up because she has blood on her head and it needs to be cleaned up."

I relax into the experience and continue to relate my story.

"Manny says, 'It's okay, baby chile. We're gonna go for a walk and let Melody sleep some more.'

"'Are you sure, Manny? Someone has to watch out for her.'

"'It's okay, darlin' Fancy, she'll be just fine. The angels will watch her for us.'

"'Are we gonna go find my mommy and daddy? They must be missing us somethin' terrible. Where do you think they are?'

"'I think that's a good idea, li'l darlin'. We'll go find them.' Manny pushes the door open with her feet, and I slide off her lap and onto the ground outside the car. She fumbles around in the car, gathering up things and takes her jacket off and puts it over Melody. For a long, slow minute, she kisses Melody on the forehead.

"It's very eerie on the road. The bridge ahead of us is washed out. There are big clouds and the sky is gray. A slight drizzle falls. The car was blown against a telephone pole next to the bridge. Lots of fallen trees and brush are everywhere. I wait for Manny to take my hand, and we walk slowly, carefully stepping over the branches and debris.

"'Where do you think we'll find mommy and daddy?'

"'Well, now let's play our game and see if we can suppose where they might be.' Her voice is shaky, and she stops walking and stands still in the middle of the road. Tears crawl down her cheek. She speaks as if in a fog. 'I'm supposing they might have gotten across the bridge and they've gone for help. What do you suppose?'

"I look up at her, 'Manny, why are you crying?'

"'Oh, chile it ain't nothin'. Just feelin' some sadness. Ol' Manny gets herself some sadness sometimes. Don't take no mind of it though.'

"'It's okay now, but remember what you always told me. Just like me, you don't want to be crying when mommy and daddy come for us. They don't like crying, you know.'

"'Yes, my little darlin' Fancy Pants. I'll be just fine.' She picks up her spirit. 'You and me, we're goin' go find us a place to be rescued from.'

"'We can't go too far from the car. Melody has to be found, too, and they have to see us.'

"'Yes, darlin'. We'll do just fine … we'll do just fine. They's gonna come rescue us, the Lord'll take care of us. The Lord'll lead them to us.'

"'Manny, I'm hungry. Can we get something to eat?'

"Manny sits down on a fallen log and rummages through her pocketbook. 'Let's jus' see if we has anythin' here, Missy Fancy.' She triumphantly pulls out a large Hershey with Almonds. 'Why looky this, Missy! Manny always has a candy bar for her little girl! Now what do you say to that?'

"'Manny! It's my favorite, and you know that!' I snatch the candy bar from her hand.

"She gently takes it back and starts to unwrap it. 'Now, li'l one, I also knows how you like to gobble these ol' candy bars up. This time we gotta be a bit careful and eat it slow like. Let ol' Manny keep it and give you special bites ever so often.' She breaks off a third of the candy bar and gives it to me.

"'Is this all I get?'

"'For now, sugar pie, you's sweet enough. Don't need no more sugar righ' now.' She takes my hand, 'Let's go find us a place to walk a bit.'

"There's a filling station across the road. Well, what's left of it anyway, because the roof has been blown off. We rummage around in the wreck and find a dirty toilet. We can't find any paper, and it doesn't flush, but at least we have a proper place to sit.

"'Manny, is this the 'colored' or the 'whites'?'

"She pauses and says carefully, 'That don't matter anymore. You just go right ahead and use it and I'll be next.'

"'You sure it's okay now? My mommy told me I wasn't to go in 'colored' an' this is lookin' dirty 'nough to be 'colored'?'

"'Don't you pay no mind to that no more, it's okay now. You just do what you need to do.' She hands me a tissue from her pocketbook.

"It's difficult stepping over and around all the debris in the street, but we find our way and start walking back toward the little town when we leave the filling station. I find a water-soaked doll in the street, and Manny says I can keep it until we find its rightful owner, but I'd have to give it back eventually.

"'Manny, I'm still hungry.'

"'Me too, li'l Miz Fancy. We'll come across somethin' in due time.'

"'Do we have any money to buy something when we find a store?'

"'We'll make do. At times like these, folks are gen'rous.'

"'I sure hope we can find someone who is gen'rous soon. I'm really starving! An' my new doll is hungry, too.'

"'How's about we talk about what we might like to be eating? If'n you could have anything you want right now, what would it be?'

"'Chocolate cake!'

"'Chocolate cake? Why darlin', you's always wantin' chocolate cake first. You's gotta have your supper, then you get your cake. Now, what you gonna have first?'

"'Cornbread and black-eyed peas. With butter and jam on the cornbread.'

"'That's a good start. Don't forget, Manny always wants you to have some greens ... what kinda greens you thinkin' about?'

"'Do I hafta' have greens even in make-believe?'

"'Why sure. Gotta stay healthy even in make-believe.'

"'How's about salad? Does that count? Can I have my chocolate cake if'n I eat salad instead?'

"'It counts every single time we talk about it, don't it now?'

"'Are we goin' count my black-eyed peas this time, too?'

"'Of course, how many peas gonna be in the first spoonful?'

"'Five, 'cause I'm five.'

"'Good girl. Now pretend to eat that spoonful. How many gonna be in the second?'

"'Six, 'cause I'm gonna be six on my next birthday.'

"While we're eating the pretend black-eyed peas, we turn down a country lane off the main road. It's the same road that goes to the cabin that we had rented for our summer vacation. The drizzle stops but the clouds are still dark.

"'Lookee there, li'l Fancy. There's a place we can go to.' Manny points to a cabin alongside the road.

"'But, Manny, it don't have a roof, the rain will get us.'

"'But the bears won't.'

"'Manny, there aren't any bears here!'

"'The 'gators then.'

"'There aren't 'gators here neither.'

"'Whatsa matter chile? Yo' don't want no place to sleep? It's starting to get dark hereabouts.'

"'But it's somebody's house. I'm not supposed to go into someone's house that I don't know. You told me that.'

"'Yes, chile, and you remember that for later. I think this time will be all right, though. This is a special occasion, an' I'm wit' you, so it's okay.'

"We walk through the debris on the pathway and gingerly push open the door. I make her knock first and holler to see if anyone is there. Her voice echoes in the vacant cabin as we enter.

"In the waning light we see the broken contents of the cabin strewn everywhere. Holding my hand as we inch forward, she brushes stuff aside with her foot and heads for the kitchen.

"'Li'l Missy, we's gonna find us something to eat here, I do believe.'

"'Are these folks gonna be gen'rous?'

"'Yes, indeed. These folks are gonna be mighty happy that somebody came along and needed the food they left behind.' She looks through the old refrigerator that has been knocked on its side with the door ajar. 'Well, we's got some broken eggs, some spilt milk, and some bacon soaking in the dirty water. That won't do us no good!'

"'Look, Manny, there are some cans of stuff on the floor.' I bend down and pick one up, 'What's this?'

"'Tuny fish. And here's a can of creamed corn. Help me find a can opener and we's gonna have us a right nice supper.'

"On our hands and knees we search the debris for a can opener. We pull out drawers and rummage through what's left in the cupboards, but we don't find one. While searching, Manny begins to gather usable remnants for a kitchen … utensils, unbroken dishes … bowls … and clears a space on the counter.

"I open a cabinet next to the stove. 'Look Manny … cereal!' I grab a box of Cheerios, tear it open, and eat a handful.

"'This'll do just fine.' She resolutely takes the box from me, pours some in a bowl, turns a chair upright at the table, picks me up and puts me on the chair, and hands me the bowl and a spoon. I prop my doll on the table next to my bowl. 'Now, chile, there ain't no milk, but you eat these here Cheerios while I keeps looking.'

"'You have some, too, please, Manny.'

"'Don't mind if I do.' She finds another chair, brushes it off, and sits down. She takes another unbroken bowl, fills it, and begins to eat the dry cereal.

"She tells me we're going to discuss things like grown-ups, and I feel very important. She says we need to 'a-ssess' the situation and make a plan. Over dry Cheerios, she tells me that she's gonna make me up a bed somehow and then she's gonna start cleaning things up a bit to see what she can find for tomorrow.

"'In the moonlight?'

"'Why yes, child, the good Lord took the roof off so's I could have light to work by when the electricity is out. Don't you know He always has a plan? That's why He put this house here … just for us to find … an' I bet He's gonna give us some blankets and a good soft spot to sleep, too.'

"'When do you think Mommy and Daddy are going to come?'

"'Soon, darling, soon.'

"'How are they going to know where to find us?'

"'The Lord will bring them back, and we'll find a way tomorrow to show them the way to this here house. Don't you worry about that at all, Manny knows what to do. Okay, now li'l darling, we have to have a bed.' She gets up and rummages in the bedrooms and finally comes back. 'Now, baby doll, we's got a bed. Just finish up them Cheerios, and we's gonna take off those wet shoes and wet clothes, and go to sleep.' She starts to undo my shoes.

"I hesitate. 'Manny, I don't want to go in someone else's bed by myself. Would you sleep with me and sing to me?'

"'Of course, of course. We don't want those silly bogeymen to get you, do we? Just let me tidy up here a bit and we'll go snuggle together.'

"I take off my wet clothes and put on a dry, flannel shirt that she found. Before we lie down, she tells me we are going to pray for Melody, who has gone to heaven to live with the angels. We kneel together and she begins, 'The Lord is my shepherd, I shall not want …' and has me repeat each sentence. When we finish the prayer, I ask her if my mommy and daddy have also gone to heaven. She tells me, with great confidence, not to worry because they are still here on earth, they miss me a whole lot, and they will be coming for us soon.

"Manny and I crawl into the bed she made for us on a mattress on the floor. I curl up almost as if I'm still sitting on her lap and hug the doll just like Manny is hugging me. She sings lullabies to me and we fall asleep under the stars and a big ol' quilt.

"The next morning, we awake and eat more dry Cheerios for breakfast. The box is almost empty. Manny spends the morning sorting out the household debris and rummaging for usable food. We never find a can opener, but we do find a large jar of peanut butter, a box of saltine crackers, raisins, and a case of soda pop bottles that we can pry open.

"Around noon, Manny finds a shovel and begins to dig a hole in the yard near a tree. I ask her what the hole is for, and she tells me that Melody needs to be buried. When the hole is big enough, Manny takes my hand and we walk back to the car to fetch Melody's body. We both cry as we place her in the grave. When our task is finished, Manny finds a few wildflowers and places them on the grave as she says goodbye. 'We's gonna come back and put a proper stone on you, Melody baby, you jus' wait for me.'

"'Manny,' I say, 'do you think my mommy and daddy are also dead?'

"'Hush, child. We can't think things like that. We has to believe in the Lord and we has to believe He will bring us all back together.'

"The fireplace in the cabin is still functional. Manny decides that a fire would be the best signal, so in the evening we find dry kindling in a shed and start a fire, burning first the broken furniture pieces and scattered tree limbs. Every time something works out the way it is supposed to, she talks about the Lord taking care of us, but I get real scared as we're waiting. Manny gives me another piece of the chocolate bar to make me feel better.

"After three days in the cabin, we hear a noise on the road and go running out to find a Red Cross Jeep. Manny stands at the door, and I run down the path thinking that my daddy has come. The man who gets out of the Jeep is a stranger in a sheriff's uniform. He picks me up and carries me up the path to speak to Manny.

"Addressing her, he says, 'Girl, you're trespassing in someone's home.'

"She proudly looks him straight in the eye. 'I saved the child's life.'

"'You know better, though, don't you? You know better than to trespass?'

"'Yes, sir.'

"'You keep that in mind.'

"We are taken across the river on a car ferry to a Red Cross shelter. Manny gives them information about my family. Beatrice is located and she comes to get me.

"When it's time to leave the shelter, I cry and want Manny to go with us. Beatrice says to the officials, 'I don't need another maid. I have someone already. She isn't needed anymore.'

"I cry and promise Manny I will come back for her.

"My aunt forces me from Manny's arms and carries me away. I cringe as I feel the red velvet of her coat clinging to me. I never see Manny again."

I fade into a silent sleep. Patricia lets me rest for a few minutes then brings me out of the hypnotic trance. I have no memory of the session, and she plays the tape for me. After hearing the tape, Patricia suggests to me that I have never forgiven Beatrice. Now that I understand what happened, Patricia says, perhaps I could consider that the time has come.

She tells me that there are other memories that could surface, but we will save them for another time. She holds me in a long hug before I leave.

. . . .

I arrive home early in the afternoon, planning to listen to the tape again. The phone rings a few minutes later. It's Bucky.

"Sugar, I haven't been able to work because I'm concerned about us. I'd like to mend fences." He pauses, and I say nothing. "If I came home right now, could we talk?"

"Of course."

"I'll be there in half an hour."

I feel afraid and leery as I place the phone back in its cradle. I fear that he will manipulate me and that I will be too weak to say what I need to say. While I am waiting, I pace the floor, practicing how I can be strong with him. I put the hypnosis tape in a portable tape recorder on the kitchen counter and listen to it as a distraction while I am waiting. When I finally hear the garage door, I rewind the tape and turn off the recorder. I am torn between my fear of a confrontation with him and wanting to share the revelations of the hypnotism.

He walks through the kitchen door, closes it, and stands still, saying nothing, just staring at me. In his hand is a single, long-stemmed, red rose wrapped in green paper. I say nothing as our eyes connect.

He walks over to me, kisses me gently on the cheek, places the rose in my hand, and whispers, "Mary Frances, I can't deal with you being mad at me. Sometimes I am stupid. I say things without thinking, I drink too much." His hand comes to my cheek and gently caresses it. "The other night, I let the alcohol and how much I missed you affect what I said. I am really, really sorry for everything, and I need you to forgive me." His eyes have a pained expression. "I love you. You are my wife. You are the only woman I have ever loved."

I can't look at him. He is doing exactly what I feared he would do. I turn away, go to a cabinet, and take out a bud vase to fill with water. I desperately want to talk to him about the hypnotism tape,

361

but I don't know how to handle myself. With the kitchen shears, I distract myself by carefully trimming the end of the rose, putting it in the vase, and placing it on the kitchen table. Still staring at the rose, I say, "Bucky. I don't understand how you can do what you do ... every day in this city ... and feel the way you do. I don't understand how you can continue to harbor racist feelings. It's wrong. What you have been saying and thinking about Benjamin is wrong. The way you have treated me over this is wrong." I breathe a sigh of relief, turn to him, and blurt out, "I can't live with it anymore. I'm sorry."

He stammers, "You're not ... not ... thinking of leaving, are you, sugar plum? I mean ... 'cause ... I don't know what I would do." He goes to a kitchen chair, pulls it out, turns it around, and sits backwards facing me. After a long pause, he starts to say something, then pauses and reconsiders. His expression changes. His eyes plead with me, and I sense a puppy that has been scolded. "You're right, I can't live with it anymore either. I need your help."

I turn back to the cabinet. I can't be too close, either physically or emotionally, because I feel drawn to him. "I can't help you. You are bound up by your prejudices and trapped by your own history. You have to help yourself."

"What can I do?" He acts helpless, shrugging, "I can't change the way I was brought up. I can't change what I was taught, I can't change the way I was formed. But I have pushed the edges, jus' like everyone else."

I turn around and lean against the cabinet, arms folded. "Pushing the edges isn't enough. Look at the way you are ... you have to have complete control over me. You have to bully me to feel like a man. I can't live with that anymore. You're also still defined by racism. I thought you were bigger than that. Respecting folks on the outside isn't enough unless you respect them on the inside, too.

I was taught the same things as you, but I don't act that way now. I changed the way I behave, I changed the way I feel, I changed the way I treat people. You can, too. You are not bound by the way you were taught."

"I need you to help me, to show me how. I need you to stay with me."

"Bucky, this isn't about us." Leaning forward, I gesture with my hands and feel drawn to his desperation. "This is about you but I can't show you anything. It's in your head. It's how you treat me. It's how you are in your private thoughts. It's how you think about other people, deep down inside, even when they are different."

Slowly, he stands up and walks over to me, gingerly taking my hands in his. "If I promise to work hard at changing, will you tell me when I mess up? Will you see me through it?"

I pull my hands away from his. Putting my hand on his chest, I push him away slightly and twist myself to the side so that I'm not facing him. "No. No, Bucky. It's not that simple."

"What do you mean, sugar plum?"

"We've been through this before. You've made me lots of promises. I have to trust you, and it's hard, given our history."

"Mary Frances." He takes my left hand and holds my fingers up so that I'm looking at my wedding ring. My gold bracelet conspicuously circles my arm, much like a larger ring. His tone is more assertive. "This is one of those 'for better or for worse' moments, isn't it?"

I am caught with my own words. "Yes, Bucky, but I'm serious. This time it has to be real, not one of your campaign promises. I'm not just a constituent. You can't blow me off with double-talk."

His arms slowly wrap around me as he talks. "There is only one vote in this election, and I'm at your mercy. As proof of my sincerity, please let me try. Let me go with you to meet your mammy. Let me meet Emmaline. Let's find out. Let me try to change."

"You're sure?" I look up at him, remembering all of the other promises.

"I mean what I say; I don't want to lose you." He looks deep into my eyes.

I listen to the voices in my head. I don't believe him. Part of me feels like a fool. But I know that I must give it a chance, just in case. "Okay, I'll take you the next time I go to Emmaline's." I allow him to engulf me in a long hug.

"Bucky," I finally say, breaking away, "I want to tell you about what happened today." I reach for the tape player and lead us over to the dining room table. I am proud of the way I have spoken to him, but I can't be sure that it had any effect.

I relax as I tell him about my lunch with Patricia and our conversation about hypnotism. My energy grows as I describe the hypnotism session ... and becomes excited as I repeat my experience. I play the tape before he has a chance to say anything. He listens with rapt attention, getting up once to pour iced tea for both of us.

Although Bucky has always disliked Patricia's use of hypnotism, he greets the story with a sense of relief. When the tape ends, he feels that I have finally found the answer that I have been looking for. In his own way, he begins to understand that a piece of my life has been missing, and I was entitled to search for it. "Darlin'," he says, "I'm not so sure that stories like that can't be planted, or can't be a figment of your imagination, but I'm not gonna make a fuss over it. All I can say is that I sure am glad that old woman saved your life for me. She jus' didn't know it at the time, did she?" He grins, leans over, and kisses me lightly.

"No, she didn't. Now aren't you glad I ran into her?"

"I sure am, and I am also glad it's over with and you got your answers. Now you don't have to be fussing about it anymore and you can stop running away from me." He kisses me on the back of the neck. "And you can start fussin' with me more."

"I have to visit her and tell her that I know the story." I rise, take his empty glass, and walk into the kitchen, not yet ready for his attention. "We can visit together."

He follows. "Well, I suppose another visit won't do any harm. After all, you were her charge for a while, and reunions are nice."

"Bucky," I rinse out and dry the glasses, "I'm perturbed that Beatrice would have been so cruel to her."

"What was cruel about that?" He leans against the counter. "She was an employee, and her employers were killed. It's jus' like when a business goes under, she lost her job."

Realizing that it will soon be time for dinner, I open the freezer and take out a package. "She was part of a family, and you can't toss family out like that. Besides, the very least is, the newspaper should have told the whole story. It said nothing about Melody dying or about Emmaline taking care of me."

"Darlin', it's the way it was back then. They'd probably tell it all now. But she wasn't part of your family, she was a servant, and she did what was expected of her." He moves because I need to open a drawer. "Beatrice didn't owe her an obligation. She found other employment. What's there to feel bad about?"

"There's something about life that requires you to be civil to people, I don't care who they are, black or white, Chinese or ... or Iraqi, whatever a person might be." I cringe while taking down dishes and glassware, thinking about the recent Gulf War. "It's respect and decency, even when they're not the same as we are. Martha isn't a servant, she's been in our family too long." I carry things into the table, "I'd be willing to bet that no one ever said 'thank you' or 'I appreciate what you did' to Emmaline, and that's the very least she deserved."

Bucky moves to the dining room and sits backward on a chair as I am setting the table. "Sugar plum, I have no problem with you wantin' to be civil to her. You jus' get yourself on out there and say 'thank you' and 'I appreciate' whenever you want, but right now, I want to thank you and show you how much I appreciate you bein' my wife and forgivin' me." He pulls me into an embrace that I don't resist.

I feel that our problems are not resolved, but my heart has gone out of being angry with him. I whisper gently, "Bucky, I'm so glad we've gotten past this one, and you understand how important it was for me to find out who she is. I'm looking forward to having you meet her."

14. NEW CLUES

"Mr. Perelli, I'm made some progress ...." I report to my detective when we meet a few days later and tell him about my trip to North Carolina and the hypnotism. "Emmaline was my nurse and she rescued me from the hurricane. I also know that Melody is the child who died. We need to concentrate on finding the child named 'Missy.'"

"Missy is most likely a nickname, which makes it harder." His face wrinkles in a frown as he reviews his notes with me. "Could be anything, most likely something starting with an 'M' ... and Mother Powers didn't get around too much ... didn't even report Melody's death ... I checked out North Carolina records for you ... but checking out every black female with the last name of Powers born in Virginia during that time period is taking some time."

"But you're making progress, aren't you?"

"I've come up with one possibility. There's a record in Virginia under her name that looks like it may be an adoption. It's both hard and expensive to get access to sealed court records, so I'm going through some of the adoption databases. A lot of people try to find their parents that way."

"Would it help for you to talk to Emmaline directly? Grace and I didn't understand what she was saying about Melody, but now it makes sense. We could ask some questions about Missy that might give some clues."

"Absolutely."

"My husband is going with me the next time I visit, but I'll take you after I return from our Easter trip."

He stares at me for a minute and pulls another file folder out of his briefcase and challenges me. "You want to know about your husband now?"

"Do I?"

"You asked, I'm delivering, if you want to hear it. But, if you would rather, I can burn this." The late afternoon sun streams in his office window as he picks up the folder while he is talking, then lays it squarely in the middle of his desk, directly in the light.

"Is it any worse that what I already know?"

"It might cause a problem if he ever wants to be a big name political force; but otherwise, it's probably too old to hurt much." He winks, "No more wives and children, if that's what you're worried about."

I'm relieved and slowly nod yes. He begins to read as he flips through the pages, "Let's see, all the data checks out ... he is who he says he is. He comes from a misanthropic family that has been slightly shorted in the gene pool ... they have had delusions of adequacy and tend to blame the world for their self-inflicted problems. A lot of financial shenanigans." He looks up sheepishly, "Sorry, that's just an old Italian cop's opinion."

He returns to his papers, "You're right about the other kid in Richmond—the girl—that checks out, too. Our boy," he grins, "other than some assorted dalliances with other men's wives, was what you would call a typical redneck Bubba in his younger days ... has had himself an assortment of trailer trash over the years but that's about it."

"How did you find out all of this?" I flush at the mention of his dalliances and cringe at the use of the reference to "Bubba."

"In my business, you develop your sources. I also have personal knowledge of wronging a woman and living to hear about it, again and again and again."

He clears his throat and continues. "Next issue ... you don't need to check his pillowcases for eyeholes now, but in the mid-sixties he was caught in an FBI photograph of a Klan function. Couldn't find any membership records though, so you're safe there. Here's one for you to think about, though ... when he was fourteen, he was in a car full of WASP boys who ran an old black couple off of the road. Both of them died, but no one was ever charged. That was the early sixties and it was swept under the rug."

He flips a page. "I also found a campus report from UVA from the late sixties that confirms a racial incident. Nothing came of it. You may also be interested in knowing that Bucky's grades in college were abysmal. I'm astonished that he got into graduate school like he did. Also, it took him three times to pass the bar exam."

Closing the file, he clasps his hands together and looks straight at me. "You seem like a nice lady, so you're probably the one who straightened him out. He's doing pretty good now ... got a good law practice and is a local political insider ... also serves on the boards of two or three charities. If I were you, though, I'd watch myself, protect my assets, if you know what I mean."

. . . .

It's time again for the monthly luncheon with my girlfriends, Katherine, Patricia, and Effi, and we decide on a picnic in the fresh spring air under the trees by the Jefferson Memorial. The picnic is a farewell for Effi, who has announced that she is leaving the area to accept a professorship while her divorce is in process. The cherry blossoms blow softly in the wind, and the sun sparkles on the tidal basin. Although tourists are everywhere, we are enveloped by a sense of seclusion as we unpack a picnic basket on a blanket in a quiet grove near the water.

Katherine's first question when she arrives a few minutes late is, "What happened with Betty Susanne?"

Patricia and Effi simultaneously ask, "About what?"

"I'll tell everything in a minute ... Effi, you would not believe what has happened to me." I take out plastic champagne glasses. "Remember how we talked about the old woman in the nursing home?"

"Sure do. Did you figure it out?"

I pop the cork on a bottle of champagne and pour it. "In fact, ladies, I solved the mystery, and we are celebrating today!"

Addressing Effi directly, I tell her how Patricia hypnotized me and that we discovered that Emmaline was my nurse and that she saved my life during the hurricane. I raise my glass in salute. "Here's to hypnotism!"

Effi chimes in, "And old black ladies named Emmaline in nursing homes!"

Katherine joins her. "Absolutely. And here's to women in general!"

Patricia is quieter. "And here's to all of us."

"Okay, Effi, the next thing … Katherine and Patricia know this already, but I think you will be surprised to hear that I discovered my husband fathered a child when he was in college."

"Ohhhhhh? No, I'm not surprised, believe me, I'm not surprised. Bucky impresses me as that type of guy."

Katherine says, "Tell her the rest …."

The three of them look at me expectedly. I take out containers and spread them on the blanket, acting mysteriously. "The mother of the child was black. I had lunch with her and I met the child."

"You're kidding! Your Bucky?" Effi whispers loudly.

"Yes, OUR Bucky," Katherine says with pleasure, opening the first container and eating a black olive.

"I need to hear all about this. Start at the beginning …" Effi instructs. As I continue with the food preparations, I obligingly tell her the details of my trip to Richmond and describe my luncheon with Angela in detail.

Effi stops in the middle of eating a carrot stick. "What did you say her name is?"

"Angela Thornton Witherspoon."

Effi's eyes widen.

Katherine notices the change. "Do you know her?"

Effi shakes her head and takes another bite. "I don't know, I might." Shaking her thoughts, she puts down her dish and raises her glass again. "Here's to miscegenation and those of us who carry the standard."

Patricia joins in the toast but stops short and turns to me. "Mary Frances, how are you feeling about all of this now?"

Holding my glass in both hands, I think carefully before sighing, "I'm bothered because he didn't tell me. It's something we should have handled a long time ago … I resent the fact that I found out on my own, quite by accident … I'm angry because he is not willing to accept responsibility for what he did and acknowledge the child. Does that cover it? But I'm not sure that this is important enough to end my marriage."

Effi thoughtfully raises her glass in the direction of the monument. "Mary Frances, how is he different from … Jefferson … or any of the thousands of other white men who have fathered mixed-race children and laughed it off?" I detect mild sarcasm. "Men, aren't they something? That's the history of our country …."

Katherine interrupts, "You forgot to answer my question. Has he told Betty Susanne?"

"No, he promised, but he didn't tell her when she was here."

"What a jerk. You're going to have to do it then."

Patricia, who has been silently watching and listening, interjects, "Katherine, hold on." She turns to me, raised fork in her hand, "You need to give him another opportunity."

"What if he doesn't tell her?" Katherine replies. "Betty Suzanne should hear it from her parents."

"Give it a little more time," Patricia says to me. "Maybe you could tell her together, next time she comes down from New York."

· ·

The next morning, I receive a call from Benjamin telling me that Emmaline took a fall, broke her hip, and is doing poorly. He suggests that a visit might help her spirits, and I make arrangements to go over in the afternoon. I call Bucky to see if he can join me. He has important appointments, he says, and can't break away but promises to go with me another time.

When I arrive at Northwest Convalescent Center, Benjamin and I catch up in the dining room while Emmaline is with her doctor. Excitedly, I tell him about my trip to North Carolina.

"Well, Lordy be. Y'all been down in God's country. I used to have kin down there in Pamlico County, but I ain't seen them since I mustered out. Those warm Carolina winds haven't caressed my cheeks in a long time."

"It's fine country indeed. It's not far, only 'bout a four-hour drive."

"That's true, but it's about forty years behind. It's hard to go back to the countryside when you seen the world like I have."

I casually sip from my cup of coffee. "Did you travel when you were in the army?"

"Me? Oh, I was a medic, so's I've been in a bunch o' those ol' army hospitals here and there. Germany some, Philippines, met my wife in Japan." He scratches the back of his head in a country-boy fashion.

"Is she Japanese?"

"Yes'm. Got a real nice one, she is. Still wears those kimono things, though."

"How does she like living here?"

"Well, now, we jus' take it a little bit at a time. When I cook, it's grits and collard greens. When she cooks, it's sushi and rice. We been together almost thirty years, but I'm still thinkin' of makin' her into an ice-cream-and-apple-pie American." He gently laughs at himself.

"They don't like to change, do they?" I muse briefly about Bucky and the concept of changing a spouse's behavior, realizing the futility. "You know what else I learned?" Without waiting for a reply, I tell him about discovering that Emmaline was my nurse and how she saved my life.

"That ol' gal did that, eh? Well, bless her soul. She's a good woman, ain't she?" He pours more coffee. "So, we know how she knows you, and it didn't even cause you no problems with your family. You's quite the de-tec-tive, ain't you? That's real good. What else did you find?"

I tell him what I've learned about Melody.

"So one of her babies is buried down there ... it's hard when you can't go see the grave now an' again. That must be what makes her sad." He looks at me quizzically. "Know anythin' about the other one yet, the other chile? You gonna bring her through that there door for us?"

"Not yet. I have someone helping me ... he hasn't found anythin' ... but he's good. I bet it'll be soon ...." The doctor comes into the dining room and reports that Emmaline is ready for a visitor.

Benjamin warns me that Emmaline is restricted to her bed and is taking heavy pain medication, and leads me to her room. The bed has been adjusted so that she is sitting up, but she looks weak and tired. He turns on a table lamp before leaving.

"Emmaline?" I peer at her to see if she is awake. "I brought you something." I take a light nightgown out of a bag and fluff it in front of her. "... this is for you."

Her eyes open slowly and her hand, touches the cloth. "You still remembers I like blue, don't you?" Her voice is barely audible as her fingers fondle the lace at the neckline. "You's always been such a good girl."

I take her hand and watch her face carefully. "How're you feeling?"

"I'm happy you're here," but it's difficult for her to talk. I give her a drink of water with a straw.

"I have a wonderful story that I want to tell you." Her skin seems to flush. She nods as an encouragement for me to tell it.

"This is a story that I think you already know ... when you remember it, squeeze my hand." I look off into the distance as I begin. "Once there was a little girl whose name was Mary Frances, but that name was too big for such a little girl, so they called her Fancy." I peek over at Emmaline, and find a sly grin on her face.

"She had a mammy, and her mammy had a name that was too big also, so the little girl gave the mammy a very special name, and that name was 'Manny.'" Her hand is weak, but I feel an attempted squeeze.

"Fancy had a friend, too. The friend's name was Melody. Manny was Melody's mother and the three of them lived together. They played a lot and the two little girls were best friends and playmates. And sometimes there was another little girl named Missy who was also Manny's baby. They all loved each other a whole lot." Emmaline squeezes harder and tries to say something, but her words are slurred and I don't understand.

"One day, Fancy, Melody, and Manny went on a trip with Fancy's parents. They went somewhere in the country, out by a big river near the ocean. I think this was a trip they took often, but this time it was different." Her eyes begin to watch mine intently.

"A big storm came up suddenly and the family was caught out there by the river. In fact, they were caught in a hurricane. They needed to go over a bridge to get back safely, but the bridge washed out and the family was very afraid." Her hand tenses; she knows this story.

375

"The winds were so strong that they blew the car against a telephone pole and knocked the mother and father out of the car, and they were blown away. And something else happened ...." I'm not sure how to broach the next piece and watch her face closely. She seems to expect it. I speak in a whisper, "The little girl named Melody died." She nods her head yes very slowly. Her eyes glisten with tears.

"But something else happened, too." I pause. "Manny and Fancy didn't die. They got out of the car and Manny took very good care of the little girl for three days, didn't she?" She nods yes again and whispers a barely audible "Missy ...."

"Manny saved the life of the little girl, didn't she? She loved the little girl very much." Her eyes light up, and the "yes" is stronger.

"But the other people, the Red Cross people, they didn't know what Manny did. And the aunt who came to get the little girl, she didn't know it either. And no one ever told Manny 'thank you' for saving the life of the little girl. They took the little girl away, and Manny never saw her again." Emmaline has stayed with me, and her face is now crestfallen with memories of how the story ends. She turns her eyes away, seeming to be reliving the moment.

I take both of her hands in mine, lean on the bed, and wait for her attention again. "Manny, thank you for saving my life. Thank you for taking such good care of me when I was little. I'm very sorry they didn't let you stay with me." I bend down to hug her and give her a kiss on the forehead.

Benjamin comes back into the room and stands near the end of the bed while I'm hugging her. She reaches up and touches my cheek before sinking back into the daze caused by her medication. I step back with Benjamin. As we are talking, I remember the small photo album that Emmaline's minister once mentioned and ask if he has ever seen it. Emmaline realizes what we are talking about and through her feeble motions invites us to open her pocketbook that is on the nearby dresser and find the small Kodak album.

In the album are several faded black-and-white photos of two small girls. One child is black and one is white. The first shots are of babies. Two or three pages later, the children are toddlers playing on a lawn. I am fascinated and want to show them to the detective. I close the album and ask Emmaline if I can borrow it to look at the pictures. She is pleased to nod her head yes.

. . . .

Bucky and I leave Washington to visit Beatrice and Martha early the next Saturday for our annual Easter visit. I take Emmaline's small photo album and browse through the pages as we drive.

"Honey bunch," Bucky says, "we know that she was your mammy, but you're not goin' to be mentionin' it to your aunt this weekend, are you? I don't think Beatrice would understand half as much as I do."

"I know I've made it hard on you, and I'm sorry you have not appreciated my interest in her. I'm very glad, though, that I followed my instinct and did what I had to do. Look at how much I have discovered!"

"Well, you're happy as a June bug now, aren't you? And we can get on with our lives. How 'bout getting back to workin' on our trip plans ... I'm really lookin' forward to taking my li'l sugar away from here an' off to Europe." He turns to me with a slight firmness in his tone while he changes the radio station. "You *can* finally put it to rest now, can't you?"

"Yes, dear." I hesitate as I flip through the photo album, somehow feeling that there is more to the story, but not knowing what it is. "Bucky, did you look at these pictures?"

"Well ... yes, I did." He seems sheepish. "You left it out on the table, and I looked at it. Few pages, maybe, belongs to someone else, so I didn't want to snoop too much."

"I looked real close at all of them."

"So, sugar plum, what are you tryin' to say?"

"Bucky, it hasn't occurred to me before, but I've never seen baby pictures of me. Beatrice never made a photo album of me. She has pictures but nothing from before I was five." I look out the window. "There *must* have been some pictures that my real mama and daddy took."

"You don't have to fault Beatrice for that."

"How many photo albums have I made of Betty Suzanne?" I flip a couple of pages and answer my own question. "There are dozens. That's something that mothers do."

"You said it yourself many times, she's never really been a mother to you. Guess that's why she doesn't do mother things, eh?"

"There's something else I don't understand about this album."

"What's that?"

"Look here ...." I start from the beginning and flip the pages. "If this white baby is me on this first page or two ... and I think it is, and then we have several pages here of Melody and then Melody and me ..." I continue flipping slowly, "... then look at this ... there are more pictures of me ... these are school pictures ... and this one I know ... it's third grade. Here ... this one is junior high. And this, this is my high school prom dress. Here's one from graduation at

378

Wellesley. This … look … this was taken at our wedding." I flip a few more. "This … look, this is Betty Susanne when she was little … and this is Betty Susanne at a play at her school, and Betty Susanne's high school graduation. That's us with her. I don't remember this picture being taken."

I close the album. "Bucky, if Beatrice took me away from her when I was five years old, how did Emmaline get these other pictures?"

"Beats me."

"I've always wondered how she recognized me that first day at the nursing home."

"Think that ol' woman was stealin' pictures from your aunt somehow?"

I'm astonished. "Bucky, how could you even think that?"

"Just joking, just joking. Let's not stir things up again. We've made peace on this one, haven't we?"

"You're doing better, but you still have a ways to go."

I become lost in thought, not knowing what to think as I watch the green fields pass. *She hasn't seen me since I was five, and I know she wasn't at the graduations or the wedding. How did she get them? What is her interest in Betty Susanne?*

15. ATTIC REUNIONS

We arrive in Richmond early on Saturday afternoon. After settling in and greeting Martha, I open the door to the side veranda where Beatrice is sitting in her rocker. As always, she looks as if she is ready to attend still another garden party. She is dressed in a flowered, fuchsia dress and a wide-brimmed, white, summer hat. She is brushing her dog, Chinaberry. Remembering Patricia's advice, I dutifully kiss her on the cheek, pet the dog with mocked enthusiasm, and brace myself to begin feeling forgiveness. "My goodness, it's a lovely spring day, isn't it, and don't you look like the governor's wife!" I sit in a rocker next to her.

She speaks like the grande dame that she is, "Yes, darlin', it's lovely today, and how y'all been up there ... how's your trip plans goin'?" Chinaberry fidgets and she doesn't look up.

"Just wonderful ... got our passports, and the tickets. I'm excited, and it's looking like a fine trip. We'll be leaving in a few weeks." I survey the spring azaleas hugging the veranda. The closest bushes are the same fuchsia color as Beatrice's dress. Forgiving her is going to feel like pretending for a while, but I have to try.

I let the rockers move in unison for a while before I speak. "I've been putting together some photo albums of Betty Susanne's childhood pictures." I know this isn't true; it's just my lead-in. These albums were finished a long time ago, but I know I can't be direct with Beatrice about Emmaline's photo album.

"How's that child doin'? I sure do wish she would come an' visit with me. I haven't seen her for mor'n two years now."

I don't think you want to, I thought, but aloud said, "Oh, she's having her ups and downs. She's pretty busy up there."

"I sure don't know why she wants to go up to Yankeeland when we have all these fine schools down here. I shouldn't have offered to pay for that school. She's gonna get into all the same kind of trouble you got into, mark my word." She points her finger at me. "You tell her she needs to visit her grandmother once in a while since I'm paying for her fancy New York City learnin'. She ought to be ashamed, treating me like this!" Chinaberry leaps off of her lap and finds a spot in the sunlight. Martha comes out with water for the dog.

She never lets it rest, does she? "Now Aunt Beatrice, it broadens her education. She appreciates all you're doing for her, I'm sure." I pause and say what I really want to ask. "When I was working on those pictures, I got to thinking about something."

"What's that, child?"

"I don't think I've ever seen pictures of me before I came to live with you … I don't think I've ever seen my own baby pictures."

"Why, there are lots of pictures of you. George was a real camera bug. Jus' look there in the library." She motions toward the room with her head. "You can see all the pictures you want in those old photo albums of his."

"No, I mean before I came here, when I was a baby, with my daddy and mama." This is my little sword. I never let her forget that she is not my mother.

Beatrice stares out into the yard, rocks in her chair, and says nothing.

"Aunt Beatrice?"

She rocks a little faster in her chair. "Oh, child, I don't think there were any. My sister wasn't much into picture taking."

That isn't true, I say to myself. I've just found pictures of me that I never knew existed. I stifle my astonishment at her falsehood but speed up my own rocking. "My mother never took baby pictures of me?"

"Well, if she did, I sure don't know what happened to them." Beatrice lifts her chin and her voice. "Why, look at Miz Wilson over there. Don't she look fine?" She waves. "Miz Wilson, how you doin' this beautiful day?"

Mrs. Wilson waves back. I realize that I've just been instructed to change the subject. We rock our chairs in silent unison for several minutes as Martha goes in the house and comes out again. "Look at you out here, just as dry as you can be. I done brung you some iced tea." She puts a tray on a low table and lingers on the veranda behind Beatrice's chair, robustly breathing the air in. "My, ain't it a grand spring day today!"

Bucky wanders onto the veranda from the library and trips on Chinaberry, causing the dog to yelp, and cussing under his breath. He collects himself, leans against the railing, and casually listens as he sips tea.

"Aunt Beatrice," I finally decide to also change the subject, "there is something peculiar that happened recently that I thought you might understand."

"What would that be?"

"I had to come down here to Richmond the other week to get a copy of Bucky's birth certificate and decided to get a copy of my own birth certificate so I wouldn't have to bother you the next time I need it. I went over to the Vital Records Department on Willow Lawn Drive."

Beatrice's forehead wrinkles, her eyes become piercing. "Now why wouldn't you just make a copy of the one I gave you last time you were here?"

"I did that. But I wanted a copy of the original from my own mama and daddy, too. It seems like something I should have."

"You were adopted, so your original records are sealed."

"That's what I found out. But I imagine you have a copy in my adoption file, don't you?"

Beatrice doesn't hesitate. "Nope." Her voice is hard and determined. She turns back to the street.

"Didn't you tell me there was a file about my adoption?"

She's rocks faster, looking straight ahead. "Yes, there is and I have it, but the only birth certificate is the one where George and I adopted you. I know that for a fact, and it's the one I gave you for your passport—that's your birth certificate now."

I hesitate, puzzled because it's such a simple thing. Why is she so nervous? I decide to keep pushing. "I did some research on the public computer at Vital Records and found something that seems peculiar about my mama and daddy."

Beatrice is cautious. "What's that?"

"It told me that there were sealed records associated with my daddy's name as the birth father, but there weren't any sealed records associated with my mama's name as the birth mother."

Beatrice is clearly agitated. "You jus' made a mistake with my sister's name, that's all. You're fussing too much about this. Probably needed her maiden name or an initial or something. I have no idea how she listed it." She rocks faster, staring straight ahead. She is going so fast now that the brim on her hat begins to flop.

"I tried all of that … every combination I could think of."

"I tol' you," her voice is high-pitched and rapid, "you're fussing too much. The records just weren't that good forty-five years ago. Somebody messed up, and you're wasting your time and mine on this silly nonsense. It certainly is clear that you were born. It's equally clear who your first parents were and that George and I adopted you, and there's a birth certificate for that, and *that* is all that matters." She stops rocking as suddenly as she stops speaking, gets up, turns abruptly, struts into the parlor, and disappears into another room, leaving Bucky, Martha, and me staring at each other.

Martha finally breaks the silence, pretending to be casual. "Miz Mary Frances, this spring air is so fine. I was thinkin' it might be time to air out the attic from the winter." She begins to back away from the side veranda into the parlor. "Why don't you come up after awhile and see if'n there ain't some of your ol' toys you might like to keep?"

"Sure," I say distractedly as Martha leaves.

Bucky takes Beatrice's seat in the rocker. "Sugar, you're getting a bit bold with the ol' aunt, aren't you?"

"Frankly, I'm really puzzled now. She would have had an original birth certificate in the adoption file, I'm sure, and there's no secret about my history. What could have set her off?"

"Beats me, she's a strange one. What did she say about the photos?"

"She says there aren't any."

"No baby pictures of you? Don't quite make sense, does it?"

"No."

"What are you gonna do now?"

"Don't rightly know, don't suppose I can do anything. She still hates my dead mama so much she won't even show me the baby pictures, or show me the birth certificate with my mama's name on it. I guess I should be glad I found Emmaline's old photo album. It's all I'm ever going to see."

. . . .

About an hour later, I decide to visit Martha in the attic, which was one of my favorite places to play as a child. A door in the upstairs hallway leads to the attic stairs. Even though Martha has it open to make a breeze with the open attic windows, I notice the musty smell of forgotten treasures as I climb the stairs. When she hears me coming, Martha calls down the stairs and tells me to close the door as I come up.

The attic is a child's dream world. The gabled roof provides nooks that contain relics from various family eras. Many years ago, Martha made one area into a costume shop using an old dress form, several large steamer trunks, an art deco dressing table, and an oval, wooden, freestanding mirror. Light from a gable window hits the mirror and reflects onto a scattered pile of bright old clothes, hats, and scarves that were salvaged from Beatrice's younger days. A wide-brimmed, feathered hat, in shades of orange, dangles on a mirror post. Long, white, ball gown gloves lay idly on the dressing table, and the three tiny pearl buttons at the wrist still invite nimble fingers. I smile, remembering many childhood days up here and realize that I haven't visited the costume shop since Betty Susanne lost interest about ten years ago.

"Oh Martha, look at this ...." I pull a pink boa off the dress form and playfully wrap it around my neck and pose in front of the mirror. "Remember how you and I used to play up here?" The dust causes me to sneeze.

"Lordy, Miz Frances, don't you go stirring up too much dust till your grandkids start coming up here. I don't want too much cleaning, y'hear, jus' gettin' too old for all this now." In spite of her large size and ancient limbs, Martha is moving cardboard boxes around. "I knows it's here somewhere." She sits on a box for a moment and contemplates. "I does want you to see somethin'." She goes to another pile of boxes and moves two sizeable cartons. "Come on over here," she motions, "looky here in this box, will you?" She moves two other sizeable boxes in order to see one that has been against the wall.

I help Martha position the bigger boxes, then kneel over the newly uncovered carton and lift the sides. I pull on the flaps so that it slides across the floor into a stream of light. Kneeling on the floor, with the pink boa still around my neck and getting in the way, I disturb more dust and watch it flutter and settle in the light.

The box is full of photo albums, framed pictures, and loose snapshots. I lift out a framed photo of a small girl about three years old, stare at it, and place it on the floor. I lift out two more photos, one of a small girl with a young woman, and another of the same child and a handsome man. I recognize the young woman as my nocturnal visitor in North Carolina. I reach for a photo album. "Martha, these are pictures of me and my mama and daddy, aren't they?"

"Yes'm."

Silently and slowly I turn the pages of the album. My eyes widen as I discover myself. "Why wouldn't Beatrice tell me about these?"

"She wanted to be your mama. She didn't want no reminders around." Martha lowers herself into an old wicker rocking chair close by. "An' you ain't never called her 'mama,' and she don't like that at all."

"She never felt like a mama." I've said this so many times, and in so many ways, it has become blasé. Pausing, I look up. "How can she still be so jealous about a woman who has been dead for forty years?"

"Your aunt makes up her mind and she don't never change." Martha's face is outlined in silhouette against the attic window. Seeing her from the floor, I have a déjà vu memory of many other times we had sat here talking, and feel a sense of warmth and familiarity.

Staring at a page, I pause. "Martha," I begin slowly, "remember when you told me about my old mammy? And you told me to look for her child? I've been visiting Emmaline at the nursing home and I've found out a lot and I know she really was my mammy when I lived with my mama and daddy. She had two daughters." I flip a couple of pages. "She showed me a photo album that she kept all these years and it has pictures of a little black girl and me." I point to a photo. "This picture here, this is the same little white girl as in Emmaline's pictures, but the black girl isn't here in this picture."

"That's right, chile, Emmaline was your mammy. An' a fine one at that. I couldn't straight-up and tell you 'cause I might find myself in trouble, you knows what I mean."

"Why didn't Beatrice want me to find out about her?"

"Well, chile, there's more to the story." She fans herself with one of the photos that I had removed from the box. "What else did you find out about her?"

"Not much else. I've talked to her, but sometimes she doesn't quite make sense to me. I did find out where she worked before she went in the nursing home. It was for a Mrs. Stanton in Washington. I went over and visited with her then I went to Emmaline's church. Her pastor told me about the little photo album that she had, so last week when I visited Emmaline, I asked her to show it to me." I continue rummaging through the box.

She stops fanning. "Why don't she make sense to you, chile?"

"She talked about her little girl who died, and I thought it was Missy, but it was the little girl named Melody. I haven't been able to find out anything about Missy yet." I recollect, "I looked for information when I went to Vital Records. I thought I might find a marriage license or maybe I would find that one of them had given birth. I even thought I would find out who the father was, that maybe he'd want to go see Emmaline. There wasn't anything useful, though."

"Oh, chile, the daddy of that li'l baby Melody is long gone from these parts." Her voice took on a concerned quality. "What did they tell you at that there records office?"

"Nothing, I went there to get a birth certificate for Bucky for his passport. That's when I tried to get my birth certificate for my real mama and daddy."

Martha's large body becomes absolutely still for a long time, and she says nothing while I continue to rummage through the photos. Her chair stops rocking. Then, with an audible sigh, she finally says, "Chile, I's gonna have to be the one to tells you somethin' and I sure don't think it's right, but it's gotta be done."

I look up from the albums, curious. "What's that, Martha?"

"Your family has a bigger story than what you knows about."

"Martha?"

"Well," she pauses, her massive breasts swell under a deep breath, "I've been wondering for a long time how this would work itself out, and I guess now I'm gonna find out." She shifts her body.

"Miz Mary Frances," she begins, then pauses and begins again, "Miz Fancy … your daddy was a fine man. He took good care of his family, he gave you everythin' you ever wanted, and he loved you mor'n anything in the world. And he loved your mama, too. But," she had difficulty saying the next words, "he was one of them men who has a hard time keepin' his britches up."

"What do you mean, Martha?"

"Your daddy had a way with other women, too."

I stare at Martha, her dark eyes glistening in the subdued light.

"Your daddy got another woman with chile, and you is the result of that." An audible sigh escapes when she finishes.

I stare at her, whispering, "You mean that my mama wasn't my real mama?"

"Yes'm."

"How do you know?"

"I've been around a very long time, you know that. I done been with your aunt since before you was born."

I let it sink in, whispering again, "Do you know who my real, I mean, my birth mama, was?"

She waits a long time before saying, "Yes'm."

389

"Martha ... will you tell me?"

"You sure you wants to know? If'n I tells you, it's gonna have a big ef-fect on a whole lot of folks." She strings out the syllables of "effect."

"I have a right to know."

"I know's you do ... that's why I finally decided to tells you, 'cause there ain't nobody else to do the tellin'. Miz Beatrice and I is the only ones who knows, an' she ain't gonna tell, that's for sure. I been carryin' this secret for so long, it done hurts my shoulders."

"Martha ...."

"Missy Frances...." Her voice lowers to an audible whisper. She stares at my face, barely seeing it in the light. "Your daddy done had his way with Emmaline when she was bran' new, workin' for him."

I am speechless. Finally I say, "It can't be. I'm white."

She finds a little bit more of her voice and leans toward me. "Chile, it's true, you is a milk and molasses baby. Your mama wanted a baby real bad and she couldn't have none. She was real mad at first about Emmaline gettin' in a family way, but she thought long and hard about it and decided that if the baby was light enough to pass, she was gonna raise it as her own."

She begins to sound like herself again. "So's she started acting like she's got a biscuit in the oven, and dressin' like it, and she kept Emmaline and her condition hid real good. She done figured that if it was a black baby, your mama would jus' tell folks that she had a dead baby, but if'n it was a white child, she would come on home from the hospital with it pretty as you please."

She looks at me like an old midwife. "Mixed chil'ren can be born real light an' they don't really show their color till about the third day or so. Emmaline had a white daddy and a white grandpappy, and you's had a white daddy, so's it was likely that you'd be plenty light-skinned. So's when Emmaline's time came, your mama done stayed away so's to make people think she was in the hospital, too. Then she went on down to the hospital where Emmaline was and she knew 'xactly what to look for … when mixed babies are born, you look at the ears and the fingernails … the cuticles … and you see what color they will turn out. She saw you was gonna be white an' then she made Emmaline sign some papers and tooks you home jus' like her own." She sighs heavily. "From that day on, Emmaline was your mammy, not your mama."

I put the album down slowly, crossing my arms and legs, and lean toward her. "How do you know all this?"

"Emmaline and I was right close. She done be related to me; she's my cousin once removed, so I looked after her. I knows a whole lot."

"What did Emmaline say about all this?"

"Well, she didn't have much say at all. It were her baby, an' she shur didn't want to even give it birth, but you can't stop that. She had that woman waiting to pounce on that baby the minute it came out, an' it scared her. They done promised her that she could stay with them and raise the chile. She finally thought it would be right good for her baby to have everythin' a white chile would get in a fine family, an' she'd be there, too."

I look down at the palms of my hands. I turn them over, staring at my skin, noticing the cuticles. A few feet away, I see my reflection in the tall floor mirror of the costume shop. I stare at myself, touching my hair and my mouth. Is it the light or am I suddenly seeing myself differently?

"You've seen her," Martha continues. "Miz Emmaline, she's light-skinned. She don't have the strong African features like some of us does. Miz Emmaline's baby came out lookin' the most like its daddy, and your mama was real happy. She done got herself a baby and she didn't have to go through no birthin' to spoil her skinny self."

I continue to stare into the mirror and finally say, "Emmaline is my mother?"

"She done take care of you most of the time anyhows. Rich white ladies don't do much taking care of chil'rens. Then you comes to me, and I done takes care of you. I done need to keep you for Miz Emmaline."

I move around and stretch out my legs as I think, finally bringing my knees to my chest and wrapping my arms around them. "Why didn't Beatrice keep Emmaline as a mammy for me?"

"When your mama died, Miz Beatrice had a chance to have her a chile. Your mama and Miz Beatrice were two sisters who couldn't have no babies and they was sure hurtin' over it. No, Miz Beatrice never allowed ol' Emmaline to see you after that hurricane, she was scared of that. She didn't want no mammy around who could say that you was hers."

"Martha, when we found Emmaline's photo album, there were pictures of me as I grew up … my graduation picture … a wedding picture … pictures of Betty Suzanne. How did she get those?"

"Ol' Martha don't forget her kin. Miz Beatrice don't know it but Miz Emmaline saw you at times without anyone knowin'. And when I could, I got pictures for her." She shifts in her chair. "Emmaline moved to D.C. when you moved there, and I tolds her about her grandbaby whatever I knowed. She watched over you but you didn't know it."

"Did she go to Betty Suzanne's school graduation?"

"Yes'm. We was all there, even Emmaline, but you didn't know about her."

I laugh. "Martha, you disobeyed Beatrice didn't you?"

Martha's voice takes on a resolute tone. "You know she gets her feathers up awful easy. You does what you has to do and you does it the way you has to do it. That's all I gotta say."

I laugh again, knowing how Martha and I always skirted Beatrice. "The other child ... the little black girl, Melody? She was my sister, wasn't she? Tell me about her."

"Ol' Emmaline was feelin' so bad about giving you up, she done got herself a boyfriend and got herself another baby. Your mama and daddy let her keep the other chile and raise the two of you together. Then she done lost both of them babies."

"Oh Lord, Martha." I rise from my space on the floor and walk to the window. Turning, I say, "What do I do now?"

"I done tol' you the truth, and you's entitled to know. I can't tells you what to do with it."

"Help me think about it, Martha, please ... the way we used to talk."

I stand by the window, appearing to look out but lost in thought. I finally turn and say, "Bucky should have been told before we got married."

"What do you think he'll say now?"

"Bucky ... Bucky is bigoted and he's never going to change, Martha. He says he wants to change for the sake of our marriage, but I don't think he can. For him to find out his wife is part black ... Martha, he would leave me in a minute." I pause. "Why would Beatrice pick him out for me? Why would she let him marry me if she knew?"

"He's a fine Southern gentleman, an' that's what your aunt wanted for you more'n anything. I don't think she expected anyone to ever tell, 'cause she sure made me promise not to." She cocks her head and looks at me. "Mr. Bucky is a fine man, and you's ain't gonna be havin' no more babies. An' it certainly ain't your fault. Don't you think he'd be man enough? Certainly won't be doin' his politicking no good up there in Washington if'n he walks out on you for this."

"I don't know, Martha. I just don't know if he has it in him. Martha … Betty Susanne … what if she had been born black?"

"Darlin', when you had that baby, I was so scared for you, I can't begin to tell you how much I prayed that chile would come out white."

"Did Beatrice ever worry about that?"

"We done never talked about it. She wouldn't even hear of it."

"Betty Susanne needs to know."

"All's I can say is, that's your job now."

"Martha, how do I tell Beatrice that I know the truth? She's gonna know that you told me."

"I reckon she will."

"How do you think she will react?"

"Well, first, she's probably gonna be mad enough to spit tacks. She didn't like you snooping around about Miz Emmaline. She was real nervous about that."

"I know, she implied she would disinherit me. Her money is her way of dealing with everything."

"Miz Beatrice is mighty stubborn."

"You know something … I don't really care. I certainly have no use for this house, and I don't need her money." I stop to think for a minute. "What do you think she will do to you?"

"I'm too old now to be working anyways. I've got some money saved; it just might be time for me to go live in one of those homes like Emmaline does. Maybe I should even go to hers."

"Do you really think Beatrice would fire you?"

"Most likely—might even be likely that I would leave on my own."

"You take such good care of her. What would she do without you?"

"I've lived in this house for almost fifty years. It might be time for a change."

"Martha …." I hesitate and wonder what to say next.

Martha anticipates my thoughts. "So, we done talked about Mr. Bucky and Miz Betty Susanne and me, now let's talk about you."

"What about me?"

"You's the one that's got to think about this. You's the one whose feelin's are goin' to matter."

I turn from the window and slowly walk back toward the costume shop. The pink boa still hangs down my back. My arms are wrapped around my waist, each hand holding an elbow. I stop in front of the mirror and stare at myself as I speak. "Martha … listen to this … this is the story of my life … my birth mother was a black woman. A white woman took me from her, but then gave me back to the black woman to raise me … so the white woman died, and the black woman saved my life. Then another white woman came along and took me away from the black woman again … then the new white woman gave me to another black woman to raise me. So … who is my mother?"

"We all loved you."

"But which one do I love the way you always love your mother?"

"I hears you."

"Emmaline was like a mother …" I stop. "She was the mother."

"Yes, baby. She was the mother."

"You've been like a mother … you took care of me … you talked to me … you played with me … and … you said Emmaline was related to you?" I hesitate and smile. "That means I'm related to you, doesn't it?"

"Yes'm, in a roundabout way. Miz Beatrice don't know that, though."

I become pensive, my thoughts taking me back to my childhood. "I don't remember Beatrice ever doing things like brushing my hair or playing paper dolls or jacks. Remember when we played jacks?"

"I sure do. Back in those days, I could still sit down on the sidewalk with you."

"All this time, I've been keeping all this love for my white mama, but she wasn't my mama."

"No, chile. She weren't. But that don't mean you need to stop loving her … you just keep on keepin' those feelings. There's plenty of room for lots of love."

"I was loving a faded memory. I didn't even have pictures of her. I made up stories about who she was and the way she took care of me when I was little."

"I know. You used to tell me the made-up stories about your mama."

"Martha, you've been so good to me."

"It was the most natural thing for me to do; I ain't never had no other chil'rens to look after."

I turn from the mirror and pace the floor deep in thought before going back to the window. "Martha," I finally say, my arms again folded across my waist, "I need some time to let it settle in, but right now I'm beginning to understand how I feel about being part black."

"What's that, darling?"

"I'm stunned, of course. This is not an easy revelation. But, I'm not feeling bad or awful or ashamed. It doesn't change who I am." I breathe deeply. "I've had a good life, relatively speaking. My ancestors don't make me different, and I don't think it makes a difference, socially, anymore. I should have been told a long time ago, that's all. I think Emmaline gave me up because she wanted good things for me, and I can understand that. It was very painful for her and still is."

I stare out of the window and finally begin again. "I'm thinking about what my life would have been like if I'd been raised black in those days, and I have to tell you, I'm really horrified thinking about it." I turn to look at her, almost as if I'm understanding for the first time. "You were treated badly, weren't you? Beatrice and Uncle George took me to church, and then they came home and taught me the most unchristian behavior toward other people, especially the blacks. And they *knew* about my situation, that's what is so astonishing!"

"I know, baby chile. It was mighty hard for me, too. I just had to close my eyes and my ears against it. It was pretendin' for them.

They always pretended that you was all white." She begins to rock in her chair.

"When I was little, the blacks had to have separate bathrooms and separate drinking fountains and sit in the back of the bus. I would have been one of them. It would have been so humiliating!" I look at her as if realizing for the first time that Martha might have been treated that way. "You had those experiences, didn't you?"

"Yes'm."

"When I was a kid, I thought that's the way it was supposed to be."

Her facial muscles tense as she remembers. "It weren't a nice time, to be sure."

"I never really imagined you as one of them. You were part of the family and you were with us ... oh, that sounds silly ... I mean, you were different but you were one of us, too ... did we treat you badly? I mean, before the laws were changed? Oh God, I know how Beatrice still treats you, and it's still not right. But ...."

She softens. "Don't you go fussing about that. I've made my peace with her and I have a good say when I want to. Dr. King said once, and I'll never forget it, he says that who you are should be determined by what you stand for, not what you looks like, and anyhows, I done lived my life by the Lord's rule, not by her rule. I treat people the way I'd want them to treat me, and I prays for the ones who don't understand that."

I walk over and sit on a box near Martha, leaning toward her. "Martha, I was raised to be a bigot like Beatrice and Bucky, and I know I was awful at times." I pause and take her hand in mine. "But I've also changed. I may not show it at times, but I'm different now. I do my best to be respectful. It may not always be exactly right, but I mean well."

I feel a deep knot rise in my throat. "There's more." I close my eyelids and lean my forehead down on my hands, then raise my head, feeling a sense of shame. "I've never said this before, but I know I've felt it and never had the courage to say it ...." I bring her hands to my cheeks and look into her eyes. "I am truly sorry for anything that I did or said as a child that was hurtful to you."

She reaches over, kisses me on the forehead, and holds my head close to her bosom. "You ain't got no reason to ever feel bad about me. That was a long time ago, and we done been fine with each other for a very long while."

We are silent for a long time, hugging each other in the attic.

I go back to the pictures with a strange and different sense of who I am. I decide on three of them that I want to take with me. I feel different now about these people, but I still want to know them. One photo is of me alone, one is of me with my white mama, and the other is with my daddy. I take the pictures downstairs to my room.

I leave the house and go for a long walk in the neighborhood, alone, thinking again about butterflies and their cocoons. I feel that my cocoon has cracked. I am stunned by the thought of wings about to unfold.

I also have to think about how I am going to approach Bucky.

. . . .

Bucky and I return to Washington late on Sunday afternoon following a day of Easter church services and socializing with Beatrice's friends at her club. In the car, Bucky says, "Sugar plum, you sure have been acting strange today. Is something up with you?"

"Now Bucky, why do you say that?"

"Just look at you … you hardly said a word to your aunt all day, much less me, and you've been poutin' around like somethin' is eatin' you up. I know you well enough to know when you've got a bee in your bonnet, and you might as well talk about it as keep in inside."

"I showed you the pictures that Martha found."

"So, you're mad at your aunt for hiding them, maybe not tellin' you when you asked, is that right?"

"Well, I'm sure that's part of it. She had no right to keep those from me."

"She wasn't none too happy when you showed them to her either. It was almost like calling her a straight-out liar." Bucky laughed, "I've never seen that old woman jump outta' her chair and get so angry as when you showed them … she was as mad as a rooster in an empty hen house. By golly, that ol' geezer still has some snap left in her garters!" He thought for a minute and chuckled, "Maybe it's gonna be a lot longer before she dies and leaves you that fortune of hers."

"I'm afraid Martha is going to get in trouble over showing me where those pictures were." *I'm also afraid Beatrice will find out that Martha told me the whole truth, not just the truth about the pictures.*

"She ain't gonna do nothing to Martha except rant and rave like she usually does. Where would she be without Martha? She knows she can't get along without her."

"I hope she doesn't do anything."

"Well, I'm glad that's all that's botherin' you. You should just cheer up now and be your own sweet self."

I stare at Bucky for a minute then look out the window, wondering how important my aunt's fortune is to him, really. *Would he stay married to me just for the money if he knew the truth?*

16. MAKING DECISIONS

Later on Sunday evening, I go into the bathroom and close the door. It's the first chance I have to examine myself alone in front of a mirror. I pull back the curtain, trying to catch the last rays of sunlight as I examine the shade of my skin next to my white satin nightgown. Is it still the creamy peach that it has always been, or does it seem darker? My hands ... are they the same, too? Am I still the person that I was last week? Once again, I examine my face, my eyes, and my features. Am I looking at a reflection of who I really am, or am I looking at a portrait of who I think I am?

I have the black-and-white photograph of my father with me. I hold it up and compare my face with his. His eyes are dark. His hair is curly black. High cheekbones ... I remember being told that he was a Black Irish, whatever that means. I'm the spitting image of him in appearance, except I see a difference, a nuance. Is it the difference between men and women, where a woman who looks like her father is often softer, or is it a racial difference?

Is there anything that makes me her daughter, Emmaline's daughter? What did she look like when she was my age? The eyes, is the slant to my eyes different from my father's? Are these her eyes? Is this her nose? Is my cheekbone his or hers? The cheekbone ... I remember a mole on her cheek. I had a mole once; the same place, but I had it removed. I had her mole … I touch the place where the mole had been and feel the tiny scar.

I practice aloud, "Bucky, I need to talk to you about something … no … Bucky, we need to talk … Bucky …" I blurt it out, "… I'm half black." My hands cradle my face. "No. It's a quarter black. I don't know, an eighth. Does it matter? I have some black blood. I didn't know until Saturday … Martha told me …."

I clutch the sides of the sink. I feel lost. *I have no family history. Beatrice is not my real aunt. Her sister was my adoptive mother. I'm not really related to the family that I have known all my life. I know very little about my real father. I know nothing about Emmaline … my real mother … I am black. I am part black. What does that mean to me? Am I any different from all the other people who have a blended racial heritage? A blended cultural heritage? How will people treat me? Will anyone care? Will everyone care? How much has really changed?*

I sit on the toilet seat, staring at his picture. The little girl is on his knee. He is hugging her and has a wide, wonderful grin as the proud papa. I feel anger welling up inside of me. *You raped her, my mother, my real mother, and she had to continue living with you. You used your position and your power to take advantage of someone else, to hurt someone else. It shouldn't have mattered who she was.* I remember Susan's rape and death and shudder with rage.

My mother had to give her baby to your wife. She had to raise that baby like a white child. She had to teach me to treat her like a servant. I had to treat my mother like a servant. You were a bastard. I clutch the photograph against my chest, feeling hopelessly angry.

I hear Bucky calling and open the door. His voice is distant. "Mary Frances ... where are you, darlin'?" He's calling from the bottom of the stairs. I grab my robe and put it on as I walk to the top of the stairs.

"Here I am, what do you need?"

"Come on down here for a minute, please."

I descend the stairs and follow him into the parlor, still holding the picture. Bucky has built a fire, and the air is filled with the sweet scent of hickory logs and the quiet cackling of wood as it becomes ashes.

He quickly goes to the mantel. "I made a place for your photos." He is proud of himself. He has moved several brass candlesticks, and has positioned two of the pictures from the attic. "Wasn't there another one, you with your daddy? You know where I might find it?" He turns toward me. "Oh, you had it! Wouldn't it look fine here?"

"Yes, dear, it would." I sit in my favorite chair across from the fireplace, a light blue velvet wingback, pulling my bare feet up under me, and leaning into the corner where I usually put my head, clutching the picture. Bucky's dark blue leather chair and ottoman is next to me, and a table and brass lamp are between us. The lamp is on, and it casts a pale yellow glow on Bucky's reading glasses sitting on top of an open book resting on the table.

Bucky starts to come over with outstretched hands expecting me to hand him the photo. He stops, sensing that something is wrong, and sits on the ottoman. The tie belt on his bathrobe comes undone and the fabric settles loosely around him, showing his pajamas underneath. His back is to the fireplace and the glow from the lamp softens his features. He reaches over and gently caresses my calf. "Baby doll, somethin' is on your mind, isn't it?"

"Yes."

"Wanna talk about it?"

"Bucky, how much do you love me?"

"Why, sugar plum, you're my pride and joy." His face exudes warmth and he leans toward me. "You are a wonderful wife, and I love you with my whole heart and soul. We've had some ups and downs, but every couple does, and we've worked through them and we're better for it. Look how well we've handled the problem from these past few months."

"I have to tell you something."

"Nothin' could be as bad as that frown on your face."

"Martha told me more than just about the pictures."

"Martha is so harmless. What in the world could she have said that is makin' you so miserable?"

"Martha has been with our family for a very long time and she knows all the secrets. She told me a story about my family that I didn't know before."

He sits still, waiting. He knows that I need a minute and there is nothing he should say right now. I know him; he is being very kind. He is ready to hug me, comfort me, and assure me that my pain can be kissed away.

"Martha knew Emmaline when she worked for my parents, they were very close. She knows about something that happened to Emmaline when she first started working for them." I stumble. "My father ... she knew my father, she knew about him." I stare at the picture.

"There is something about your father that's botherin' you, isn't there?"

"Yes."

He's patient.

"My father raped Emmaline."

He is quiet for a long minute. "That happens. It happened a lot more back in those days. It's not a nice thing, and those men should be ashamed, just like you've made me ashamed about Corinne. But, baby doll, that's not your problem. It happened between them a long time ago. That's hers to deal with."

"I was born as a result."

His face freezes as he comprehends. The hand that has been massaging my calf stops. The expression in his eyes changes from jovial warmth to hardness. A long moment passes. "I think Martha is not telling you the truth. You're white," his voice shakes.

"White babies can be born to black mothers, just like little black babies can be born to folks who think they are all white. Beatrice and my white mother were sisters. Neither of them could have children. When my white mother found out about Emmaline being pregnant by my daddy, she decided to take the baby if it was born white enough, an' that's what happened."

I have finally said my piece and I stop. My heart beats loudly and my body is tense as I lean back into the corner of the chair and slowly put the picture facedown on the table.

"Do you have any proof?"

"I think if we take some steps, we could get the original birth certificate. The indications are all there."

"You can't trust folk tales. Coloreds like to make up stories like this. It gives them status."

I notice that he has reverted to using the word 'colored' again. "I know this will seem silly to you but it means something to me." I stop to collect my thoughts. "Emmaline has a mole on her left cheek. Here …." I lift my finger and touch my face high on my left cheek. "I don't know if you remember, but I had one just like it and I had it removed many years ago. I can still feel the little scar."

"That's foolishness. Doesn't mean anythin'. Anybody can have a mole."

"I think they can be inherited."

He takes his hand from my ankle, turns, gets up from the ottoman, and paces in front of the fireplace, thinking. The fire continues to crackle behind him, and light flickers on the folds of the robe as it brushes his legs.

"Who all knows this rubbish?"

"Beatrice and Martha, and now you and me."

"No one else?"

"No."

"Martha can't be trusted. Beatrice will need to confirm it."

I speak softly, "We should think long and hard about bringing it up to her, you know how she is." Looking at him carefully, I finally continue, "What are your feelings about me now?"

He stops at the far end of the fireplace and stares at me. "If it's true, and I can't believe it yet, Beatrice should have said something before we were married." He sounds a little angry. "This is not the kind of thing you keep from a husband." He looks down into the fire for a long time, collecting his thoughts. "This means that my daughter has colored blood in her veins ... that we could end up with a colored grandchild."

"The way Betty Susanne is acting now, if she ever gets married, she might marry anyone of any color and any nationality. Nothing would surprise me."

"I don't think she should marry under these circumstances."

"I don't think we have any say in the matter, dear."

He begins pacing again.

"You didn't answer my question."

"What question?"

"How do you feel about me now?"

He raises his voice and continues to pace. "How do you think I feel? I'm shocked, deeply shocked, disturbed. Not at you, darlin', but at the circumstances. I'm trying to sort out how this will affect us, how it will affect my future. What will the constituents think?"

He has spoken only of the external world. He sees our relationship as a structure to be examined only as it relates to his ambitions. I absorb his behavior, finally asking, "Will there still be an 'us'?"

He stops and stares at me. He says nothing for a long time. With carefully measured pacing, he begins, "My first reaction is that I was deceived. When you marry, you are choosing a family, a social environment, and a social history. You are choosing the genetic makeup of your children. You are choosing the relatives that your children will grow up with. I should have had proper information. But …" his voice softens, "… this is not your fault. You are blameless in this. Beatrice courted me as much as I courted you."

I am overcome by his reaction, by his narcissism. I feel abandoned, but I also begin to feel free of my fears and powerful in a different way. It is significant that he cannot tell me that he still loves me, and that he is thinking only of himself. In this moment of decision, I need for him to do the right thing, to make the honorable choice. The worst he can do is to do nothing. I also know that I must make decisions for myself, to operate within the framework of who I am, who I really am. The voice that I hear must be mine. Each day, each minute, is also mine and I must move forward slowly, living one day at a time.

I stare at him and see someone that I have never seen before. Where once I thought him to be ambitious to improve himself and the world around him, I now see him as exploitative and opportunistic, someone who projects a desirable image and garners attention and admiration without having an underlying sense of values. He has learned what it takes to be noticed and to be in demand, but his image of himself depends on his idealized public image and on the perfect combination that he believes is necessary for him to be judged. For him, a wife with a mixed racial background is an imperfection. I have ceased to be his wife and have become a political issue. I am the rook in Bucky's chess game of life, useful but not necessary.

His words hang in the air like a dark cloud. Our marriage has just crashed like a huge wave folding over itself in a storm. Our vows to each other many years ago, and our promises to love, honor, and cherish, have dissolved like water rushing in and wiping away a castle built in the sand. The meaning of our marriage seems to disappear like the water receding back into the ocean, taking our sand castle memories with it.

I realize that it is my decision, not his, and I speak slowly. The power of my words gives voice to the reality that my marriage is over. "I will give you a divorce and I will tell Betty Susanne the truth."

"Don't tell her."

"Why not?"

"I … I don't think she is mature enough to handle it yet."

I remember Susan's parents and the way they caused me to realize how I had lost my direction in life. Now I feel on the brink of a new direction. I hear Angela's words and feel the power of choosing uncertainty, courage, and growth. I remember the old quilting women in Louisiana many years ago and their sacred memories, and realize that I have nothing to lose but my pain. But I also realize that growth as a person is a lonely process.

I rise from my chair, wrap my robe carefully, tie the sash, and walk to the door of the parlor. "How is your maturity, Bucky?" I turn and stare at him while saying the words that he should have said, "And, by the way, I still love you."

I go to my bedroom and call Katherine to tell her what has just happened. She invites me to pack a small bag and come to her house, which I do. As I close the kitchen door behind me, I realize that I am leaving Bucky alone and he will, no doubt, continue to contemplate his political strategies.

. . . .

I spend the next few days alone at Katherine's place ... sometimes quietly listening to my thoughts ... sometimes putting them on paper. Often I ponder the meaning of my life as candles flicker in my darkened room. I watch the magic of the light on the walls, while flutes play on a CD in the background.

The shock of leaving Bucky hits me hard, but it also merges with a realization that something was wrong between us and with our marriage. Beneath its successful exterior, our life together had been a deadly fungus of fear, hatred, and confusion. It was based on one person being powerful by making the other one powerless. I realize that my old life no longer works and I am a new person who must find a new path. Katherine and her husband, Peter, respect my need for solitude and provide solace only when I ask for it.

Words flow much like they did in my days of solitude at Wellesley. Deep within the questions that I ask myself, I notice an emerging sense of freedom, a reawakening. I question myself, my sense of what life should be about. But this time, the answers are mostly happy and uplifting. Sometimes the words feel poetic. Other times, I feel the need to put my life story in writing.

A few days after I moved to Katherine's, I call Benjamin and arrange to meet him for lunch at the nursing home. When we meet, I tell him about the conversation with Martha in the attic. He has become my friend, and I notice again how kind and gentle he is.

"You're scared, ain't you?"

"Absolutely."

"You're a brave woman."

"I don't know about that. There is another feeling, though, and this amazes me."

"What's that?" Benjamin looks over his glasses at me with kindness.

Slyly, with playfully flirtatious eyes, I continue, grinning, "I met a caterpillar when I went to North Carolina." I pause for effect. "Caterpillars turn into butterflies, you know." I take a bite. "Do you know that butterflies are not allowed to hide in cocoons, once they have been set free?" I raise my hands similar to a preacher dramatically exploring a spiritual concept. "I feel like my soul has just opened up and is about to soar." My outstretched arms turn into a full-body stretch.

His smile is like the warmth of an old friend who understands.

Together, we go to see Emmaline. She is sitting in a solarium with the sun shining through the windows. Benjamin stands at the door and lets me go to her alone. She has recovered from her fall and is sitting in her wheelchair staring out at the plant-covered deck. She looks asleep, but lifts her head when she sees me come in. I sit on a stool at her feet and take her hands into my own.

"Manny," I say gently, "Manny, I know who you are now."

411

Her face beams with expectation.

"You're my mother, Martha told me the story." I pause. "I'm Missy, the one that was taken away from you, Missy Fancy Pants."

She says nothing, but her eyes gleam with moisture. Her facial muscles relax and she smiles gently. Finally, she reaches over to touch my cheek. "Martha? Is Martha still alive?"

"Yes."

"Martha has always been so good to me."

"Manny, I've missed you all these years and didn't know it. You have suffered so much. I'm so sorry for everything that happened to you." I take both of her hands in mine and speak slowly, "I'm sorry for what my father did to you … I'm sorry for what my aunt did to you … I'm sorry for what my mother, my white mother, did to you."

She hears these words and seems to remember something far away and long ago. It also seems as if she is slipping away. "Darlin' chile, you's my darlin' li'l chile. Manny is here. You're safe with me. Manny will always take care of you."

"I know, and I'll take care of you."

I feel the same connection that I felt four months ago.

"Li'l Fancy, you've finally come for me, haven't you? You've always been such a good little girl. I knew you wouldn't let me down." She holds my hand firmly and doesn't let go. I feel glad to be alive, to be with her.

Sitting on the stool, I look up at her, much like the child from many years ago. "Mama … I can call you mama now, can't I? I want to read something that I wrote the other day … it's a poem. I like to write poems." I take out a piece of paper, unfold it, and read aloud,

THE BUTTERFLY

On a yesterday summer day
A creeping caterpillar crawled into a flaxen shell
And hid away from the world
No more to let the elements of time
Play havoc on her mind.

The wind blew the flaxen shell far away
To a field of flowers and the aroma of happiness
And laid her at a stranger's feet.
He nurtured her, and cared,
Until her beauty, with him, she shared.

A crack appeared in the flaxen shell
And a wondrous creature appeared. But the aurora
Of unfolding wings blinded the stranger's
Sight, and in his stride,
He brushed the butterfly aside.

Her wings have been clipped and torn
And she reaches for her flaxen shell to hide again.
But butterflies are not allowed to hide
Once they have been set free,
And she must gather strength to fly away,

…with me.

"Come away with me, mama," I whisper in her ear.

PART TWO

17. NATURAL CONSEQUENCES

"Katherine, I'm feeling so confused. Sometimes I soar and sometimes I'm not sure of who I am or what I'm doing. I'm frustrated because I have to start my life all over again." We have just left her home near the southern edge of Rock Creek Park to go for an early morning jog. "It's both exciting and scary."

"I know. You'll do fine, though." We move at a good pace along Adams Mills Road, hearing faint sounds of animals from the zoo and catching whiffs of drifting zoo breezes, until we reach Beach Drive and find the jogging path leading down into the park. I realize how much I trust her capacity to see things that other eyes miss. She has never belonged to a tradition, to a role, to a set way of thinking that pulls dark velvet curtains around a person's essence. Because she is different, because her footsteps march to a tune that only she knows, she reasons with a more piercing freedom.

My thoughts go deep within my psyche. An irrational melancholy about my childhood becomes my hidden heartbreak and it reverberates with each pounding step along the pathway. I sense an irretrievable loss and anger for those who caused it. I feel cheated out of a life force, out of a soulfulness. I have not gathered

414

the energy around me that I once longed for and I do not know how to proceed.

We stop at a park bench, and I express these thoughts, ending with a sigh. "Am I being immature? Is it finally time for me to grow up?"

"Yes, m'am." As always, she has listened carefully, and has devised her own solution. She contemplates for a minute, then dribbles from her water bottle onto her fingertips and playfully sprinkles the drops over my head. "I hereby baptize you as an adult, and your sins and omissions are absolved. There ... you have courage now. You can do anything you want."

I laugh at her playfulness. "Is it that easy?"

"It's never easy." She becomes more serious. "But it's worth doing. It's a matter of attitude. You were born a strong and powerful woman; you simply haven't noticed it yet." She drapes an arm around my shoulder. "Mary Frances, be who you want to be, do what you want to do, whatever it is, just don't let your own magical song go unsung or your tale untold."

• •

In late April, shortly after leaving Bucky, I recognize that I must have a conversation with Betty Suzanne, and take the train to New York to see her over a weekend, leaving early on Saturday. She meets me at Penn Station around noon. I am comforted by her appearance, which is a little more normal. She has on black jeans and a black sweatshirt with a Columbia University logo, although her hair is streaked with purple this time and she still has a ring in her eyebrow. Walking out of the train station, I notice that she is slightly taller than I am even without the thick-soled shoes, something I hadn't noticed when she visited in late February.

We take a cab to my hotel, The Plaza on Central Park South. Along the way, she tells me that her father has already called to tell her that I am suffering from a mental breakdown. She is very concerned about me and seems to have dropped much of her earlier attitude and antagonism. Bucky's words surprise and annoy me, especially since I'm feeling a renewed sense of sanity. After checking in and dropping off my luggage, we cross the street to take a walk in Central Park.

I feel eager to absorb the beauty of the awakening spring and the energy of the city. The afternoon sun is spectacular and full of life, blending a palette of splendid colors and subtle shadows. A line of horse-drawn hansom cabs beckons quietly along Central Park South, while costumed drivers call to the crowd and yellow taxies whiz past. The air is crisp, and a gentle breeze lifts the odors and scents of the city and tosses them carelessly.

Betty Suzanne detours over to a street vendor to buy popcorn for the pigeons and I follow, feeling a spirit in my step. We meander down alongside the pond, finally sitting on a bench. I watch a mother swan gently nudging her two cygnets, and Betty Suzanne teases the ducks with her offerings, sometimes pretending to throw the popcorn and then eating it. When she tires of her play, she asks, "So, Mom, what's up? Why's Dad calling you crazy?"

Although I have spent considerable time mulling over my feelings and Bucky's reaction, I still wonder how to talk to our daughter. "Your father calls anyone crazy who doesn't agree with him. I'm feeling better than I have in years."

"What's he pissed about?"

"I've left him. I'm staying with Katherine."

"You're kidding, of course? Jeez, he didn't tell me that." She shakes her head and looks at me with a twinkle. "Does that make you crazy?"

"I suppose, in his eyes anyway."

"What happened … do I have a right to know?"

"There are several things, I guess." I'm pensive. It's hard to explain this to my child, and I worry about her reaction. "Now that I'm away from it, I wonder if it wasn't building for a while."

"Was I in the middle of something when I was there at spring break?" She pauses then acts like she understands. "I know, Dad was having another affair and that's really why you hired the detective, isn't it? The other thing was just an excuse, wasn't it? You finally got fed up with the affairs and you wanted the foolproof evidence. Did the PI get it for you?"

"You knew about the affairs?"

"Come on, Mom. Everyone knew, even you knew underneath it all. We wondered when you would wise up."

I look at her, wondering what "everyone" was thinking. Was Bucky's need to dazzle women so obvious? "That wasn't the immediate cause. It really goes deeper, maybe it's a bigger difference in our values than anything else, and I never realized it before."

"Come on, Mom, tell me. He's a nice dad, but sometimes he's a jerk, too." She stares at me, her eyes beckoning closeness. "And you're beating around the bush on something, aren't you?"

"There's a lot to talk about and I'm not sure where to start."

"Come." She gets up, grabs my hand, and pulls me with her, locking her arm in mine. "Start at the beginning, and it works better when you're walking." We meander down the pathway, slowly working our way north on East Drive, passing roller skaters, bicyclists, and many strolling couples. I begin by reminding her of the woman I met at the nursing home and lead into telling her the story of the hypnotism, the hurricane, how Emmaline rescued me, and how Aunt Beatrice took me away. I talk about the sense of relief that I feel, knowing the story and understanding my feelings toward both Emmaline and Beatrice.

"So the old lady was your mammy, that's what you thought, isn't it? That's neat, to find her like that." She waits for me to say more. "Didn't you say something last time about a kid? You were looking for a kid. Did you find her?"

"Well, yes, there's more to it, I'll get there in a minute." We are near the Conservatory Water, and pause to watch the elaborate, miniature sailboats gracefully ease across the basin. Betty Suzanne stops to play with a beautiful, black greyhound that belongs to one of the boat owners. She picks up a tennis ball and tosses it several times for the dog and waits for him to bring it back to her.

"Okay, Mom, next chapter." She comes back to me. "Get to how the old lady affects you and Dad. I need to hear it all." She grabs my arm again and leads us toward the Hans Christian Andersen statue. "Oh ... look at the butterfly on his book. It looks like it belongs. See how the duck seems to be jealous?"

Jealousy, I thought, is a good operative word, and I begin again as we turn north. "So, okay, she had two children. Martha told me about them. It turns out that Martha is related to Emmaline, she's a cousin ...."

Just above the Conservatory Water, we reach the bronze statue of Alice in Wonderland with her friends, the Mad Hatter and the Cheshire Cat. A couple of small children are climbing on it. "Look Mom, remember when I was a kid and we came here, and you took pictures of me on that?" Betty Suzanne sits on the mushroom next to the Doormouse, just like she did then.

"Yes, dear." The two children leave, and I lean against the White Rabbit. "You know how *Alice in Wonderland* is the story of things not being what they seem to be? The story about Emmaline is the same thing. It turns out that nothing is as it seemed to be."

"What do you mean?"

I take a deep breath. I don't know how she will take this news and I try to understand how I feel about telling it. "Emmaline had two children while she was working for my parents. One of her children was with us when the hurricane struck, and that little girl died." I have to pause here; she looks at me with expectation. I sigh deeply as I speak. "The other little girl, well, she had that child because my father had sex with her. My father got her pregnant, and I was that little girl. The little girl that she saved in the hurricane was really her own child."

Betty Suzanne stares at me. I can't read her reaction. She says nothing for a long time. "Say that again. I'm not sure I understand."

"My father got her pregnant while she was working for my parents. My mother couldn't have children, so when Emmaline's baby was born white, my mama took it as her own and let Emmaline stay on as the mammy."

"But Aunt Beatrice knew, didn't she? She's very racist. Why would she take a child as her own who was a mixed baby?"

"Beatrice wanted a child very badly and couldn't have one either. The whole world thought that I was her niece, so she just kept it up and made allowances for the deception."

"Beatrice was your mother's sister, but then she really wasn't your mother. That means you're not really related to the wicked witch, doesn't it?"

"Betty Suzanne, we may have our problems with her, but we do not call her a wicked witch. I don't know how this whole situation will work itself out, but for now you still need to think of her as one of your grandmothers and respect her."

She gets up from the toadstool and begins to pace, attempting to absorb everything she has heard. "So, this is why Daddy thinks you're nuts! He can't come to grips with it, he needs another reason." She turns and addresses me. "Mom, he must be having a meltdown. You know how he is with racism. Jesus Christ, Mom. So ... if you have some black blood, then so do I." She turns, looking at me, her face alive with the new discovery. "How do you think I would look in cornrows?"

"It really isn't necessary for you to do anything to change, darling. There is nothing about you that is different than you have always been."

"No, it's cool. I'm multiracial, I'm multicultural." She shrugs her shoulders, "I can get away with any shit I want ... join any groups I want and be one of them." I'm awestruck because she doesn't respond from a racial point of view. "Hey, do you think you can also find some Jewish somewhere? I mean, I live in New York City, I need to have some Jewish, too."

"I'm sorry, darling. I can't laugh with you. This situation is very hard on me because of what it's doing to our family."

"I know, Mom. It's also hard on you because you found a new mother. That has to be rough, especially when you never knew the old one."

"I struggle with it daily. I have the same life history that I have always had, but it all seems strange now. Something has changed. I now feel more akin to a whole lot of people. Well, I *am* kin to them. I'm curious about a culture that I know very little about, but it's now my culture, at least in part. I need a whole new sense of who I am." I sigh thoughtfully. "But I don't think I need a mirror for that."

"'Shit, man' … 'Hey, don't bug me' … I like that stuff. I have to practice it, it's what blacks say … this is cool." She is energized. "Come on … we gotta talk about this." Walking back to East Drive, we head around the Boathouse. A juggler entertains children near the entrance, and a busy, late-lunch crowd enlivens the area while the lake swarms with boaters. We head northwesterly into the heavily wooded area of the Ramble. Roaming up and down the sloping pathways and rustic steps, absorbed into the shadows of the trees, we create our mother-daughter bond anew. She asks questions about Emmaline, wanting to know exactly how the story unfolded, wanting to know everything about Emmaline, wanting to know how she could meet her new grandmother and what she looks like. I tell Betty Suzanne that Emmaline knew where we lived and would secretly come to her school events and watch the playground from afar. My daughter is amazed.

When we reach the gazebo near the Bow Bridge, I lead us in for a rest, also knowing that there is more that I must tell and knowing that the time has come. New buds and fresh blossoms add bright colors to the reflections in the water, and we watch two cameramen carefully photograph a high-fashion model in an evening gown on the crest of Bow Bridge. Boaters silently skim by. One boat carries three Hasidic Jewish men, who seem absorbed in the unfamiliar details of rowing, and several boats carry couples of wide-ranging ages and ethnic backgrounds.

Leaning back against the wooden seat, I begin the next revelation. "Betty Suzanne, there is one more thing. I wish your father had told you this earlier, but he couldn't bring himself to do it."

"Listen, nothing would surprise me now. I would try to guess, but you're already past my ability to imagine. What now?"

"Something else has come to light recently. This is what was going on when you came down to visit last time. I had just found out, and your father and I were battling over it."

She leans forward, resting her elbows on her knees, her eyes wide open and waiting. "Spit it out, now."

I dread having to make the next statement, but I do. "Many years ago when Bucky was still in college, he fathered another child."

"My family increases by the hour," she says without missing a beat. "Is it a boy or a girl? Do I have a brother or a sister?"

"A sister."

"It's about time I had a sister. She must be older than me. Hmmm, I have a big sister, good. I can continue to be the brat in the family. When do I get to meet her?"

"You can't. She doesn't know who her father is. The mother doesn't want to tell."

She stands and walks to the edge of the gazebo. Turning, unable to comprehend such a rejection, she says, "Why not?"

"She is also multiracial."

"What do you mean?"

"Her mother is black, African American. The child was raised in a black social environment and has a strong identification with that culture. I can't tell you her name, but I want you to know that she is out there somewhere."

"Daddy fathered another child? A black child? No, she's a multiracial child. Why didn't he tell us about this a long time ago?" She leans against a post, sounding angry, then defensive, staring out into the water. "Wait a minute, she is mixed, like me ... don't you think she would want to meet me? Wouldn't she want to know about her white relatives, or her other relatives, I guess is the way to say it?" Whirling around, she says, "Hey, he did the same thing as grandpa, how can he be mad about Emmaline?"

It feels good to be talking to her in an adult way, but I need to explain about him without finding fault. "Your father comes from a different time and place. He was raised with a different set of standards and he feels bound by the way he was raised." I have never before given voice to these thoughts and attempted an explanation that recognizes Bucky's point of view. "He has attitudes about race that he can hide but he can't let go of. In his world, white men could have their way with black women and they didn't have to be responsible for what happened. They were just considered randy boys."

"Sounds like my grandpa was that way, too."

"Yes, it's an ugly part of the old South."

"But weren't you raised with those same standards? You and Daddy were both raised as racist; it's part of your culture."

For days, I have been examining my thoughts and rehearsing what I should say to her and finally have the chance to say it. "I can't change what I was taught. It's like a tape recorder, I still hear those voices in my head ... all that old racial stuff ... the fear of someone who is different ... it will always be there, and I will always notice it. But what matters is how I react. At some point in my life, I decided not to be that way; I decided that prejudice is wrong. I don't want to make decisions about people because they are different. Every time I hear it in my head, I have to make a choice, and that's what I do. I think I have changed a lot, maybe not enough, but a lot."

I'm opening up to my daughter for the first time in my life. "When I first learned that Emmaline was my mother, I worried about how people would treat me. I remember how it used to be … you were considered to be black if you had any black blood at all. It all seems so ridiculous now. Thank God, some people were brave enough to stand up for civil rights and change things. You're very lucky that you were raised in a different era. We didn't instill prejudice in you … society would not have permitted it."

I breathe a quiet sigh of relief at having said my piece. I also need to bring it back to our family situation. I give her a few minutes, and then go to her side. I end my comments very gently, my arm around her shoulder, with both of us watching the water. "It has reached a point where I can't tolerate Bucky's racism anymore, especially in view of what I have learned about myself."

"Mom, are you and Dad going to get divorced?" Her eyes are childlike and her face is fearful.

"Darling, it would be very hard to stay married after all of this."

We continue to talk and to walk in the park, heading south along West Drive past Strawberry Fields and back toward the hotel. As best as I can, I answer her questions and explain the circumstances of her half sister without revealing details.

We continue to spend time together over the weekend. Coming home on the train, I feel a sense of relief that Betty Susanne has been told the truth.

. . . .

I continue living with Katherine and her husband and file court documents for a legal separation in June.

Bucky throws his hat into the ring as an independent candidate for mayor, running against Marion Barry, and becomes enmeshed in his political activities. He invites me to attend some of the functions, insisting that I must be the dutiful wife, but I choose not to be present. Reading the newspaper reports, I notice his tendency toward bragging, exaggeration, and relentless self-promotion, a trait that exceeds even the outer limits for a politician.

He is not handling our separation well. Privately he refers to me as "being confused" and "struggling with PMS and menopause." He tells our mutual friends that I am seeing a psychiatrist because I am dealing with emotional problems. To my face, he belittles me whenever he can and accuses me of various infidelities and inappropriate behavior. He seems to be intent on punishing me.

Emmaline's health is still frail, but she gets stronger, and I visit her several times a week. I ask questions about her life and her history in an effort to make it my own, and I take some of our family pictures to show her. Effi, Katherine, and Patricia accompany me on visits. Betty Susanne comes down once in the summer and goes with me to meet her new grandmother. Bucky refuses to meet her, indicating that it would not be appropriate until I am ready to reconcile with him.

Grace leaves the law firm and represents me in the divorce as her first client. Grace indicates that she has personal knowledge that Bucky misused my trust funds and she wants to hold him accountable in court. She has the court consolidate the legal issues surrounding my trust fund with the divorce case. Bucky's approach is to hold tight to the purse strings, refuse all requests for information or for an accounting, and force a lengthy court confrontation, but he does not give me sufficient money to pursue this legal action. Finally, based on Grace's knowledge, I file a petition to have him removed as my trustee. At our first hearing, the court is reticent about making changes and postpones the hearing so that further information can be presented.

Aunt Beatrice and I become alienated because she supports Bucky in the divorce and in the management of my trust. Prior to the first hearing, she signed an affidavit describing her intentions when Bucky first assumed responsibility for my assets and claimed that I was naïve and unable to be financially independent. She claimed that the trust document permits her to control who the trustee is, and it is her desire that Bucky remain in charge, even if I choose to divorce him. She becomes extremely rude and unbearable to Martha, who is torn by her sense of loyalties.

Martha comes up on the train to visit Emmaline several times. Their reunion is tearful, touching, and even a little boisterous as they recount their lives together. Seeing Martha is a tremendous boost, and Benjamin is thrilled to see the changes in Emmaline. He enthusiastically reports her progress to me. When Martha is in town, we have long conversations about Beatrice's behavior, and I can only offer comfort.

Patricia is my emotional lifesaver both as a friend and a therapist. In moments of despair, I have sought meaning and clarity from her, and she counsels me to stay connected to the process of change, to feel my emotions and respect my pain, to work through the complications, and to continue to look for the mysterious and poetic aspects of life. During long walks and frequent cups of tea, we talk about the bittersweet nature of a new beginning brought about by the end of my marriage and the discovery of my birth mother.

I rekindle my friendship with Mr. and Mrs. Devereaux and their son, Eric, and take pleasure in showing them the museums of Washington and attending cultural events together. Even though they never met us as a couple, they become aware of Bucky's foray into local politics and are saddened to hear of our separation.

In mid-August, Bucky sends a copy of the Beaux Leander Foundation's tax return to me at Katherine's house with instructions to sign and return it immediately. I casually mention the tax return to Katherine and Grace as we sit on the deck, enjoying a glass of wine while dinner cooks on the grill. Grace tenses immediately and asks to see it. Carefully, she flips through the pages, seeming to examine certain numbers, and lays it on the table.

Katherine notices with curiosity.

"Mary Frances, as your lawyer, I'm advising you not to sign this." Grace is careful but suddenly professional. She gets up and walks to the edge of the deck.

"I've been signing these for years. Is something wrong?"

Grace looks at Katherine hesitantly. "I don't mean to be disrespectful, but unfortunately, I can't say any more."

Katherine reaches over, picks up the return, and flips through it casually. "What happens if I ask questions? Is anyone prevented from answering them?"

Grace, leaning against the railing, takes her time. She looks thoughtfully at Katherine and then at me. "Mary Frances. You are the secretary-treasurer of this organization. You certainly have a right to disseminate information or to seek advice through any sources that you wish. Katherine is your close friend and is very knowledgeable, but she is also a reporter. It's up to you to judge how you wish to handle this."

"Katherine," I turn to her, sensing a message in what Grace said, "as my friend, but not as a reporter, would you look at that return to see if anything looks unusual to you?"

Katherine takes a close look at the document, speaking aloud as she peruses. "The charitable purpose is to raise funds to support athletic activities for disadvantaged children in an effort to reduce juvenile delinquency." She looks up. "Am I reading these notes correctly? Are most of the funds raised through the donation of used automobiles and boats to the foundation?"

"Yes," I respond quietly, moving over to the grill and turning the pieces of chicken.

"My first question when I look at charities is how much of the value of the donations actually goes out in benefits for the children." Katherine continues. "Is this a fair question here? How does this work?" She looks to Grace first, as if she is checking to see if she is on the right track.

Grace's expression does not change, but she carefully shifts her gaze from Katherine to me. "Mary Frances, I did the record keeping for this foundation and worked with the accountants. If you wish to ask me questions, you have a right to do so, but I must bring it to your attention that Katherine's presence removes the attorney-client privilege."

"Grace, would you answer Katherine's question?" I say as I carefully pour more wine into our three glasses, sensing that Grace is attempting to lead me somewhere.

She chooses her words carefully. "Vehicles are donated to the foundation and title is signed off by the taxpayer. The full value of the vehicle is taken as a tax write-off. The foundation has the law firm handle the vehicle, which is turned over to a wholesale car operation. They sell it, take their commission, and remit the balance to the law firm. The firm takes its fees, and remits the balance to the foundation."

Katherine looks at the tax return again. "How much are the commissions and legal fees? Where are they reported here?"

"The commissions and fees are not reported on the foundation's books."

"What percentage are these commissions and fees?"

"Both the wholesaler and the law firm combined, seventy-five percent of the sale price of the vehicle."

Katherine looks at Grace cautiously. "The taxpayer takes the full deduction, but you're telling me that the foundation only reports twenty-five percent on its books?"

"Yes."

"Is that legal?"

"I don't think it is."

I speak again. "Grace, how long has this been going on?"

"Several years that I know about."

"Have I been signing tax returns like this?"

"Yes." Her answer is barely audible.

"Does Bucky understand this situation?" I ask cautiously.

"Yes. When I brought it to his attention, he told me to mind my own business and keep quiet. After that, he assigned the management of these accounts to someone else."

The front door opens and closes, and Katherine's husband, Peter, walks through the living room onto the deck with a cheerful greeting.

I carefully place the tax return inside a folder and take it back into the house.

18. THE GOOD, THE BAD, AND THE UGLY

Eric Devereaux calls to invite me to be his guest at a state dinner at the White House honoring the president of the island country of Trinidad and Tobago. Members of Congress whose states have strong economic and social ties to the Caribbean have been invited. I am thrilled to be going to a dinner at the White House for the first time.

Eric picks me up in a limousine with another congressman and his wife, and we are driven to the North Portico, where the butlers guide us into the foyer and to the East Room for the reception. Once the invited guests have gathered, President and Mrs. Clinton are announced along with their guests, President Noor Hassanali and his wife. The small orchestra strikes up "Hail to the Chief," and we patiently watch the press corp avail itself of a photo opportunity. My first reaction to seeing the Clintons in person is that he is much more handsome and she is much younger looking than they appear on TV. As we go through the reception line a few minutes later, President Clinton comments about the education bill that Eric is co-sponsoring, and Mrs. Clinton recognizes me as the wife of the local mayoral candidate. "I'm impressed," I comment to Eric as we begin to mingle.

At precisely eight-thirty, dinner is announced in the State Dining Room, and President and Mrs. Clinton escort their honored guests in first. The rest of the group is shown to their assigned seating while compliments are paid regarding the lovely flowers and small flag decorations in the red, black, and white colors of Trinidad and Tobago.

I am seated across from Eric and between an ambassador from the island of St. Thomas and a senator from Florida. Much of the conversation during the evening centers on Newt Gingrich's proposed Contract with America, and speculation regarding the upcoming mid-term election. Our dinner is an exquisite presentation of either a striped bass or a beef filet entrée, and superbly cooked fresh vegetables. Over the fresh peach and almond ice cream dessert, Eric and I reminisce about our summer in New Orleans.

Eric accompanies me back to Katherine's house after dinner and is invited in for a late-night drink with Katherine and her husband. Later, as he says goodnight at the door, he kisses me lightly. Before going to bed, Katherine slyly winks. "Nice guy!"

Two days later, a photo of Eric and me at the state dinner appears in the *Washington Post* gossip column, and Bucky is furious. He calls to find fault with me and uses inappropriate insults to get his point across.

Meanwhile, Katherine and Grace pursue additional information regarding the tax return and confirm that the foundation's accounting practices are questionable. They call in the detective, Mario Perelli, and ask him to research the sale prices of the automobiles that were donated to the foundation. A week later, he provides all of the requested documents, and Katherine and Grace confirm that the foundation is only reporting twenty-five percent of the donated funds and the rest slips through the cracks unreported.

When I am apprised of this, I realize that I could become implicated in this tax fraud. I call Bucky's office to talk to the person who handles the Beaux Leander Foundation, but she refers all questions to Bucky, and his response is, "Don't try to tell me how to run things; you don't know anything about accounting. There's nothing wrong with those returns, and you should just sign them. Don't ask questions; it's none of your business."

. . . .

Beatrice calls late one afternoon. She is curt and businesslike. She tells me that I need to come to Richmond immediately, but she won't tell me what is on her mind. I make plans for the following day.

Beatrice and I have been very distant since I moved away from Bucky, and I haven't seen her since Easter. Once, she called me with a lecture on the importance of staying with my husband. I couldn't tell her how much Bucky's racism offends me. It was shortly after that call that she wounded me deeply by signing the affidavit asking that Bucky remain the trustee of my funds.

When I arrive in Richmond, Martha answers the door and hugs me warmly. "Darlin' chile, I's been so worried about you." She is using a wooden cane to steady herself.

"Martha, is anything wrong? Are you injured?"

"No, chile, it's just my age. Ain't nothin' wrong with me that a few aspirin won't cure, but it's mighty nice to lean on somethin' once in a while."

"How's she treating you now?"

She closes the door behind me and quietly limps along. "Not good. Not good at all. It's still bad around here." She shakes her head sadly. "That woman has become mean, very mean. She's got the devil in her now."

"I'm very sorry that you're bearing the brunt of this."

"I's can hold my own." She takes a deep breath. "Now, you run along into the library, Miz Beatrice is waiting for you. Don't you let her jump on you, though."

The library door is ajar, and I knock lightly as I push it open. Beatrice is sitting in a gray chair near a window, with Chinaberry at her feet chewing on a bone. She closes her book. "Come, sit down." She motions to a nearby chair.

Her tone is cold, but she seems to be attempting friendliness. "Thank you for coming, Mary Frances. How was your drive down?" Then, without waiting, "I'm sorry to hear that you cancelled your trip to Europe. I know how much you and Bucky were looking forward to it."

"Under the circumstances …."

"Yes, yes, I know." She seems agitated. "Much has happened since the last time you were here." She looks straight ahead, avoiding eye contact. "I presume that you need an explanation regarding … well, regarding your circumstances, before we continue."

I wait quietly. Her words stumble out. "Your Unc … well, George and I, we did what we thought was best at the time." She pauses to create an effect. "Things were different back then, you know." She seems slightly assertive. "Margaret, my sister, had adopted you."

"Emmaline was my birth—"

She interrupts me, "Margaret and James adopted you. You had become their child. You had become part of our family."

433

"They kept Emmaline as part of the family. That was their deal with her. She had a right to be with me."

"She gave up her rights. This talk about keepin' Emmaline is only speculation. No one can prove it."

"You knew what happened. Emmaline was supposed to be kept on. You took advantage of a bad situation."

"You're not making this easy for me. What I'm trying to say is—"

"What you are trying to say is that you think you did the right thing, and I should just accept it, regardless of how wrong it was, or who was hurt. You want it to be right because it is what you did."

She ignores me and sighs deeply. "Let's not be uncivil. Since we can't talk about it reasonably, let me get to the reason that I called you here." She stirs in her chair, unsettled. "Bucky called me yesterday. He said I should talk to you."

"About what?"

"He said you were suddenly being uncooperative, and I needed to talk to you."

"Excuse me, about what?"

"To be quite frank, he described you as acting like an 'uppity nigger.' What did he mean by that?"

"Beatrice ... I have a great deal of difficulty hearing myself referred to in that manner, by anyone." I take a deep breath, inwardly furious at the name used by my husband. I get up from my chair, needing to do something physical to alleviate the anger. Chinaberry stops gnawing on the bone and watches me. "I will not respond when called names like that." A large, floor-model world globe catches my attention, and I purposefully walk over and spin it, focusing on the twirling action.

"Those were not my words, they were his."

434

"You did not need to repeat them. You have insulted me."

"You're thowin' a conniption fit over nothin'. He's using an expression, and you're taking it personally."

I spin the globe again, not wanting to continue the argument. "What do you want from me?"

"Why does Bucky have his drawers all in a twist?"

"I have no idea what's bothering Bucky. The only thing that has happened is that I asked some questions about a tax return that he wanted me to sign. It was one of the foundations that he manages, and I'm the secretary-treasurer."

"Mary Frances, it sounds to me like you are questionin' his integrity and his authority, his ability to do a job that he's been doin' for years. That is not the way you should treat your husband, especially now, when you have already caused problems with his political aspirations by livin' away from him."

"Some questions came up. I didn't understand what I was supposed to sign."

"And you expect to understand complex financial and legal matters? Isn't that why we hire people to do it for us?" She leans forward. "This is the reason that I oppose having you manage your own trust fund. You don't understand these things and you can't be expected to."

I turn to her, go back to my chair, and sit defiantly. "Beatrice, given everything that has happened, I intend to divorce Bucky. I think I should have the right to manage my own money if I'm not married to him. I also think I should have the right to question matters on a tax return that I am asked to sign."

Beatrice rises from her chair, tapping her cane noisily as she starts to pace. Chinaberry gets to his feet and follows, always a step or two behind her. "Does that also mean that you have the right to embarrass your husband by fraternizing with a black man in public?" She has reached one end of the room and turns back, pointing her finger at me. "That may be part of your blood heritage, but you have to realize that you were fortunate enough to be raised in a respectable white family and you are expected to keep the social customs of that family."

"For God's sake, Beatrice! I was invited to a state dinner at the White House. How much better could an invitation get?"

She stops in her tracks, her voice rising. "Do you realize what it does to Bucky's campaign when his wife is seen on a date with someone else?"

I turn in my chair to face her. "He was my escort, not my date. That's common at these functions. Besides, I can't worry about Bucky's campaign right now."

The veins on her temples throb. She firmly plants the cane in front of her. "You have the best husband we could find for you, and you are throwing it away over something that happened a long time ago!"

I try to stay calm. "Maybe that's the problem, Beatrice. I did not find him, you found him for me." I take a deep breath. "I wasn't really part of the decision, was I?"

"Oh, for God's sake child, come to your senses! You should consider yourself very lucky. My family took care of you. We took you in as our own. We gave you everything." The tapping of her heels on the hardwood floor echoes in the room as she resumes pacing. "But you couldn't be happy with that, could you? Even now, you can't see how fortunate you are to have the husband that you have, to have the family that you have, to have the money that you have. You should be grateful, not spiteful ...."

Beatrice's body jerks as she continues, "I promise ... you ... that you will ... pay for this!" Her speech slurs as she speaks. Her hand suddenly clutches her head and her left side seems to stiffen as her cane tumbles to the floor with a bang. Her eyes glaze over and lose their focus, and she collapses. Chinaberry barks excitedly.

"Martha!" I scream and sink to the floor next to her.

Martha rushes to her side, cradles Beatrice's small body, and gently lays her out on the floor. I quickly call an ambulance.

The medics arrive within minutes and hustle Beatrice into the waiting ambulance. Martha and I follow in my car. At the hospital, she receives immediate care in the emergency room and is admitted. The doctor tells us that Beatrice has had a stroke.

Soon after arriving at the hospital, I call Bucky's office. I don't reach him directly, but talk to his campaign assistant. Bucky had already left for a fundraiser and will be notified as soon as possible. I call Katherine and Grace also, and cancel a lunch the next day with Renee Devereaux.

By seven o'clock, I am alone in the hospital room with Martha. Beatrice has stabilized, but she is still in a coma, and her condition is serious. The doctor believes she will survive, but does not know whether she will have her mental and physical capacities. He advises us to go home, assuring us that nothing will happen during the night and we need our sleep.

Martha and I cannot leave. We are each lost in thought and say little to one another. She sits on a straight-back chair near the bed, watching and waiting. Clutching tissues, she occasionally wipes her nose; at times, she seems to be praying. I, on the other hand, still feel a great deal of anger about her most recent tirade and cannot sit still. Twice I leave the room and walk up and down the hall, my thoughts are full of hatred and animosity, but are commingled with compassion and a sense of family tragedy.

Martha looks up when I return from the second trip down the hall. "Dumplin'," she says, "let's you and me talk." Using her cane, she slowly pushes herself up from the chair. Without a word, she reaches over and takes two more tissues from the box. She seems much older than the Martha I have always known; long ago I forgot her age.

Silently we catch the elevator down to the main floor and leave the hospital for a nearby park. The heat from the summer night is stifling as twilight settles on the city, fireflies flicker among the bushes, and crickets hum relentlessly. We walk slowly, arm in arm, weighed down with the gravity of the situation and mindful of Martha's age. The glittering water of a fishpond in the park catches my attention when the streetlights come on, and we find a bench nearby.

"Martha," I begin, "most likely, she will be in the hospital for a while. Do you want to stay in the house alone, or would you like to come back with me?"

"I's have to stay nearby. I can't be no two hours away."

"I know."

"You don't let this afternoon make you feel bad in any way, y'hear?"

"Why does she keep doing this to me?"

"Chile, it ain't you. That woman in that there hospital bed ain't neva been able to give to anyone. She's been too fearful. Miz Beatrice is someone who has gained the whole world, but has lost her soul, and now it's time for her reckonin', and I's so afraid for her." She dabs her eyes with the tissue.

"Martha, you have been so good to her, but there isn't anything anyone can do. She spent her life hurting people, especially you and me and Emmaline. She will sit in judgment on what she has done."

Martha barely hears me. Her words tumble as if this is her last chance to say them. "She done be distant from her husband and from you, an' it's because she grew up with more pain that she ever wanted anyone to know. Her daddy done think that money was everything, and when he lost it all in the Crash of 1929, he done killed himself and your aunt became poorer than church mice. She vowed that she would neva be poor again an' she kept her word on that. Her world was all about having money and pretty things and stuff, not about having love in the home."

Her voice becomes more plaintive. "Chile, she has a monster called greed that controls her heart and hides many parts of who she really wants to be. There was a mother inside of her that wanted to come out, to be your mother, but she couldn't let it out on her own. She kept askin' you to call it out for her, but you was too young to know what that was all about."

In spite of her bulk and age, she stands as her feelings rise. Leaning on her cane, she takes on the quality of a minister speaking to her congregation. "The worse people act, the greater is their need for healing, and Beatrice acts real bad sometimes, which tells me she needs a great deal of loving an' healing." She looks at me intently, almost pointing with the tissue in her hand. "We all done be a family, even if it ain't what everyone else thinks is family, and we's got to keep on being that family and lovin' and healin' each other." She pleads, "We's got to let our loved ones go to their Maker in peace."

439

She leans down further, staring hard at me, speaking with the passion of a revivalist. "I'm askin' you, Dumplin', to think about how she tried, even if it wasn't much to you, and how much she needed you, and how much she still needs you. You is the only one who can give her peace. You done hated her long enough. It's time to let go and to let her soul pass over peacefully, if that's what's suppos' to be."

"Martha, I can't."

"Dumplin', even if you is shaking inside, it would be real important for you to do this. All's I'm askin' is for you to think about it before it's too late."

It isn't long before we find our way back to the hospital. Martha decides that she needs to sleep and takes a taxi home.

I am troubled by Martha's words and my inability to respond in any way. I rest in the visitor's lounge near Beatrice's room. About two o'clock in the morning, I awaken from a fitful nap and feel fidgety; Martha's words must have stirred me while I slept. I begin to walk restlessly in the room and finally go into the hallway. No one is about; even the night janitors have completed their tasks. I feel drawn to Beatrice's room and quietly slip through the door.

The stillness of the night has an ethereal quality. Eerie moonlight flows through the window almost as if her Maker is calling her with the light. My shoulder nervously rests against the wall near the window, and my arms fold across my chest as I stare at her. I am struck by her frailty; she hardly seems like Beatrice.

I whisper, barely realizing what I am saying, "I want to hug you right now, but I can't, my anger won't let me." Feelings overwhelm me. "Even though you can't hear me, there is so much I need to say."

440

Quietly I move closer, one slow step at a time. "To be your daughter, or not to be … that has always been the issue between us, hasn't it? Should I have been the real daughter that you wanted, and pretended not to have any pain; or should I have pretended to be your daughter, which is what I did, and allowed myself to feel the pain and suffer through my sorrows? I couldn't do either. I was too young and I hurt too much. I didn't know how to make the pain go away, and I finally had to seek the truth."

By this time, I'm standing in the stream of light, and I turn to look out of the window, searching somewhere for a spiritual answer. I speak to Beatrice's reflection in the glass, my arms still tight across my body. "As a child, could I have met your needs? Would that have been possible?"

Turning toward her again, my voice quivers, "Would it have been so hard for me to call you 'Mother'? For the single ounce of courage that it would have taken, did I have a whole pound of cowardice?" I shake my head slowly. "I never understood the cost for you, and you never understood what I lost."

I begin to feel like the child from long ago, asking her to love me. "I needed you to do the little things … sing with me … play with me … hold your arms out and wait until I was ready to run to them." I walk closer to her as tears form. "I needed you to kiss me once in a while, like I want to kiss you right now and can't. Perhaps, in a very small way, I can finally understand how hard it was for you to reach out to me."

Wiping away the tears, I turn away from her and use the foot of the bed to create a distance between us. "You and Bucky both worked hard and you accomplished a great deal. Martha believes that you lost your soul in the process. I believe Bucky also lost his. Beatrice, he's not strong, he's built of sand. He's not powerful inside as a human being. He has to control others, to make them small, in order to be powerful. I can't be one of those people anymore, someone who makes other people powerful, for you or for him. I'm afraid for him, for what has happened to him.

"Beatrice … Aunt Beatrice, yes, you are still Aunt Beatrice. Martha has been your friend and cared for you and cared about you your whole life, even now. Do you understand, even with everything you have done to her, that she is generous with her love for you? She tells me to forgive you. She tells me to understand the pain in your life, and she tells me that I must allow you to end it with peace."

I absorb my thoughts and decide what to do. Stepping around from the end of the bed, I approach her, finally taking her limp hand in mine. "Do I need to make you suffer? Even if I continue to blame you, I still have to live my life; I have to be the person I want to be. I have found out the truth about me and I can let go of my pain and be free, well, almost free. I can be five years old again and go back to the arms of the proud woman who is my mother. If I continue to withhold forgiveness and love from you, it will diminish my ability to see the goodness in my new life, to see the goodness in who I am.

"Can I forgive you? Can I walk away from our years of hurting each other? There are words floating in my head that cry out for revenge, but I must move ahead with my heart not my head, and I must be the person that I want to be … yes, I can forgive you, for everything … for everything."

I lift her hand and kiss it. "I will be here for you when you need me. I will be the daughter who cares for you in your old age. I will find a name for you that will be similar to 'mother'…that will mean 'mother' between us. I won't leave you."

19. TRUE COLORS

Eric Devereaux is the first to arrive at the hospital the next morning to comfort me. I am exhausted after a restless night in the visitor's lounge at the hospital. He hugs me, and I rest my head on his shoulder, slowly letting go of the strain of the past eighteen hours.

Bucky walks in and sees us embracing. "Take your hands off of my wife," he commands. I awkwardly introduce Eric as my old friend from Louisiana. Eric maintains a sense of presence and introduces himself as Congressman Eric Devereaux of Louisiana. Bucky recognizes him as being on the House Committee that oversees finances for the District of Columbia, then abruptly takes charge and acts as if he is now responsible for Beatrice's affairs.

"No, we will do it my way," I assert, "I am her closest relative."

"We'll see about that. After all, you really aren't her relative. She was going to put me in charge of her affairs and her estate. If she has already done it, then you will have no say in anything."

Very little needs to be accomplished at the hospital, arrangements are made quickly, and the three of us awkwardly leave the hospital.

Grace immediately files papers and represents me in the temporary guardianship hearing the following week. Bucky files an opposition detailing the vast financial holdings at stake, claiming in his documents that I am not related to Beatrice at all and am, in fact, the child of a maid and have been a golddigger all my life. He gives an impassioned and highly slanted account of my life and assigns great weight to our separation, claiming that he was forced to ask for the separation because of my infidelities, and attaches the affidavit that Beatrice had signed regarding my trust funds.

"This is what Miz Tyler wants," he repeats during the court hearing, picking up the affidavit from the documents spread in front of him and quoting legal cases to support the continuation of her desires. "Precedence in this jurisdiction requires that the wishes of the incapacitated person be maintained. Miz Tyler recognizes that the child that she cared for her whole life does not meet her expectations. This same person is now asking for control over Miz Tyler's money. When Miz Andrews became an adult and should have been legally authorized to assume control over her own funds, this did not happen. We must ask ourselves why.

"Why?" he repeats. "Your Honor, it is because throughout her life, Miz Andrews has shown a lack of prudent and sound judgment, a lack of wisdom, a lack of intelligence. For instance, when Miz Tyler sent her ward to the best women's college in the country, the opportunity was squandered, and the young Miz Andrews flunked out. She had to appeal to the school administration and use personal connections to get her grades changed so that she could graduate. She was not an honorable student, Your Honor.

"Under my tutelage, she has managed to lead a normal and respectable life, but Your Honor, even with an expensive college education, she has never worked a day in her life. She does not understand how the financial world operates. For years, I have tried to encourage her to take part, but she has never grasped it. I have given her simple tasks ... she is the treasurer of a small foundation that I manage ... two weeks ago, I gave her the very simple task of signing the foundation's tax returns so that they could be filed by the deadline. In years past, this was easy for her because I made sure it was done. But now, on her own, she could not do it, and the returns are late and will cost the foundation a hefty penalty. Is this the sense of responsibility that she will show toward Miz Tyler's vastly complex financial involvements?

"Let me take the court's valuable time to take this situation one step further." He steps out from behind the table, walks halfway to the judge's bench then abruptly turns to me, almost as if he is speaking on behalf of the court. "Miz Andrews saw an opportunity with those tax returns. She went to Miz Tyler in Richmond ... ol' Miz Tyler ... incapacitated Miz Tyler ... the same Miz Tyler that has only recently asked the court to continue the prudent management of these trust funds ... the same Miz Tyler who has wisely conserved these funds for years. Miz Andrews was angry ... she was angry because her attempts to get control over these funds had not succeeded. Miz Andrews went there with the intention of forcing a confrontation, of blackmailing ol' Miz Tyler. Miz Andrews had a scheme ... if she could not get access to these funds one way, she was going to do it another way. Knowing how ill her guardian was, Miz Andrews agitated Miz Tyler until her age and physical weaknesses took over. Miz Andrews caused this stroke and now she wants to reap the benefit of what she sowed. She should not be rewarded for her bad behavior, Your Honor." He sits down.

Grace rises slowly. She quietly looks down and speaks softly. "Your Honor. I'm an orphan, just like Mrs. Andrews. I was rescued from Vietnam and raised in an orphanage in Baltimore. Early on, the nuns taught me to read, but I read good literature. I was never allowed to read dime-store trash ... dime-store trash like the story that Mr. Andrews just told this court." She turns to Bucky. "Thank you, Mr. Andrews, for reminding me how much I continue to give thanks to the nuns for their literary training."

She walks around the table and stands in the middle of the courtroom, speaking more professionally. "Mrs. Andrews is the only child of Mrs. Tyler. Granted, she was adopted. She was also adopted by Mrs. Tyler's sister before her death. Two families loved this woman, two families provided for her financially as she was growing up. But, Your Honor, we are not here to discuss her funds. We are concerned with the day-to-day personal and financial guardianship for Mrs. Tyler, who may well recover sufficiently to resume control herself. We are talking about the person who will oversee her medical care and will pay her daily bills. We are talking about her only living relative, a relative who wants to care for her, who is able to care for her."

She crosses to the side of the courtroom away from Bucky and leans against the railing of the jury box, looking directly at him. "While it is true that Mr. Andrews has been totally and completely in charge of his wife's funds during their marriage, the court should be aware that Mrs. Andrews trusted him completely and acquiesced to his management of her money. Since her separation, she has become aware of possible discrepancies and mismanagement. She has asked for a report, for an accounting of her money. Mr. Andrews has refused her requests. It remains to be seen how Mr. Andrews' management will be judged.

"Let me also address the tax return. Mrs. Andrews has not signed it on advice of counsel. There is a concern that the tax return is not accurate, and that the foundation run by Mr. Andrews has practiced deception in reporting its income."

She turns to the judge. "Mrs. Andrews is the only daughter of Mrs. Tyler. While their relationship has had its ups and downs as any parenting relationship does, she cares about her mother. She has her mother's best interests at heart and has the ability to hire the advisors necessary to adequately maintain her funds while Mrs. Tyler recuperates."

The judge, a black woman, seems to mull over her response as she delivers it. "Mrs. Andrews, it appears that you do have a troubled relationship with your mother." She turns to Bucky. "We are not here talking about probate and the distribution of this woman's estate, although that may loom in the near future. We are not talking about the difficulties that you and your wife are having in your marriage. We are talking about the care of someone who is in the hospital and the daily management of her financial affairs. Mr. Andrews, in focusing on the overall value of this elderly woman's assets, and in focusing on your desire to control both Mrs. Tyler's and Mrs. Andrews' money, I am concerned about your priorities and about your conflicts of interest."

She looks down at the file in front of her. "I am awarding the guardianship to Mrs. Andrews. She is to consult any financial and medical experts that she desires and she is to be bonded according to the requirements of the law. She will have the full authority of a general power of attorney to manage as she sees fit. Proper accountings will be required, and you may review them, Mr. Andrews, if you wish." She closes the file. "That is all." She stands and returns to her chambers.

Outside the courtroom, Bucky approaches us. His hair and moustache are in need of a trim, and his tie doesn't match the suit he is wearing. Grace steps in front of me when he gets too close. "This is what affirmative action bullshit leads to," he bellows as he attempts to brush her aside. "I'm going to appeal. Once we get this before a real judge, a man who knows what he is doing, the court will come to its senses. I will see to it that you never get access to her money, or to yours, for that matter."

I face him. "Bucky, Aunt Beatrice gave you the career that you wanted. You are successful in your own right … why do you want to do this? Why do you need to do this to me?"

20. BUCKY'S COMEUPPANCE

Bucky campaigns for mayor against Marion Barry, playing up Barry's recent criminal conviction for drug use and the six months that he spent in jail. In his public appearances, Bucky talks about his own credibility, his work with the Control Board, and his active involvement in helping the poor and disadvantaged people of D.C. The polls show a concern among whites and middle-class blacks regarding Barry's behavior, and Bucky leads all of the candidates among voters who are most likely to vote.

The press asks about his apparent marital separation. He dismisses their questions as a non-issue, indicating in a press release that I am staying out of the election because of my aunt's grave illness. He asks the press to respect me by leaving me alone with my sadness and anticipates that everything will be fine soon. I have heard that he jokes among his friends that the divorce filing is only my emotional reaction to the situation and that I don't really mean it. He tells them that I am too ambitious and would never turn down an opportunity to be the mayor's wife.

As soon as I receive the guardianship papers for Beatrice's affairs, I issue documents replacing Bucky as the trustee of my funds and assign a professional financial manager. I also make a formal request of the new trustee for an audit of the records during Bucky's management. Bucky brings a motion in court to halt this replacement and to prevent the audit. I ask for an immediate hearing, and we are assigned a date two weeks before the election. Bucky desperately tries to change the hearing, but a postponement is denied. However, his request to bar reporters from this proceeding is granted.

We gather in the hall outside the courtroom for the hearing. Grace had advised me to dress so that I feel strong and she approves of my navy dress with red trim. Katherine is elegant in a stylish black-and-white suit rather than her usual tweedy attire.

Katherine walks over to Bucky and asks for a word with him. She leads him back to where Grace and I are standing. He seems very self-assured and jovial, although I notice that his suit is wrinkled and he missed a couple of spots when he was shaving. "Mary Frances, you've already lost this one once, haven't you?"

"The first decision was temporary because the court is awaiting your accounting. Besides, the circumstances have changed."

"Not that much, we already have her affidavit on file. You don't have enough power as a guardian to change it. You'll lose again today." I wonder if I smell liquor on his breath.

Katherine steps in. "Bucky, I have some business with you."

He turns to her, his voice reflecting the sneer on his face. "And what could you possibly want with me? You're a reporter and I've had you barred from the courtroom."

She ignores him and continues, "I have records that prove that you have been skimming funds off of the Beaux Leander Foundation, and the children of D.C. are not receiving all of the money that is donated for that purpose."

"You're full of shit; you don't have any clue what you're talking about." His words are confident, but his demeanor changes in a way that only I can read. His stare is intentionally focused on Katherine for a moment too long, and the sweep of his eyes around the group is too intense. Finally, he stares at Grace but says nothing.

Grace speaks in a firm but even tone, never breaking her eye contact with Bucky. "I assure you that I fully understand what has transpired with the foundation, how the finances were misreported, and the ramification of not reporting the commissions and management fees as expenses."

Bucky's eyes shift back to Katherine without a word. She says, "Bucky, I will give you forty-eight hours to withdraw from the election. I have already written a feature article exposing this situation and I will have it printed in the Sunday edition of the *Washington Post*. If you have not withdrawn, it goes to press in seventy-two hours."

He sneers, "You can't blackmail me like this. If you try to take me down, you will also take Mary Frances. She's implicated, you know. She's been signing the tax returns for years. You can't do that to your friend, can you?"

"This isn't blackmail," Katherine says, her voice even and resolute. "I have written the story showing her innocence and laying the entire blame on you. And, I can print it. She has authorized it." She pauses. "Think about it seriously before you shrug this off."

He turns to me with a sarcastic grin. "Sugar plum, nice friend you have here; she's going to destroy you. I had nothing to do with it; you signed all of the papers." In spite of his words, I see panic rising in his eyes, and his hand begins to shake.

I maintain his stare. "I understand the risk to me and support Katherine in this. I'll take my chances on the exposure."

Katherine, Grace, and I turn and walk into the courtroom together, leaving Bucky stunned and shaken. We join Eric and Patricia who have come to the hearing to support me as friends and are already sitting inside.

Bucky joins the associate from his firm who will be conducting the hearing, Travis Taylor, and they take their places at the counsel table as Grace and I take our places.

The judge is the same one that presided over the previous hearing regarding my trust funds, and I worry that Bucky's prediction of a loss will come true. When the case is called, Travis stands to begin his statement and Bucky rises with him, buttoning his suit jacket. Travis looks confused as Bucky interrupts and introduces himself. He makes a half turn as he tells the court and Travis that he won't need his associate because he will be representing himself. Bucky has a strange look on his face that I have never seen before. Travis looks worried as he sits down.

Bucky reminds the court that reporters have been banned from the hearing and asks that Katherine be removed. Grace states that Katherine is on our witness list and can't be removed without a prior hearing. The judge agrees with her.

"Then I want all of the witnesses removed!" Bucky bellows.

"Mr. Andrews, this is a courtroom. Please control yourself," the judge warns. "I will treat that as a motion and I'm going to deny it."

Bucky calls me as his first witness, but turns to the judge, "Your Honor, I want this witness to be declared a hostile witness."

"Denied." The judge's face is very stern.

I'm intimidated that anyone would consider me hostile.

While the preliminary questions are being asked, Travis searches through his files, puzzled. He is also observing Bucky closely and seems concerned. Even before the first real question is asked, Travis jumps up, politely excusing himself for interrupting, states that Bucky is not addressing the issues in this case, and asks the court for a recess.

"I don't need a recess, Your Honor." Bucky turns to Travis before the judge can respond. "You're not needed here anymore, boy. You're fired. Go back to the office and clean out your desk."

The judge looks at Grace. "Ms. Ngyuen, do you want a recess?" She shakes her head no. The judge contemplates Bucky with a cold, hard stare. "You may continue, but I don't want any more of your antics, Mr. Andrews. Don't waste my time."

Bucky is leaning against the railing that separates the seating area for the visitors, his arms folded across his chest. I have a déjà vu feeling of having been through this many times before with him. Katherine, Patricia, and Eric are directly behind Bucky, and are temporarily obscured as he moves back and forth. "Miz Andrews, who are your parents, your real parents?"

"Objection, Your Honor, irrelevant." Grace is instantly on her feet.

"Your Honor, I would be proud to answer that question. May I?"

The judge stares at Bucky again. "Mr. Andrews. I don't know where you are going with that. I will allow the question only because the witness seems to want to answer it. However, I don't have all afternoon and my patience is wearing thin."

"Thank you, Your Honor." Bucky nods his head to the court. "Again, Miz Andrews, who are your real parents?"

"Your Honor." I acknowledge the court and turn back to Bucky and repeat the circumstances of my birth.

"Ah," Bucky breathes loudly, "what race was this maid who seduced your father?"

"Bucky, she didn't seduce."

"Please, Miz Andrews, this is a court of law. Address me with respect. Now, I ask you again, what race was this maid?"

"I understand that her mother was black and her father was white."

Bucky looks at the judge and repeats, "You're the mulatto child of a black maid, aren't you?" but it is said as a statement, not as a question, and he immediately poses the next question. "Isn't it true that you try to pass?

Grace jumps to her feet. "Please, Your Honor. This is not permitted."

"I understand completely, Ms. Ngyuen. Mr. Andrews, this is your last warning."

Before realizing that the judge is not permitting the question, I respond, "I don't understand."

"Yes, you do. You pretend to be white, don't you?"

The judge pounds his gavel three times.

I look Bucky straight in the eye. "Bucky, it doesn't matter who my ancestors are. It doesn't matter what shade my skin is. What matters is that I treat people with respect and I am honest."

The judge has been watching Bucky closely, anger showing in his facial expression. Grace jumps to her feet, but before she says anything, the judge motions for her to sit down. It seems as if the he has decided to let Bucky play out his cards and take the consequences.

"Ah, honesty, that's a good one. After the death of your first adoptive parents, you were taken in by Mrs. Roche's rich sister,

Beatrice Tyler, weren't you? But, you've hated her your whole life, haven't you?"

"Bucky," I sigh at his tone, "Aunt Beatrice and I have had very difficult times in our lives together. I now know why."

Bucky reiterates, louder, "Even though you hated her, you still want her money, don't you?"

"I am her closest living relative; in fact, I am her only living relative. She is in the hospital in a coma. She needs to be looked after. Her affairs need to be managed."

"Excuse me, you are not a blood relative, are you? You are no more related to her than I am." He is leaning against the railing backwards, his head extending toward me.

"I am her adopted daughter. I have already been appointed to manage her affairs by the court in Richmond."

"Isn't it true, Miz Andrews, that Miz Tyler set up a trust fund for you many years ago?"

"Yes, it was money I inherited from my father."

"Did you ever gain access to those funds?"

"No."

"Why not? Isn't it true that Miz Tyler did not trust you to manage the money? Isn't it true, Miz Andrews, that she never intended for you to have control over the money because she didn't trust you?"

"I don't know what her reasons were. I recall that you had much more interest in the money than I ever did."

"Isn't it true that Miz Tyler filed an affidavit in this case only a few weeks ago, stating her desire that I should remain as the trustee?" Bucky's voice is loud, his tone angry. "Isn't it true that you are now intentionally going against her wishes?"

455

I speak quietly, but firmly. "The circumstances, Bucky, are that you and I are getting divorced. I don't think you should have control over my money after we are divorced."

Bucky begins to pace the courtroom floor. "You are the child of a black maid, but you chased after me, promising me all of Beatrice's money and influence, and you had the most lavish wedding in the Richmond social season, didn't you?"

"I recall that you and Aunt Beatrice both wanted me to marry you, and you and Beatrice made most of the wedding plans."

He angrily turns to the judge. "Order her to answer the question, she isn't answering the question!"

The judge calmly says, "I think she is answering the questions very well."

His demeanor becomes more out of control. "During our marriage, you weren't faithful to me, were you?"

I'm shocked. "I don't understand. What do you mean?"

Pointing to Eric, he yells, "This is your 'old friend' from Louisiana. You said that a few weeks ago. I caught you with him, in his arms, in an embrace. You have maintained a secret affair with him for years."

"Bucky, that's not true."

He acts humiliated. "You and he are after my money." Something seems to snap. I recognize the same crazed demeanor as the night we fought last spring when I returned from North Carolina. He walks over and points to Katherine and Grace. "You and your Christ-killing Jew reporter and your gook lawyer." He turns around, plaintively addressing the judge. "Everything I have, everything I have ever done, has been because of Beatrice. She and I managed that money as my career. It has been my whole career." He walks over to me, sounding like a child. "It isn't yours. It's mine. I earned it.

It's my life and you are trying to destroy me, blackmail me." He looks around the courtroom wildly, as if addressing an invisible audience. "No lying, cheating, stealing, gold digging, fucking nigger bitch and her friends are going to take it away from me! It's mine!"

Those in the room are stunned. Bucky is left standing in the middle of the room, his face reddened with anger, his fists clinched. He slowly turns around, looking at each of the frozen faces, realizing the enormity of his error. His eyes are wild.

He awkwardly moves to his counsel table, carelessly shuffles the papers into his briefcase, and locks it. No one moves as we watch him. He starts to approach the bench and backs off, facing Grace. She stares at him. He turns but avoids my eyes. Finally, he swivels and walks out of the courtroom.

Bucky is reclusive at home for three days. The rumor is that he will not speak to anyone, even on the phone. His campaign manager is frantic as reports about his meltdown creep into the daily conversations of Washington officials.

On the fourth day, Katherine publishes her story in the *Washington Post*.

#

ABOUT THE AUTHOR

In 1999, when Bonnie Moore moved to Washington, D.C. from the West Coast, a much more racially integrated area, she noticed memories of childhood training in racism, and how she consciously monitored her behavior to change these old rules. She also observed subtle but racially motivated attitudes among some of her peers, and became interested in the long-term impact of the Civil Rights Movement on those who had lived through it.

Her novel, MIZ FANCY, grew out of this experience and follows Mary Frances Andrews, a child of the changing South.

Bonnie Moore is an accountant and attorney, working as a management consultant. She has published in two literary magazines. *MIZ FANCY* is her first novel.

Printed in the United States
26160LVS00002B/34-222

9 781418 453213